D1483818

IN THE EYE OF THE STORM

Kurt Riezler, 1950

IN THE EYE OF THE STORM

KURT RIEZLER AND THE CRISES OF MODERN GERMANY

Wayne C. Thompson

University of Iowa Press

Frontispiece: *Courtesy, New School for Social Research, New York*

University of Iowa Press, Iowa City 52242
© 1980 by The University of Iowa. All rights reserved
Printed in the United States of America

Library of Congress Cataloging in Publication Data

Thompson, Wayne C.   1943-
  In the eye of the storm.

  Bibliography: p.
  Includes index.
  1. Riezler, Kurt, 1882-1955. 2. Statesmen—
Germany—Biography. 3. Political scientists—Germany—
Biography. 4. Germany—Politics and government—20th
century. 5. Europe—Politics and government—20th
century. 6. Political science. I. Title.
DD247. R48T46   943.08'092'4 [B]   79-24251
ISBN 0-87745-094-3

TO SUSIE

CONTENTS

PREFACE

During sixteen years as professor of philosophy at the New School for Social Research and at the University of Chicago, Kurt Riezler (1882-1955) provided American students and scholars with a classical perspective from which to view politics, literature, art, and natural science. His students and colleagues knew him as a learned man whose intellectual horizon extended to all aspects of human endeavor.

Few Americans were aware of Riezler's German past or of his anti-Hitler resistance activity while in the United States. Few suspected that this eminent scholar of Parmenides and Thucydides, Michelangelo and Goethe had, at the age of twenty-five, attracted the attention of the German kaiser, for whom he wrote speeches, and had become a political adviser to Chancellor Theobald von Bethmann Hollweg. Few knew that he had advised Bethmann Hollweg on the dangers and prospects of war in July 1914, had helped place Lenin into power in 1917, had guided Germany's diplomatic mission in Moscow in 1918, had helped arrange peace with the United States in November 1918, and had helped create the Weimar Republic.

After leaving Germany in 1938, Riezler did not wish to discuss his earlier political activity because he believed that Americans would not understand the political and intellectual setting in which he acted. Americans' views on politics are forged by circumstances unique to this young and dynamic land. For this country, protected by two wide oceans and bordering two friendly nations, wars are seen to be fought only on distant continents and do not unleash domestic forces which can seriously threaten the American democratic regime. Indeed, politics, in the American mind, seems inherently to include the characteristic of stability, despite periodic economic crises. Perhaps most significant to Riezler was the Americans' faith in human progress which, in his opinion, was unjustified in light of the terrifying events in Europe during the twentieth century.

The political setting in twentieth-century America was characterized by occasional wars on distant continents, by the memory of one successful political revolution in the distant past, and by long periods of peace. By contrast, the setting in which Riezler had acted was characterized by wars at one's own doorstep, by numerous revolutions springing from those wars, and by uneasy peace which seemed to be only a postponement of war.

This book will focus on that European political setting and on Riezler's insights about politics in general. Riezler was a participant in and observer of European politics for more than a half century. In the critical decade and a half from 1906 until 1920, he was a political observer and actor at the very heart of German decision-making. He preserved his observations in diaries which offer the closest existing record of the German political leaders' actions and motives during the First World War.

However, since Riezler himself was more than just an observer, his diaries and other writings are more than mere descriptions of events. Riezler was unique in that he was both a man of action and of contemplation. He had a significant impact on great events, but he also kept a certain critical distance from them. Therefore, his writings constitute a valuable assessment of those great events. Further, the fact that he was both a political theorist and a practitioner of politics greatly enhances the significance of his views on such political matters as international law, international trade, treaties, diplomacy, military force, nationalism, imperialism, pacifism, and domestic reform. Riezler shared many of the values and attitudes of Germany's educated elite to which he belonged. Indeed, a large part of the significance of the Riezler story is the way in which he applied or altered these values and attitudes to deal with the grave political problems of his time. He had the opportunity to apply political wisdom both in and after the event. Thus, he differed from most scholars of politics, who apply political wisdom only in retrospect. As he wrote in 1946: "Ours is a time in which action tends to be thoughtless and thought inactive."

As a philosopher, historical observer and political actor, Riezler was able to understand the true context of statesmanship. Blending his own political experience with a careful study of man, Riezler wrote in his last work that

the political action of each and every acting ruler, be it an individual or a collectivity, occurs in a human context, which ties together the necessary, the possible, and the desirable; man cannot help looking at each one of these three under the aspect of the two others. . . . Man in political action is man in his totality.

Biography helps to describe one of Riezler's major political concerns: man's interaction with and impact on the world around him. Political systems, societies, and political and philosophical trends have no life of their own. They originate, are preserved, altered, or developed, take on meaning and are passed on by specific persons living under specific circumstances at specific times. Riezler was a person who was charged with high responsibilities and who reflected on everything he heard, read, or witnessed. Therefore, through Riezler's biography an entire age is illuminated, an age which spans two world wars, revolutions which decisively affected the twentieth century, and no fewer than a half dozen

German regimes. Through the eyes and mind of Kurt Riezler the conflicting views and events of more than a half century are seen and judged.

In the course of writing this book, I have become greatly indebted to
many persons and institutions who have assisted me. I am especially
grateful to Professors William L. Bischoff, Arnold Brecht, Peter Celms,
Erich Hula, Harry V. Jaffa, Konrad H. Jarausch, Richard Kennington,
Adolf Lowe, Werner Marx, Harry Neumann, James L. Owens, Rosario
Pérez, Stefan T. Possony, Donald B. Pryce, Joachim Remak, Harold W.
Rood, John R. Scudder, M. Wesley Shoemaker, Hans Speier, Hans
Staudinger, and Leo Strauss, as well as to Mrs. Charlotte Beradt, Mrs.
Emil Lederer, Mr. Mark Mullin, Dr. Fabian von Schlabrendorff, Dr.
Toni Stolper, and Mrs. Howard White. All generously shared their
memories of Kurt Riezler, offered invaluable over-all guidance, or
critically read the manuscript. I wish also to thank the archivists of the
Archive Nationale Paris; the Geheimes Staatsarchiv and Kriegsarchiv of
the Bayerisches Hauptstaatsarchiv Munich; the Hauptstaatsarchiv
Stuttgart; the Hoover Institution on War, Revolution and Peace; the
Militärgeschichtliches Forschungsamt Freiburg; the National Archives
Washington; the Politisches Archiv des Auswärtigen Amts Bonn; and the
Zentrales Staatsarchiv Potsdam, who kindly granted me access to
documents in their possession relevant to this study. I am further
grateful to the Deutscher Akademischer Austauschdienst, the Earhart
Foundation, Lynchburg College, the National Endowment for the
Humanities, and the Woodrow Wilson Foundation, which provided the
financial support needed for this project. The assistance of Linda Alber,
Suzanne Thompson Horst, and Daniel R. Leamy was indispensable in
the preparation of the manuscript. Finally, I am most indebted to my
wife Susie, whose encouragement and patience and continuous help were
essential for the completion of this book.

Chapter One
EARLY YEARS

Study Molière, study Shakespeare, but above all study the ancient Greeks, ever and always the Greeks.

—Goethe

Kurt Karl Josef Riezler was born on February 12, 1882, into one of the most prominent families in Munich. For centuries his family had been settled in the Walsertal, a valley within Austria located a few miles south of Oberstdorf. Riezler showed continued attachment to the area of his forebears by returning to Oberstdorf on holidays throughout his life in Germany.[1]

Riezler's great grandfather, who had acquired a considerable fortune as a merchant and broker, had moved to Munich after his marriage to the heiress of the Ruedorffer banking family. Riezler later honored the enterprising Ruedorffer family by using the name as a pseudonym both before and after the First World War. His grandfather, Josef, and his great uncle, Franz Xaver, were cofounders of the Bayerische Hypotheken und Wechselbank and were pioneers in the development of a private insurance system. The Riezler family's prosperity was evident by its palace on Brienner Strasse. As Magistrat and as a member of the Bavarian state legislature, Franz Xaver was also an active and important figure in public life. However, the prominence of the family declined somewhat in the 1850s when the Ruedorffer banking house went bankrupt.

Riezler's father, Heinrich Riezler, who held a modest position as head clerk for an industrial firm, was very fond of painting and music, and his mother, Etha Riezler, was from the artistic Heffner family of Würzburg. The family in which Kurt Riezler grew up was thus one in which music and art were appreciated and emphasized. Riezler's own strong interest in art was one reason for his attraction to his future wife, Käthe Liebermann, the beautiful, vivacious, and extremely witty daughter of the German impressionist Max Liebermann. Riezler's own interest and expertise in art intensified after he left public service in 1920, and he devoted a portion of his later scholarly activity to art. His brother, Walter, who was

1

four years older than he, gained a reputation as an archaeologist, music critic and Beethoven biographer.[2]

Riezler's father had been killed in a boating accident on Lake Starnberg in 1899, and his father's two brothers assumed guardianship of the Riezler family. Emanuel Riezler held the rank of major in the Bavarian War Ministry, and Ritter Sigmund von Riezler was a professor, whose work on Bavarian history earned him many honorary positions and a title of nobility. As a *Festschrift* dedicated to him indicated, Sigmund Riezler had participated in the "war of German unification," which "positively influenced" his work. As a student of history, he had learned Ranke's "historical-critical method," which allegedly kept him above the "fluctuating quarrels of parties and opinions." It became clear that Kurt Riezler had inherited this portion of his uncle's outlook. However, instead of concentrating on the struggle among states for power and territory, Sigmund worked with "genuinely German patient diligence on the legal, economic, social, artistic and scholarly life" of Bavaria. He did this, not in a "romantic," but in a "cool, realistic" way.[3]

During his early childhood Riezler acquired his deep attachment to Bavaria, his strong artistic inclination, his interest in history and economics, and his desire to participate in public affairs. These interests and inclinations were strengthened and deepened by his education. In 1891 he entered the Luitpold Gymnasium, and in 1896 he transferred to the Theresien Gymnasium. In these elite, academically demanding high schools he gained a thorough knowledge of Greek and Latin. This training prepared him well for the study of philosophy and the classics, which were to remain his constant and enduring interests throughout his life. The last book which he requested the evening before his death in a Munich hospital on September 5, 1955, was the Greek edition of *Timaeus*, Plato's myth of creation ending with the birth of mankind.

Before commencing his studies in Munich, Riezler served a year of active military service as an enlisted man in the prestigious Second Royal Bavarian Infantry Regiment. Throughout his studies he continued to perform his reserve duty, and in 1903 after performing well in a military exercise, he was promoted to the rank of corporal in the reserves.

Several years later in Berlin, Riezler took note of the immense social prestige accorded to reserve officers and felt that it would benefit his career to have such a reserve commission. On June 12, 1908, he requested promotion to officer in the Royal Bavarian Reserves. Riezler pledged officially that he had never had "an affair of honor, whose settlement was in any way inappropriate to one's rank." He also swore that he had never been arrested and that he "neither belonged to nor would ever belong to a

2

secret society or any kind of association whose purpose is unknown to the
state or, disapproved by the same, is foreign to the interests of the state."
Riezler's request was granted, and although he had to be excused from
several required maneuvers because of his official duties in Berlin, he
continued to fulfill his reserve obligations satisfactorily, and was
periodically decorated and promoted. By 1918, while on assignment in
Moscow for the German Foreign Office, he was promoted to captain in
the reserves.[4]

He began his study of classical philology at the University of Munich
in 1901. His student years were serious ones of stimulation and challenge.
Characteristically, Riezler refused to join a fraternity, whose frivolous activities he disdained. It was a time when his philosophical thinking was
taking shape, a time when he was already grappling with the concept of
"being," a central question in the philosophical thinking of the later
Riezler. Shortly after the First World War he reminisced with a friend
about these years of questioning and search:

Do you still think about our first boyish efforts? Even if we were uncertain and
groping, we were nevertheless on the right track. We considered ourselves to be so
great when we discovered Kant and, provided with his insights, proved our right
to discard the wasteland of the prevailing university philosophy with its measure-
ment and spying out of sensations, notions and associations. We wrestled with
the terminology of the view of being (Wesenschau) and grasped initially that the
observed being, drawn from the fog into the light, was at best a Platonic idea. We
thought that we had made much progress with these insights. However, then
began the difficult struggle which we [did not know] how to resolve or come to
grips with—the attack of our Hellenic inheritance against reason, or, if you will,
the battle of our feelings and our pleasure of sense against Kant, the battle over
the unity of nature and the intellect. . . . We did not want to pit reason against
feeling, the intellect against nature, or to honor the one and diminish the other.
Ultimately we were helplessly led astray along the limits of understanding. In
vain we fumbled around with a stick in the fog and sought the direction of a sun,
which we did not see.

In his student years he had already rejected Platonism and had decided
that the essence of things was in the things themselves, not apart from
them. Riezler also revealed that the part of Greek thought which he had
"inherited" from his earlier education was not that Greek tradition established by Socrates which argued the primacy of man's rational
faculty. He had already rejected reason as the absolute measure for all
things; nature and history did not operate under the dictates of a
prescribed rationality.[5]

Riezler's original career goal was to teach ancient philology in royal
Bavarian high schools. He even considered writing an habilitation work

3

Wayne C. Thompson

in classical philology, which would have entitled him to become a university professor. His military records indicate, however, a gradual change of interest. He became interested in two professors who, as we shall see, helped broaden his academic interests beyond classical philology: the national economist, Lujo Brentano, and the ancient historian, Robert Pöhlmann. In 1903 he called himself a "student of history," and in 1906 he called himself a "historian." He also took a minor in economic history. The great extent to which he blended classical philosophy, history, and economics in his work was a major reason for the great popularity of his writings before the First World War.

On March 1, 1905, Riezler was granted a Doctor of Philosophy degree, with the superlative evaluation: *"Examinibus Rigorosis Summa Cum Laude Superatis."* His education at the gymnasium and at the university placed him into an elite which enjoyed not only enormous status in Wilhelmian Germany, but enormous influence as well. This elite did not claim its status on the basis of family descent, land ownership, wealth, or entrepreneurial success. It was an aristocracy of learning *(Bildung)*, an "educated elite," made up of Germany's university professors, secondary school teachers, government officials, doctors, lawyers, and clergymen. The values and attitudes which were transmitted by this aristocracy of learning in the classical German education formed the conceptual framework within which he operated. Riezler and other highly educated Germans applied these values and attitudes to the problems which Germany faced in the twentieth century. This conceptual framework, therefore, had a very significant impact on him and on German politics in general.

The education which this aristocracy of learning received was a humanistic one, focusing on classical Greece, as well as on the arts, literature, and philosophy. The object of inquiry was "pure humanity," which in the words of Ludwig Curtius was "not a pale abstract theory, but a moral command, directed at each individual, for the reconstruction of his moral life." Thus, "self-fulfillment" and the cultivation of the "whole man" were the ends. "Pure learning," the absolutely disinterested contemplation of the good and the true, and the cultivation of one's own spirit to the fullest possible extent were held to be the principal vocations of man. While this orientation was humanistic in that it focused on "pure humanity," it cannot be said that it guided man toward humanitarianism. A respect for the highest potential in man, not for the cares and aspirations of the common man, was inculcated. Nor can it be said to have cultivated cosmopolitanism in Riezler's time. Few in this elite, including Riezler, doubted Fichte's pronouncements that "to have

4

character and to be German undoubtedly mean the same" and that the Germans are the people "in whom the seed of perfection most unmistakenly lies."[6]

This highly individualistic emphasis required first and foremost a high degree of "inner freedom," or, in Riezler's words, "intellectual freedom, not practical freedom." With such intellectual freedom the German mind could, in the words of Friedrich Meinecke, indulge its "often stormy inclination to rise up suddenly from the limitations of the reality which surrounded it . . . to soar up suddenly into a metaphysical world, which was supposed to emancipate it." This freedom, Germans believed, had permitted the enormous eruption of creativity from 1770 to 1830 when such figures as Goethe, Schiller, Beethoven, Kant, and Hegel set the high standards for German idealism. This freedom was also the precondition for the flowering of romanticism during this golden period. The romantic tended to spring above universally valid reason, laws of nature, eternal values, and tradition. His spirit had its own laws, and he could be boundlessly subjective and emotional.[7]

Without a doubt, German idealism enriched not only Germans, but people throughout the world. However, it dominated the minds of Germans at a time when the Western countries were experiencing their democratic revolutions. At a time when Western nations were implementing political freedom, the Germans were tending to concentrate on "inner freedom." Thus, German idealism had a retarding effect on German politics in many respects. It steered many Germans away from political affairs altogether. It dominated political rhetoric. Germans, including Riezler, felt compelled to think and talk of politics in highly abstract and metaphysical terms. This predilection was, of course, nourished by the enormous authority of Immanuel Kant and Friedrich Hegel, who subordinated ideas on politics and freedom to their larger metaphysical and moral systems. It inclined one to search for total philosophical and moral verities, to comprehend "the whole." Meinecke noted that "specifically German was the tendency to elevate something primarily practical into a universal world theory." Also, the concepts of individuality and self-fulfillment were easily transferred to entire cultures, nations, states, and even to epochs. It became widely believed that each of these embodied its own unique spirit and developed organically and fulfilled itself in the same way that a human being does.[8]

Therefore, the state could not be viewed as a mere administrative instrument; it too had to have cultural and spiritual content and objectives. Such a *Kulturstaat* (culture state) was taking shape in Germany at a time when Prussia and other German states had been politically and militarily weakened by Napoleon. King Frederich William III declared that "the state must replace by spiritual forces what it lost in material strength." For most of the educated elite, this meant that they would serve the temporal authorities in return for the state's support of cultural pursuits. The arrangement was, of course, advantageous for both. The former, as grantors of indispensable academic titles, became the brokers for access to prestigious civil service positions. They also became the interpreters of the nation's spiritual values. In return, state authority became gilded and underpinned with philosophy and idealism. Thus, not only were absolutism and intellectual individualism apparently reconciled, but culture and power were seen to fructify each other. Absolutism and, later in the nineteenth century, nationalism thereby gained a moral self-confidence in Germany which was lacking in most other countries of the world. The higher the values the state served, the greater its perceived right to assert itself domestically and abroad. Of course, as Fritz Stern has observed, when by the end of the nineteenth century culture as an ideal became embodied in institutions, it degenerated "into little more than the ritualistic repetition of phrases and pieties." Nevertheless, these rituals are powerful forces in politics. Stern noted: "There is pathos in the fact that the Germans used their greatest achievement, their culture, to augment and excuse their greatest failure, their politics."[9]

The ideal of the culture state could be maintained in Germany after the French Revolution only by diverging from fundamental elements of Western political thought: modern natural rights and contract theory, which provide standards for rule derived from nature and therefore valid everywhere and always. Natural rights doctrine places limits on rulers. Obligations of rulers and ruled toward one another are established by consent in contracts. Because all men are equal in the possession of certain rights, a ruler must at all times govern not only in the interest of the whole people, but by consent of the ruled. Few educated Germans could accept the implications of modern natural rights theory, which is inherently democratic, and which establishes consent, not superior wisdom, as the basis for legitimate government. To be sure, liberal reforms were introduced in Germany to protect the individual's thought and person, and a majority of the educated elite, including Riezler, consistently defended these liberties. Also, most educated Germans advocated a "government of laws" (Rechtsstaat) grounded in fixed and rational principles which are clearly and publicly stated; they rejected capricious rule. However, without a grounding in modern natural rights and contract theory, the conviction that popular participation in government was necessary and desirable was very slow to develop. For example,

6

Heinrich von Treitschke, who often fancied himself as a liberal, rejected the very thought of universal suffrage: "Our idealism has always been our strongest national asset; thus it is absolutely un-German to let stupidity and ignorance have the decisive voice." Theodor Fontane put the matter a little more mildly: "Freedom of course. But evil looms large wherever the masses are left in charge. Even the freest of souls will concede the wisdom, the prudence, the utter need (why not admit what we all understand) of clear and firm laws, of the clear firm command." For most Germans freedom continued to mean only the freedom of the individual and of the entire nation from mental and physical coercion at the hands of capricious rulers or foreign powers.[10]

In the minds of Germany's educated elite, the absence of widespread effective political participation was quite natural and desirable. Educated Germans had much at stake in the *Kulturstaat* and *Rechtsstaat*, which had brought them great influence, privileges and status. Also, their elitist education had bred in them a condescension toward those who had been denied or who were intellectually incapable of such cultivation. For instance, the worst thing Riezler could ever say about a person was the he was "uneducated." The kind of individualism which they had been taught to admire had nothing to do with equality as it was coming to be understood in the West. Instead, it had instilled in them a cultural Philistinism and intellectual snobbery which added a powerful justification for the social barriers which already existed between the educated and uneducated classes. German idealism remained an obstacle to the amelioration of class divisions in Germany; indeed, it tended to give them ideological rigidity.[11]

It is certainly ironic that while the educated elite belonged to the ruling strata of Germany, its members tended to consider themselves to be apolitical. This attitude stemmed in great measure from the strong anti-utilitarian bias of their training. "Pure learning," not practical learning, was the aim. This lopsided education, this emphasis on "inwardness" *(Innerlichkeit)*, inclined many educated Germans toward becoming somewhat estranged from, and in many cases, outright disdainful of day-to-day affairs. They frequently failed to develop the capacity to deal with practical matters in practical terms. When they did descend to practical political questions, they often tended to apply moral and spiritual terms to them. This tendency often blocked a realistic view of problems and limits. Also, an unavoidable problem with converting political issues into matters of principle was that diplomatic or domestic compromise became much more difficult. It also inclined a person such as Riezler toward an aversion for "interest politics" of any kind, and for govern-

7

ment responsible directly to parliament, where the interests of competing groups are accommodated. "Government of the best" was strongly preferred. When practical politics became too difficult, the educated German frequently escaped to idealism again. He saw little ultimate danger in this flight from civic responsibility; he was convinced that each person could through learning enrich his own spirit quite independently of the prevailing political conditions. Each always maintained his most important freedom, his "inner freedom."[12]

By the end of the nineteenth century, Germany's educated elite found certain developments within Germany disturbing and threatening. These developments stemmed from Germany's extremely rapid industrialization and urbanization which by 1900 had transformed Germany into one of the world's foremost industrial, trading, banking, and urbanized countries. All Western countries experienced difficulties in adjusting to the social consequences of industrialization. However, the suddenness of German economic and population growth had no equal in Europe and had at least two major negative consequences for Germany. First, the intoxicatingly rapid growth provided the foundation for a rapid increase in German military power and stimulated in many Germans a hubris which manifested itself in the form of impatient imperialism, something which Riezler later had to oppose publicly. Many Germans, including a majority of the educated elite, embraced a *Machtpolitik* (power politics) with an exuberance which became difficult to control. An increasing imbalance developed between German power and the political maturity to moderate or control it.

Second, industrial and population growth changed the face and character of German society. The German Empire, which had become united territorially in 1871, became increasingly divided socially. Expressed in an over-simplified way, German society became more and more polarized. A class conscious, somewhat doctrinaire and fairly well-organized proletariat confronted a semifeudal ruling class. This ruling class was, in the main, stubbornly conservative and was composed of the surviving aristocracy and the educated and wealthy (*Bildung-* and *Besitz-*) bourgeoisie. In between stood both a growing sector of salaried white collar workers dependent upon industry, and the declining elements of small farmers and of the old middle class, such as small shopkeepers and petty officials. This middle group always showed in Germany a greater susceptibility to appeals from the ruling elite than from the proletariat. Neither idealism nor nationalism was able to overcome the extreme antagonisms which arose out of these changes in German society.[13]

The educated elite had grave misgivings about the rise of an urban proletariat and a wealthy entrepreneurial class. Both challenged its cultural leadership and values. The urban proletariat, organized in the Social Democratic Party of Germany (SPD) or in fast growing trade unions, demanded universal suffrage and government responsible to parliament. At the same time, Germany's new industrial leaders were beginning to demand more attention to the development and application of technology, rather than to ideals and culture. The educated elite feared that its values were being threatened by utilitarianism, "mass tastes," consumerism, realism in politics, and materialism in business; in short, by what it saw as British and American values. Thus, that elite interpreted the changes in German society as a decline. There was in that part of the ruling strata a strong "cultural pessimism" which gradually infected large numbers of Germans who did not belong to that elite. German spirit was in decline, they lamented, and many agreed with Nietzsche, who in 1888 claimed: "German spirit: for the past eighteen years a contradiction in terms."[14]

It would be misleading to imply that all Germans who had received the kind of elite classical education in which Riezler was trained formed a completely homogeneous group. They did not. Interest and involvement in politics varied greatly. Almost all of them supported an exuberant German foreign policy; however, some were strident nationalists, while others, such as Riezler, were not. Some, such as Riezler, were willing to make some adjustments to changing times, while others were not. Nevertheless, most remained more or less committed to the idealistic values of "self-fulfillment," "pure learning," government by the best, "government of laws" and the cultural state. Most tended to be uneasy about, or even openly hostile to, government responsible to parliament, interest politics, popular sovereignty, practical politics, utilitarianism and "mass values." That is, most tended to apply the values of the late eighteenth and early nineteenth centuries, an era of German weakness, to the problems of the twentieth century, an era of German power. It will be shown that Riezler shared some of these values all his life; others he discarded out of practical necessity. A large part of the significance of the Riezler story is the way in which he applied or altered these attitudes and values to deal with the grave problems of his time.

After his prize-winning and widely-praised dissertation, it is rather surprising that he chose not to pursue what undoubtedly would have been a very successful university career. Instead, he traveled through France, Italy, Switzerland, Belgium, Austria-Hungary, the Balkans, and Russia; afterwards he took a job for a short time as a tutor in a Polish home, where he became very interested in Eastern European and Russian affairs. In the spring of 1906 he became foreign affairs editor in Berlin for the *Norddeutsche Allgemeine Zeitung.* This prestigious newspaper was a semiofficial mouthpiece of the German government, and it provided Riezler with the visibility needed to move into a high government job.[15]

Riezler mastered his newly chosen profession, journalism, very quickly. "Due to his exceptional knowledge in the fields of history and culture and due to his journalistic talent," he attracted the attention of Foreign Office Press Chief, Otto Hammann, who brought him into the press office on October 1, 1906. Riezler was offered this job mainly because of his series of articles on Russian affairs. His new responsibilities extended to both foreign and domestic affairs, and he was occasionally sent on foreign assignments. He published an article on November 29, 1906, entitled "Der Reichstag und die Presse," which attracted the attention of Kaiser Wilhelm II. In this article Riezler praised the "instinct of the possible" and criticized both the Pan-Germans and the Social Democrats for their "utopian thinking." The kaiser asked who had published the "excellent" essay and expressed satisfaction that "such a clever man was won for the press office."[16]

Riezler also initially impressed Chancellor Bernhard Fürst von Bülow, for whom he composed drafts of personal and official letters and occasionally of parliamentary speeches. Riezler even wrote drafts advocating an aggressive colonial policy and rapid naval armament, policies which he strongly criticized several years later. He also did domestic political chores for Bülow. For example, after the Reichstag elections of 1907, Riezler met with Friedrich Naumann in order to dissuade him from advocating so vigorously reform of the Prussian three-class electoral system. He stressed in his conversation with Naumann that the government did not exclude the possibility of an electoral reform, but that this reform should be held within certain limits. Bülow found Riezler's report of this meeting "very good." Only a few years later, however, Riezler himself advocated this very reform with no less vigor than had Naumann.[17]

Not until after Bülow had left the Chancellery in the summer of 1909 did his favorable opinion of Riezler change radically. When Riezler later criticized Bülow's policies, the vain Bülow was enraged. His description of Riezler in his memoirs reflects this rage:

In the press office during the last few years of my chancellorship served a young official, Dr. Riezler, who came to my attention because of his ostentatious admiration of me. After my resignation he transferred this enthusiasm to my successor, incidentally after he had correctly and in written form assured me of his respectful gratitude for the goodwill which I had shown him during the years when he had the fortune to work under me 'and to learn.' Empress Fredrick, who combined intellect with humor, liked to tell the following story: Once while taking a walk through the splendid rooms at Windsor she noticed a parlour-maid who was weeping bitterly. She asked the poor child whether she had perhaps lost her sweetheart. The young girl answered, not without a certain indignation, 'Oh no! It is not for love, that I feel unhappy. Thank God I can love any man.' Riezler was one of those ambitious people who can love anyone and who does love anyone who has in his hand the cornucopia of favors. . . . At a party in Berlin during the second year of the world war Riezler coincidentally met a Viennese guest, who remarked in a general conversation over war and prewar literature that political literature in Berlin had produced some excellent works except for a few entirely bad books, and then he mentioned in this connection the book by Ruedorffer (Riezler). The person next to him gave him a gentle nudge. When the man from Vienna thoroughly damned the Ruedorffer book once again, it was followed by a more forceful jab in the ribs and an indication toward Herr Riezler, who had become very red across from him. Then the Austrian said: Huh, and what does the idiotic book of Ruedorffer have to do with Herr Riezler? Tableau! as the French like to say in such cases. . . . During the world war Riezler played a hardly fortunate role under Bethmann Hollweg, whose confidential collaborator he soon became, and belonged with Hans Delbrück to those advisers who pressed for a reunification of Poland, the greatest political mistake which was made since the beginning of the war. In 1917 the following poem made the rounds in Berlin:

> Ein schöner Wahn schafft uns nicht Frieden,
> Der Hohlweg sperrt den Blick zum Horizont.
> Ihm ward durch einen Riez die Welt zu sehn beschieden,
> Doch hinter diesem Riez war alles leer.

Wahnschaffe was a so-called fine man, Bethmann Hollweg led us down the empty road to war, and Riezler was in fact empty. The best thing about him was his cute wife, a daughter of the painter, Liebermann. Naturally after the fall of the Empire Riezler jumped with equally agile feet into the ship of the republic, just as he abandoned me after my resignation and turned to Bethmann. After the November Revolution he thrust himself onto Federal President Ebert as staff chief. The upright Ebert did not put up with this Adlatus long, who did not measure up either as a person or as a subordinate, and he soon showed him [Riezler] to the door.[18]

Throughout his life Riezler was a somewhat controversial person who aroused strong feelings in those around him. However, those feelings were by no means always negative. For example, Bülow's obviously one-sided description of him, written in the tone of a jilted lover, is balanced by a favorable description of him by Theodor Heuss, first president of the Federal Republic of Germany after the Second World War:

11

When we saw each other for the first time, our student days just over, he intrigued me. He was then moving in the border regions of the German Foreign Office, an expert observer, prepared to give advice on matters of publicity to those who sought it. I was not among his clients. However, it was alluring for me to watch his performance. Soon followed the second phase in our relations, my admiration for his wide knowledge, ever at his command and never overbearing, and also for the almost sprightly power of mental combination which blessed conversational thinking with elasticity, yes, with sheer elegance. He had the gift of improvisation, and, combined with his intellectual wealth, this might have been a temptation to indulge in playful artistry. Nothing of the sort! The trenchant sarcasm which was ever at his call—sometimes apt to hurt (and sometimes meant to hurt)—was his defense against mediocrity and highflown dramatics.[19]

Germany before the First World War was becoming isolated diplomatically and was already divided domestically. Nevertheless, most Germans were enthusiastic about the prospects for Germany's future. Her unification and her rapid economic and population growth had given her a strong hand to assert her claims in the world. How did the young Riezler think Germany should play this strong hand? What should Germany attempt to achieve at home and in the world? What contribution could he make to Germany's political future?

Chapter Two
OUTLINES OF CONTEMPORARY WORLD POLITICS

No man, however rich in attainment, can live on without longing; true longing cannot but look for the unattainable.

—Goethe

All of Riezler's political writings pointed in the direction of a change in German policy. In these writings the philosophically oriented Riezler described with great accuracy the prevailing political constellations, explained the tendencies at work to change or maintain those constellations, and made recommendations on how Germany should both operate within and effect changes in the world political context. His linkage of the philosophical and theoretical with the immediately observable aspects of politics greatly increased the significance of his writings and the attention which was paid to them. It was this quality which attracted the attention of two imperial chancellors for whom Riezler worked.

Riezler's writings and his concrete proposals reveal that he was diverging in some important ways from the attitudes and ideas of Germany's educated elite. He was becoming increasingly flexible and was taking a broader and more balanced view of the problems of his time. This divergence stemmed from the realization that the process of industrialization and the resultant pressures for democratization could not be reversed and that a stubborn refusal to come to grips with this new reality could only lead to revolution or stagnation. Both of these consequences would ultimately weaken the higher values on which the educated elite thought that Germany's future depended. Along with such figures as Friedrich Naumann, Friedrich Meinecke, Max Weber, and Ernst Troeltsch, Riezler saw a pressing need for an accommodation with many of the demands of modern life, both in domestic politics and in foreign policy. The former involved a firm support of civil rights, a move toward broader political participation which would include especially the working class (albeit somewhat short of full parliamentary government) and a drastic reduction of Prussian conservatives' hold on German

13

politics. Riezler believed that the masses could then be helped to respect the best of German cultural traditions and ideals and that they would accept guidance by those who could create social harmony by satisfying the common needs of all Germans. Further, by pursuing a restrained imperialist policy, Germans would find that their objectives would be more acceptable to the other members of the international community, and therefore could be successfully achieved. The German masses would then have more sympathy and understanding for the needs of the German state and would help form a domestic consensus for that foreign policy. These more realistic "accommodationists," such as Riezler, generally argued for a foreign policy based on enlightened self-interest. Indeed, their foreign policy views invariably became unrealistic and unpromising whenever they departed from the standard of Germany's interests and proposed meaningless abstractions, such as "the German idea," as the standard for German foreign policy. They could, it is true, be called "enlightened conservatives" with regard to domestic policy. However, it must not be forgotten that all modernization involves to a great extent a *rapprochement* between continuity and change.

During his entire political career Riezler advocated a course which stood between political fronts. Before the outbreak of the First World War he was a proponent of a patient imperialism and steered a course between the advocates of ceaseless German growth and conquest, by war if necessary, and that minority which opposed imperialist politics altogether. During the war, he stood between the advocates of large-scale direct annexations and advocates of the *status quo ante bellum*. After the war he opposed the extremes of left and right which wanted to destroy Germany's first republic. This middle course was not without its weaknesses and illusions. A large part of the German catastrophe in the twentieth century resulted from Germany's inability to develop in the general direction in which the accommodationists pointed.

GREEK IMPERIALISM AND MODERN GERMANY

In 1905 Riezler received his doctorate with a major in classical philology and minors in history and economic history. The philosophy faculty of the University of Munich granted him a prize for his doctoral dissertation, *Das Zweite Buch der pseudo-aristotelischen Ökonomik (The Second Book of the Pseudo-Aristotelian Economics)*. This was indeed an ambitious project. Riezler wanted to do no less than to develop on his own a new total theory for the economic development of Greece. "An extreme joy stemming from the magnitude and significance of the problem

14

may excuse the bold venture."[1] This work, published in 1907 under the title of *Über Finanzen und Monopole im alten Griechenland (Concerning Finances and Monopolies in Ancient Greece)*, is very significant for a study of Riezler's political ideas because it contained the basic thinking of his other three major prewar works. This is the only one of his four major prewar works which does not deal explicitly with contemporary political questions. However, the reader senses that Riezler's thoughts are not directed exclusively toward ancient Greece. Insight gained through his study of a period of classical Greek history, which he could observe from beginning to end, reinforced what he observed in the present and enabled him to speak confidently of general tendencies in history.

In *Finanzen und Monopole* Riezler set out to correct the way in which earlier scholars had studied Greek economics. Previously, Riezler wrote, scholars had looked at Greek economics almost exclusively through the eyes of the Greeks themselves. The weakness of this method was that the scholar was unable to see developments because he saw only the isolated economic facts which any living Greek saw in a lifetime. Also, scholars observed only the economics of the city, "its influences and motivating forces." Riezler, of course, preferred to deal with long-term developments although he realized that the shortage of data from the time being observed made his work much more difficult. In the introduction to *Finanzen und Monopole* one finds two characteristics of Riezler's approach in all his early works: first, he expressed the need to look at a subject in its entirety in order to arrive at a concept of the whole. Riezler never focused on isolated events or phenomena, but always sought their relationship to the whole. Second, he showed the modesty of a single individual who realized that he alone could offer no more than an "attempt," an "outline," a "prologue."

Riezler began the second—and for our study the most important—part of his dissertation with historical background. Before 700 B.C. the Greek *polis* was independent economically and politically. The *polis* dominated the economic structure, and this domination was not challenged by the citizens of the *polis*, who considered it to be "the primary factor of life," "the only form of life." Economics served the state. The chief means by which the *polis* drew income from outside itself were war and plunder, which in the eyes of the ancients were "the most venerated category of revenue." In the long run such plunder contributed to economic decline; "disruption of traffic, uncertainty of trade, colossal losses of national wealth . . . threw economics off its natural path of development." Nevertheless, the idea of "the state as primary factor of all life" and "the

15

desire for riches, fame, and freedom" made all "striving for political domination," which would secure these, seem entirely natural to the Greeks.[2]

Riezler observed that Greek economic life reached a period of crisis after approximately 700 B.C.: As a result of colonization the "consumption and production even of necessities expanded beyond the framework of the *polis*." This expansion, Riezler explained, resulted from the Greek nation's enormously rapid population growth; the problem resulting from such rapid growth could neither be solved by more intensive cultivation of the soil nor by extermination of excess population. The expansion was in both an easterly and westerly direction and across the Mediterranean Sea, and as a consequence the Greek nation had not only to take control of and to transport the rich Mediterranean raw materials but also to supply the colonies and their hinterlands with necessary products from the home city. The cultivation of the hinterlands brought the home cities a supply of cheaper foodstuffs and raw materials but at the same time brought a demand in the colonies for finished products from the city. Thus, the city no longer had to produce everything it needed. The result was trade. Interlocal exchange, which had always taken place for specialized goods, began to develop for ordinary goods.[3]

Trade created serious problems for the *polis*. Division of labor among cities, and thus interdependence, developed. Such dependence on the outside contradicted the autarchy of the *polis*. Riezler saw the resulting conflict between the inward organization of the *polis* and the outward movement of economics as "the great struggle between life and economic forms." Such a struggle was good, Riezler argued, because every historical development is a

struggle between the old forms, which indicate both the torpid life principles of a long vanished time and the new living forces, which produce a new life impulse and which drive forcefully ahead. The new impulses destroy the old forms, within which they originated and grew, and elevate their own forms to the stage of law: This is the eternal struggle of the 'becoming' with the 'has been'.[4]

This kind of language, as well as this kind of thinking is characteristic of Riezler before the war. It reminds one of the language of Hegel or of the social Darwinists.

Can one merely label Riezler as a social Darwinist and explain his political theory simply as an expression of that school of thought? It is certainly true that the application of Darwin's conclusions in *The Origin of Species* to human society was frequently made in the late nineteenth and early twentieth centuries by many persons in Europe, Great Britain, and the United States. It is also certain that Riezler had read Darwin and later social Darwinist writings, and it is known that Riezler's later superior, Theobald von Bethmann Hollweg, was very influenced by Darwin and David Strauss, who applied Darwinist thinking to nineteenth-century international relations. Although Riezler frequently spoke an apparently Darwinian language, it is unlikely that he was decisively influenced by Darwin. The idea of forms struggling with one another and of peoples and states as organisms can be found in Hegel's and Ranke's writings, and this kind of thinking preceded and was thus not restricted to the social Darwinists. Also, Riezler showed strong disagreement with some of the characteristics which are attributed to social Darwinism. He did not find war to be natural and ennobling. As we shall see, he believed that struggle was the fundamental characteristic between nations, but he advocated conducting this struggle in non-warlike ways. Riezler by no means saw only force, expansion, and the right of the strong over the weak. He criticized his own countrymen for not grasping *"l'impuissance de la force,"* for stressing only external expansion, and for believing only in the "steamroller." Furthermore Riezler did not see races struggling against one another, as the social Darwinists did. Riezler was increasingly cautious about the concept of race; not races, but nations struggle with one another; and since nations are bearers of ideas, what Riezler saw was fundamentally a conflict of ideas. Riezler would certainly have agreed with Max Weber, who criticized those who propagated a "shallow and empty, purely zoological nationalism." Finally, Riezler never accepted the domestic political implication of social Darwinism, namely unrestrained competition.[5] Such domestic competition disrupts the organic unity of the nation and weakens it. In short, one cannot consider Darwin as a decisive influence on Riezler's thinking.

The problem which the *polis* faced was in many ways the same as the problem which states still faced in Riezler's day: how could the incongruity between the limits and limitations of the state and the widespread economic involvement of the state be resolved?

What position will the state take? Will it find a possibility of adjusting its forms to the new movement, or will it be obliged forcefully to throw the development off its natural course in order to preserve itself . . . the inherent drive of life in these states is toward independence. However, there is no political independence where there is economic dependence.[6]

17

Riezler observed that there were three ways by which Greek *poleis* could overcome this difficulty: through a network of alliances with other cities, through enforced self-isolation, or through imperial expansion.

Through a network of alliances cities could attain a condition of equilibrium. Theoretically the resulting reliance on another city would be mutual. In this way political independence of the individual city could be combined with interlocal division of labor. In order for this to work in practice, a system of alliances and commercial treaties had to be created which could insure effective communications, travel, and regular delivery of necessities. Also, a general international order had to be created as the foundation for interlocal commercial agreement. The beginnings of this legal order were visible in Greece. Consuls and protective law were created, and interlocal trade agreements were made.

For a while this system worked relatively well. Riezler's analysis of the temporary success and subsequent failure of this system is very important because he applied it again in *Grundzüge der Weltpolitik* to twentieth-century European conditions. The reason for temporary success was the possibility for parallel expansion. As long as there were new areas which could be controlled politically and economically and which could be colonized, a city's economic expansion could be accomplished in harmony with other cities and not in conflict with them; there was room enough for all. Even after further territorial expansion was no longer possible, the league of all Greek cities prevented member cities from directing their drive to expand against one another. Also, the development of industry within the *polis* and the possibility of exporting finished goods and importing foodstuffs relieved the pressure to send excess population into colonies. While equilibrium through alliances was temporarily successful, it failed in the long run. Buyers of finished products and suppliers of foodstuffs tended to be the same territories. Competition to dominate those large, economically important territories led to open hostility. In the end economic interdependence did not result in lasting equilibrium and a general need for peace, but in war. Riezler made the observation: "These states all want to dominate: the political situation allows them only the choice between destroying or being destroyed."

The most radical solution to the conflict between the inner needs of the state and outward economic development was the solution which Sparta sought: enforced isolation of the city. This involved expulsion of all foreigners and prohibition of all grain exports and of all foreign trade. Excess population which could not be fed was exterminated or expelled from the city. However, this economic isolation made full exploitation of

18

the productive capabilities of the city impossible, and while the obligations of the city increased, the financial resources of the city remained the same. Thus, those cities which chose this alternative ultimately weakened themselves.

Athens chose the third possibility, imperial expansion. Because Athens was the first city to turn "in grand style" from isolation to expansion, it gained undisputed domination of the seas and therewith the allegiance of all those states which depended upon imports from overseas territories. Soon those powers which had voluntarily joined the Athenian Naval League found themselves forced to stay in the league because of Athenian supremacy at sea.

Crucial for Riezler was the question: how did Athens use its domination of the other cities? He observed that Athens used it very poorly, for it was unable to widen the narrow horizon of its concept of the state and to absorb the subjugated cities by giving them a share of the benefits of domination. Also, Athens retained a purely narrow Athenian economic policy and was unable or unwilling to develop an imperial economic policy. It transformed itself into an economic metropolis at the expense of the other parts of the empire. For example, it forced the cities on the island of Keos to export its ruddle, the best in all of Greece, only to Athens. The result of this narrow policy was a general and violent reaction against Athenian domination and a long series of wars which led the Greek nation politically and economically to the brink of ruin.

The parallel with Britain is striking here. Like most Germans of his time, Riezler was irritated by Britain's supremacy at sea, her supervision of the trade routes, her domination of many of the best areas for colonization, her financial center in London, and her parochial horizon, which, according to Riezler, the British always confused with cosmopolitanism. Riezler's view of Britain changed later, as we shall see in greater detail when we examine British imperialism. Perhaps this change of view was due to his realization that Britain, far from being inflexible, was able to change her imperial policy in order to strengthen and save her empire. Riezler came to accept British supremacy at sea and to admire her financial centralization and her handling of colonies. During the First World War Riezler concluded that Germany, not Britain, used Athenian methods of domination. Britain followed more closely the Roman methods of domination. Of the ancient cities only Rome was able to overcome the "horizon of the limited territory"; only Rome had the skill to include, not merely to exploit, conquered peoples. Germany, Riezler regretted, never acquired this skill.

Riezler's conclusion in his first work was that no Greek city could go

19

beyond its very limited constitutional foundation in order to cope with the outward economic development which characterized Greek economics after 700 B.C. The Greeks themselves could not grasp this problem of the inflexible character of their constitutions because they could not grasp economic relationships. Since economics had to serve the *polis,* Greek economic theory was devoted to the question, "what should be," instead of "what actually is." According to Riezler both Plato and Aristotle looked at economics from the point of view of "what should be" and were thus unable to recognize and to deal with the problem of adjusting a constitution to outward economic development.

Economic development beyond the *polis* eventually led to its rapid decline. Rulers, trying to control such economic development, became tyrants, and interest groups and classes arose. In Riezler's opinion, these interest groups and classes struggled for political power because political power brought economic privilege. Economic development created drives within the individual which brought the individual into conflict with the state, and individual interest began to outweigh the interest of the whole. Often the state even encouraged individual performance in order to make itself great. However, once individuality was permitted, it became an end in itself. The homogeneity of the populace and the former unity of will disappeared. "States emerged within the state," as Plato wrote, and "the state . . . became the tool of individual interests, the primary means to wealth, the most profitable business corporation." Revolutions followed one another in rapid succession, and the cities tried to offset the resulting economic losses by predatory wars against other cities. Thus, the riches of all cities were consumed by war.[7] The Greek example, as Riezler understood it, helped shape his view of war as unprofitable, in most cases unnecessary, and in almost all cases undesirable. It also taught him that the unity of will within a state could never be regained or maintained by the application of force within the state.

In *Finanzen und Monopole,* Riezler concentrated on ancient Greece without explicitly dealing with his own time, although parallels with contemporary circumstances are obvious to the reader. Riezler's journalistic career gave him an opportunity to deal with the politics of his time. For instance, he did this in his first widely recognized article, "Die Weltpolitik im Jahre 1906" ("World Politics in the Year 1906"), published in January 1907, in the *Norddeutsche Allgemeine Zeitung.*

In "Die Weltpolitik im Jahre 1906," Riezler dealt, of course, with the important events of the year, but he characteristically asserted that "no single question in international politics forms in itself a whole which can be observed and isolated from all others." Following his usual approach, he wrote that "the observer cannot refuse at least to try to discover the actual essence, the powerful antitheses *(die treibenden Gegensätze)* in the jumble of appearances." An observation of events

must give us the opportunity to look in depth at those tendencies which are not always visible, but which remain that which leads politics and which ultimately causes the great decisions. These great tendencies of development are exactly the ground on which diplomacy is forced to build its most delicate house of cards.

Here one finds the basic ideas behind Riezler's analysis of the political constellation which he presented in his two books published shortly before the outbreak of the world war. In this article he only touched upon the basic tendencies in world politics of his time. His mention of them indicates how early in his political career he formed his basic opinions of politics and how little these fundamental views changed until after the war. It also shows what an original thinker he was and indicates that Riezler's political ideas were not fundamentally influenced by Bethmann Hollweg, despite the fact that Riezler admired him greatly and discussed politics and philosophy in detail with him.[8]

Riezler wrote that in democratic states people often believed that international complications were the work of an evil, deceitful, and bickering diplomacy, while the peoples of the world, disregarding such bickering, peacefully sought friendship with one another. Such views, in Riezler's opinion, rested on the false assumption that states were institutions which could exist peacefully with one another, if only the right formula for cooperation could be found. States are not institutions, he stated, but organisms which have a need to grow, and this need for growth leads them into conflict with other states.[9] These are only hints of what he argued in great detail later: enmity, not friendship, is the basic relationship among states; the national tendency is stronger than the cosmopolitan tendency; the state is an organism.

Riezler's article reveals three things which may be regarded as characteristic of his thinking. First, one can find economic considerations in even the smallest and most insignificant political question, although it is impossible to register and describe exactly the relationship between politics and economics. Second, population increase is one of the most significant factors in international politics. "The degree of population increase, differing between countries, determines realignments of power—unstoppable but definite changes of those fragile balancing circumstances of power factors upon which the game of international diplomacy is dependent." Third, Riezler observed that "the legal claims of one state on the other tend to grow when it has a superiority of military power." To him military force was by no means everything, but he never underestimated its importance in international politics.[10]

By the end of the year 1906, Riezler noted that the Triple Alliance, composed of Germany, Austria-Hungary, and Italy, remained as strong as ever, that Russia was still greatly weakened as a result of her revolution in 1905, and that Britain had improved her relations with both France and Russia. Nevertheless, he was confident that Germany's relations with Britain had not suffered much during that year and that good Anglo-German relations could be expected.

His conclusions about world politics in 1906 were almost identical with those he reached eight years later. The nations of Europe had the possibility of moving into unsettled areas; thus, the political situation was characterized by coexistence, not hostility. These unsettled areas were large enough to prevent for years the peaceful competition from changing into open hostility. "The old year has not bequeathed the new one a single problem which cannot be resolved peacefully."[11]

A THEORY OF POLITICS

In 1909 Theobald von Bethmann Hollweg replaced Bülow in the Chancellery. Bethmann Hollweg, "the philosopher from Hohenfinow," life-long Prussian public servant, and most recently state secretary of the interior, fascinated Riezler, who became the liaison man between the press office and the chancellor. "Bethmann's character firmly ties me anew to my profession." Bethmann was to many, including Riezler, a "Hamlet figure," whose inclinations toward both the contemplative and the active life corresponded to Riezler's own inclinations. Bethmann Hollweg was indeed a man who was inspired by the classics and by philosophy but who felt himself unable to fit what he had read into a whole. His study resulted in many open questions. In contrast, Riezler always seemed to have a grasp of totality in his own thinking. Therefore, Riezler's attraction to the contemplative chancellor was matched by Bethmann's attraction to the erudite Riezler, who could help him put order into his own thoughts.[12]

Before Bethmann Hollweg became chancellor, he had scarcely expressed opinions on foreign politics, and it is unlikely that he had thought much about Germany's position in the world. Like Bülow, Bethmann Hollweg believed that Germany was encircled and that this circumstance was dangerous for Germany. He was advised by Bülow on March 6, 1909, to strive for better relations and a naval agreement with Britain; Bethmann Hollweg worked toward such an agreement until the outbreak of the war. Finally, he adopted the *"Nibelungentreue"* (Nibelungen loyalty) to Germany's chief ally, Austria-Hungary. Bethmann's inexperience in foreign affairs can explain why he chose Riezler, who had already shown considerable interest and perception in foreign affairs, to work with him; and it indicates the great likelihood that Riezler's foreign political ideas had some impact on the chancellor before the war. One must be careful, however, not to assume an identity of the two men's views.[13]

Riezler's job gave him additional opportunity to travel. In 1909 he was sent to Paris and London for three months, and in 1912 he was sent on a courier mission to Istanbul. Early in 1914 he made his longest journey, traveling by land over Siberia to Shanghai and by ship through the Suez Canal back to Germany. His travels sharpened his observation of the global political tendencies of his time.

Riezler had broad responsibilities which included press affairs and the writing of speeches and position papers for Bethmann Hollweg. As a well-informed conversation partner, he could aid the chancellor in working out many of the fundamental aspects of German government policy.

Bethmann Hollweg's most pressing problems were in the field of foreign affairs. Germany's position in the constellation of powers had deteriorated considerably since 1890, the year in which Kaiser Wilhelm II dismissed Bismarck from the office of chancellor of the German Empire. Germany had become practically isolated diplomatically, and there was much talk that only war could emancipate Germany from the diplomatic stranglehold. As Hans Plehn, strong proponent of a German rapprochement with Britain, wrote in 1913: "In the years since the last Morocco crisis [1911] the feeling in the German nation has become almost universally accepted that only through a great European war could we fight for a free hand in our world political activity." Bethmann Hollweg and Riezler saw great danger in such attitudes because public opinion in the German Empire, as elsewhere, was becoming an increasingly strong force to be reckoned with by statesmen. To educate the impatient German public about the realities of the constellation of powers and about the limits on German foreign policy and to give a well-reasoned plea for support of Bethmann Hollweg's foreign policy, Riezler wrote *Grundzüge der Weltpolitik in der Gegenwart (Outlines of Contemporary World Politics)*. This book was an elaboration and practical application of the political ideas he had already presented in *Die Erforderlichkeit des Unmöglichen, Prolegomena zu einer Theorie der Politik und zu anderen Theorien (On the Indispensable Character of the Impossible, Preface to a Theory of Politics and to Other Theories)*. In

23

Grundzüge der Weltpolitik, Riezler dealt with two things with which we are already familiar from *Finanzen und Monopole:* tendencies and the present constellation. He argued that tendencies do not follow their course without hindrance, as in a vacuum. The possibility for success of a tendency depends on the constellation, most importantly for Riezler's purposes the constellation of powers, which necessarily sets limits on purpose.[14]

Die Erforderlichkeit des Unmöglichen, published in 1913, is a collection of essays, of which the most important for us is the final one, "Grundriss einer Theorie der Politik," (Outline of a Theory of Politics). The timing of the book's publication was probably not determined by political events of the day because, unlike *Grundzüge der Weltpolitik,* published one year later, it is above all a theoretical work containing primarily essays which did not deal with important issues of the time. The fact that Riezler did not use a pseudonym for this book as he did for *Grundzüge der Weltpolitik,* despite his important position as adviser to the chancellor, indicates that he did not expect the work to be drawn into current political debates. The political chapter is a refinement of many of the ideas he had presented in *Finanzen und Monopole* and in "Weltpolitik im Jahre 1906." This extremely important chapter forms the theoretical foundation for his much more popular and widely read *Grundzüge der Weltpolitik.* A thorough examination of the philosophical aspects of *Erforderlichkeit des Unmöglichen* and *Grundzüge der Weltpolitik* would be study in itself, and the essential points are mentioned only briefly because they help one to understand Riezler's politics.

Riezler characteristically attempted to place politics in a total concept. "The highest task of philosophy is to search the unity of totality for ideas." At the beginning of his chapter on politics he dealt with the question of what one can know about the subject of politics. At the end of the nineteenth century and beginning of the twentieth century a methodological dispute arose in Germany concerning how to study history. The dispute centered around the question of how historical-political knowledge (i.e. cultural scientific as opposed to natural scientific knowledge) was possible.[15]

Riezler thought that a theory of politics was necessary, although he offered only a sketch, a first step toward this theory. Riezler argued that the nature of the things to be dealt with, namely man, the nation, the state, etc., does not enable one to observe them in a mathematical way. The nature of these things is characterized to a great extent by irrationality and constant development. Thus, no "laws of politics" can be established. A political theory must be modest, and the theorist must continue to strive toward such a final theory of politics although he must remain conscious of the impossibility of attaining that goal. Such a modest political theory will never be able to give to an active statesman a clear indication of what to do in any one political event; nevertheless, it will at least protect the statesman from naive and shallow views, and it will help him understand more about political reality.[16]

In nature and in human affairs Riezler saw the relationships of things to each other as one of conformity *(Gesetzmässigkeiten)*. However, when he spoke of conformity he did not mean in all cases causal determination. Some things are subject exclusively to causal determination, but human beings are not. Human beings are, to some extent, determined beings, but they are not wholly determined beings. To human beings Riezler applied the concept of "finality," instead of "causality." Man is guided by purpose, by an "after" in time, not by a "before." That is, man is also oriented toward "ends."[17]

The primary influence of Aristotle is clear in Riezler's theory of politics in which he postulates a unity of the world from the point of view of a finality which is inherent in the things themselves. Aristotle's influence can be seen in Riezler's speculation that all being *(alles Seiende)* contains within itself the potential to realize itself in the form appropriate to itself. However, the young Riezler did not see this pathos as a blind, irrational drive like Nietzsche's will to power or like the many forms of voluntarism popular in Europe at the time. Pathos was for him oriented toward the "higher" and ideally toward the "unity of the highest purpose," although this "unity of the highest purpose" could never be attained.[18]

The key to understanding the title of the book, *Die Erforderlichkeit des Unmöglichen,* is to realize that it is not a demand for a specific political program, a call for a "struggle for the German Empire's position as a world power with equal rights, an attempt to force through impossible demands with all means available." This view overlooks the philosophical dimension of necessarily striving toward the impossible. Riezler wrote: "God is unattainable; the highest necessity is impossible."[19] He often thought of the tragedy which resulted from the necessity to strive toward the unattainable. In his private diary he also wrote about the tragedy of Germany's attempt to be a world power and to assert the "German idea" in the world although such attempts may well prove in the end to have been impossible. The important thing at this point, however, is that in none of his prewar writings did Riezler consciously advocate a concrete political program which he knew was unattainable. On the contrary, he advocated a program which he believed was attainable

25

and attacked those nationalist programs which he believed were unattainable.

The individual human being is not the only organism which must be dealt with by a political theorist. The *Volk,* the nation, and the state are also organisms and must be treated as such.

Riezler avoided giving a definition of *Volk.* That such a term was left largely undefined was something which would hardly have bothered most Germans in his day, for the concept of the *Volk* as a subjective and undefinable concept was taken for granted by most Germans. Riezler's purpose in writing these two books, especially *Grundzüge der Weltpolitik,* was as much to counteract harmful political influences during Bethmann Hollweg's administration as to provide a sketch, an outline, or a beginning of a theory of politics. Tight, logical definitions were not needed to persuade the many: "It is not our task to present the philosophical and sociological foundations and consequences of this concept *Volk.*"[20]

Riezler acknowledged that the difficulty in defining *Volk* lay in the nature of the thing. "The essence of this living unit called *Volk,* that which makes this a unit, is a mystery as with all living things." The *Volk* cannot be conceived of as a sum of individuals; the whole is not the sum of its parts. It is not a whole by virtue of a common language, as Ernst Moritz Arndt and Johann Gottfried Herder believed, or of a common citizenship. "The *Volk* is a unity of personality." The essence of the *Volk* is never what it seems to be at any one time; it is not to be found in that which has already been attained. The essence of the *Volk* is in the future. Riezler applied the same reasoning concerning the finality of human beings to the *Volk;* as an organism the *Volk* strives continually toward something higher, but it can never attain what it strives for. The *Volk* supports each human's striving in that the *Volk*'s purpose is "the unity of a striving toward the higher." In *Erforderlichkeit des Unmöglichen* Riezler described the *Volk* rather romantically as follows:

It is like the rolling wave which the heavenly storm-wind drives across the endless sea, always growing and shooting higher, carrying on its back smaller waves and the light curl (and in everything stronger or weaker the same pathos of the wind), goes through material only as a form and never abides in that form, shooting too high, strikes foaming over or breaks against a reef; however, under the foam it rolls the same as before and finds itself behind the reef.

Unlike the individual human being, who knows he must die, the *Volk* does not recognize the need·for death. A *Volk* may suffer setbacks, but it never stops developing. The goal, according to Riezler, is "becoming more and more organic, becoming in a higher and higher sense an

26

organism." The *Volk* must aim toward a "more and more inward synthesis."[21]

Riezler saw four "manifestations" of organic unity: space, race, culture, and a state. These are four sides of "possible attainment" and are for a *Volk* "paths to itself." These four elements may be mixed in different ways in different peoples, and a theory of politics has the obligation of seeking the "constant relationship of the variables to each other." Riezler admitted that in such a "fleeting outline" such as *Erforderlichkeit des Unmöglichen,* the four elements could only be touched upon separately.

Riezler regarded a unified space or territory as a necessary precondition for the formation of a unified *Volk* as well as for the formation and the protection of the race and the state. He pointed out that the condition of space heavily influences the *Volk,* an observation made before him by many important Germans including Ranke and Bismarck. In other words, geography influences the character of a *Volk.*

Riezler believed that the element of race had to be treated with great caution. The word was generally used very loosely, and one could not deal with this topic by looking at blood alone. It was true, he admitted, that antipathies and sympathies based on blood relationships and racial-political measures had played an important role in the past and in his time. He observed that a blood relationship is in most cases a precondition of the *Volk* and that whenever it does not actually exist it is usually a goal of the *Volk* to establish a blood relationship. However, Riezler believed that a theory of politics had to deal carefully with the role which the factors of blood mixture and inheritance, space, culture, similar environment, and similar living habits play in the formation of races. His underplaying of the role of race stirred criticism from Professor Hans Freiherr von Liebig, who in 1915 wrote a pamphlet strongly critical of Bethmann Hollweg. Liebig complained that the proper concept of race is "completely excluded" from Riezler's nationalism. In writing a book for prewar Germans, Riezler could not completely exclude race from consideration, but it is abundantly clear that for him the concept of race could not be used as a theoretical justification of any government policy.[22]

Much more important for Riezler and, in his opinion, much easier to grasp, was the element of culture. "There are no peoples without at least the beginning of a unity of culture." Culture, wrote Riezler rather vaguely, was to be understood as the "possession of created forms and the capability to create such." "The created forms are images of the highest purpose"; "they are direction signs to God." These created forms help

27

mold the personality of the *Volk* or nation, just as they help mold the personality of the individual.

Riezler discussed four things within the category of culture which specifically aid a *Volk* in seeing itself and in developing itself intensively: language, art, ethical ideas, and religion. Language is not only a means through which countrymen can maintain contact with each other; its sounds and thought patterns help to shape the personality of the countryman. Language helps to show the *Volk* or nation its uniqueness. A language is also the greatest tool for the expansion of the spirit of the *Volk (Volksgeist)*, and peoples have the desire "to conquer through language." Art is created by individuals who have within them the "idea of the *Volk" (Volksidee)*. Nevertheless, a nation can benefit from the art of other peoples and nations, and the art of a nation promotes the national idea best when it best captures "humanity." Such art advances the "national character" toward the ultimate goal. Ethical ideas are attempts to translate the "highest," which is striven toward, into "shoulds" which regulate the individual's relation to the whole. Religious beliefs are also reflections of the "highest," and each religion considers itself the true vehicle to "the highest," to "humanity." Although religions can be powerful cosmopolitan forces, they tend to become "national religions," and God most often becomes the bearer of the idea of the *Volk*.[23]

At an advanced stage of development after a "higher degree of cultural uniformity and uniqueness, a defined and comprehensive personality" has been attained, the *Volk* becomes a nation. Riezler gave no standard by which to judge when a *Volk* had become a nation.

He by no means considered the nation the highest value for man. The highest goal for man is, in Riezler's words, "that totality, whose conceivable fulfillment for man is humanity itself." Humanity, "as the nation of nations," is "the highest." Every nation wants to become humanity and is the starting point to it. The nation must believe itself to be the only correct starting point, and for most humans it is both the best starting point and the best orientation point throughout life. Close to the goal of humanity "all paths come very close to each other," but the final goal has never been and never will be reached. Falling short of that goal, but striving toward it, "all nations as nations are arrogant, intolerant, and one-sided; the more so they are, the more they are nations." This arrogance is honorable, not calculating or hypocritical.[24]

German thinking regarding the state had been greatly influenced by Hegel and Treitschke, both of whom saw the state as a personality with the task of effecting some kind of synthesis of the individual will and the will of the whole. Both saw a much loftier task for the state than merely preserving the lives of its citizens. Both thought that the state should fit its appropriate *Volk*. Bismarck had regarded the state neither as an organism nor as a personality, but merely as a tool which statesmen employ in the conduct of politics. Riezler's concept of the state drew from all three of the above. Although he did not devote much attention to the origin of the state, Riezler, like Hegel and Treitschke, rejected the idea of a contract as the origin of the state. Instead, a state is established by violence, but soon law and custom replace that violence.

While Riezler saw the necessity for a state, he did not see it as an independent personality merely using the subjects for its own ends, as Veblen characterized the German concept of the state. To Riezler, the state is mainly an instrumentality of the *Volk,* the "corporeality of the supra-individual form." He compared the state to a body and the *Volk* to a soul: the state "needs a unified and internally homogeneous *Volk* as its soul as much as the inner-community of the *Volk*, as a soul, demands a body which not only protects it and gives it the power to act but actually enables it to develop in the first place. For that reason *Volk* and state need each other: they want to become a unit and in this way to achieve a still higher form of organism." In this statement we find the kernel of his concept of the state. The state is outwardly an instrument of the *Volk* and enables the *Volk* to act; it "makes the outward struggle possible." Inwardly, however, it is an element of organization, not simply to keep citizens in their place, as Bismarck believed, but to help the *Volk* develop itself. Also, *Volk* and state actually search for each other; this search is "the final content of all political shoulds." The highest purpose of the state is "the *Volk* which is becoming."

Though Riezler found that a state without a *Volk* was like a body without a soul, he did find that the state could not always follow the *Volk* which it served. The reason for this is that the international environment in which the state must operate places certain demands on the state to which the state must respond. For example, to provide protection for itself and the *Volk*, it may often be driven to conquest although the *Volk* is not yet developed enough to absorb the conquered territory. In this case when the state advances faster than the *Volk*, it must draw the *Volk* to it. It can also happen that the *Volk*'s idea *(Volksidee)* advances faster than the state. For example, the idea of a unified German *Volk* had developed before there was a unified German state to accommodate it. In such a case the *Volk* must draw the state to it. In any case, although the "rhythm of development" is often different, the state and *Volk* must continually seek each other.

29

While readers today are unaccustomed to such concepts as states and peoples seeking each other, it is important to understand Riezler's view of these concepts, which greatly affected his thinking on imperialism, annexationism, occupation policies, and particularly German domestic and constitutional reform. We shall deal with Riezler's concept of the state in greater detail when we discuss his activities in the Chancellery during World War I.

Riezler's belief in the concept of the organic *Volk* set him apart from Hobbes, Locke, and Rousseau, who attempted to build a theoretical structure on the "normal man." The pathos to develop, which is in all organisms, renders such a "normal man" nonexistent. He did not even bother to deal in detail with such thinkers: "Neither Rousseau's geometry of the state nor the teachings of the English rationalists about the greatest good for the greatest number as being the purpose of the state need to be disproved." Also, he denied Hobbes's concept of self-preservation as the basic desire of man. The "self," in Riezler's opinion, is not something which can be preserved; it "is" only insofar as it develops and "becomes."

Like Hegel, Riezler saw the individual acting primarily as a member of a community, not as an isolated individual. Such a community could be a tribe, a *Volk*, or a nation, but by far the most important of these is the nation. Nevertheless, the individual continues his own process of self-realization. Personal and collective self-realization proceed simultaneously and, logically, can conflict with one another. Which self-realization process takes priority? Half of politics revolves around this question, Riezler wrote. His criterion in such a conflict was as follows: "Which of the opposing demands . . . leads closer to the highest goals?" Riezler admitted that no one can know exactly which demand leads to "highest goals." He did venture to assert, however, that the right of the individual personality is superior to the claim of any instrumental organization produced by men (e.g. the state), but is subordinate to the "deeper ethos of the *Volk*."[25]

By means of the "ethical idea," Riezler thought it possible to observe from a distance the "ethos of the Volk." This "ethical idea," as Riezler understood it, is an individual's "attempt to secure one's own . . . law as an idea in his struggle with his environment," or vice versa, "to determine the idea of a general law of the world and then to adjust one's own law in accordance with it." He did not want to present this as a "spirit establishing values" opposed to a "blind and evil nature." He merely wished to unmask those ethical systems claiming absolute validity, but not limiting themselves to a definite form of life, as heroic attempts of the intellect *(Geist)* to raise one's own law to the level of idea and to expand it to a "law of the world." This thinking shows the influence of both Nietzsche and of historicism: ethical systems and ideas of justice are "horizons" of the philosopher or are understandable only in relation to a certain time and place. On the one hand, they are a result of the will to self-realization, but on the other hand, as elements of reflection, they are possible correctives to the elementary will of peoples to realize themselves.

Riezler asked whether there is a place for ethics in human affairs, whether there is a differentiation between good and evil. He did not want to neglect the question of this ethical differentiation, and he himself called the goal of all striving "the highest good." However, there is a great difficulty in deriving ethical prescriptions from a secular evolutionary process and from goals which can be neither attained nor defined clearly. Unlike Aristotle, who established from nature an ethical system which each man could apply to his own life, Riezler, who denied "normal man" and who stressed an evolutionary process with unreachable goals, could not determine ethical principles. Ethical principles could hardly be derived from "the impossible."

This absence of clearly defined ethical principles leaves individual organisms, including man, in a difficult position and leads easily to tragedy, a word which appears very often in Riezler's writing. He explained the source of this tragedy as follows:

That man in his deepest experience is only vaguely conscious of his own law, which he does not comprehend as such; that to live according to his law is the greatest happiness of earth's children; that rather than avoiding it men suffer death and the greatest hardships and know that they can lose everything if they remain what they are without being able to recognize what they actually are. . . . We call it character, admire it as personality, sense the happiness to be a self. . . . We sense regret if we are traitors to a puzzling law of our self which we do not know. We search eternally for this self and hope eternally to find it, happy to utilize it and unhappy to miss it. It is no material unit . . . and is no form which is finally grasped and held onto. It is a form of a much more puzzling kind. It is a part of its essence to be in that it develops, becomes, and never completely reaches the end—thus, a something of deep tragedy and incomprehensible . . . being cast eternally back and forth between expansion and limitation, between the striving toward both diversity and unity as both directions of an unending synthesis. Man, driven by the deepest pathos, never arrives at any kind of final realization. The same pathos which drives him out of peace and into the struggle, which forces him to expand in order to be, drives him out of his peace in order that he can find that peace again and does not even let him remain there. The monk on the post and the horseman in battle seek in principle one and the same thing.[26]

31

Riezler did not stop at the difficulty of deriving ethics and at the tragedy which results from organisms striving for self-realization. He was working on a theory of politics, and, as already mentioned, a theory of politics must protect the statesman from naive and shallow views.

It was important, he felt, for the statesman to know what to expect of relations among nations. Observation indicated that the most basic and the most obvious fact in international affairs is the battle of men and peoples. This is an "open or hidden war of all against all" and is called by Riezler the "national tendency." He observed, however, that this war is not waged continually, but appears at times to give way to peaceful coexistence and cooperation. Such peaceful coexistence must, in Riezler's opinion, be understood only as a postponement of hostility. He did not believe, as Kant did, in the possibility of eternal peace. He called the postponement of hostility the "cosmopolitan tendency." The predominance of one tendency over the other gives an epoch its character; he argued that the epoch in which he was living was characterized by the national tendency.

Riezler's study of history as well as his observation of his own time convinced him that overt or latent hostility among states predominated despite the necessity for statesmen to pay lip service to the ideals of peace and international justice. Coexistence "dominates in many ways the speech which practicing statesmen use," but hostility "dominates their thoughts." Such "peace phraseology" is employed by statesmen to support national interests and is thus a political tool. "We have to concentrate on the concrete and on that part of historical development which is open to us." Riezler's own time was, in fact, dominated by nationalism; hostility was the basic observable relation among nations, and national borders were more often drawn through wars rather than through peaceful means. This observation was very important for him.

While Riezler's own observation and classical study indicated the fact of hostility among nations, other factors pointed to the desirability or at least the inevitability of this hostility. First, a nation is a nation in that it feels a sense of mission and a sense of being chosen over other nations to come closest to "the highest good." Since each nation feels that it alone takes the right path, it tends to be intolerant of other nations which make the same claim; it tends to be hostile to those nations. Second, "the organism is a process which needs a hostile environment against which it can develop itself in action and reaction. It needs the other. Strength needs opposition in order to be a strength." A nation, in Riezler's opinion, could not exist without this hostility; since the nation was the surest

32

path to the highest, hostility had to be considered good. "The pacifists will not see peace on earth until war against the inhabitants of Mars has become possible and necessary." Third, the necessary expansion of a nation as the more highly unified *Volk* must eventually bring it into conflict with other nations. There must be no theoretical limits on this expansion. "Theoretically every *Volk* wants to grow, expand, dominate and subjugate without end, wants to consolidate itself more and more firmly and organize itself more and more, to become an ever higher unity until totality has become an organic whole under its domination."[27]

For some modern readers this is a shocking passage, a "philosophy pregnant with war," "an idealistically embellished, militant philosophy of the merciless struggle of all against all," "an ideological justification of German aspirations to be a world power." Indeed, it does on the surface appear to lend itself to various interpretations. Is this, however, an adequate analysis of Riezler's views which were given practical application in *Grundzüge der Weltpolitik?* Was he simply a civilian Bernhardi who was trying to give a philosophical foundation to the exorbitant demands of the Pan-Germans, and can one interpret the above passage as an active program of conquest whose acceptance Riezler was advocating? As the word "theoretically" indicates, it was not. Contemporary criticism of *Grundzüge der Weltpolitik* clearly showed that it was not regarded in his time as being any such thing. A careful reading of *Grundzüge der Weltpolitik* indicates that Riezler was strongly criticizing the loud nationalists of his time, that he did not regard war as timely or useful, that peaceful expansion was possible, and that a reorientation of German policy in the direction of moderation and patience was both necessary and possible.[28]

Riezler was convinced that German nationalists in prewar Germany understood only one dimension of national expansion—the extensive dimension. He believed that growth must be in two directions; there must be both a growth in breadth (territorial growth) and growth in depth—both extensive and intensive expansion. Riezler rejected Aristotle's idea that the size of the community should be limited. He did not doubt that all peoples and nations desire to expand territorially, and he thought this desire to be good. However, this territorial expansion in no way exhausts necessary national growth.

A *Volk* which spreads out conquering foreign lands does not become more of a nation because of it. On the contrary, if it does not become a tightly jointed nation at the same time that it expands and conquers, it appears to have to perish and disintegrate precisely because of this expansion.

A *Volk* which stresses only conquest is like a tree "whose branches grow too long, cannot be nourished any longer, fade away, and endanger or destroy the life of the tree itself."[29] A strengthening of the inner organic structure must accompany growth in breadth.

He believed that Germany was in a period of intellectual decline.

The great intellectual conceptions, according to which the uniqueness of peoples and their cultures took shape, are a thing of the past; our time can show no such conceptions through which the inner essence of peoples reshapes itself, develops itself further, deepens itself.

Germans were beginning to have doubts about the possible supremacy of the German spirit. They had forgotten Napoleon's experiences with *"l'impuissance de la force,"* and exaggerated the "power of force." Due to her craving for recognition, Germany lacked judgment and goal orientation, and her nationalism showed "the manners of a young dog." She lacked "political sense," and was laden with "envy and resentments," both of which were poor advisers for an "upstart" who did not know how to "let things ripen." German nationalism was "primarily extensive," and sought the expansion of German power without comprehending the limits and considerations which arose out of the complexity of world and colonial politics. Riezler asked if the exclusive extensiveness of German nationalism could be reduced or whether "the well was beginning to run dry." This was for him a crucial question upon which "the fate of Germany" depended. The "decline of peoples" always began with "the decline of their cultures."[30]

Riezler's message was clear: national extensive expansion was natural and could in the right circumstances be good, but those who think exclusively in terms of the extensive development of a nation damage or destroy the true national idea, an idea which Riezler clearly considered to be superior to the cosmopolitan idea. In fact, the neglect of internal development would prevent a nation from either becoming or remaining a nation.

He could hardly have been more explicit when he discussed the "nationalists," who have a place in every healthy modern nation. One spoke, wrote Riezler, of Pan-Slavists, Pan-Germans, Pan-French, Pan-American, and even Pan-Italian. "Pan" movements usually had a "pan-party"; without question he had the Pan-Germans in mind. The pressure which the Pan-German Union put on Bethmann Hollweg was such that he declared in 1912 almost in despair: "Politics cannot be made with these idiots!"

Riezler softened his attack on the Pan-Germans by stressing that these representatives of extensive expansion belong in any nation which is not "weak or tired." Nevertheless, they are usually not those people who "understand in the deepest sense the national idea and the national interest."

> They are certainly the most impatient and most determined representatives of the national idea, who push forward, express demands and desires before they become ripe, move far in advance of developments, and for that reason are mainly a nuisance to governments, which try to follow them slowly and when appropriate, to use them.[31]

The irritation felt by Bethmann Hollweg and his supporters in government circles is clearly expressed in this sentence. *Grundzüge der Weltpolitik* clearly is no "ideological justification of German aspirations to be a world power," but an attempt to instruct Germans about the requirements of world power.

While Riezler feared that perhaps "the nations cease being the bearers of ideas" and that "an epoch of new cosmopolitanism would follow the epoch of nationalism," he maintained that such an epoch of cosmopolitanism would only be temporary since other peoples would always rise up. "National organisms have always proved themselves to be the strongest principle of life, and as it always was, so it will always be."[32] In *Grundzüge der Weltpolitik,* Riezler presented the national and cosmopolitan tendencies as cohabiting forces in world politics and maintained that the understanding of these forces was essential for statesmen. Let us look briefly at some of the cosmopolitan tendencies.

Riezler discussed certain aspects of the "general modern ideal of culture," that is, those values which could be called international and which form the general mark of an epoch. Such a value in his time was "the enormous estimation of human life as an absolute good." Most people no longer saw life primarily in terms of the kind of life, as the ancients and a few modern peoples (e.g., the Chinese)[33] had viewed it. Today "the struggle against death binds all peoples." This view of life was the foundation for the modern "condemnation of war as an evil." It now took courage to see "war not only as something necessary but also as something good under certain circumstances," but anyone who held this view certainly found himself in opposition to conventional thinking of his time. The general condemnation of war was the basis for pacifism, which "has become an organized movement in our time." All governments must pay respect to this movement, at least in the external aspect of their actions or in their way of speaking, and this movement placed certain restrictions on governments. Riezler in no way wanted to be identified with this movement, which he scorned. However, he did think that the present constellation was favorable to peace and that governments' stress on peace was basically compatible with the peculiarities of the present constellation.[34]

Related to the pacifist movement was the "internationality of pity." This phenomenon was easily seen in the political significance of publicized atrocities in far-away places and revealed a characteristic partisanship for the weak, something wholly foreign to the ancients. This type of international pity was "one of the most essential characteristics of German public opinion." It was also seen in the protection which small states enjoyed *vis-à-vis* their large neighbors. The international morality, which "observers" uphold, condemned the assertion of "raw superiority." However, this international morality, which in "the political phraseology of the time" was summarized in such vague expressions as "civilization" and "humanity," was applied only to the relations of great states with each other and with neighboring small, but civilized, states; the very same international morality was used to justify national expansion and colonial expansion at the expense of "uncivilized states."

The cultural idea created an atmosphere of idealism which dominated only the "exterior form" of international politics. This atmosphere could in some cases place certain limitations on political actions. Nevertheless, the human intellect's art of interpretation provided much latitude for political action. It was merely the necessity of the epoch's "style of diplomacy" to bring political action and the atmosphere of idealism into harmony. One should not be deceived concerning the "thinness and bloodlessness" of the cultural ideal. "It is like a garment, which one is used to putting on; this garment has no influence on the inner nature." The "living power" of the national tendency was much stronger. This cultural ideal

is more smoke than fire. The forces and ideas which dominate human life are of another kind. They are as much alive as earlier. The only difference is that they reside under the surface. The surface of international phraseology lies over them like a veil, but only the opportunity is needed to call them out of the depths, and the veil rips apart.

Riezler's derisive language indicates his clear disagreement with the cultural ideal of his time, but it does not mean that he favored doffing the garment. On the contrary, he spoke out in his diary and in his wartime articles for mastery of the art of appearance in politics. Germany's failure to master the use of appearance and her preference for "the steamroller" made it impossible for Germany to win sympathy in Europe for her war aims.

Related to the cosmopolitan tendency of regarding human life as an "absolute good" was another cosmopolitan tendency: "the general going-to-sleep of idealism, the skepticism against all ideals, the valuation of personal pleasure . . . in short . . . materialism." The chief danger of this tendency was that it had a moderating and enervating effect on "all strong and forward driving forces which find their expression and direction in ideals." It can even affect the "national drive for life." This materialism was an expression of a certain "fatique of the epoch."[35]

A further cosmopolitan tendency was international socialism. Riezler believed that the popularity of socialism necessitated a certain lip service to socialist "peace theories," which would affect only the form, not the substance of politics. He observed that for the Social Democratic Party of Germany (SPD) and for all other socialist parties in countries where strong national feeling prevailed, the national bonds were stronger than the socialist bonds. The patriotism of socialist parties in all belligerent countries after the outbreak of the First World War offered clear evidence that Riezler was right.

Up to now we have discussed cosmopolitan tendencies which affected only the form of politics, not the substance. Riezler indicated one cosmopolitan tendency, however, which profoundly affected the substance of international politics—capital. Capital had a cosmopolitan and a national aspect, and these two aspects were closely related to each other. Here Riezler applied to present-day circumstances the central problem with which he had dealt in his first work. As in ancient Greece, economic life had expanded far beyond the borders of the nation state. "The possibility of capital investment is internationalized, and as a result the economic interests of the capitalist have become detachable from the economic and political fate of the country to which he belongs." What was the result? "The world has become a single, interrelated economic area"; autarky had become impossible. Instead of being like a forest in which the trees touched each other only with the tips of their branches, the world had become like "a thick, untrimmed hedge, in which at every point branches of many trunks are inseparably entwined and bound."

Riezler thought that capital had a cosmopolitan effect because capital had an interest in peaceful development and for that reason resisted a policy of nationalist territorial expansion. Destructive wars against other countries meant losses of one's own investments in that country. This did not mean that capital operated against the struggle between nations; it operated only against a special form of the national struggle—war. Thus, capital affected the form, not the substance, of the national tendency; it softened the expression of the national tendency.

Riezler could not be sure that this cosmopolitan tendency would be weaker than the national tendency in the event of a serious conflict. Whether the "businessman" would be stronger than the "countryman" depended to a great extent on the strength of materialism, which "has gradually become the Weltanschauung of the common man in the second half of the previous century." The common man believed that money could buy all pleasures, and pleasures were supreme. "Modern hedonism is eminently cosmopolitan. It is because it is individualistic."[36] If it were true that money were everything, then business interests would overrule national interests. However, there had been no serious trials in the few decades prior to 1913 to test the superior strength of materialism. The fact that the national tendency seemed to be gaining strength was significant and indicated to Riezler the likelihood that the citizen would be stronger. At the beginning of the First World War there was, in fact, resistance from financial circles to fighting a war, but once war became inevitable, the "citizen" did prove to be stronger than the businessman, just as Riezler suspected.

A final significant cosmopolitan tendency with which Riezler dealt was international law, which sought to eliminate force from relations among peoples and to replace it with law; "what can be understood to be more cosmopolitan than the unity of legal community binding all men?" The desire for binding international law was great and helped to create and maintain an "idealistic atmosphere." While this was "only appearance and a soap-bubble," this "idealistic atmosphere is in itself . . . a real force." He observed that "even appearances are real forces, especially in politics. It is an imponderable." "The idealistic atmosphere . . . is a soft and invisible net over the politicians of the civilized world, which makes it difficult for them . . . to challenge the rules and customs and forces them all to cover up these challenges. . . . As a result, the struggle is refined and slowed down, the beast of prey is tamed." In Riezler's opinion one should not overestimate the power of international law. Accords such as The Hague agreement dealt only with the form of war, not with its abolition. International arbitration was successful only when it was in the interest of the conflicting states to submit disputes to arbitration. However, this kind of common interest is not genuine cosmopolitanism. International courts of arbitration are nothing more than the "organized postponement of national struggles." Never are vital national questions settled in courts nor are "wars which are wanted" avoided through courts. International treaties, like international arbitration, are dependent upon the national interests of the states involved.

Whenever these treaties are respected, it is not due to the power or authority of a superior court, but to the interest of the parties themselves. . . . In excited times when a *Volk* has to fight for its existence, the national will to live will neither regard the moral condemnation of the observers nor have any difficulty in withdrawing from the suggestion of the idea of justice, but will keep or break treaties as its interest dictates. That is very simply the lesson of history.[37]

While Riezler was correct in seeing a strong link between national interest and the observance of international law, he was surprised later to see how much strength some treaties had in the minds of men. Violation of neutrality or of Hague agreements did lead to more than just "observers' showing their fleeting indignation to the violators only in a few flighty newspaper articles." Disregard for certain treaties helped cement the alliance against Germany, gave the Allies a sense of a mission, and strengthened the will to fight until Germany surrendered.

Riezler's belief in the priority of national interest remained unchanged throughout the First World War. Although he was frequently critical of German policy and advocated basic changes in the German society and constitution, he did so because he wished to see German strength and influence maintained or increased. That is, his criticisms and reforms were in Germany's national interest.

CONTINENTAL POLICY VERSUS WORLD POLICY

In the years before the outbreak of the First World War there were numerous reminders that the national idea was not dead or even outdated. The second Moroccan crisis of 1911 and the increasing advocacy of war by numerous influential Germans revealed how urgent it was to show Germans how to give vent to their powerful national drive without resorting to war. Riezler saw a pressing need to add specific feasible proposals to his theoretical insights in order to gain support for Bethmann Hollweg's policy of peaceful cooperation with the nations of Europe.

Riezler was well aware of the damage to Germany's political position due to the first Moroccan crisis of 1905-06. "The Moroccan question threw a net over German freedom of movement." "One sought a way out of this net." Germany, with only one firm ally, Austria-Hungary, now felt

39

herself surrounded by hostile powers, and Riezler believed that this ring had to be loosened. Germany tried to make a start toward this by signing a German-French Moroccan Treaty in 1909; Germany recognized French political interests in Morocco in return for French recognition of German economic interests there. This treaty proved to have been a correct calculation; "Europe felt relieved." "The diplomatic encirclement," Riezler wrote, "was broken." The relief in Europe was soon shattered. Feeling her interest in Morocco threatened by the French dispatching of a military mission to Fez in the spring of 1911, Germany sent the gunboat *Panther* to the Atlantic port of Agadir on July 1, 1911. France's action was clearly wrong, for it was a violation of the agreements of Algeciras; however, the German reaction caused Europe to overlook this point. German bellicosity concerned Europe more than a questionable French interpretation of treaties.[38]

From Riezler's diary entries it is clear that he favored a firm stand in Morocco. He was sure that reasonable compensation could be obtained from France only if Germany held territory in hostage. More important, he thought that if Germany challenged France so resolutely that France's allies would not dare support her, then the Entente would be weakened, if not entirely broken up. However, strong British intervention eventually forced Germany to back down and to accept a compromise solution. Germany declared its disinterest in Morocco in return for a colony of highly questionable value—the Cameroons. The German government spoke of a "prestige success," but this evaluation was by no means accepted by vocal German nationalists. German Colonial Secretary von Lindequist resigned rather than sign the agreement, and a majority in the Reichstag accused the government of "spinelessness." Many Germans now spoke of the "humiliation" of Agadir.[39]

There is no evidence whatsoever in Riezler's diary, in *Grundzüge der Weltpolitik,* or in Bethmann's memoirs that either Bethmann Hollweg or Riezler "wanted war" or "were disappointed that the Empire conceded at the last minute." This is true despite a diary entry on July 30, 1911, in which he spoke of "the genuine German idealistic and correct conviction that the *Volk* needs a war. Bethmann also shares this conviction." Immanuel Geiss found that this statement placed Riezler and Bethmann Hollweg in fundamental agreement with those who "wanted war and were disappointed that the Empire conceded at the last minute." Geiss's stress on this point is questionable. Geiss proceeded as follows: He found it unimportant that Bethmann Hollweg did not consider it the goal of German policy to bring about a war. More important, wrote Geiss, was Bethmann's opinion "that we must hold firm and bear the risk of war."

Most important, Geiss continued, is the information that even Bethmann Hollweg at that time had "the genuine idealistic conviction that the *Volk* needs a war." Why should one not reverse these statements in order of importance? Are not those statements containing conditions more important for German policy than the "idealistic conviction" that the people needed a war? That the people should only accept the "risk of war" and that war should not be Germany's objective are of considerably greater importance than the "idealistic conviction" that the people needed war.[40]

In his prewar writings Riezler made it very clear that he was not a pacifist and that he did not rule out the use of military force in international affairs. Indeed, his thinking on war in general was no different than that of most of his contemporaries, regardless of educational, social, or national background. Nevertheless, it must be remembered that to accept war as a legitimate instrument in international affairs and to accept the risk of war in specific cases are not at all the same as wanting a war and being disappointed when it does not come about. Furthermore, if Bethmann had wanted a war, he would not have been so concerned about the apparent dangers of open hostilities; he could have urged the kaiser to steer a war course, and indeed he might have been successful in accomplishing this goal. Riezler's diary indicates that the chancellor advocated caution and wanted to keep alternatives open. Riezler was aware that many Germans would be disappointed if Germany backed down. Pressure from nationalist groups and the press was so intense that "if we offer anything, we will receive nothing but press tumult and war cries." Thus, the German public seemed to be uncompromising.[41]

A war in 1911 would have been a radical break with the deliberate foreign policy which Bethmann Hollweg had pursued since 1909. In matters of actual policy, Riezler did not seek the "impossible"; he wanted Germany to pursue a rational policy within the limits imposed by the constellation of powers. Riezler found nothing wrong with the increasingly strong national tendency in Germany, but he was strongly critical of its manifestations: the German *Volk* overestimated "the power of force" and lacked "judgment and sureness of aim." It showed "the manners of a young dog" and "lacks political sense." It was impatient and stressed only "extensive expansion." This, Riezler noted critically, was the *Volk* which felt in 1911 that it needed a war.[42]

The diplomatic consequences of the second Moroccan crisis were not favorable for Germany. Germans not only felt that the ring around them had been tightened, but they could no longer count on the unconditional support of Austria-Hungary. France experienced a *réveil national,* and

41

Wayne C. Thompson

Britain regarded Germany with greater apprehension. The international goodwill toward Germany's foreign policy, for which Bethmann Hollweg had worked, had disappeared. As Churchill wrote: "For the first time she had made British statesmen feel that sense of direct contact with the war peril which was never absent from continental minds." Riezler described the significance of the second Moroccan crisis as follows:

> This chapter of German world policy illustrates as no other the uniqueness of the Empire's world political situation, the limits of its possibilities to expand, the linkage of world politics to continental politics, the complexity of the factors which German world politics has to take into consideration. All of these difficulties spring from a geographic situation which binds great power and hems in freedom of movement.[43]

The need to show Germans peaceful outlets for their energy was made particularly pressing by the increasingly open advocacy of war since the second Moroccan crisis. Such advocacy was an embarrassment to the German government, which was seeking accommodation rather than direct confrontation to further German interests in the world. The kaiser began to speak of an approaching war between the Germanic and Slavic races, and he called his military leaders (but not the chancellor) to a "war council" on December 8, 1912, to discuss the matter. That same month, he wrote:

> The battle of Germans against the Russo-Gauls for their very existence is coming. No conference can soften that because that is not a great political question but a race question. It is a question of the existence or non-existence of the Germanic race in Europe.

In general, the kaiser acted much more cautiously than he spoke. Nevertheless, his careless statements did have an influence on public opinion and thus had considerable political significance.[44]

The German general staff was by no means silent on the subject of a war in the near future. Helmuth von Moltke, chief of the general staff, suggested to Foreign Secretary Jagow that perhaps a preventive war against France and Russia would be wise, considering the increasing Russian military strength resulting from a reform of the Russian armed forces. However, the most significant military influence on German public opinion was a book first published early in 1912, which by 1914 had been released in nine editions and which had been translated into almost all major languages of the world, including Japanese—*Deutschland und der Nächste Krieg (Germany and the Next War)*. The author, General Friedrich von Bernhardi, a retired officer and,

42

according to Gerhard Ritter, an "outsider," noted that the Germans "have reached a crisis in our national and political developments" and therefore had "the duty to make war." He wrote:

War is a biological necessity of the first importance, a regulative element in the life of mankind which cannot be dispensed with, since without it an unhealthy development will follow, which excludes every advancement of the race, and therefore all civilization . . . . Without war, inferior or decaying races would easily choke the growth of healthy, budding elements, and a universal decadence would follow.

Since "strong, healthy and flourishing nations require a continual expansion of their frontiers, conquest . . . becomes a law of necessity." Bernhardi was exactly the kind of nationalist whom Riezler criticized for emphasizing only "external expansion." Whereas Riezler criticized Germans for not seeing *"l'impuissance de la force,"* Bernhardi asserted that "might gives the right to occupy or conquer."[45]

Bethmann Hollweg also faced opposition from the Pan-German League, from the crown prince and from the Reichstag, where a majority accused Bethmann of "spinelessness" after the Moroccan crisis. The crown prince was held by nationalist circles to be one who, according to the Pan-German *Kreuzzeitung,* "would have preferred another solution to the Morocco conflict" than the chancellor or Wilhelm, whom Pan-German and Free Conservative journals had openly called "William the Peaceful" and "Guillaume le timide." Bethmann frequently had to seek the aid of the emperor in order to block the crown prince's attempt to thwart his policies.[46]

Prevailing German public opinion hampered a foreign policy which would have been most successful in advancing Germany's political interests in the world. Something had to be done to educate the public. On June 25, 1913, Bethmann Hollweg wrote:

I have had enough of war and bellicose talk and of eternal armaments. It is high time that the great nations settle down and pursue peaceful work. Otherwise it will certainly come to an explosion, which no one wants and which will hurt everyone.

Fritz Fischer stated the purpose of Riezler's *Grundzüge der Weltpolitik* so:

Kurt Riezler's book, written in October, 1913, sought to disprove or at least to control the continuous attacks by the nationalist press that the government had no power political program whatsoever.

43

This is essentially correct. Riezler was not putting nationalism into question; nor was he denying that the German government had a "nationalist-imperialist orientation."[47] He was merely questioning the extensive brand of nationalism which was so popular in Germany. He did not advocate a strictly continental policy, and he spoke out strongly in favor of supporting German economic interests throughout the world. He had only ridicule for those who spoke seriously of "eternal peace," and he emphatically denied that war was an evil which should be avoided at all costs. *Grundzüge der Weltpolitik* was to a great extent a journalistic work which was aimed not so much at pacifists or cosmopolitan Germans but at the extensive nationalists who, in Riezler's opinion, represented the greatest danger for Germany at that time. Since he was attempting to persuade such extreme, but confused nationalists, he did not hesitate to use language which would appeal to them. The Hegelian, Darwinian, and Nietzschean language in *Grundzüge der Weltpolitik* shocks many modern readers, but Riezler saw that he could convince with greater success if he were seen as being in essential agreement with his opponents but simply disagreeing with their methods. Moderation can very often be more effective than a frontal attack. One need only compare the language in *Grundzüge der Weltpolitik* with that of his diary to see how his language differed when he was attempting to persuade and when he was merely writing down his thoughts.

One may argue that Riezler's nationalism differed only in degree, but not in kind, with that of the more stridently nationalistic opponents of the chancellor. Perhaps that is true. Nevertheless, many important differences in human affairs are matters of degree or proportion. The differences in the consequences of policies which differ only in degree can be enormous. Certainly, one can expect great differences in the consequences of a nationalism which stresses moderation, patience, and peaceful cooperation and of a nationalism which impatiently preaches external expansion by whatever means, although both remain nationalist in kind. Also, judging by the fact that most nations of the world maintain armed forces, it can certainly be said that most statesmen, then and now, are willing to use military force in international affairs; however, the crucial questions are: for what causes, under what circumstances, and to what extent? That is, their differences concerning the use of force are essentially ones of degree, not of kind.

Based exclusively on Riezler's refusal to take a diametrically opposed position to those he was trying to persuade, one cannot assume that *Grundzüge der Weltpolitik* was merely "an ideological justification for German aspirations for world power," "that Riezler may have been well aware that his demand could be fulfilled only through war," or that by the summer of 1914 Riezler in fact strove for "world domination."[48] A careful reading of *Grundzüge der Weltpolitik* reveals that such assumptions are untenable. Let us look at Riezler's description of Germany's dilemma and his proposals for extricating Germany from that dilemma.

Before July 1914, Riezler considered war to be untimely and inappropriate. There were several reasons for this. The first reason was the interdependence of economics. There was, as a result, "a community of economic interests in the civilized world." Wars were economically destructive for all participating nations. National rivalries continued to exist, but they manifested themselves in more moderate ways.

Second, Riezler believed that the constellation of powers was not such that war was unavoidable. He argued that an understanding of the political constellation is essential in predicting what is politically possible. That which happens is determined by forces and their laws; he calls these forces "tendencies." If one wishes to know how these "tendencies" will manifest themselves in individual events, then one must consider the present constellation, which "is the foundation for the activity of these forces. The forces operate within a constellation." In politics one cannot predict events based on knowledge of the tendency and constellation as exactly as one can in the natural sciences. One cannot conduct experiments with the political constellation, and the individual factors of politics cannot be isolated. Nevertheless, the relation between tendency and constellation remains in politics whether one has perfect understanding of it or not. Riezler was interested in the basic trends or "outlines" *(Grundzüge)* of the political constellation of his time; these outlines gave contemporary politics its specific character.[49]

That which was the most obvious characteristic of modern politics was that it was world politics.

That means that the world has become a unified political arena, that any political event anywhere in the world affects, or at least can affect, everything else. It means that it is no longer possible to view any territorial area and special question as fully isolated.

Riezler held this development to be more than fifty years old. World politics was considered by the neo-Rankean school as the transition from the system of European powers, about which Ranke wrote, to a system of world powers. The European balance of power was to be transformed into a world balance of power. Thus Germany, already a strong European power, had to have an active world policy. Bülow popularized the slogan for such world politics in a speech before the Reichstag in December

1897: "We do not want to force anyone into our shadows, but we also demand our place in the sun."[50]

Colonialism and economic interdependence were important reasons for the emergence of world politics. However, Riezler was not so interested in the origins of world politics as in its consequences. He asked the reader to imagine himself in the position of a statesman responsible for the foreign policy of a modern great power (e. g. Bethmann Hollweg).

The man has to be aware of the interests of his own empire on the European continent, in the Mediterranean, in America, in Africa, in the Near or Far East. Because of world political linkage, the position which he takes in one question affects the political situation in other areas.

Interests pursued in one area should not adversely affect interests in another area. Almost as if anticipating the outbreak of the First World War, Riezler noted that "the attempt to isolate the diplomatic constellation locally can be successful only temporarily and to a limited degree."[51]

Because of such interrelationship of interests, it was very unlikely that the interests of two powers would clash in every area of the world. Therefore, such interrelationship had a moderating effect on the hostility of the great powers. When two powers were divided on one question, they were brought together by another. For example, tension between Britain and Germany during the Moroccan crisis of 1911 could be partially overcome by cooperation in the Near East in 1912-13.

Did not the existence of two opposing alliances, the Triple Entente and the Triple Alliance, make cooperation with hostile powers more difficult? Riezler warned of interpreting political questions solely in terms of this duality because one would then overlook the threads running between single powers in one group to single powers in the other group. Very seldom did these two groups confront each other directly. One must not deny entirely the reality and significance of these groupings, but they applied only to the European problem. They had, in Riezler's opinion, "no actual world political character," although they could at times influence the line-up of powers in world political questions. As we shall see in the following chapter, he greatly underestimated the strength of the bonds between the Entente powers.

Riezler believed that all powers should act according to a careful consideration of national interest. All statesmen must distinguish between vital and non-vital interests, and he stressed to his readers that for European continental powers, European interests were the vital interests. "World politics for these states is always a compromise with continental politics and thus limited in many ways in its freedom of movement."

Riezler, of course, wished again to emphasize the crucial point that German political activities in the world should never endanger German vital interests on the European continent.

To the complexity of the constellation, the interpenetration of interests, and the multiplicity of political considerations Riezler added another important characteristic of the general political constellation of the time—the possibility of "parallel expansion." In *Finanzen und Monopole* Riezler had described how the economic activity of the *poleis* beyond their borders led to war because the cities' competition for markets was not conducted in cooperation. Riezler found that this was no longer the case in his time. Asia and Africa offered European powers "free room for growth." "All political agreements in recent years have come at the costs of these parts of the world." More important, through economic development there were now possibilities for growth which did not necessitate political conquest. "States now have room not only to develop next to one another but into one another." Such development "into one another" postpones or at least limits hostility. Growth would follow the "direction of the least resistance." This possibility gave "the political character of the time the stamp of peaceful cooperation and of peaceful solutions to conflicts which arise." When conflicts arise between two states, both would have an interest in postponing the struggle because both would benefit from a compromise. No longer was it a question of "either you or I," but "both of us! This to you and that to me!" That is, territories could be exchanged or interest spheres established. Any change in one area could be compensated in another.

Another factor of the "constellation of coexistence" was that as a result of modern industry, land was no longer the exclusive prerequisite for expansion. No longer was growth simply the conquest of land; growth could be accomplished through economic expansion. "A country can grow in wealth, power and population in accordance with the quantity and quality of the goods which it produces and markets." It could now support a growing population without exporting part of its population. To a great degree "the struggle for land has become a struggle for markets." Also, these markets did not need to be controlled politically. The likelihood of peaceful rivalry thus became greater because while the quantity of land could not be increased, the ability of markets to absorb goods could increase almost indefinitely. The prosperity which would result could be enjoyed by all nations. That which would be earned by one country would not be taken away from another. Value would be created from what was nothing. "Rivalry is now only a question of percentage of profits." In this rivalry no great economic power had to be eliminated; on the contrary, elimination of a great economic power could be ruinous. Specifically, economic downfall of either Britain or Germany, which were each other's best customers, would very seriously damage the other.

Riezler did not deny that the struggle over the percentage of profits was at the same time a struggle for political and cultural influence. Political influence aided in receiving important concessions (e.g. for railways), and through financial loans, etc., states could increase their countrymen's share in profits. "The use of political influence for economic purposes is half the contents of modern world politics." Although political domination might have been most desirable, the constellation made political domination, economic monopolization, or banning of all competition impossible. The necessary program was: "freedom of trade for all powers."

Despite the peaceful effect of parallel expansion, Riezler was not willing to guarantee that wars could not arise out of conflicts in certain areas. Many questions such as the possession of the Dardanelles, the strategic exits from the Adriatic Sea, the domination of the Mediterranean Sea and Alsace-Lorraine, and, of course, the Balkans (which he failed to mention) could set off a war. While coexistence characterized world politics, European politics could still only be characterized by hostility. Parallel expansion merely gave Europe "a certain rest." Nor was he willing to argue that economic coexistence would be possible forever. Economic competition was not limited by territory, but it could become increasingly sharp. When such competition increases too much, then political conflicts are carried more and more into economic life, and political power is employed increasingly against economic competitors. He concluded rather pessimistically that "even economic coexistence is on the way toward turning into political hostility."[52]

This did not mean that Riezler foresaw a new era of wars in the near or distant future. On the contrary, he was convinced that the destructiveness of modern wars practically prevented states from ever engaging in them on a grand scale. Riezler proposed that Germany pursue a policy of peaceful expansion and cooperation, a policy which he thought could be successful.

He saw German unity as the beginning of a new development toward world politics, and he saw several crucial tasks which Germany's statesmen had to accomplish. All required world politics. "The young German people are pressing outward into the world." In order to provide the rapidly increasing population with jobs and necessities of life, Germany had to step up her industrialization and to find increasingly large markets abroad. On the one hand, Germans could not think exclusively in continental terms; on the other hand, Germany's geographic position in the middle of the great powers had lost none of its traditional strategic significance. Indeed, "this development of economic interests and of world political feeling on the one hand, and the consequences of the continental position of the German Empire on the other hand form the uniqueness of the political situation of modern Germany." All of the great powers had possibilities of expansion right before their doors: Russia had Asia; Austria-Hungary had the Balkans; France and Italy had the North African coast; the island power, Britain, had the world. These states had "more or less only one side to defend and the other is free." Germany's central position made her more dependent than her neighbors upon the constellation in Europe. To strengthen his argument, Riezler invoked the greatest authority in the eyes of his readers, Bismarck, whose policy was built around this principle. He modified Bismarck's policy enough to allow for world politics, but he asserted that in dealing with any world political question German statesmen always had to examine the consequences for the European constellation.

Riezler found that Germany's first world political activities had influenced the European constellation in a manner unfavorable to Germany. For example, the Berlin-to-Bagdad railway had facilitated a *rapprochement* between Russia and Britain, and German opposition to France in Morocco had had a similar effect on Britain and France. Riezler felt that Germany had to place limits on French expansion because Germany could not allow any other colonies to fall completely under foreign influence, but this problem simply illuminated Germany's own dilemma of being caught between world political and European continental considerations.

In this relation between world and continental politics lies . . . the *circulus vitiosus* of the German Empire's foreign policy. World political activities affect continental politics, under whose influence the German Empire must limit its world political activities.

German politics had to escape from this vicious circle. In Riezler's view, this was the main problem in Germany's foreign policy; "everything which happens must be conceived as an attempt at its solution." The less Germany was constrained by the European constellation, the more world political flexibility she would have.[53]

To break the vicious circle, Riezler offered three concrete policies: (1) increase Germany's military power on land, (2) cease challenging Britain's navy, (3) seek an understanding with Britain.

49

Riezler sought a military situation in which "Germany is so strong on the continent that regardless of the political constellation, the chances for victory are on her [Germany's] side." That is, Germany should be able to repel an attack on the European continent by any combination of powers whatsoever. Only in this case would Germany's position in Europe be immune from negative reactions resulting from world political activities. "The decision over German world politics is made on the continent." In open support of Bethmann Hollweg's policy, Riezler called for a strengthening of Germany's land forces at the same time that he called for a reduction of the German fleet in order to reduce British fears of a strong threatening Germany. Riezler noted that the "German public opinion has not yet thoroughly grasped the relationship between the military position of Germany on the continent and its world political freedom of movement. The fleet seems to it [public opinion] to be the primary instrument of world policy." This statement was as much aimed at the kaiser as at the general public. When Bethmann Hollweg had proposed to Wilhelm in January 1912 that colonial agreements be pursued instead of a new fleet law, the kaiser retorted: "To be a great colonial power means at the same time to be a great sea power." Riezler disagreed; no matter how important a fleet may have been to add to the "imponderabilia of power . . . the army is more important" for Germany because German world politics was impossible without it. Riezler was convinced that such a strong army would certainly cause potential enemies, primarily France, to end their opposition to Germany's world politics, "if reason and understanding of the real situation determine the actions of men."[54]

Of course, reasonable men can evaluate the "real situation" in different ways, but the stress on "reason and understanding of the real situation," and the general accuracy of Riezler's description of the contemporary constellation, militate against the conclusion that his political philosophy manifested an "idealistic irrational character" which reached for the "impossible."[55] On the contrary, it followed the example of sober Bismarckian *Realpolitik*. At the same time, while viewing politics unemotionally, Riezler too often underestimated the strength of emotions in politics. When confronted by the concatenation of war declarations in 1914, by Russia's refusal to accept a separate peace with Germany even when revolution threatened the very existence of the state, and by the confused and short-sighted policies of European states after the war, Riezler was baffled by the fact that states so seldom act reasonably and according to their interests.

Riezler's argument was a clear defense of Bethmann Hollweg's military policy since 1911. Bethmann had opposed Tirpitz's advocacy of a stronger fleet. The admiral had argued that a policy of naval armament would in the long run force Britain to reach a *rapprochement* with Germany and would guarantee for Germany "complete political and military equality." Bethmann Hollweg, on the other hand, wanted to reduce the danger of war with Britain through a slower build-up of the fleet and through a build-up of land forces. He found support, although for different reasons, in General Moltke and Secretary of the Treasury Wermuth. The kaiser, who according to the imperial constitution was responsible for settling all conflicts between military and political leaders, sided with Tirpitz. He warned: "If the Imperial Chancellor, Kiderlen and Wermuth do not wish to cooperate, then they can leave!"

Riezler found it wiser and more realistic for Germany not to challenge British mastery of the sea in the hope that Germany's real interests of continental security and world political success could be realized. Germany's challenge of British naval supremacy was, in Riezler's opinion, one of three fateful mistakes which were made before the war. As his diaries show, he hated Tirpitz perhaps more than anyone else. In Tirpitz, "the father of lies," "the lying spirit," Riezler saw the fate of German policy.[56]

His entire hopes for a successful world policy hinged upon a *rapprochement* and cooperation with Britain. Indeed, Riezler's entire world political concept was oriented toward Britain. We will see throughout his political career that although he criticized some aspects of British politics, Riezler also found much to admire about the British: their model nationalism, the consistency of their sense of world mission, the intelligence and the discretion of their political method, the far-sightedness of their economic life, and their live-and-let-live attitude. Since British world politics was Riezler's model, and since the British example would play an important role in his later thinking about German occupation policies, it is helpful to look first at his description of the British before proceeding to Bethmann Hollweg's attempt to reach a political agreement with Britain prior to the outbreak of the Great War.

"The most important result of the last two centuries and the primary fact of the present world political constellation," Riezler wrote in *Grundzüge der Weltpolitik*, "is England's domination of the world." Her success stemmed "from a wonderful consistency and goal orientation." To Riezler the factors which contributed to the origination of her empire were the same as those which guaranteed her maintenance:

mastery of the seas and the guarantee of a balance of power on the European continent. These factors gave British politics its "simple and unified character."

Riezler warned his readers against thinking that what Britain had created had been primarily due to "deeds of violence," to military victories.

Even with these or more glorious victories, the work which we admire today would not have been possible without the spirit which dominates these island dwellers, without an unusual political talent and without a rare mixture of political flexibility and energy. It is to a much greater degree the work of diplomacy than of weapons. The military history of other countries is richer in glittering victories, heroic deeds. What England has over other states is not the victories but the favorable consequences of her victories. These are the work of politics.

Riezler saw a Britain which had what she had because of her own excellent qualities, because of her politics and not her arms. This passage, as well as so many others in which Riezler criticized those Germans who overestimated "the power of force," was obviously overlooked by those who assert that for Riezler "there's only force, expansion, the right of the strongest over the weakest."

He did not attribute long-standing British political success to great geniuses, as many Germans attributed German political success to such leaders as Frederick the Great or Bismarck. Britain did not produce more geniuses than any other country. It was "the political spirit," which one found in Britain; it was "a broad political elite," whose tradition and way of thinking "guarantees a good average, . . . assures talent in the leadership, . . . does not tolerate the bungler."

British nationalism differed from the nationalism of other peoples in that it was one of "those in possession." For other peoples it was "striving for world domination, which they do not yet possess and which they can perhaps never possess." For this reason British nationalism masqueraded as cosmopolitanism. It did not know that "drive of dissatisfaction, that fierce desire, that passion" which characterized nationalist movements in other countries.

Had Britain, Riezler asked, obtained all that it wanted? Foreign Minister Sir Edward Grey had announced in 1912 that Britain was saturated. However, this contradicted the essence of the national tendency, which Riezler thought was insatiable. He wrote that "England is saturated because it digests." This is an important point which Riezler brought up again during the First World War when German military leaders showed an interest only in territorial conquest, but not in digesting what they had conquered. Germany "only understood the steam roller," whereas Britain understood the sympathetic embrace. Riezler was sure that further British expansion would follow, but only after patient attention to the problems of the existing empire had been given. Also, the British had a good political instinct for that which was possible and that which was not. German ambassador to London before the war, Prince Lichnowsky, also noted: "The Briton is matter-of-fact; he takes things as they are and does not tilt against windmills."

Aside from the fact that Britain was "digesting," there were two other factors which gave Britain the appearance of a saturated state. Unlike young nationalism, which becomes intoxicated on the external appearance of power and which thrives on prestige, British nationalism had long outgrown its "joy of appearance." While Britain no longer reveled in the appearance of power, she had not forgotten how to employ masterfully the real power of appearance. Here we discover another aspect of Britain's ruling talent which Riezler admired and advocated for Germany throughout the First World War. Germans never fully grasped the importance of appearance in politics. Finally, British power extended much farther than the territory which it occupied; thus, Britain had no great need to annex new territory to the British Empire. Through mastery of the sea, expert diplomacy and British capital, such states as Spain, Portugal, Argentina, and to a lesser extent Japan were dependent upon Britain. In order not to create an Anglo-Russian border, Britain also left states bordering on India nominally independent. The British simply did not share the joy of young nationalism, "which measures the power of the fatherland according to the size of the territories which bear on the atlas the color of the fatherland."

In addition to her sea power and mature nationalism, Britain had two other pillars for a successful empire: British cultural cohesion and the London Stock Exchange. Riezler admitted that the power of British culture was an "imponderable difficult to grasp," but it resided in the British "ideal of man." "The British type is infectuous" and had for individuals of other origins something "seductive." It was easily adopted by others because it was a "mediocre ideal," not the "highest," ideal.

Duty, health, rational pleasure of life, practical efficiency—an ideal of the masses, which renounces all striving toward the heavens and all longing for the unreachable, perhaps even all true greatness and the deepest pathos of man. This type is not the highest ideal of man which can be devised, but it is politically the most useful.

53

Wayne C. Thompson

There is an apparent contradiction between Riezler's argument that an ideal of the masses "which renounces all striving toward the heavens" can strengthen a nation and his basic argument that a nation is a "path to God." Riezler did not attempt to deal with this contradiction.

He saw "uniformity" in this ideal man, and it was this quality which guaranteed that freedom would not be dangerous and which made possible self-government. Freedom and self-government appealed greatly to other peoples and enabled Britain to maintain the loyalty of her colonies, which themselves enjoyed great freedom. This was an important aspect of British power which, in Riezler's opinion, Germans could not grasp. Germans had the naive belief that "the English global empire must collapse with the destruction of the English fleet." Riezler conceded that some of Britain's tropical colonies and Egypt and India might slip from her control if the fleet were defeated, but her control over the dominions would remain intact; "the power of its culture does not sink with the cannons of British ships." The only way the British global empire could fall, Riezler thought, was if Britons began to question their own ideals, and if general skepticism set in. This he felt to be so because the strength of Britain was supported by what he saw as the naive belief that British ideals were the best possible ideals. Of course, Riezler was the victim of the same kind of naiveté concerning undefinable German ideals.

The final pillar of British supremacy was economic interest: "There is no doubt that affiliation with the British global empire is very good business for the colonies. For all their enterprises they have the London Stock Exchange behind them." Unlike Germany's colonial empire, which was highly unprofitable, Britain's empire was very profitable. However, like naval supremacy, economic interest was not enough to hold states and empires together. A successful empire depended on a blend of economic interest, of the "power of the idea and of feeling," of "national imponderables," and of the "impulse to freedom." Britain knew how to harmonize these perfectly.

Riezler's analysis of British imperialism in *Grundzüge der Weltpolitik* differed greatly from the hidden criticism of Britain in *Finanzen und Monopole.* In his earlier work he had criticized Athenian imperialism. Despite the fact that it had been the first Greek city to turn "in grand style" from isolation to expansion, to gain undisputed control of the seas, and to maintain its allies because of that control, Athens had been unable to absorb subjugated peoples and to develop an imperial economic policy. Athenian imperialism was supported by power alone. On the other hand, Britain did not make these mistakes. Nor did she, or would she, fall as a result of that element which had doomed the Greek cities to

54

ruin—an inflexible constitution. For example, when the expense of maintaining a global empire had become too great for Britain to bear alone, the colonies were asked to share the burden of expense. As a result, the colonies demanded and received a greater voice in imperial foreign policy. The British constitution was flexible enough to accommodate these demands; this constitutional flexibility was backed up by "the political intelligence and common sense of Englishness."[57] Britain should not be compared with Athens, but had to be compared with that ancient power which had showed true imperial talent—Rome.

Riezler's profound admiration for British imperialism not only influenced him during the First World War but helped persuade him before the war that German interests were best served by good relations and close cooperation with Britain. Of course, advocacy of a policy of cooperation with Britain was not popular in Germany: Germans felt humiliated after the second Moroccan crisis, in which Britain had supported France. The national feelings of the broad masses had been hurt by Germany's retreat under British pressure, and the indignation was still directed against Britain. This was given expression by Ernst von Heydebrand, leader of the Conservative party, in the heated parliamentary debates of November 1911: "We now know where the enemy is."[58]

As Churchill wrote, "the Bismarckian system . . . always included the principle of good relations with Great Britain." However, the policy of the "free hand," pursued in Germany after 1890, German naval armament, and German aggressiveness during the first Moroccan crisis led to strained relations between the two countries. From the time he entered the chancellery, Bethmann Hollweg was intent on improving relations between Britain and Germany. In a private letter written in 1911 he stated: "I see a *modus vivendi* with England . . . as the order of the day."[59]

The most important diplomatic step toward such a *modus vivendi* would have been a reduction of naval expenditures, a step which the chancellor was never permitted to take. However, despite the naval tension, Bethmann Hollweg was successful in arranging a series of talks with British leaders. The most important of these talks was the Haldane mission to Berlin in February 1912. In the course of these talks Britain's minister of war, Richard Haldane, became convinced of Bethmann's sincere desire for peaceful relations with Britain, but he gained the impression that there were both a peace and a war party in Berlin. The reason for this impression is clear; on the one hand, Germany was obviously seeking an understanding with Britain. On the other hand, German leaders committed two great errors. The Germans placed emphasis on an agreement to achieve British neutrality "should war be forced on Germany." This demand must be seen as the continuous attempt to weaken the Entente and break the encirclement around Germany. We have seen that Riezler considered this an essential task of German diplomacy. Churchill wrote that such neutrality "would have carried us far beyond our original intention. . . . It would certainly have been regarded as terminating the Entente." The British were most interested in discussing the limitation of naval armaments, a topic which the Germans relegated to secondary importance. The significance of this subject increased even more after the most untimely publication during the talks of the new German fleet law on February 7, 1912. This new naval law called for an "extraordinary increase in the striking force of ships of all classes, . . . and increase . . . in this year's estimates for submarines," and the dangerous fact that "practically four-fifths of the German Navy were to be placed permanently upon a war footing." Successful negotiations with the British could hardly have been expected after such a naval law had been announced.

The failure of the Haldane mission disappointed Bethmann Hollweg greatly, and on March 6, 1912, he offered his resignation, which was declined by the kaiser. Bethmann Hollweg continued his policy to establish a good working relationship with the British, although the new fleet law made this difficult; he called this task "the squaring of the circle." A year and a half later Riezler noted in *Grundzüge der Weltpolitik* that the "deepest and most dangerous conflict of the time . . . the English-German" had lost its dangerous character as a result of "gradual agreements." Churchill recognized that "the policy of Germany towards Great Britain had not only been correct but considerate" and that "British and German diplomacy laboured in harmony . . . Germany seemed, with us, to be set on peace."[60]

Riezler's policy of restrained, patient imperialism, which clearly recognized the limits of power, which regarded war as neither timely nor useful, and which rested on the assumption that peaceful expansion was possible, did not collapse primarily because of its own weaknesses. It was prevented from coming to fruition by the momentous events of the summer of 1914. Perhaps it would have failed in any case; one cannot know. Of course, his approach was not free of some noticeable weaknesses.

First, Riezler maligned some very important surface features of international relations, such as the "peace phraseology," "internationalization of pity," the "enormous estimation of human life as the absolute good," and generally the "atmosphere of idealism" which dominates only the external form of international politics. One is struck by the accuracy with which he described the actual weakness of these facets of international politics when they come into conflict with basic national interests. Indeed, this weakness is almost as great today as it was in his own time, and one can only pity the statesman who does not recognize this fact. Nevertheless, this atmosphere of idealism and of international morality, as shallow as its roots are, does place some constraints on statesmen and their nations. Riezler recognized this effect, but he spoke disparagingly of it. There are obvious limits to the strength of international morality, but negative consequences can flow from speaking too often or cynically about these limits; they lose all too quickly what little force they have if they are ridiculed. They are easily corroded.

Second, it was unwise to base so much of German politics on a vague notion of the "German idea." Not only was Riezler himself unable to define it, and not only was there no domestic consensus behind it, but he clearly suspected that the Germans themselves no longer possessed such an idea. Such an abstraction could easily distract Germans from pursuing actual German interests by means which could offer reasonable promise of success. Also, this vague notion bore in itself an arrogance, as well as presumptions which, when confronted with actual modern developments, gave rise to a deep cultural pessimism which became dangerous to Germany. Further, the faith in this abstraction contributed to the unwillingness of Germany's leaders to accept the fundamental premises of liberal democracy. Here, Riezler remained attached to a tradition which greatly retarded the political modernization of Germany.

Third, Riezler's description of man's condition in terms of tragedy, namely man's continual "becoming" and striving toward something which he can never achieve, not only provides a good rationalization for failure, but it leaves man in an ethical quagmire. Values tend to become individualized and thereby relativized. No standard which applies universally appears to be possible. How can a person derive from this concept ethical standards by which to judge his own and his nation's behavior? This is not to say that Riezler had no ethical standards of his own; he simply did not convey such a standard in his writings.

Unlike most of the German educated elite, Riezler not only presented grand theory, but he also publicly advocated actual political solutions to contemporary problems. He did not share an open disdain for the practical. For this reason, one is able to see without great difficulty the actual implications of his theoretical writings. The actual policies which he recommended and supported before the First World War unquestionably reflected the implications which he intended his theoretical writings to have. A balanced analysis of his philosophical

Wayne C. Thompson

writings and the policies which he advocated protects one from the serious pitfalls of placing Riezler's political conception close to the Pan-Germans or in the outer realm of "pre-fascist ideology," however this vague notion is defined.[61] It is quite true that the superficial reader of his time could misunderstand or misinterpret some parts of Riezler's message. His theoretical formulations were often more strident and romantic in tone than were his actual proposals. These formulations sounded very good out of context. For instance, his statement that "theoretically every *Volk* wants to grow, expand, dominate, and subjugate without end . . . until totality has become an organic whole under its domination" could be quoted with relish by the wildest of German "hurrah patriots." This kind of formulation may have had a more lasting impact on some readers than Riezler's careful analysis of why German nationalism should be restrained and channeled into peaceful paths. Also, some readers may have had difficulty reconciling his theoretical argument that it is a good sign when nations are arrogant and intolerant with his strong argument that Germany should not act that way in the international community. In truth, Riezler was often too vague, too abstract, or too subtle in his theoretical treatment. Nevertheless, it is curious, that the modern reader appears to be far more vulnerable to such misinterpretations than Riezler's own contemporaries.

Hermann Oncken, in 1915, praised Riezler's treatment of the calculation of war but criticized him for arguing that coexistence was "the most probable or in any case the most desirable from the standpoint of German politics." Dietrich Schäfer disapprovingly saw in *Grundzüge der Weltpolitik* a "plea for peace." Hans Rothfels remembered that the book "was held to be a document of German programmatic, whose optimistic basic idea" was that one "no longer counted on wars."[62]

In 1923 Hans Herzfeld held Riezler's book partially responsible for the fact that "a completely misleading peaceful and optimistic atmosphere" existed in Germany before 1914. Karl Alexander von Müller, an acquaintance of the Riezler family in Munich, found the book a stimulating and "most unusual fusion of abstract philosophy and contemporary politics." However, he criticised Riezler's apparent denial of the "power of personal will in the modern world . . . . Everything depends on the constellation. . . . Everything is rational calculation of risk, nothing will, nothing passion." Could one, Müller asked, imagine Balfour, Morley, Cromer, Curzon, Churchill, Clemenceau, Poincaré, Isvolski, or Masaryk writing such a book? He asked if Riezler's entire presentation were not above all "an inner justification of the German government's own indecision." In a review in *Zeitschrift für Politik* in 1916, Riezler was criticized for having shown too clearly his preference for the national tendency over the cosmopolitan tendency, for having shown man as being too determined, and for having neglected the "ethical dimension."[63]

Much stronger criticism was made by the extremely nationalist *Alldeutsche Blätter* in December 1914, and in January 1915. Riezler's work was compared to the widely read work of Hans Plehn. The only difference was that instead of influencing only one facet of German foreign policy, Ruedorffer's book "is very simply the guide . . . to current German foreign policy . . . Herr Ruedorffer is one in the know." Riezler allegedly made the mistake of attacking the "sinister nationalists," whose superior political talent had been shown by the very fact that a world war had broken out a few months after the book had been published. Equally serious was his neglect of the crucial significance of racial factors in international politics. Without the concept of race, Riezler's national state became "an unrealizable concept, devoid of content." He turned the world into "a trading house." Finally, Riezler failed to comprehend the fact that while an industrial nation could support its population without external expansion, it could not remain "healthy both physically and spiritually" without such expansion. This was a rejection of Riezler's criticism of the nationalists' emphasis on external expansion at the expense of spiritual and cultural development. On the contrary, argued the authors, such inward development could not occur in a country which neglected its external development.

Using the pseudonym, Junius Alter, Franz Sontag described Riezler's "world political distortion" as a "mixture of misunderstood ethical principles and naked business considerations. All the drives which determine the inner lives and mutual relations of peoples, such as the will to life, national pride, the feeling of power and honor, the drive to expand, race peculiarities and contrasts . . . have no room." Alter criticised Riezler's condemnation of war and his idea of parallel expansion. "Whoever seeks to satisfy the vital needs of peoples through trade agreements and open doors must necessarily see his policy fail sooner or later."[64] Sontag's and others' criticism of *Grundzüge der Weltpolitik* clearly indicates that Riezler's message was not interpreted by his contemporaries as a call to arms.

Peaceful cooperation and parallel development was in fact official government policy until the final few days before the outbreak of the First World War. Bethmann Hollweg was working on cooperation with Britain in the Near East, and negotiations concerning the establishment of a Central African Empire showed great promise until general war suddenly ended almost a half a century of peace in Europe.

59

Chapter Three

OUTBREAK OF WAR

*Our modern wars make many unhappy while they last and none happy
when they are over.*

—Goethe

A THEORY OF WAR

As the year 1913 approached its end, the thirty-one year old Riezler sat in
his Chancellery office, "filled with books and documents," and directed
his thoughts to the coming year. His office

faced the peaceful garden to the rear of the Imperial Chancellery. It was in the
house of Bismarck; behind the large desk and through the window the leafless
tops of his beloved trees swayed phantomlike; his giant shadow swept through
the rooms, in which he at one time built up the Empire.[1]

Riezler anticipated a new year which would be as peaceful as the garden
outside his window, a new year which would present no mortal dangers to
the nation which Bismarck had unified barely four decades earlier.

Riezler's optimism was not based on an illusion that there were no out-
standing diplomatic problems among the nations of Europe. He knew
that there were. Nor was it based on the hope that the possibility for
parallel expansion would exist forever. He knew that it would not.
However, he believed that another development had made it inappropriate, if not impossible, for great powers to engage in warfare with
one another: the destructiveness of modern weapons and the expense of
armaments had reached such a high level that the costs of war now out-
weighed the possible gains. Hostility would, of course, not cease in this
situation, but wars would probably no longer be fought; they would only
be calculated.

Riezler described in *Grundzüge der Weltpolitik* how the nature of war
had changed by the turn of the century. The interests of nations and
states were by that time completely intertwined; therefore "the comba-
tants themselves [are] so entangled that none of them is able any longer

60

to work himself loose from this knot in order to strike a blow at the opponent." This international entanglement does not mean the cessation of national struggles, but only the elimination of war as "an almost antiquated form of struggle."

Unlike states in former centuries, which fought wars with few people and little money, today's states "set in motion armies with millions of soldiers and spend billions." The entire economic bases of states are at stake. The costs of wars have greatly outstripped that which can be gained from wars; "the risk has grown more rapidly than the utility. . . . For all European great powers the loss of a war to another great power means political and economic ruin." Further, the great power which wins a war and that power which benefits most from the war will probably not be the same. Due to the intertwining of interests, not the victor but the observer who does not participate in the war reaps the greatest benefit.[2]

The complexity of all of the above mentioned factors—the preponderance of risk over gain and the observer as the real winner—makes the calculation of wars practically impossible. Two additional factors make precise calculation absolutely impossible: armaments and the grouping of great powers.

Riezler noted that the movements for disarmament showed no hope for success.

Arms are the necessary expression of the nations' limitless will to life on the one side and the general constellation . . . on the other. All nations conceive of coexistence as a preparation for hostility, as a postponement of hostility.

"Armaments are the modern form of postponement" and are used by modern states to back up diplomacy. "Cannons do not shoot, but they speak in negotiations." An unarmed state is compelled to give way to a well-armed state in every conflict of interests. In such cases the well-armed state would be doing nothing more than firmly defending its own interests. Riezler saw this as perfectly legitimate because "there is no other standard by which a state can claim its right than its own interest." International law and the cultural perception *(Kulturempfinden)* of the time are so vague that much flexibility is given to interpretation. In any case, they influence only the methods, not the goals, of an action.[3]

Arms not only strengthen the negotiator but prepare a state for a possible war, which Riezler claimed no power wanted in 1914. A high degree of military readiness, in his opinion, makes it less likely that states resort to war. "That is why our age is that age of the greatest arming for war and of the longest peace. . . . Wars are no longer fought but are calculated." The

61

estimate of one's own military might compared with that of the opponent, combined with the complicated factors of the entire diplomatic situation, determine the compromises to be demanded or granted. Thus, the purpose of armaments is to affect the calculation of war in one's own favor. In effect, they replace wars.[4]

The calculation of war involves two factors. The first factor concerns the relationship between the advantages of a victory to the costs of a victory on one hand and the costs of a defeat on the other. The second factor concerns the probability of a victory over a defeat. Here Riezler saw the "dilemma of world armament": the attempt to change the second factor in one's favor affects the first factor "in a way favorable to peace." The first factor is composed of two elements: the advantage of victory, and its costs in terms of "blood and property." The first element remains constant, whereas the importance of the second element is enhanced by increased armament. "The more one arms, the greater the imbalance between the advantages and disadvantages of wars moves toward a stress on the latter, thus in favor of peace." Riezler admitted that this calculation was an abstraction; in reality many accidental circumstances have to be considered, but the calculation is always made at least unconsciously.[5]

Riezler thought that a calculation in favor of war had become practically impossible. Thus, wars which might be fought between great powers would only be fought out of "necessity," not as a result of calculation of advantages. Wars of necessity are also extremely unlikely because no opponent would have an interest in forcing a great power to fight a war. No great power would be interested in seeking a military solution to a conflict with another great power.

Since powers considering war now think in terms of relative destructiveness instead of relative advantage of a war, the bluff "has become the chief requirement of the diplomatic method."

If between two conflicting parties no one wants war, then the most powerful, that is, the one which can most easily bear a war, will not always win the diplomatic confrontation, but the one who can hold out the longest with the claim that he is ready to fight: that is, he will win who has cooler nerves, composure, tenacity and flexibility.

Thus, even the weaker power has a chance to be successful.[6]

Riezler was not blind to weaknesses in his argument against the likelihood and desirability of war. The bluff could indeed lead to danger.

Out of the characteristics of this method comes that element which contains the greatest danger of war in our time. It is not the case that the actions of a state are always a pure expression of calculation, that the governments are always able or willing to do that which corresponds to the interests of the nations. If a government gets itself into difficulty as a result of the method of the bluff, dared to too great an extent, or as one says, bluffed itself into a corner, then it is perhaps unable to retreat, even if such a retreat were the best move. Respect for personal interests, ambition of governments, or the storm of indignation which can be expected from the nationalists can bring about a war, which objective interests alone would never have justified. For that reason the danger of war in our time lies in the domestic politics of those countries in which a weak government is faced with a strong nationalist movement.[7]

The alliance system, wrote Riezler in 1913, is another factor which contributes to peace because it makes the calculation of war much more difficult. He did not yet see any direct conflict of interests between the Entente and the Triple Alliance. In his opinion, such conflicts of interests exist only between individual powers in both alliances, and in no controversy are interests of each ally within an alliance equally strong. Riezler optimistically argued that such unequal intensity of interests suffices to cause the allies with the greatest interest in peace to avoid an open conflict. For example, France would apply pressure on Russia in the event that the latter threatened the peace over a matter which was not of direct interest to France. Riezler concluded that allied states are less inclined to go to war than individual states, and thus alliances contribute to peace. In private he was less optimistic about this peaceful influence of alliances. For several years he had shown uneasiness about the *"cauchemar des coalitions,"* and he continued to do so throughout the July crisis.[8]

Riezler maintained that on the European continent large-scale military actions are unlikely because no power could gain from such actions, and no power would risk the total ruin which could result. This does not mean that all nations would accept the status quo without trying to change it in their favor. Every nation, Riezler wrote, seeks here and there a "gradual realignment" of the constellation in its own favor. However, such realignments have to be accomplished "without shaking the entire structure."

Many small unnoticed advantages are added together. The realignment should not be perceived until it is already a *fait accompli,* when it can no longer be undone by war or can be undone only through war. Under such circumstances it is the goal of politics to avoid, if possible, the application of force or to leave the decision to apply force to the opponent.[9]

63

Riezler asserted that all great powers in his day had already mastered this tactic to a greater or lesser degree. All engaged in the slow and quiet attempt to change the constellation. He merely recognized this fact and presented it in his *Grundzüge der Weltpolitik*. For example, France had waited almost ten years in order to build up its Moroccan position to the status of a protectorate. Russia, Riezler argued, was using this gradual method to gain control of Mongolia and had already practiced it in Persia with some success. All of these slow realignments took place under the slogan of maintaining the status quo. For example, during all the recent Balkan crises, while European powers always called for the maintenance of the status quo, they always accepted the changes. This was merely an expression of their disinclination toward sudden and radical changes. In general the status quo was a term which merely referred to "the slowness and the caution of political movements in our time."[10]

Slow and cautious political movements in certain respects conflict with the national tendency. Nationalism, which Riezler understood as that extensive component of national growth, is insatiable, impatient, and uncompromising.

It demands the joys of power and loud confirmations, complete successes and the brilliance of the deed. Indeed, it demands such things all the more, depending upon the weakness of the political education in the country and upon the inability to see into the complicated machinery of foreign policies. Particularly, nationalisms of young world powers have a certain longing for a more robust method, whereas the older and more sophisticated, such as England's, do not allow themselves to be distracted from the true task.

Riezler reminded his readers that "it is not the time for prestige politics."[11]

The small realignments are only directed by diplomats; they are not conceived by them. The main force behind these realignments is the people. Here Riezler returned to his concept of the *Volk,* which must expand and progress or die. The role of diplomacy is no more than to protect the development of the *Volk* from disruptions and to create the external conditions for its activity. Diplomacy differs somewhat according to whether it is practiced by a people which is "advancing" or "standing still." The diplomacy of an advancing people (e.g., the German people) is in the fortunate position of being able to let time work in its favor. It can "postpone conflicts with calm assurance and tell itself that the position of its people must improve according to elementary natural necessity." The diplomacy of a people (or of a state containing several nations such as Austria-Hungary) which is standing still has to be on constant guard against advancing peoples and is thus essentially more restless, nervous, and unsteady. Riezler admitted, however, that politics in all nations tends to operate in short time spans and that patience is not always practiced. Impatience and miscalculations are always strong dangers in politics. Although he thought that war had become very unlikely, he had to admit that it was not impossible.[12]

Riezler saw a further problem in conducting a rational foreign policy oriented toward national interest. Whereas power was formerly concentrated in few hands such as a monarch and his court, it is now distributed in many countries such as Germany among parliamentary leaders, government ministers, newspaper owners, editors, and financiers. The kaiser, military, and chancellor have to consider the influence of such groups. "It is not the age in which one man conceives far-sighted plans and proceeds to realize them." Few governments had the freedom suddenly to offer friendship to a former enemy:

The domestic distribution of power forbids it. . . . Many governments in our time have very little freedom to plan or avoid wars. . . . The power of the government in general operates in the broad or narrow limits which parliaments and public opinion allow.

Riezler found that in his time "lasting success" no longer belonged to

the single bold deed, also no longer to the genius of the individual statesman, but to the quiet, plodding work of millions. . . . In the last analysis the better average decides. The deed of the individual disappears behind the great number.[13]

In Riezler's view of modern warfare risks outweigh potential gains; therefore, wars no longer are fought but calculated. The bluff becomes the main diplomatic act, and under the cover of a bluff, calculated risks can be taken which can work on cracks in the alliance systems and can result in small realignments. When engaging in this calculated risk, the vital interests of a great power must never be threatened. Finally, in the unlikely event that a war does come, then the "advancing" people would always be victorious.

Perhaps there is some wishful thinking mingled in with some aspects of this analysis; there is certainly no historical evidence that "advancing" peoples, however they are defined, always win wars. With reference to the alleged decreasing likelihood that modern states would resort to war, events would soon show that he had committed the same error of which he was often guilty: of assuming, in his own words, "that actions of states

65

and governments always were a pure consequence of rational considerations." Nevertheless, his over-all analysis of modern war and its effects
was quite accurate. The problems in calculating the outcomes and consequences of wars were, and still are, important constraints on political and
military leaders; indeed, in the nuclear age such constraints have become
many times more significant.

Before a half year had passed, Riezler's optimism that the year 1914
would be a peaceful one proved to have been entirely ill-founded. An un-
expected event produced radically changed circumstances in all of
Europe. On June 28, 1914, Austrian Archduke Franz Ferdinand and his
wife were murdered in Sarajevo by a Bosnian student named Gabriel
Princip. The shots of Sarajevo awakened the world from the exceptional
tranquility of the spring and summer of 1914 and sounded the end of
almost fifty years of respite from major war among European great
powers. Bismarck had predicted shortly before his death that "one day
the great European War would come out of some damned foolish thing in
the Balkans."[14]

Within six weeks after the assassination of the Austrian Archduke, all
of Europe's major nations were locked into a war which was to last four
years and which far exceeded all previous wars in terms of casualties and
destruction. Of course, the origins of that war, or of any war for that matter, cannot be sought exclusively in a violent act by a fanatical individual. Nor can the causes of war be adequately explained by the often
confused events which occur during the few feverish weeks preceding the
actual commencement of military operations. Wars do not simply "break
out" suddenly, as do natural catastrophes. They have their roots in long-
range developments, as well as in immediate causes.

Long before June 28, 1914, there had been much dissatisfaction in the
capitals of Europe. Indeed, only two countries in Europe were at all interested in maintaining the *status quo:* Austria-Hungary and Britain.
Both of those powers had grown increasingly nervous about threats to
that *status quo.* Austria-Hungary felt threatened by Russia and by what
it saw to be Russia's client state, Serbia. Britain had become rather nervous about the growing naval power of Germany and by periodical German saber-rattling. In general, Riezler's conclusion about the out-
standing characteristics of world politics in his time appears to have been
correct: that enmity, not amity, characterized nations' relations with one
another.

The decade preceding the outbreak of war in August 1914 had
produced numerous crises which could have served to ignite a war.
However, in order for a crisis actually to lead to a war, several powers

must conclude that they are in a favorable position to gain from such a war, if a war were actually to come. That feeling of confidence prevailed in many European capitals in July and August 1914. Events in those months revealed that most major European countries were willing to risk war by that time in order to improve their strategic positions. For her part, Germany certainly decided in the course of the July crisis that a local war between Austria-Hungary and Serbia, or at least a significant prestige success for Austria-Hungary, would help retard the erosion of Germany's strategic position and the growth of Russian power.[15]

German nervousness about the worsening of her strategic position stemmed in great part from a drastic increase in the Russian defense budget in 1914. Early in that year, Russian Prime Minister Vladimir N. Kokovtsov, announced the intention to allot an additional five hundred million rubles for defense spending, a sum which was three times as high as the entire Austro-Hungarian defense budget. This new army organization program became law on July 7, 1914. The German defense bill of 1913, which had already been rendered obsolete by France's introduction of three-year compulsory military service, was now mightily over-trumped by the Russian program. If at this time Austria-Hungary were to collapse, then seventy-eight German divisions would face one hundred ninety-four Russian, French, and Belgian divisions. That is, the potential opponents of Germany would have a superiority in divisions over Germany by a ratio of two and one-half to one. Within four years, this ratio would grow even more unfavorable to Germany.[16]

A few weeks before the Russian defense bill became law, Anglo-Russian naval talks concerning a possible naval agreement with each other were taking place. The Germans were completely informed about these talks through the Baltic German, Renno von Siebert, who was the second secretary to the Russian ambassador in London. Among the things discussed was the provision that in wartime the British navy should cover the landing of a Russian expeditionary corps in Pomerania. This news unleashed great concern in Germany that the Entente was tightening its relations even more and that a more aggressive Russian foreign policy would be the natural result.[17]

Of course, no European leaders had contemplated, let alone wanted, the kind of war which actually came in August 1914. In the minds of most statesmen at that time, war was a relatively violent action lasting a month or six weeks and conducted as a part of intricate diplomatic games. The memory of the Napoleonic wars having faded, they had not yet had the opportunity to observe the consequences of wars which unlocked powerful emotions stemming from nationalism and democracy.

67

They also vastly underestimated the capacity of countries in possession of modern industry and technology to conduct theretofore inconceivably destructive wars for long periods against one another. Although Riezler had been mistaken in believing that technical advancements in weaponry had made their actual use unlikely, he certainly foresaw better than most others of his time the true significance of war in the modern age. On January 10, 1917, in a letter to historian, Eduard Meyer, who had been very critical of Riezler's *Grundzüge der Weltpolitik,* Riezler argued that his predictions about modern warfare had been borne out by the destruction and suffering which was actually occurring in the war. He wrote, probably correctly, that by 1917 the governments of all belligerent countries wished that they had never gotten involved in such a war.[18]

The purpose of our examination of the events of July and August 1914 will not be to solve the question of guilt for the outbreak of the First World War. That question is one of the most controversial and complex problems with which scholars have felt obligated to deal in the twentieth century, and it is one which cannot be treated adequately in this work. Our purpose will be more modestly to place Riezler in the context of the events and decisions of July and August 1914.[19]

RIEZLER IN THE IMPERIAL CHANCELLERY

In order to place Riezler more accurately in the context of July and August 1914, we must examine his official position and responsibilities within the Imperial Chancellery. The German constitution of 1871 provided for an imperial chancellor and a chief of the German General Staff, appointed solely by the kaiser to assist him in political and military affairs. Each office was entirely outside the control of the other. In cases where military and political interests conflicted, the kaiser's decision was final. Thus, there were at least three decision-making instances. The chancellor could not overrule the military without the support of the kaiser, and under no circumstances could he overrule the kaiser.

The Imperial Chancellery was the central bureau through which the chancellor could coordinate the work of all administrative branches. The chancellor, who at the same time had the titles of president of the Prussian State Ministry and minister of foreign affairs for Prussia, guided the work of three distinct governmental organizations: the ministries of the empire, the ministries of Prussia, and the Imperial Chancellery itself.

First, the chancellor appointed all state secretaries, whose job was to guide the day-to-day affairs of the various departments. These state secretaries answered directly to the chancellor, and the most important were those of the interior and of foreign affairs. Bethmann Hollweg's Secretaries of the Interior Clemens von Delbrück (until May 22, 1916) and Karl Helfferich (until October 23, 1917) also bore the title of vice-chancellor. All important instructions from Bethmann Hollweg's State Secretaries for Foreign Affairs Gottlieb Jagow (until November 22, 1916) and Arthur Zimmermann (until August 5, 1917) were sent out in the chancellor's name. All state secretaries had an under-state secretary, as well as a staff guided by directors and counsellors.

Further, the chancellor had responsibilities within the Prussian government also. He had to work with Rudolf von Valentini, the chief of the Privy Council of the Prussian King and with such important Prussian ministers as Friedrich Wilhelm von Loebell, Prussian state minister of the interior from April 18, 1914, until August 5, 1917. All of these figures had their own staffs which assisted them in their duties.

Finally, the chancellor oversaw the work of the Imperial Chancellery. His chief assistant was Under-State Secretary Arnold Wahnschaffe, and almost all the business of the Chancellery ran through Wahnschaffe's fingers. He assigned tasks and made certain that the work was completed. He attended all meetings of the Prussian cabinet, and more importantly he managed all governmental business in Berlin while the chancellor was outside of Berlin, especially while Bethmann Hollweg was serving at the Supreme Headquarters. Wahnschaffe was highly respected and trusted by Bethmann Hollweg. Bethmann biographer, Eberhard von Vietsch, called Wahnschaffe the chancellor's "closest collaborator," and another Bethmann biographer, Konrad H. Jarausch, referred to him as a "close collaborator" and "Bethmann's domestic advisor."

Below the under-state secretary was the position of *Vortragender Rat* (chief counselor). Although Riezler did not officially rise to this post until April 1915, he had already performed the most important function of the chief counselor while he still had the title of *Legationsrat* (counselor). That function was to brief the chancellor on all communications coming into the Chancellery. The chief counselor not only briefed the chancellor, but also drafted replies to important communications before speaking with the chancellor. Naturally, the chancellor was responsible for approving or amending the replies.

In addition to the briefing function, Riezler was called upon to perform whatever other tasks Bethmann Hollweg or Wahnschaffe assigned to him. Riezler's own diaries, as well as the files of the Imperial Chancellery, indicate the variety of these tasks. He was particularly responsible for press affairs, and Delbrück referred to him as a "journalistic attaché." He not only reviewed the daily press and scholarly publications

69

and briefed the chancellor daily on the contents, but he also recommended how the authors should be answered or otherwise dealt with. He helped establish guidelines for censorship, and he dealt directly with newspapers and with news agencies to insure that certain pieces of information did or did not go to print. In addition, he planned many of the details for the chancellor's travels, and he disseminated information about Bethmann Hollweg's appearances. He was particularly careful that all ovations and enthusiasm directed toward the chancellor were reported to the press.

Riezler was often asked to write policy papers and speeches covering a variety of subjects for both the chancellor and for the kaiser. He also performed liaison activities with the Parliament and with the German General Staff. He was frequently directed to gather information on subjects of special interest to the chancellor, such as the American harvest. He was regarded as the chancellor's chief adviser for Bavarian affairs. Riezler devoted much of his time meeting with individual citizens or representatives of private organizations who wished to make recommendations to or to gain information from the chancellor. He also answered much of Bethmann Hollweg's correspondence and thanked those who had sent advice or books to the chancellor. He was occasionally called upon to initiate police checks on Germans being considered for employment at important German governmental missions abroad. Because such chores occupied much of Riezler's attention, Conrad Haussmann, parliamentary leader of the Progressive Party and a later friend of Riezler, referred to him as the chancellor's "private secretary."[20]

Riezler's duties were not clearly delineated, and perhaps his most important role, as far as Bethmann Hollweg was concerned, was that of a well-informed, philosophically oriented conversation partner. Bethmann Hollweg, who was often referred to as the "philosopher of Hohenfinow," was drawn to the young Riezler because of the latter's breadth of knowledge and ability to place single events into the largest context. Through conversations with the young Riezler, the chancellor could explore the consequences of his own thinking and thereby formulate his thoughts more clearly. This in no way meant that Riezler's views ultimately became the chancellor's own views also. Many instances showed that this was not so. It did mean that Riezler's political influence cannot be understood merely in terms of his official duties.

JULY CRISIS

There was general shock and indignation in all of Europe when Archduke Franz Ferdinand's assassination was announced. At first few leaders outside of Austria-Hungary considered war with Serbia an appropriate response to the assassination. The German Foreign Office, in contrast to German military circles, expressed the hope that an Austro-Serbian war could be prevented.[21]

In order to clarify Germany's possible attitude toward retaliatory measures, Austro-Hungarian Emperor Franz Joseph sent Count Hoyos, under-state secretary in the Austro-Hungarian Foreign Office, to Berlin. Hoyos delivered a memorandum written before the assassination proposing a diplomatic ring in the Balkans around Serbia, whose appeal to Balkan Slavs threatened the weakening cohesion of the polyglot Austro-Hungarian Empire. He also brought a personal letter from Emperor Franz Joseph to Wilhelm II, in which Wilhelm was reminded that "the assassination is a direct consequence of the agitation conducted by Russian and Serbian Pan-Slavists with the sole objective of weakening the Triple Alliance and of fragmenting my Empire." Russian activity in the Balkans presented "a lasting danger for my house and my lands." He asserted that "the efforts of my government in the future must be directed toward the isolation and reduction of Serbia." He closed with the appeal:

You too will be convinced after the latest terrible events in Bosnia that a reconciliation of the conflict between us and Serbia is unthinkable and that the European monarchies' policy of maintaining peace will be threatened as long as this focus of criminal agitation remains unpunished in Belgrade.

These documents clearly revealed Austrian willingness from the beginning to resort to war in order to deal with Serbia. Indeed, since no reconciliation with Serbia was considered possible, it is difficult to imagine how Serbia could have been "diminished" and how such "a focus of criminal agitation" could have been punished without some war-like measures. In any event, on the morning of July 5 Kaiser Wilhelm assured the Austrian ambassador in Berlin, Count Szoegyény, that "Germany will stand on Austria's side in traditional loyalty to its ally." Szoegyény reported Wilhelm's comment that

if we really saw the necessity of a military action against Serbia, then he [Wilhelm] would find it regrettable if we did not take advantage of the present moment, which is favorable from our point of view.

Wilhelm indicated that he could not make any commitments regarding military activities in Serbia without consulting Chancellor Bethmann Hollweg, but he told Szoegyény that he did not have the slightest doubt that Bethmann Hollweg would agree with him fully.[22]

Bethmann Hollweg and Zimmermann met the kaiser in the afternoon of July fifth. Bethmann had already been informed of the contents of the two documents. The kaiser expressed his opinion that the matter was serious. Nevertheless, he indicated it was not Germany's business "to advise the ally what is to be done about the bloody deed of Sarajevo." Germany should especially abstain from hints and suggestions because "we should use all means to work against the growth of the Austro-Serbian controversy into an international conflict." The kaiser said that Franz Joseph must know "that we would not abandon Austria-Hungary in a grave hour. Our own vital interest demands the safe maintenance of Austria." Bethmann concluded: "These views of the kaiser correspond to my own views."[28]

Later on the fifth Wilhelm called together his military advisers for consultations, and according to Adjutant General Plessen, "the opinion prevails here that the sooner we move against Serbia the better and that the Russians—although friends of Serbia—will not intervene." However, War Minister Erich von Falkenhayn told Helmuth von Moltke, chief of the General Staff: "The chancellor, who was already in Potsdam, seems to believe as little as I that the Austrian government is serious about its recently more forceful language."[24]

On July 6 in a conversation with Hoyos, Szoegyény, and Zimmermann, Wilhelm confirmed the famous "blank check" for an Austrian action against Serbia: Austria should determine its policy and Germany would support it. The kaiser recommended immediate action against Serbia as the solution to the Balkan problem because the momentary international situation was more favorable than it would later be. These meetings on July 5 and 6 became known as the "Potsdam Crown Council."[25]

The kaiser's monarchical loyalty had been touched by the assassination of a crown prince, and it is unlikely that any German chancellor in 1914 could have openly opposed the kaiser in this matter. Also, the kaiser's conversations with his military advisers were at least as important for his decision as his conversations with the chancellor. Bethmann's approval did lend added weight and constitutional sanction to the German policy as it was expressed to the Austrians on July 5 and 6, but his opinion alone did not decide the issue. On the contrary, the decision was, in the words of Konrad Jarausch, "a tenuous compromise between the conflicting views of the decision-makers, Bethmann, William II, Zimmermann, Falkenhayn and the military entourage."[26]

Riezler's diary entries immediately after July 5 and 6 indicate that he was neither present at the high level meetings where the crucial decisions were made on those days, nor was he with the chancellor. In the days before July 5 Bethmann Hollweg was at his estate in Hohenfinow outside of Berlin while Riezler remained in Berlin. Bethmann Hollweg traveled by rail to see the kaiser four times from June 29 to July 5, but it is unknown whether he saw Riezler during these short visits to Potsdam. Seldom did Riezler ever accompany the chancellor on official visits to the kaiser. Of course, it can be assumed that Riezler maintained telephone contact with the chancellor and that he continued to do paper work for him while the latter was absent.[27] There is no question that Riezler, along with other high level advisers, such as Jagow and Zimmermann, advised Bethmann on the political strategy and tactics which the chancellor himself then recommended or decided. Undoubtedly, some clues as to the advice which Riezler gave can be gotten from his prewar writings.

Andreas Hillgruber maintains that the German policy adopted at this time "corresponded to a definite political calculation which the chancellor had developed in constant close contact with Riezler." Hillgruber was referring, of course, to Riezler's theory of the calculated risk, but he does not indicate when this "definite political calculation" had been developed. Although there is no supporting documentary evidence, it is certainly possible that in 1913 Riezler had discussed with the chancellor some of the arguments he made in *Grundzüge der Weltpolitik,* including that concerning the calculated risk. Also, although Riezler does not mention it in his diary, it is possible that they discussed Riezler's calculated risk argument, even if only by telephone, in the days before the Potsdam "Crown Council" and that the theory formed part of the general conceptual basis for the chancellor's approach to the crisis. It is true that the chancellor, as well as Riezler, strongly felt that the growing Serbian threat to Austria-Hungary was ultimately a serious threat to Germany's own vital interests. It is also true that, in contrast to previous Balkan crises, both sensed that the time had come for a bolder policy, even at the risk of a local war or, if unavoidable, a continental war in order to achieve a diplomatic realignment in the Balkans and thereby to reverse the steady deterioration of Germany's diplomatic and military position. The chancellor did not want war; nevertheless, he accepted the risk of war, and as Joachim Remak noted, this risk proved to be "immeasurably too high." Further, we know from Riezler's diary entries that throughout the July crisis, the chancellor and his young assistant rationalized German support of Austria-Hungary since July 5 and 6 in terms of the possible diplomatic realignment which could flow from that policy. Indeed, the kind of favorable outcome resulting from a calculated risk such as Riezler described in *Grundzüge der Weltpolitik* would have been the optimal outcome of the July crisis, from the chancellor's point of view.

Nevertheless, as will be shown, Riezler's prewar theory of the calculated risk can in no way be viewed as the operational guideline for German policy during the July crisis.[28]

On July 6 Riezler returned to Hohenfinow with Bethmann Hollweg, and that evening he was given a report of the situation by the chancellor. What Riezler heard surprised him greatly and seemed so important that he resumed his diary the next day for the first time since the second Moroccan crisis:

Yesterday I drove out with the chancellor. The old castle, the wonderful, gigantic lindens, the avenues like a Gothic arch. . . . In the evening on the veranda under the darkened sky a long conversation on the situation. The secret news which he tells me gives an unnerving picture. He views the Anglo-Russian negotiations concerning a naval agreement and a landing in Pomerania with great concern, the last link in the chain. Lichnowsky is much too gullible. He allows himself to be taken in by the English. Russia's military power growing rapidly; with the strategic extension into Poland the situation is untenable. Austria increasingly weaker and immobile; the undermining from the North [Poland] and Southeast has advanced very far. In any case incapable [for Austria] to go to war as our ally over a German problem. The Entente knows that; as a result, we are completely paralyzed.

I was completely horrified. I had not viewed the situation as being so bad. One does not receive the secret news if one does not truly belong to the inside circle—and everything which is in the realm of high politics and which is also military is top secret. The chancellor speaks of difficult decisions. The murder of Franz Ferdinand. Official Serbia involved. Austria wants to get right to work. The message of Franz Joseph to the kaiser with the questions concerning *casus foederis*. Our old dilemma with every Austrian Balkan action. If we encourage them, then they say we pushed them into it; if we discourage them, then it is said we left them in the lurch. Then they go to the Western powers, whose arms are open, and we lose the last reasonable ally. This time it is worse than 1912 because this time Austria is in defense against the Serbo-Russian intrigues. An action against Serbia can lead to a world war. From a war, regardless of the outcome, the chancellor expects a revolution of everything that exists. That which exists has long outlived itself, is wholly without ideas. Heydebrand said a war would lead to a strengthening of the patriarchal order and way of thinking. The chancellor is furious about such nonsense. Generally, delusion all around, a thick fog over the people. The same in all of Europe. The future belongs to Russia, which grows and grows and thrusts itself on us as a heavier and heavier nightmare. . . . His [the chancellor's] cleverness is indeed as great as his clumsiness. . . .

Riezler continued on July 8.

Message delivered by Hoyos to Franz Joseph. Hoyos with Zimmerman. The chancellor thinks that perhaps the old Kaiser [Franz Joseph] will in the end decide against it. If the war comes from the East, so that we go to war for Austria and not Austria for us, then we have the prospect of winning it. If the war does not come, if the tsar does not want it, or if a perplexed France counsels peace, then we still certainly have the prospect of maneuvering the Entente apart over this matter.[29]

These entries give us insights into Bethmann's and Riezler's attitudes and roles during the July crisis. We learn, for one thing, that Riezler did not have access to all sensitive political or military information; he did not belong to the "inner circle." Although he was undoubtedly aware of the alternatives which were being considered, he received confirmation of the decision to support Austria in whatever policy she chose only after the crucial decision of July 5 and 6 had already been made. We see in his scornful remarks about Lichnowsky the first indications of a serious miscalculation concerning Britain's stake in a potential European war. We see Riezler's concern about the steady decline in Austria's strength and his exaggerated anxiety about the possibility of Germany's losing her last ally if firm support were not granted to Austria.

Riezler's conviction that Germany's security depended upon Austria's continued existence was shared by most Germans in 1914. It is true that Germany was unwise in tying itself so closely to Austria-Hungary, which, in Riezler's words, was "a relic of the Middle Ages." In the age of nationalism a polyglot state could hardly be held together by a dynasty alone. Though Riezler had doubts about the wisdom of "eternally squatting behind this weak state and [having] to squander our youthful strength on the postponement of its disintegration," he believed in July 1914, as did most Germans, that the Austro-Hungarian state had to be preserved. The fact that the existence of Germany's only ally was at stake took this matter out of the realm of a "small realignment."

Riezler's thinking was similar to Bethmann Hollweg's during the two Balkan wars of 1912 and 1913. In 1912 the Balkan states had fought against Turkey in order to enlarge themselves at Turkey's expense, and in 1913 the same Balkan states had fought each other over the booty. To Austria's chagrin the chief winners in both wars were Serbia and, indirectly, Russia. In both wars it was Germany's policy to oppose any Austrian attempt to declare war on its threatening southern neighbor, Serbia, and Germany cooperated with London to achieve a settlement. As a result Anglo-German relations improved greatly, but Austria-Hungary became more and more irritated by Germany's apparent infidelity and began to contemplate an alliance with other major powers. While no German, including the chancellor and Riezler, contemplated allowing the very existence of the Austro-Hungarian state to be threatened, the fear that Austria would seek allies elsewhere became one of many considerations in German policymaking by July 1914.[30]

This fear was hardly justified, however, for with what other major powers might Austria have allied? An alliance with Russia was out of the question because of disputes in the Balkans and because of Russia's support of Serbia. Also, Austrian weakness was quite apparent to Britain and France, and the latter could therefore have had no interest whatsoever in abandoning their neutrality or alliances in order to squander their resources backing a dying power. In short, Riezler and the chancellor feared the impossible.

Riezler's remarks reveal a deep pessimism about the chance for Germany and Austria to resist an ever-expanding Russia. His concern about Russia was considerably less than Bethmann Hollweg's. The chancellor's strong feelings about the inevitability of Russian expansion was perhaps best shown by a remark which he made to Hans von Flotow, Germany's ambassador to Rome at the time of the outbreak: Bethmann Hollweg, "looking out over the park on his estate at Hohenfinow doubted whether there were any purpose in planting new trees because the Russians would be there in a few years anyway."[31]

Both Bethmann Hollweg and Riezler knew from the beginning that an Austrian action against Serbia could lead to a world war. Nevertheless, Riezler was displeased with the prospect of war, especially a general war in Europe. This was indicated by his description of the "unnerving picture" Bethmann Hollweg had presented him. He, of course, hoped that a minor readjustment of the European diplomatic constellation in Germany's favor would be a consequence of the crisis. For example, on July 11 Riezler stated how he wanted the crisis to be handled: "a quick *fait accompli* and then turn to the Entente in a friendly manner; that way the shock can be endured. And then with good and overwhelming material which permits no objections speak out openly against the Serbian intrigues."[32] Such was Riezler's desire—not for a European or world war, but for a diplomatic success, possibly following a rapid Austrian war against Serbia. He undoubtedly recommended such a policy to Bethmann Hollweg.

The above passage also indicates the difficulty, as Riezler saw it, of controlling Austria's policy from Berlin. In this entry Riezler reported "differences" between Austro-Hungarian Foreign Minister Leopold Graf von Berchtold and Hungarian Minister-President Count Tisza. On July 7 the Austro-Hungarian Council of Ministers decided on war with Serbia. The majority of the cabinet in Vienna agreed with Berchtold that a rapid military action without previous diplomatic negotiations should be undertaken. Tisza, who initially opposed war with Serbia entirely, wanted to make concrete demands on Serbia with an ultimatum and mobilization to follow a Serbian rejection. Tisza's plan was finally adopted. Riezler wrote: "Apparently they require a terribly long time to mobilize. Konrad von Hoetzendorff says sixteen days." He made the important observation: "It is hardly possible to lead their hand from Berlin." Germany had no control over Austria's policy toward Serbia and over her timetable because on July 5 and 6 Germany had granted Austria a free hand in this matter. Sidney Fay's observation was correct that "Germany by no means had Austria so completely under her thumb." Throughout the crisis control of the situation remained in Austrian hands, and only in the final days of the crisis did Bethmann Hollweg try desperately to regain control. As George Peabody Gooch wrote, "the mistake in Berlin was not in promising aid but in allowing Berchtold alone to steer the ship."[33]

Subsequent events revealed that German interests would have been better served by a tighter German rein on Austrian policy. However, in the eyes of German leaders there appeared to be no alternative to their policy of allowing Austria to deal harshly with Serbia at this time. Certainly no policy which would have resulted in a significant weakening of Austria-Hungary would have been acceptable to Germany, and, as we have seen, Bethmann Hollweg, the kaiser, and Franz Joseph considered Austria-Hungary to have been threatened by Serbia, which they saw as the agent of Russia and of all threatening nationalist movements. Thus, some kind of strong measure against Serbia would have been considered essential. No policy would have been acceptable which would have allowed Russia to strengthen herself greatly in the Balkans; it is clear that the conviction was strong among the German military, the kaiser, and Bethmann Hollweg that inaction on this occasion would have considerably strengthened Russia's position in the Balkans. Bethmann Hollweg's fatalism regarding Russian expansion was not so great that he would have passively accepted a sudden and dramatic increase of Russian influence in the Balkans.

After approving the decision to back whatever policy Austria chose, and after recommending rapid Austrian military action against Serbia, Bethmann Hollweg ceased taking a direct hand until the last few days of the crisis. While Germany's ambassador in Vienna, Heinrich von Tschirschky, continued to urge Austria to take rapid action against Serbia, Bethmann Hollweg attempted to create a calm atmosphere by persuading the kaiser not to cancel his annual cruise in the North Sea and by returning to his own estate at Hohenfinow. He was careful not to give the impression that Berlin was preparing for war.

Riezler accompanied the chancellor to Hohenfinow. By mid-July there was still no appearance of a crisis, but Riezler wrote on July 14 that "the gravity of the diplomatic situation overshadows everything." Riezler's pessimism about Germany's situation and about the chances to maintain peace continued to grow. "Our situation is terrible." The lack of control over events gave Riezler a feeling of helplessness.

As the prospect of war became more real, his mind dared to ponder the positive aspects of a war. "If the war should come and the veil [of friendliness which covers the real enmity among peoples] should fall, then the entire *Volk* will follow, driven by a sense of emergency and danger. Victory is liberation." His use of the words "emergency and danger" indicated that he was thinking primarily of "liberation" from the *"cauchemar des coalitions,"* from the encirclement of which he wrote in *Grundzüge der Weltpolitik.* There is no question that Riezler hoped that the Austro-Serbian crisis would loosen or break some of the ties which existed among Britain, France, and Russia. However, he reflected upon another aspect of a war which he discussed with the chancellor: The "liberation" from petty things, the adventure of being a part of a great movement. "The chancellor thinks that I am too young not to be lured by the uncertain, the new, the great movement. For him the action is a leap into darkness and this [is] the gravest obligation."[34]

Riezler had not abandoned his hope that a negotiated settlement could be reached. In his entry of July 14 he mentions a discussion in Vienna over whether the ultimatum to Serbia should be issued before or after French President Poincaré's talks in St. Petersburg (July 21-23) with Russian leaders. Riezler preferred that the ultimatum be issued before Poincaré's trip: "Then there is a greater chance that France, suddenly shocked by the reality of the war dream, will press for peace in St. Petersburg."

Unfortunately Riezler's preference was not the preference of all governments concerned. On July 14 the Austrian government decided to present the ultimatum within hours after the French president had departed from Russia; Austrian leaders feared that the chances of direct French and Russian intervention in the crisis would increase if the French president and the tsar had the opportunity to discuss the ultimatum. Bethmann Hollweg was informed by the German embassy in Vienna on July 14 and again on July 17 that this ultimatum was to be presented on July 23 and was intended to be unacceptable:

Graf Berchtold revealed his hope that Serbia would not accept the demands since a mere diplomatic success would unleash here in this country a lax frame of mind, which is absolutely the last thing which is needed.

Although German leaders had not directly influenced the decision, the news that the ultimatum was designed to be unacceptable to Serbia did not alarm them. Certainly, the German chancellor favored "an energetic decision" on the part of Austria-Hungary, in order "to put an end to the intolerable conditions in the southeast."[35]

Riezler wrote on July 20 that "a very serious mood" prevailed in Berlin. "A heavy blanket of open sadness and of the greatest responsibility hangs over the men and over all conversations, broken only here and there by the children's need for gaiety. The chancellor is determined and taciturn." Riezler continued to speak of the chancellor, whose personality clearly fascinated him:

In many petty things unbearable; in the great things admirable. . . . I always considered him as basically a very intelligent and educated bureaucrat; that is entirely wrong. He is great as a man through the breadth and independence of his intellect. He is entirely free from all prejudice and narrowness and entirely independent of that which is common opinion and suggestion. His judgment moves completely independently; so often he says the unsaid and unheard.

Riezler also revealed an irritating element of his relationship with Bethmann Hollweg, which indicates an important task which Riezler performed: even when Bethmann had a "firm opinion about something," he "pretended to doubt" and said things "which he himself did not believe in order to hear the opposing position from the other."[36] Riezler served as a sort of wall against which Bethmann Hollweg bounced ideas in order to confirm his own thinking. Undoubtedly, Riezler's greatest influence on the chancellor was exerted in such daily briefings and informal conversations.

After supporting Austria-Hungary in a critical moment by tolerating the unacceptable ultimatum against Serbia, Germany turned its attention to insuring that the almost inevitable Austro-Serbian war would not expand into a European war involving the European continental powers; Germany wished to see the war localized. Few German leaders wanted such a European war, but all were well aware of the danger that the local war could lead to a larger conflict. Therefore, efforts were made to decrease the likelihood that this would happen. On July 21 a preliminary "white paper" was sent to German ambassadors in London, Paris, and

St. Petersburg explaining Germany's stand and emphasizing Germany's conviction that the crisis was no more than a quarrel between Austria-Hungary and Serbia. The German Foreign Office recommended to the Austrian government that only a part of its army be mobilized in order "not automatically to provoke a Russian countermobilization which would force us and thereafter France to adopt the same measures and in the process would ignite a European war." Furthermore, calm was maintained. High German military officers were sent on leave, and the German press was ordered to avoid all provocation against France in order not to stir up French public opinion. Riezler, whose job included drafting replies for the chancellor, probably worked on Germany's "white paper," and as the chancellor's press adviser, he was certainly involved in the efforts to tone down provocative press statements directed toward other European powers.[37]

Riezler's diary entries during the remainder of the crisis indicate an increasing apprehension about Russia; he even considered meeting this growing danger by reaching an agreement with Russia. He wrote on July 20 of

. . . Russia's growing claims and enormous explosive force. Uncontainable in a few years, especially if the present European constellation remains. If successful in changing it [constellation] or in loosening it up, then one must consider whether and how the entire present alliance system must be overturned and changed. But whether that is possible? Only if Russia is not supported to the end by the Western powers in the Serbian affair, if it sees that it must come to an agreement with us. However, Russia will be very expensive. It has become too powerful and must use Pan-Slavism for domestic political reasons and as a counterweight to revolutionary movements.[38]

Although Bethmann Hollweg continued in all official correspondence firmly to support Austria-Hungary in the Serbian affair, Riezler began on July 23, the day the Austrian ultimatum was delivered, to question whether Austria-Hungary should be supported at all and whether an alliance with Russia might have served German interests better. He was pleased that Austria had acquiesced to German pressure by openly declaring that it had no territorial aspirations in Serbia; "such a declaration perhaps restrains Russia from a mobilization and directs them toward the path of negotiation." Riezler no longer believed in the "vitality" of the Austro-Hungarian state. He wrote:

It is certainly characteristic for the entire political mess in Austria, which does not let go of the inherited lures of a world power, but which cannot even begin to maintain itself. We will certainly squat behind this weak state and will squander our youthful strength on the postponement of its disintegration.[39]

Bethmann Hollweg and Riezler actually considered a possible solution to this dilemma. Throughout the crisis they saw no better solution than to reduce the pressure on Austria by weakening the Franco-Russian alliance, thereby eliminating the backing for Russian penetration and political warfare in the Balkans. On July 23 Bethmann Hollweg and Riezler discussed a remarkable conversation which had taken place a few days earlier between Russian Foreign Minister S. D. Sazonov and Berlin banker Robert Franz von Mendelssohn. Sazonov said to Mendelssohn: "Si l'Allemagne lâche l'Autriche, je lâcherai immediatement après la France." One cannot be certain that Sazonov meant this remark to be taken seriously; it is also highly unlikely that Sazonov could unilaterally have made such a radical shift in Russian policy. Nevertheless, Riezler wrote that Bethmann Hollweg actually thought seriously about that possibility. A lasting arrangement with Russia might have been better than an agreement with Britain. However, Riezler sensed that the difficulties in such a radical change in German policy would have been

perhaps much greater. Russia much more demanding. Yes, if she wanted only to infringe upon the Balkan aspirations of Austria but not upon the very existence of Austria. The Balkan aspirations of Austria disappear if we do not support them.

One wonders what kind of agreement would have been acceptable for Germany? Riezler noted that "we must preserve Austria itself. If Russia reaches for the southern Slavs, we are lost. At most a German-Russian agreement for the preservation of Austria." Even this, Riezler saw, would have been artificial and temporary because it would not have solved Austria-Hungary's nationalities problem, which, after all, was the fundamental problem. Therefore, he had to conclude that at least for the time being:

Utilization of Sazonov's remark to Robby Mendelssohn impossible; Sazonov would only give the appearance of negotiating and let Vienna know via London in order to blast Austria away [from Germany].

Riezler, as an earlier entry indicated, was unnecessarily concerned about the possibility of Austria's defecting to the Entente. Therefore, if an agreement with Russia were desirable, it could only be considered after the present crisis had passed. He wrote:

If the Serbian affair goes well, without Russia's mobilizing and thus without war, then there would perhaps be no danger in reaching an understanding with a Russia which would be disappointed with the Western powers, even at the expense of a satisfied Austria-Hungary.[40]

81

As we shall see in the final chapter, Riezler often toyed during the war with the idea of abandoning Austria in order to reach an agreement with Russia.

On July 23 the political situation seemed very uncertain and mysterious to Riezler.

Sat and strolled for a long time under the great linden trees and reflected on everything. What will happen? Will the German *Volk* be saved or will it perish? Nature unconscious and unconcerned . . . greater than the greatest event.[41]

On July 23, at 6:00 P.M., the Austrian ambassador in Belgrade, Wladimir Baron Giesl, presented the Austrian ultimatum to the Serbian government. In forty-eight hours the ultimatum had to be answered, and no extension of the ultimatum could be considered. The major European governments were not informed of the ultimatum until the next day. This ultimatum transformed the local quarrel into a world crisis. Russia's foreign minister accused Austria of "setting Europe aflame," and he predicted war. British Foreign Minister Edward Grey warned that all European powers could be drawn into the conflict, but he assured Lichnowsky that Britain would remain disinterested in an Austro-Serbian conflict so long as no war between Austria and Russia resulted. Finally, Germany's and Austria's ally in the Triple Alliance, Italy, protested the Austrian move; Italian leaders implied consequences which were actually realized after the outbreak of war when they declared Italy neutral and even declared war on the Central Powers.[42]

Szoegyény reported from Berlin on July 25 that German leaders had again urged Austria to proceed quickly against Serbia in order to minimize the danger of intervention. It was still hoped in Berlin that the war could be localized. Nevertheless, as Riezler's entry on July 25 shows, the military, economic, and diplomatic preparations for a possible war with France and Russia were being made by Germany before the invasion of Serbia had begun:

Almost the entire time the last few days the chancellor has been on the telephone. Apparently preparations for every eventuality, talks with the military about which nothing is said. Merchant marine is warned. Havenstein financial mobilization. Until now nothing could be made which would be conspicuous. Great movement.

Without question Riezler, along with the chancellor's other aides, was deeply involved with these economic and diplomatic preparations for an

82

eventual war. Unfortunately, there is no documentary evidence which indicates exactly what he was doing at this time.

The philosophic Riezler pondered the meaning of this confusion and uncertainty. "What does fate want? But fate is mostly stupid and unconscious and muddled in many coincidences. Whoever takes hold of it has it." Riezler believed that individual human action could help control events. Nevertheless, he continued to see difficulties. Fate "in this cursed, confused modern world has become so multifarious, can neither be calculated nor comprehended. Too many factors at the same time."[43]

On July 25 at 6:00 P.M., Serbia presented its answer to the Austrian ultimatum. Despite the fact that Serbia agreed to almost all of Austria's demands, Austria rejected the Serbian note and broke off diplomatic relations. In response, Serbia ordered immediate and full mobilization. The rejection of the Serbian note did not lead immediately to panic or to a sharp escalation of tensions in Europe despite the fact that Austria had answered immediately with partial mobilization. Riezler wrote that the first reports on the reactions in Paris, St. Petersburg, London, and Rome were "not unfavorable . . . . The main thing," Riezler continued, was "that Sazonov, though furious, avoided committing himself. Paris dismayed. England's coldness: an Austro-Serbian conflict is none of my business. Italy's attempts to blackmail." Riezler saw the crucial point in a possible Russian mobilization; "everything depends on whether St. Petersburg mobilizes immediately and whether it is encouraged or held back by the West." Riezler was in complete agreement with Bethmann Hollweg, who on July 23 stated that "if war comes, it will come through a Russian mobilization *ab irato,* that is, before possible negotiations." The chancellor now saw "a fate greater than human power lying over the European situation and over our people."

The excitement in Germany on the evening of July 25 showed that the crisis was approaching a peak. Arriving in Berlin, Riezler observed:

Movement on the streets. Crowds of people in Unter den Linden waiting for the Serbian answer, even before the reports of the *Lokalanzeiger.* However, the people have not yet been awakened fully from the dream of peace, which they still take for granted, still disbelieving, amazed and curious.

There was an air of excitement in Berlin which Riezler detected at this critical point:

In the evening and on Sunday people singing. At first the chancellor thought that only juveniles were taking advantage of the opportunity for racket and excitement and were letting their curiosity run wild. However, there is more and more of this, and the tones are becoming more genuine. In the end the chancellor is deeply moved, deeply stirred, strengthened especially since the news [of such popular emotion] is coming from the entire Empire. In the people an enormous, if confused, urge to act, a yearning for a great movement, to rise up for a great movement, to rise up for a great cause, to show one's ability.[44]

Bethmann Hollweg had reason to be pessimistic because on July 27 the crisis entered its most serious stage. Riezler recorded on this day that "all reports point to war." Austria decided to declare war on Serbia, and the actual declaration followed the next day. Riezler correctly identified the critical points: Russia and London. He reported "obviously hard struggles over mobilization in St. Petersburg." On July 26 and 27 the German Foreign Office received reports from Germany's ambassador in St. Petersburg, Pourtalès, of Russia's partial mobilization in the four military districts of Kiev, Odessa, Kasan, and Moscow. Also, the Baltic and Black Sea fleets were mobilized, and the "war preparation period" was introduced in the entire Russian Empire.[45] These orders had been given on July 24 and 25, thus before, not as a direct result of, the Austrian rejection of the Serbian note.

Riezler also observed that "England's language has changed," and indeed it had. On July 26 and 27 Lichnowsky sent Berlin four telegrams reporting a sudden change in Grey's thinking and warning Berlin against believing that a war between Serbia and Austria could be localized. Grey frankly believed that such a war could lead to a world war and warned that if Berlin did not restrain Vienna, Britain would take sides with Russia and France. Riezler believed that the British policy had changed because "obviously in London one has suddenly seen that the Entente will have a crack in it if one is too lukewarm toward Russia." He was irritated by the warnings of Lichnowsky, who had "completely lost his composure." Nevertheless, he and Bethmann Hollweg certainly took the reports seriously. Riezler saw the

danger that France and England promise support because of fear of irritating Russia, perhaps without actually considering the fact that mobilization means war for us; perhaps they consider everything a bluff which they answer with a counterbluff.

Germany's stand was clearly not a bluff.[46] There is no clearer indication that Riezler's theory of the calculated risk was not being applied. Britain's perception of the significance of Austria's Balkan action shocked the Central Powers out of the belief that a world war was unlikely. Bethmann Hollweg was never positive that Britain would remain neutral in a major conflict, but he had hoped that both his recently improved relations with Britain and the latter's general interest in peace would insure British neutrality.

Britain's new hostile attitude changed the atmosphere in Berlin. Riezler writes that there was "hectic activity in the Chancellery. No one sleeps any more. I see the chancellor only for seconds. He is entirely changed, has not a single minute to ponder and for that reason is fresh, active, lively, and relaxed." This frantic activity had no letup; after July 27 Riezler was so busy in the Chancellery that he had no opportunity to write in his diary until August 14. "In the intervening time, not a single minute for a notation."[47]

From July 27 events went so rapidly that in a meeting of the Prussian State Ministry in the afternoon of July 30, Bethmann Hollweg had to admit that "all governments including Russia's and the great majority of the peoples are basically peaceful, but all direction is lost and the stone has begun to roll." Indeed, by July 31 war was certain. Riezler made very few notes about events in these crucial days, so we cannot determine exactly what duties he performed. His name or initials appear in no relevant official documents located in the German Foreign Office files.[48]

July 27 was a turning point in the crisis for two reasons: first, the Austrian government decided on that day to declare war on Serbia. Second, strong doubt was cast on British neutrality; Britain began intervening directly in the Austro-Serbian dispute. On July 26 Grey proposed a four-power conference to deal with this dispute. Germany rejected this fearing that such a conference would only condemn Austria as that power which threatened the peace. Germany asserted that only Austria-Hungary could determine what was necessary in the defense of her vital interests. The only kind of mediation to which Germany would have consented was between Austria and Russia.[49] However, two important events rendered mediation almost impossible: Austria's actual declaration of war on Serbia and Russia's mobilization.

On July 28 at 11:00 A.M., Austria-Hungary declared war on Serbia. At the same time a discussion was taking place in Berlin concerning the proper interpretation of Serbia's answer to the Austrian ultimatum. In the night of July 27-28 Bethmann Hollweg had sent a telegram to Tschirschky in Vienna that the Serbian reply only seemed to make concessions and was thus unacceptable. On the other hand, the kaiser, who had returned unexpectedly from his North Sea cruise on July 27, read the Serbian answer and was very impressed with Serbia's concessions. He saw in the reply a "capitulation of the most humiliating kind" and found "no more reason for a war." He ordered Bethmann Hollweg to request the

85

Austrians to "stop in Belgrade," a city which he hoped could be used as a hostage to insure that Serbia fulfilled its promises. However, Bethmann Hollweg did not forward this order until the evening of the twenty-eighth. It is beyond dispute that Bethmann Hollweg did not want to restrain Austria at this point; indeed, after numerous recommendations to Austria throughout the crisis to move quickly against Serbia, an appeal for Austrian restraint would have seemed incomprehensible. He hoped that British mediation could prevent the conflict from spreading before Vienna had captured Belgrade. Then Austria could negotiate with Russia before Russian mobilization.[50] Bethmann's policy had little chance for success, though. The likelihood of full Russian mobilization had become very great, and Russia's leaders knew well that Germany would interpret such mobilization as war.[51]

As we know, at this point Bethmann Hollweg was not interested in preventing an Austrian war against Serbia; on the other hand, he did not believe that such a war would inevitably lead to a world war. If a larger war were to come, then Bethmann Hollweg and Riezler were sure that Russia would be responsible for it. Naturally, they both wanted the Russians to be seen in the world's eyes as the guilty party. No country which goes to war for any reason wishes to be branded as the guilty party. For example, Jules Cambon, French ambassador to Berlin, advised his government on July 30, 1914, not to announce mobilization measures until after Germany had done so ". . . in order that English public opinion . . . cannot attribute to us the initiative which led to war." Also, Grey had informed Lichnowsky that Russia would have to seem to be in the wrong before Britain would put restraining pressure on France and Russia. In any case, the German chancellor's reaction to the news of partial mobilization revealed quite clearly that Bethmann Hollweg did not want a general war. That reaction was not one of relief that the Russians had blundered by mobilizing and now had to live with the war guilt. The reaction was a frantic and desperate one.[52]

Riezler wrote that following the first report of Russian mobilization, "we now had to work at top speed for five days in a row until five or six o'clock in the morning." To be sure, much of this frantic effort was directed toward diplomatic preparation for an eventual war; Bethmann Hollweg was fully aware by this time that recent events could lead to a larger war. Riezler mentioned some of those preparations, and there can be no question that Riezler was deeply involved with them. Efforts were made to invoke the agreements of the Triple Alliance in order to insure Italy's participation in the war on Germany's and Austria's side. However, it was already apparent to Riezler that "Italy is not coming with us." The Italians maintained that they were obliged to go to war only in the event of an unprovoked attack against one of their allies, and Austria, they argued, had provoked general war by declaring war on Serbia. Riezler saw another motive behind Italy's refusal to cooperate: "The Austrians (bureaucrats run wild, narrow-minded and stupid) keep them [the Italians] at arm's length instead of offering them Trentino as a good gesture." Austria was intent on keeping Italy out of the Balkans. Germany redoubled her diplomatic efforts to win Turkey, Bulgaria, and Rumania as allies. Also, a preliminary white paper was prepared to present Germany's view of war guilt.[53]

While diplomatic preparations for a possible war were made, the chancellor's staff was occupied with "the question of how far one should go in accepting the English proposal for negotiation." Bethmann Hollweg was interested primarily in seeing Austria accomplish its objectives without a general war, not in simply having Russia bear the guilt for such a war. In an effort to stop the movement toward general war, Bethmann Hollweg made what can only be considered a grave diplomatic blunder. At 10:30 P.M. on July 29 he made a pledge to the British ambassador in Berlin, Sir William Edward Goschen: if Russian aggression against Austria-Hungary compelled Germany to fulfill her treaty obligations, "we can assure the English cabinet—presupposing its neutrality—that even in case of victorious war, we will seek no territorial aggrandizement in Europe at the cost of France." Dutch neutrality would be observed in any case, but with regard to Belgium,

we do not know what countermeasures French actions in a possible war might force us to take. However, assuming that Belgium does not take sides with our enemy, we would be willing in this case to give the assurance that Belgium's integrity would not be permitted to be violated after the war.

The conversation ended with the suggestion that Anglo-German cooperation in the present crisis could possibly be extended to a "general neutrality agreement in the future."[54]

This message to Goschen was interpreted by the British as a crude move designed to remove Britain from an imminent European war, and it created indignation in London. Under-Foreign Secretary Crowe noted: "The only comment that need be made on these astounding proposals is that they reflect discredit on the statesman who makes them." Indeed, this conversation appeared to presume a general war with France and Russia and did not seem consistent with Bethmann Hollweg's belated efforts on July 30 to apply genuine pressure on Austria to consider negotiations with St. Petersburg. Previously he had either refused to do this at all, or he had assured Vienna that his official attempts to mediate in Austria's affair were no more than a formality designed to please the British.[55]

On July 30 Bethmann Hollweg sent the first truly sharp note to Vienna, which had shown reluctance to negotiate with St. Petersburg. In it Bethmann Hollweg stated:

> We are certainly ready to fulfill our treaty obligations; we must, however, refuse to allow ourselves to be drawn into a world conflagration by a Vienna which is careless and disregards our suggestions.

The answer as to why there was such a rapid change of policy in Berlin can be found in a report from Lichnowsky on his meeting with Grey the afternoon of July 29. In this conversation Grey stressed the importance of mediation at this critical moment in the crisis. He informed Lichnowsky that Britain would "stand aside so long as the conflict is limited to Russia and Austria, but if Germany and France were drawn in, the situation would immediately become entirely different, and the British government would see itself under certain circumstances forced to make rapid decisions."[56] The message was clear: if the conflict could not be localized, then the only other alternative would be world war.

The chancellor's last minute efforts to stop the development toward general war were doomed by another powerful influence in Berlin—the voice of military necessity. He informed the Prussian Ministry of State on July 30 that "we have lost control." Military aspects had become overriding after reports of Russia's partial mobilization had arrived in Berlin. Nevertheless, the chancellor had been able to prevent German mobilization in response by agreeing to send telegrams to Paris and St. Petersburg warning against further military preparations. Bethmann wanted time to make mediation possible. On the thirtieth Moltke openly advocated immediate full mobilization of German forces. In fact his advocacy was so indiscreet that at 2:00 P.M. that day the *Berliner Lokalanzeiger* reported in an extra edition that full mobilization had been ordered. The chancellor immediately denied these reports and had the newspapers recalled. In a meeting at 1:00 P.M., the chancellor had successfully resisted Moltke's pressure for the proclamation of "state of imminent danger," a state of military readiness short of mobilization. That evening Bethmann made a final effort to persuade Vienna to agree to negotiations with Russia, but Moltke was successful in having the telegram bearing these instructions stopped.[57]

At 9:00 P.M., on the evening of the thirtieth, Moltke, Falkenhayn, and the chancellor made a crucial decision. According to the only available report of this meeting, Falkenhayn argued that all the *démarches* had been unsuccessful and that "the advisers of the Imperial Chancellor counted in vain on a miracle." Finally, Falkenhayn and Moltke were successful in gaining Bethmann Hollweg's agreement "that by noon of the next day at the latest, a decision concerning the proclamation of the state of imminent danger must be reached."

In view of his hopes at that time that Germany's objectives could be attained without war involving Germany and Entente powers, it is almost certain that Riezler was one of these advisers who "counted on a miracle." What kind of "miracle" might these advisers have counted on? This "miracle" was not merely a hasty Russian mobilization which would have given Germany the political advantage of being able to mobilize in apparent response to Russia's move. Russia's general mobilization seemed very probable in Berlin the night of July 30, especially since Germany's displeasure at a last-minute Russian proposal was evident to the Russians. Sazonov had proposed that Germany put pressure on Austria to strike several points of the Austrian ultimatum to Serbia; in return Russia would cease all military preparations. However, Jagow rejected this as a humiliation for Austria. Thus, it would not have been a "miracle" to bring about a Russian mobilization in advance of German mobilization. Bethmann and his advisers hoped that somehow "miraculously" the Austro-Serbian conflict could still be localized, perhaps as a result of Russia's acceptance of Austria's "stop in Belgrade" declaration or as a result of Austro-Russian negotiations.[58]

Hopes for a "miracle" were indeed "in vain" because on July 30 Russia made the critical decision to order general mobilization. Sazonov had become convinced that Russian general mobilization was necessary, and he supported the Russian military in urging the tsar to order it. He also announced to the foreign missions in St. Petersburg that Russia would continue its military preparations until Austria accepted Russia's demands. At 3:00 P.M. the tsar agreed that general mobilization be ordered at 6:00 P.M. In retrospect, it can be seen that with that mobilization, the last thin thread which held together the peace in Europe had been broken.

The Russian decision was not, as Geiss argued, a mere "alibi" which all German leaders, including the chancellor, had awaited in order to issue Germany's own general mobilization in apparent defense. Two important factors concerning the decision taken in Berlin the evening of July 30 militate against such an interpretation: first, it was agreed that no decision concerning German military preparations was to be made until noon the next day; this meant that all alternatives had not already been foreclosed. Second, the decision which was to be made the next day concerned the "state of imminent danger," a type of military alert short of general mobilization.[59]

At 7:00 A.M. July 31, Moltke received the first news of the Russian mobilization; at 9:00 A.M. he and Falkenhayn personally presented this news to Bethmann Hollweg and Jagow. The political leaders insisted on waiting for confirmation from St. Petersburg. The message did not arrive until 11:40 A.M.: "General mobilization of army and navy ordered. First day of mobilization July 31." If Bethmann Hollweg had simply wanted to place the guilt for the war on Russia, then he would now have had all that he needed. However, at 1:00 P.M. he consented only to the proclamation of the state of imminent danger which he stressed was not general mobilization. At 3:30 P.M. he sent messages to Paris and St. Petersburg stressing the extreme seriousness of the situation and announcing a twelve hour time period within which "every war measure directed against us and Austria-Hungary" had to cease. A negative answer or no answer at all meant mobilization, and as he stressed to the French, "mobilization inevitably means war."

When no answer was received from Russia and France within twelve hours, general war with German, French, and Russian involvement became a virtual certainty. At 10:00 A.M. August 1, the chancellor approved of the declaration of war against Russia and France. The declaration was sent immediately to Russia, but the uncertainty concerning Britain's stand and the hope that Britain might remain neutral caused the declaration of war on France to be delayed until August 3. On August 1 Grey had made it indisputably clear that British neutrality was out of the question so long as such neutrality would be to France's disadvantage.[60] France proved its loyalty to its Russian ally by mobilizing its forces on August 1. In this situation, with Germany's eastern and western neighbors fully mobilized for war and with war already declared against Russia, German political leaders lost all influence on policy; military necessity became decisive.

With Russia, Germany, and France carrying out general mobilization, a European war had become unavoidable. Britain's entry into the war transformed the European war, which Germany probably would have won, into a world war. The most important step in bringing Britain into the war was Germany's violation of Belgian neutrality. Before the German invasion of Belgium on August 3 the British cabinet was "overwhelmingly pacific," and according to Winston Churchill, "at least three-quarters of its members were determined not to be drawn into a European quarrel, unless Great Britain herself were attacked, which was not likely." However, "the direct appeal from the King of the Belgians for French and British aid raised an issue which united the overwhelming majority of ministers." Churchill admitted that by the time British troops were being sent to the continent, "it was not Belgium one thought of, but France." For at least a century Britain had been conscious of the strategic importance to the British Isles of Flanders and the Belgian coast, but the prevention of any one country's hegemony over Europe had been a cornerstone of British foreign policy for centuries. As Grey had made clear, Britain would not have allowed France to fall under German domination, thereby witnessing the establishment of German hegemony over Europe.[61]

The violation of Belgian neutrality was in conformity with the German military plan worked out in 1905 by Count von Schlieffen and modified by Ludendorff in 1912. His plan was designed to meet the danger of a two front war through a strike at the heart of France instead of through a frontal assault on the well-fortified Franco-German frontier, which extended 150 miles from Switzerland to Verdun. German forces were to be concentrated on the right flank, which would sweep through Luxembourg and Belgium into northern France; Paris would be enveloped, and the French troops would be pushed back toward the Moselle where they would be met by the German left flank.

Although later modifications and mistakes in the actual execution of the policy caused the plan to fail, the plan itself was, in Liddell Hart's words, "the logical military course." Nevertheless, as Gerhard Ritter concludes, "every war plan which is worth anything must be well thought out politically as well as militarily." Did Bethmann Hollweg or Riezler see the political danger in the German plans for troop deployment, known as the Schlieffen Plan? Before December 1912, they were not even aware that such a plan existed. Although the military updated these plans annually, no war council was ever held during Bethmann Hollweg's chancellorship at which military plans were discussed with political leaders. The isolation of military thinking from politics was characteristic of Wilhelmine Germany, and during the war Riezler bitterly remarked that "the concept of the purely military is celebrating orgies." However, there is no evidence whatsoever that either the chancellor or Riezler at any time objected to the Schlieffen Plan or were concerned about its negative consequences. Bethmann Hollweg wrote after the war that it would have been an "unbearable responsibility" for a civilian leader to have intervened in a military plan which had been well thought through and which was considered necessary by military experts.[62]

Although Bethmann Hollweg had shown little apprehension about the political consequences of the Schlieffen Plan, and although he attempted to hold back the German invasion of Luxembourg only at the last moment, he and Riezler were incensed that Britain actually declared war on Germany. They had never given up the hope that Germany's good relations with Britain during the past few years would help Britain accept what they believed to be Germany's defensive action. Lichnowsky strongly warned against this illusion, but his warnings were disregarded. Riezler wrote scornfully: "Lichnowsky trembles like an aspen leaf, [displaying] only understanding for the English position and without bearing and dignity."[63] In fact, it was Riezler who had unfortunately failed to grasp the British position.

Shortly before noon on August 4, the British government issued an ultimatum: if the German invasion of Belgium were not stopped by midnight, a state of war would exist between Britain and Germany. It is unlikely that any German chancellor could have stopped the invasion of Belgium at this point. In his speech before the Reichstag at 3:30 P.M. Bethmann Hollweg argued that "Russia put the torch to the house. We are faced with a war with Russia and France which has been forced upon us." He also stated that "only in the defense of a just cause should our sword be drawn from the sheath." Riezler, who may very well have written the chancellor's speech, agreed entirely with the chancellor and never changed his mind that Russia was responsible for the outbreak of war. However, it proved to be impossible for Germany to make its case that the execution of the Schlieffen Plan was merely an offensive military tactic in a purely defensive war. Indeed, any country which conducts military operations must be concerned about how its actions will be interpreted, and offensive operations always present problems to a country which wishes to make the case that it is conducting a purely defensive war. Bethmann Hollweg publicly confessed that the German invasion of Belgium was an "injustice," but he claimed that necessity had forced Germany to commit this injustice, which "we will make good as soon as our military goal has been attained."[64]

Despite his realization that the violation of Belgium was an injustice, the chancellor could not believe, as he confessed to British Ambassador Goschen in an emotional encounter on August 4, that Britain would go to war against a friendly nation "just for a scrap of paper"—for Belgian neutrality. In his memoirs Bethmann Hollweg admitted that "a scrap of paper" had been a very unwise choice of words, as Britain's effective use of this statement in her war propaganda later revealed. We recall that Riezler regarded national interest as the foundation of treaties, and it was difficult for both Riezler and the chancellor to see how British national interest was served by a defense of Belgian neutrality in August 1914. It is therefore entirely possible that such a phrase was on the tip of his tongue as a result of recent conversations with Riezler.[65]

Riezler's diary is the closest and most complete immediate account of the German leaders' thinking during the July crisis. Of course, any person so close to the center of power had important functions to perform. Riezler worked on press matters, official communications with other governments, and unofficial German communications to the chancellor. He wrote speeches for him and for the kaiser. Most importantly, he regularly discussed the changing political and military situation with Bethmann Hollweg. He therefore was in a position to bring his own thoughts and interpretations to the attention of the highest political official in Germany. It is very likely that Riezler had an influence on at least the tactics which the chancellor adopted during the crisis, although it is impossible to determine the extent of that influence. Nevertheless, for us, Riezler's greatest significance is as a political observer during the crisis.

His diary indicates that from the beginning, not merely at the end of the crisis, German leaders recognized the possibility that Britain would side with France and Russia and that the local war could expand into a European or world war. Riezler and Bethmann Hollweg were willing to risk such a world war although both hoped that the Austro-Serbian war could be localized. It cannot be argued that the chancellor "accepted the risk of war with unbelievable nonchalance."[66] It is clear that Bethmann Hollweg neither deliberately led Germany into war nor saw the assassination at Sarajevo as a cue to rush into a long prepared war.[67] The idea of Germany's conducting a preventive war against Russia was not a leading motive in either man's mind, although they certainly perceived a long-term Russian threat to Germany and were aware that it was a relatively favorable time to deal with that threat.[68] However, their desire to weaken or split the Entente was great, and they believed that this could have been accomplished through the humiliation of Serbia and through French refusal to support Russian policy. At the same time, Riezler's prewar view that alliances helped preserve peace in that they made the calculation of war more difficult proved to be incorrect. Instead of foreclosing the alternative of war, the alliance system gave many statesmen the feeling that the likelihood of losing a war had been greatly reduced.

Riezler's diary reveals no deliberate attempt on the part of the leading German policymakers to start a war either to establish German hegemony in Europe or to clear a path for German territorial annexations.[69] Both the chancellor and Riezler were convinced, however, of the necessity to support Austria-Hungary in order to maintain Germany's position as a world power. Neither saw any realistic alternative to supporting Austria. There is no indication that "monopoly capitalists," industrialists, or any economic motives played a significant role in the decisions made in Berlin during July.[70] Security considerations were foremost in their minds.

Based on Riezler's diary entries during the July crisis, direct pressure from nationalist groups had little or no influence on the chancellor's decisions. Nor was the chancellor decisively influenced by parliamentary leaders, newspaper owners, editors, and financiers. Bethmann Hollweg never capitulated easily to public opinion and to parliamentary and industrial pressure; his opposition to a naval build-up a few years before the war and to the use of unconditional submarine warfare during the first two and one-half years of the war offered evidence of this. It is true that Bethmann Hollweg and Riezler had probably not forgotten the indignation which the nationalists had shown after the "humiliation of Agadir." However, during the July crisis Riezler saw Russia and not Germany as having gone too far.

Riezler's theory of the bluff which he elaborated in *Grundzüge der Weltpolitik* did not apply to German policy during the crisis. German leaders did not want merely to give the impression that they would risk war. In light of the dangers which the German leaders saw—threat from Russia and dissolution of Austria-Hungary—they were absolutely serious about risking war for they saw no alternative. Also, there is no indication that Riezler's prewar calculated risk theory was the operational model for the chancellor's policy. This is so despite the fact that Riezler thought that a German diplomatic victory short of general war would have been an ideal conclusion. German control over events was relinquished too quickly for an effective application of the kind of calculated risk which Riezler had described.[71]

Finally, Riezler's entries reveal a certain measure of fatalism which crept into his and the chancellor's minds. Riezler saw events slipping out of human control. They also reveal no trace of criticism of the chancellor's policy during the July crisis. Once war was unavoidable, Riezler showed enthusiasm and optimism. Though he criticized Austrian conduct during the crisis, he wrote that "it is just as well. The [German] *Volk* is indestructible. It may suffer defeats, but they can be turned into blessings if it is clever."[72] With peace no longer possible, Riezler set about to help achieve a German victory.

Chapter Four
A NEW CONCEPTION OF EUROPE

Never was a Volk *more capable of conquering the world and more incapable of ruling it!*

—*Kurt Riezler*

Riezler had willingly risked war although he had hoped that reason would dictate a peaceful settlement to the crisis. Once the war had actually begun, he was greatly impressed with the German people's response. On August 14, 1914, he wrote:

. . . war, war, the *Volk* has arisen—it is as if there were nothing there before and now suddenly it is powerful and moving. Everyone has crawled out of his corner, on the surface the greatest confusion and yet the most meaningful order; by now millions have already crossed the Rhine.[1]

Riezler's enthusiasm for the impressive way Germans responded to the national threat and his conviction that German culture was at stake were shared by most of his countrymen. The intense national feelings at the time of the outbreak, which seemed to make individual desires give way to total devotion to the national cause, were known as the "ideas of 1914."[2] These "ideas of 1914," which were seen to be in opposition to the lower "ideas of 1789," and with British "commercialism," helped many Germans, including Riezler, to view the war as something more than a mere defensive war in the territorial sense. The war was regarded as a defense of German culture, as a higher necessity arising from the irreconcilable differences between German spirit and culture on the one hand and the spirit and culture of the enemy powers on the other.

The most significant difference, it was continually pointed out, was between Anglo-Saxon "shop keepers' spirit" and German idealism and heroism. The result was often Anglophobia. On September 30, 1914, Riezler spoke of "the tragic character of our relation to England" and of

96

my hatred against this Western European freedom phrase. It would certainly be horrible if the domination of this flat spirit should eternally hold the world captive. Above all, it is clear that the German spirit has not yet spoken its last word.

In May 1915, Riezler spoke of the "empty and meaningless English-American dullness which internationally dominates and typifies the present time." He asserted that the main issue of this war was whether "a German spirit could not only exist for itself but could also leave its stamp on the world."[3] Riezler was impressed that the "ideas of 1914" had contributed greatly to the mobilization of the German public behind the war effort and to the unlocking of great reserves of strength in Germany. Only later did he realize how little substance and lasting strength these vague and undefinable ideas had.

Unlike most Germans, Riezler sensed from the beginning that a German victory was not assured. On August 14, 1914, in his first diary entry after the outbreak of war, he noted that although "everyone was apparently happy to be able for once to dedicate himself unreservedly to a great cause, . . . no one doubts or appears to consider even for an instant what a gamble a war is, especially this war." Riezler also realized that the "ideas of 1914" would not retain their strength forever. "Just as the storm frightens the vermin out of the air—when it becomes quieter again, everything crawls out of its refuge—and emerges again in the state as well as in individual human beings."[4] This realization protected Riezler from the naive belief of the conservatives, whom he criticised so sharply throughout the war, that Germany could bear a long war without an obvious effort to achieve a negotiated peace, without a new European order which allowed Germany only indirect control and without domestic political concessions to the German masses.

On August 16, 1914, Riezler accompanied the chancellor to the Supreme Headquarters, and in January 1915, he was officially assigned to the Imperial Chancellery. Riezler's duties were not clearly defined and included a variety of things: he worked on war aims, parliamentary speeches, revolutionary movements, and domestic political questions. He helped interpret the chancellor's policies to the press, establish guidelines for censorship, and write anonymous articles supporting Bethmann Hollweg's policies. He could be called Bethmann Hollweg's assistant for political warfare.[5]

Erdmann summed up the leitmotiv of Riezler's wartime activity as "the calculation of the possibility and the shape of peace"; that is, how could peace be achieved and what kind of peace should it be. The basic topics which will be covered in this and the following chapters concern

Riezler's conception of Europe which resulted from the greatly changed
circumstances after the outbreak of war, the domestic reforms which the
new circumstances made necessary, and the Russian Revolution. All of
these main areas of Riezler's activity revolve around the question of how
and what kind of peace should be achieved.

The basic outlines of Riezler's thinking concerning Europe and
domestic reform were remarkably clear within three months after the
outbreak of hostilities. In September 1914, Riezler wrote an important
proposal concerning German war aims in the West, and in October he
wrote a memorandum which revealed his domestic political conception.

On August 22, 1914, Riezler wrote:

One is already beginning to make plans for the victory booty . . . . We looked at
the map today. I always preach the erection of vassal states. Today the chancellor
had me come to him, asked me about peace conditions and my ideas.

Bethmann Hollweg was faced with a barrage of demands which needed
to be summarized in position papers with which he could work. Many industrialists desired markets and sources of raw materials, while some
landowners wanted territory in the East. Traders and shipowners pressed
for channel ports, coaling stations, freedom of the seas, and access to
colonies. Numerous scholars expressed the need to reestablish the former
borders of the Holy Roman Empire, and some financiers argued for a
large indemnity. Riezler wrote to Hammann on August 29 that this "annexation Hydra," which was being propagated by unofficial, but respec-
table and reasonable people, and which was creating such confusion in
the Supreme Headquarters, should be countered in the press. The confusion during the first few weeks of the war was reflected in the conclusion
of Riezler's letter to Hammann:

It is no wonder that the people here do not yet know what they will want in the
end, considering the complexity of the problems, the diverse tendencies, and the
uncertain [military] situation.[6]

As a result of these and later conversations, Riezler produced on September 9, 1914, the famous "September Program," which combined elements of all major demands. This document, partly typed and partly
handwritten by Riezler, was discovered by Fritz Fischer, who saw in the
document clear proof that Bethmann Hollweg, who initialed the draft of
the document, did have war aims which he consistently pursued before
and throughout the war. Indeed, Bethmann Hollweg did consider certain

annexations, but the "September Program" was neither an exact expression of his goals in September 1914, nor was it applicable to Bethmann's war aims throughout the war.[7]

In his document Riezler listed six specific demands. First, France must relinquish to Germany the iron deposits at Briey, which were "necessary for our industry's iron ore supply." Military experts were to decide whether the acquisition of Belfort, the coastal strip of Dunkirk to Boulogne, the western slope of the Vosges Mountains, and the demolition of the strategic fortresses were necessary. France was to pay reparations to Germany high enough "that France is not capable of spending considerable sums on armaments for the next eighteen to twenty years."

Bismarck had said after the Franco-Prussian War: "Our enemy whose honest friendship can never be won must at least be rendered somewhat less harmful." Likewise, Riezler saw in September 1914 no chance of a Franco-German reconciliation. After a few weeks of war Bethmann Hollweg had considered making France an offer of alliance in order to achieve a separate peace; he also considered dividing Belgium with France, an idea which the kaiser also supported. Riezler, however, advised against such a policy calling such reconciliation a "fantasy." He wrote on August 22, 1914:

It would be false to hope that France would reconcile herself with us simply because that would be the most reasonable. France's elasticity would be enormous, her vitality entirely fantastic. . . . France, with half of Belgium, would be even stronger than before.

Riezler advocated a trade agreement "which would lead France into economic dependency on Germany, make her our export land, and make it possible to exclude English trade from France." On October 11, 1914, he emphasized the importance of such a harsh economic policy: "We spoke of France, of the *feu sacré,* and of power of hatred. It is entirely impossible to destroy this *Volk* other than economically."[8]

Second, Belgium should continue to exist outwardly as a state but should sink to a vassal status under Germany. Liège and Verviers should be annexed to Prussia, but the annexation of Antwerp should be left open. Germany should perhaps have occupation rights in the militarily important ports, and the coastline should be at Germany's military disposal. Economically, Belgium was to become "a German province." He noted that the strength of this plan was that Germany would have "the advantages of annexation without the domestic political disadvantages, which cannot be eliminated."

Third, Luxembourg "will become a German state and receive a strip of land from the present Belgian province of Luxembourg and perhaps a corner of Longwy." The fourth demand referred to Holland although Riezler thought that the appropriate methods for bringing Holland into a closer relationship with Germany would have to be worked out later. In any case, Holland should not be forced to work more closely with Germany nor to enter into any military obligations with Germany. The goal should be "to leave Holland seemingly independent while bringing her into dependence on us." Fifth, a colonial empire in Central Africa should be acquired.[9]

All of the above demands were merely parts of the sixth and most important demand—a "middle European economic union," known as *Mitteleuropa*. Riezler described the *Mitteleuropa* which he envisaged as follows: "It is to be created . . . by common customs agreements and is to include France, Belgium, Holland, Denmark, Austria-Hungary, and perhaps also Italy, Sweden and Norway." There would be no constitutional head, and all of its members would outwardly enjoy equality of rights. *De facto,* all would be under German leadership; "this union must stabilize the economic predominance of Germany over *Mitteleuropa.*" Riezler had stressed the economic aspects three days earlier in a letter to Matthias Erzberger, leader of the Center Party. He wrote "that next to the military safeguarding of Germany for the foreseeable future, economic possibilities must be kept in mind as a goal in this was."[10]

Mitteleuropa under German leadership remained central to Riezler's thinking and was his major foreign policy goal for the rest of the war. His advocacy of limited German territorial expansion on the European continent and of indirect control over Germany's European neighbors was, in Bethmann's words, a "path between annexationism and defeatism" and was a clear break with his prewar ideas.[11] Riezler never mentioned such expansion or control in any of his prewar writings, and Bethmann Hollweg never spoke in public or private of such. The answer to why Riezler changed his thinking regarding annexations and control can be seen in the radically changed European and world political situation. Even before the war Riezler had indicated the relationship between continental and world politics; to be an effective world power, Germany's continental position had to be secured. Before the war Riezler had thought that such security could be achieved through an invincible land force and a navy which in no way threatened Britain. By September 1914, however, France, Russia, and Britain were at war with Germany, and one of these powers, Russia, had actually invaded German territory.

France, in Riezler's view, was filled with hatred toward Germany and would therefore be a threat for years to come. More important, British participation in the war had led to almost immediate loss of all German colonies. Finally, the loss of reliable contact with the rest of the world made peaceful parallel expansion impossible. Thus, a more powerful continental position was needed in order for Germany to remain a world power. Riezler had never questioned the notion that Germany needed to be a world power.

A stronger continental position was seen to be a strategic imperative for Germany in order for it to be able to continue the foreseeably long war with Britain. Riezler had no illusions about Germany's limited ability to defeat Britain militarily. On September 20, 1914, he wrote:

I believe that England will hold out—then we must construct a European constellation with a modern form of continental blockade and wait until this . . . leads to a favorable conclusion.

Everything depended upon which power "had the longer breath." To outlast the colonial and sea power, Britain, Germany had to dominate the European continent. As he wrote on November 11, 1916, "the only way to overcome England is to unify Europe from the middle." A unified continent would have been "hidden help against England."[12]

The evidence indicates that Riezler's document of September 9, 1914, was neither a reckless attempt to acquire as much territory as possible "in the expectation of an imminent German victory over France," nor a formal "war aims program" for which Germany had allegedly started the war in the first place. In reality Bethmann Hollweg did not expect immediate victory in the West. In a letter to Otto Hammann written on August 29, 1914, Riezler reported the chancellor's opinion that "it is improbable that we are on the brink of an impending peace with France; it is completely uncertain whether we can actually dictate conditions to England." On September 5, 1914, he wrote:

The French Army is apparently moving back southward (not toward Paris) in order to prolong the war. This is certainly the tactic in England. Under these circumstances there is for the time being no prospect for an end. It would be good to prepare the press for a long siege.[13]

Thus, Riezler's "September Program" was written at a time when a long war against the Entente was anticipated.

Was the "September Program" the basis for Bethmann Hollweg's war aims until his dismissal in July 1917? Was it, as Fischer argues, "no

101

triviality, but an outline for a position of world power," conceived long
before the outbreak of war and pursued resolutely by the German government throughout the war? Little evidence supports this argument. This
draft was expressly labeled by Riezler as "provisional." Also, on the same
day that Riezler's document was written, Zimmermann wrote a letter for
the chancellor addressed to Delbrück in which he spoke of the guidelines
which the chancellor had established:

> Even if the outcome of the war is not yet decided, and if it seems that England
> will succeed in holding her allies to a resistance à *outrance,* we will have to be
> armed anyway for the eventuality of sudden negotiations, which would then not
> have to be long and drawn out. . . . Shortly after the outbreak of war we discussed
> verbally the economic program of the Central European customs union and were
> able to reach a basic agreement on the general outlines.

Zimmermann indicated, however, that there were great difficulties when
details were discussed. He also indicated that such a union would adversely affect some private interests, and he continued:

> I would like to advise, therefore, that the interest groups be brought in as little
> and as late as possible. Considering the magnitude of what must be accom-
> plished, we will, in the interest of the whole, have to ignore some very legitimate
> special interests here and there.[14]

Since there was no expectation of a sudden victory, maximum demands had been drawn up so that they would be available "for the eventuality of sudden negotiations." It is customary for negotiators to enter
talks with far more sweeping demands than they expect to achieve. This
provides the basis for apparent compromises. Negotiators always have a
"fall-back position" which represents what they actually hope or expect
to achieve in the talks. Fischer did not attempt to determine what the
German fall-back position might have been in the autumn of 1914, if
peace talks had actually taken place. On September 19, Bethmann
Hollweg, in a letter to Delbrück, gave a clue about his fall-back position:
If the maximum plans were not possible to achieve, then Germany must
still insist on a minimum program which would be a customs union.[15]
That is, only ten days after Riezler's document had been written, the
chancellor indicated that he was not inflexibly committed to achieving
five of the six demands of Riezler's draft.

The "September Program" written by Riezler was a provisional
catalog of possible war aims drawn up for negotiating purposes and
passed on to the Ministry of the Interior, where Delbrück noted that it
lacked coherence, and to Bethmann Hollweg, who soon showed that he

was not bound by this temporary list of war aims. For example, in November 1914, the chancellor wrote to Hammann that

Belgium is a hard nut to crack. I had repeated the phrase of a half-sovereign tributary state. I now consider that a utopia even if we had already slain the bear. An Egypt in the middle of continental Europe is certainly not possible.

Also, on October 22, 1915, in a paper dealing with conditions for a possible peace treaty, the chancellor no longer spoke of a large European economic unit. We shall see that during the war he never felt bound to the other specific points in the "September Program." He was justified in his claim that he had "no plans but only ad hoc ideas which could be influenced through changes in the fortunes of arms."[16]

While Bethmann Hollweg ignored most of the specifics in Riezler's document, and while he did not feel bound to a larger European economic unit, neither he nor Riezler ever rejected the possibility of establishing *Mitteleuropa* and indirect domination of Germany's neighbors. Riezler's public support of *Mitteleuropa* did not begin until March 1916 because in December 1914 the chancellor had banned all official discussion of German war aims in order to retain flexibility for possible negotiations. In fact, in October 1914, Riezler had been given the task of drawing up the guidelines for press censorship and for limiting the public discussion of war aims. In these guidelines Riezler forbade all journalism which threatened German unity, which advocated suppression or the "barbaric treatment" of foreign peoples, which did not use a language worthy of "the purity and greatness of the movement," and which criticised the government's foreign policy. Foreign policy, he wrote, was "difficult business, which cannot be conducted at the beer table." He closed with a warning: "Newspapers which disregard the guidelines will be banned temporarily. Extraordinary conditions require extraordinary measures. Wherever self-censorship and political intelligence is absent, compulsion will be applied."[17]

By spring 1915, Riezler had come to disagree with Bethmann on this matter, arguing that only public discussion of war aims could enable Germany to develop reasonable and generally acceptable aims. Free discussion, he thought, would regulate and thus moderate the demands and would enable the chancellor to demonstrate "the positive aspect of his activity." Bethmann's silence on war aims increasingly irritated him: "In such a time a man must operate like a grenade slid into the world. He must strike, and if he misses twice and then finally hits the mark, then there is progress."[18]

103

Wayne C. Thompson

The concept of *Mitteleuropa* was not reintroduced to the German public until the well-known liberal journalist, Friedrich Naumann, published his book *Mitteleuropa* in the fall of 1915. By 1917 more than 137,000 copies had been sold, and the extreme popularity of the work was due to the idealism of Naumann, who hoped to direct German nationalism into new channels. Naumann argued that the time had come to create a large community of Central European peoples which should include Germans, Hungarians, eastern and western Slavs, and, if possible, Rumanians. Many other smaller peoples could associate themselves with this community, but they would become members of a type of federation, not of an empire dominated by a single nation state. Only a community of states and peoples with common institutions could enable Central Europe to resist the pressure of the great world empires in the East (Russia) and West (Britain). Small nation-states were now politically and economically outdated. Naumann presented numerous arguments why *Mitteleuropa* would be economically advantageous to all European peoples. The creation of such a great Central European community would, however, require a complete reorientation of thinking on the part of those peoples involved. Narrow nationalism and mutual distrust would have to be replaced by a more liberal understanding of foreign ways and interests and by a mutual readiness to cooperate. Only if this could be done could a better and freer future for Europe and Germany emerge from the war.[19]

We shall see that the similarities between Naumann's and Riezler's ideas of *Mitteleuropa* were very great. Both were idealistic and far-sighted, and both greatly overestimated the Germans' talent for such an enterprise. Riezler's diary indicates that his conception of *Mitteleuropa* was developed long before the publication of Naumann's book. Also, there is little evidence that Riezler and Naumann had much contact with each other either before or during the war. Nevertheless, the great success of Naumann's book probably influenced Riezler's decision to publish anonymous articles in 1916 supporting *Mitteleuropa*. The journalistic tool was one which Riezler could use at least as well as Naumann. Also, Riezler had a better opportunity than Naumann to advocate *Mitteleuropa* in those circles where policy decisions were made.

Riezler clung to the idea of a Central European federation under German hegemony until the end of the war. What did he hope could be gained through such a federation on the European continent? Riezler believed that such an arrangement would offer advantages not only for Germany but also for the associated European states and for the entire world. His argument reveals very well how he sought unsuccessfully a

104

synthesis between modernization and the German idealistic tradition.

In addition to the strategic reasons for *Mitteleuropa,* Riezler also saw its economic benefits. He did not predict whether economic union would be in the form of a customs union or a free trade area, but he was sure that a far-reaching regulation of production would be necessary if struggles among industries of the member states were to be prevented. The German government would supervise the formation of cartels and would act as codirector of these cartels. In the interest of consumers and workers, these industries would no longer be in private hands.[20] "Economic individualism" would be reduced in the interest of the whole. Riezler admitted that he was advocating nothing less than socialism, but all Germans, not merely the working class, would have derived the greatest benefit from this socialism.

Riezler did not think that the resulting economic strength should increase the profits of "monopoly capitalists" but that it should increase German national power and establish the necessary preconditions for the advancement and, in some cases, transformation of European culture. Riezler applied his earlier thinking concerning the critical importance of culture for a *Volk* and a state; if such a union did not have "an idealistic unity," then it would be incapable of living and "would necessarily bring about a terrible confusion." Thus, Riezler saw far deeper reasons for *Mitteleuropa* than mere economic ones. He saw in it the possibility to preserve and strengthen the "German idea," to save Europe, and to offer an alternative between the British and Russian Empires.[21]

In May 1916, Riezler wrote an anonymous article entitled "Deutsche Mission" (German Mission) in which he asked why there was such general agreement outside Germany with Prime Minister Asquith's statement that Germany had to be liberated from militarism. How could such a view arise? Basically, Riezler felt that the world had not been able to understand the "German idea," but it is clear that he was really trying to say something more: many Germans did not understand and therefore could not believe in a "German idea" either. He directed his appeal both to Germany's potential allies and to his fellow Germans.

Riezler reviewed nineteenth-century European history in order to emphasize his argument that the source of strength for powerful nations was not military prowess, but ideas, or at least the appearance of representing ideas. Britain, for instance, had become "the protector of everything free and progressive." She had developed the basic principles of bourgeois freedom, self-determination of peoples, and freedom of trade. She was also a haven for those individuals persecuted in their own lands for advocating these freedoms. Britain combined this reputation

105

with political and military power, whose broad foundation she had laid during her war with France. Thus, Britain was equipped with great power, authority, and prestige, which she continued to enjoy in Riezler's day. Her prestige was greatly enhanced by "the generous way in which she allowed everyone, regardless of nationality, to participate in the great political and economic life."[22] Riezler's admiration for the British style of domination was again obvious; *Mitteleuropa*, as Riezler conceived it, drew heavily on his conception of the British precedent.

There would certainly have been one important dissimilarity between the British Empire and *Mitteleuropa;* the "idea" which would have been the core of *Mitteleuropa* would have been much higher than the British "idea." Although Riezler asserted without hesitation that the German idea was superior to that of the British, he was never able to offer a clearly defined alternative. Perhaps that was why Riezler felt compelled to write such an article entitled "German Mission," emphasizing the fact that great world powers always represent great ideas; Germany had no great idea. In the privacy of his diary he wrote: "The people today do not have a single idea which corresponds to the greatness of the time." This was, of course, the greatest weakness of his conception: It rested on a chimera.

In "German Mission" Riezler addressed both Germans, who had no great idea, and non-German Europeans, who had failed to take notice of German cultural contributions. Riezler found that the great task of forging a unified Germany had caused the "cultural ideas" to be underemphasized. Despite this, Germany had made great cultural contributions which were not regarded as German. German artistic creations were seen only as the creations of individual personalities, not of Germans or of the German culture. Also, with regard to discoveries in the natural sciences, one tended to lose sight of national origin. Finally, the difficulty of the German language had tended to restrict admiration for German intellectual contributions to very small circles outside of Germany.[23]

Riezler hoped that Germans would become aware of their own spirit and that their cultural contributions would no longer be unseen by the peoples of Europe.

We Germans have . . . awakened powers in us the magnitude of which we would never have imagined. Above all, we have discovered within us a spiritual essence through which we can gather these powers in such a way that they mutually support each other and are thus enhanced.

Germans had discovered the "foundation of national solidarity" and had subordinated individual interests to it. Culture, economics, and politics had become a "complementary powerful unity." Riezler predicted naively that Germany would show interest in the problems of European peoples and would cooperate with others while serving her own interests. Germans would be "the allies of everything new and progressive."[24] There was obviously far too much wishful thinking in these predictions.

Riezler was confident that Europeans would not fear the "German idea" because it was allegedly the closest of any national idea to the "idea of humanity." With regard to the national tendency, he had shifted his emphasis from the intolerance and arrogance which results from the national idea to the common goal of all national ideas—humanity. By unifying Europe around the central idea of humanity, Germany would save Europe. This is the second basic reason for *Mitteleuropa* aside from the preservation of the German idea—the salvation of Europe. On October 11, 1915, Riezler wrote that one of two things would emerge from the uncertain political and military situation in Europe: "Either Europe perishes, or a Central European imperialism with a soft touch develops." Four months later he wrote that "Europe must embark upon a new course or it will fall." The Entente solution to the problems in Europe—"the sacrificing of Germany"—would, in Riezler's opinion, have eliminated Europe from any future world political significance.[25] This maintenance of Europe leads us to Riezler's third justification for *Mitteleuropa*—to offer the world an alternative between East (Russia) and West (Britain and the United States).

Never during the war did Riezler advocate German world domination. His diary entries clearly show his conviction that Germans did not have the political talent for such world domination.[26] He did hope, however, that they would develop the political talent to establish *Mitteleuropa*. "If the solution of the Central European question is found, then the great world political question of choosing between England and Russia has lost a great degree of its difficulty." Further reading reveals that Riezler was not solely concerned with giving the world a third choice; the preservation of Germany was at stake. "If the solution of this problem is hopeless, then in spite of all our victories we will in the long run be crushed between the great world empires, above all between East and West, between Russia and England."[27]

Thus, in addition to the strategic and economic advantages, *Mitteleuropa* was needed to preserve the German idea, to save Europe, and to provide an alternative between East and West. While recognizing

107

Wayne C. Thompson

the necessity of *Mitteleuropa,* Riezler had some doubts about Germany's capacity to construct such a federation of states on the European continent. He knew that Germany would at least have to maintain herself militarily; a victorious Entente would never have agreed to a federation in Europe under German leadership. Nevertheless, more than military strength was necessary for its realization. Germany would have to develop new techniques of rule if control over other European states were to be successful. The proper techniques, in Riezler's opinion, were indirect rule and mastery of the art of appearance; in general, Germany should learn from British imperialism and should be prepared to change her concept of the nation.

German rule had to be indirect because no other kind of control over Europe or over any empire was possible in the long run. Riezler had in no way changed his estimation of power since the outbreak of war. In *Grundzüge der Weltpolitik* he had clearly criticised the exaggeration of power and had questioned its significance in maintaining an empire. For example, with regard to Japan, Riezler had noted that hers was

an imperialism of power. However, in our time power alone cannot maintain that which it has acquired. True imperialism, which not only dominates the acquired outwardly but which adjusts itself inwardly, presumes many capabilities which have nothing to do with the use of the sword.

During the war Riezler continued to complain about the "intoxication of the violent method. That there are limits to power, that everything depends on whether the application of power pays off in the long run—no one wants to consider that."[28]

While direct control through power is not appropriate anywhere in the world, it is especially inappropriate in Europe. Europeans must be treated with respect, tact, and intelligence. Such respectful treatment is necessary at any time, especially while the enemy still has undefeated armies in the field; "one cannot dictate if the enemy is not yet beaten."[29]

In his articles published during the war Riezler was never specific about exactly how *Mitteleuropa* should be organized. He wrote only in general terms about a new federal organization of Europe in which direct rule by any one nation would have no place. For more specific indications of how Riezler envisaged the new Europe, we must turn to his private diary. As early as April 1915 one can see his thinking on the new Europe taking shape.

On April 18, 1915, Riezler wrote that he had presented "my new Europe, that is, the European disguise for our will to power." His new

108

Europe was to be "a Central European empire of the German nation," which would be like a joint-stock company. Just as Prussia had a majority of shares in the German Empire, Germany would always retain a majority of shares in the Central European empire. No increase in the number of cooperating states would ever deprive Germany of her majority, that is, of her hegemony. Riezler did not believe that it was necessary to speak of an association around the central power (Germany); "the European idea . . . will lead unavoidably to this." Nor needed one worry about pacifism, which could be expected to emerge from the war-weariness. Germany could even use this pacifist thinking to her own advantage by promising the world eternal peace. Finally, a new concept of the balance of power would replace the traditional British concept, "which is like a house, which is in such perfect equilibrium that it collapses when a sparrow sits on the corner." This new organization was "economically and politically the world historical task."[30]

Fifteen months later Riezler devoted a long entry in his diary to *Mitteleuropa*. In this entry Riezler mentioned Constantin Frantz, who in opposition to Bismarck had advocated a "greater Germany," as distinguished from a "smaller Germany" excluding Austria-Hungary. In 1879 Frantz had called for a Central European federation of states which would guarantee the European balance of power. Although Riezler found Frantz wrong in his practical criticism of Bismarck, he saw one basic truth in Frantz's thinking: "A state in the middle of Europe based on power and the appearance of conquest is untenable. The temptations for the neighbors, whose backs are guarded, forbid such." "In the center of Europe there should be a political formation which is federal in all directions, which has the effect of attraction, not of repulsion and conquest."[31]

It must be noted that Riezler did not imply that Germany should not have a hegemonial position in Europe. His criticism of the military was based on their "explicit stipulation of German hegemony." Riezler's point was that "hegemony itself can be accomplished; only the caudinian yoke of its formal recognition cannot." Riezler was frank in his diary about the goals which he hoped Germany could accomplish through *Mitteleuropa:* "I always work toward German domination over *Mitteleuropa* and over all the small states under the pretense of a Central European confederation but without any sacrifices of German power." Riezler knew from the British example that domination was possible without the appearance of domination. A mastery of the art of appearance was crucial for Riezler if indirect rule of Europe were to work.[32]

The importance of appearances was not new to Riezler's thinking during the war. In *Grundzüge der Weltpolitik* Riezler had written about "the

109

real power" of appearances which were always "imponderables" in politics. His discussion of them was aimed, however, at those who might confuse appearances with the actual substance of politics. New to his thinking during the war was that he advocated deliberate German use of them in order to disguise actual German domination of Europe. He wanted the Germans to learn to do exactly that which the British were already able to do very successfully.

Riezler's advocacy of the use of appearance stemmed not so much from study of such political thinkers as Machiavelli but from observation of its actual power in politics. Riezler's favorite model was always Britain, although he often privately expressed exasperation at what he called "English mastery in the use of humanly inferior methods." While complaining of "enormous hypocrisy," Riezler recognized the "compulsion to the same. . . . The exasperation over England combined with the imitation of English methods." He advocated the application of the secrets of British imperial success to *Mitteleuropa:* sober recognition of the possible; cementing the empire through strong cultural ties and common economic interest; representation of the ideals of freedom and self-government.[33]

Riezler knew what was necessary for a successful establishment and maintenance of *Mitteleuropa,* but he harbored strong doubts that Germans were capable of doing what was necessary. For the kind of empire Riezler advocated, recognition of the power of appearances, mastery of the freedom and culture "phrases," renunciation of saberrattling, and a feel for indirect rule were necessary. However, the German "does not have at his disposal all the modern means to power; has nowhere his own phrase, has only one means—power. With it how is he to rule the world, even if he is able to conquer the entire world?" Riezler saw this dilemma as tragic.[34]

Riezler saw one further crucial precondition for the establishment of *Mitteleuropa,* and indeed for the preservation of Germany's "national power and greatness": domestic reform within Germany itself. Athenian imperialism had taught Riezler that the inability of a nation to change its own constitution makes the long-term maintenance of an empire impossible. Although he was apparently not primarily guided by Christian, humanitarian, or democratic convictions, his willingness to introduce domestic reform when he saw the necessity clearly distinguished him from the unbending, conservative majority within Germany's ruling elite. He saw the wisdom in Theodor Fontane's observation: "Cases of states that were ruined by bold reforms demanded by the times are rare. I know of none. But the reverse shows itself a hundred-fold."[35]

On September 25, 1914, the chancellor directed Riezler to draft a memorandum with recommendations for domestic reform. This document, which was finished and dated October 27 and 28, 1914, is very revealing and significant. In his introductory remarks, Riezler stated his three general goals: (1) to create a liberal majority which would include the SPD, (2) to attract more classes to participate in the tasks of the state, (3) to establish a broader base for the Prussian state since the "aristocratic-military foundation" of the Prussian state was obsolete. The war, Riezler wrote, had placed Germany into an entirely new situation:

What is new is that the broad masses of the *Volk* have proven themselves to be capable of serving this state and its idea. From that flows the obligation to win for the state even further segments of the *Volk*, or to hold to the state those strata which have been newly won through the great movement. . . . This favorable hour would pass quickly if it were not preserved through a generous practical program, which engages the new attitude in new tasks. Without new practical tasks the nation will rapidly sink back into the old clash of slogans.[36]

Riezler proposed four principal reforms. First, the long outdated Prussian three-class electoral law had to be modified, although Riezler did not advocate full parliamentary government. Second, all discriminatory measures directed against non-German minorities within the empire had to be forbidden in order both to create greater unity within Germany and to make a more positive impression on other Europeans who were to be included in the new Central European federation. Third, the position of the working class in Germany had to be elevated. Before 1914 the prevailing attitude in Germany had been to integrate the German nation against the party of the working class, the SPD. Despite such traditional hostility, the German workers showed their patriotism at the time of the outbreak of the war. The outbreak had offered the chancellor a great opportunity to attempt to break down the barriers which had always existed between the left and right in Germany; the Social Democrats' patriotism had freed them in the minds of many Germans from the suspicion of being enemies of the state and made it possible for a German chancellor to work with them. Riezler was of course relieved: "Thank God that the chancellor intervened energetically." He also noted that "the Social Democrats are being worked on from all sides." Negotiations with SPD leaders were conducted in order to prevent socialist agitation for peace and to secure them as a counterweight to the "wild annexationists." Riezler even recommended that labor union leaders be drawn into the government.[37]

111

Not only did Riezler want to bring the German left into the state, but he thought that the political left and center should become the basic foundations of the German state and of *Mitteleuropa*. He wrote in June 1916 that the time for policies based on the support of "the great masses of the more democratically oriented middle and working classes" had come.[38]

A new domestic orientation which did not involve a basic change in the structure of the state raised one important problem with which Riezler wished to deal: those high civilian and military officials and those classes which traditionally bore political responsibility and had the most privileges had to be taught to understand and to accept the new political orientation. Therefore, Riezler in his October Memorandum proposed, fourth, that the political education of the *Volk* be intensified, that political science be given more serious treatment at the universities, and that a "political academy" be established where a "cadre" of bureaucrats and officers could be trained in the ideas and methods of the new orientation. Throughout the war Riezler complained of the German officers' lack of political education, and it is therefore understandable that he should propose a solution to this problem.

Riezler wanted the career path for higher officials in the bureaucracy to be opened to representatives from all classes. In his diary entry on December 24, 1914, he spoke of his new social policy as the "ascendancy of the talented into the higher classes." For Riezler, the key to this policy was that promotion to responsible positions would be based exclusively on talent, not on family or class background.[39] Indeed, throughout his public life Riezler always believed that the affairs of the nation should be guided only by those whose exclusive claim to leadership is talent and education. He remained convinced that the best government was always government by the best.

In summary, Riezler hoped that the "German idea" would become widely recognized as attractive, that the Germans would acquire the skill to apply the "modern means to power," and that domestic reforms would be introduced. If all these were possible, then perhaps a middle course could be steered between the wild annexationists, on the one hand, and the proponents of the *status quo ante bellum,* on the other. However, the hollowness of the "German idea," German treatment of occupied peoples, a highly unfavorable diplomatic situation, and insurmountable domestic opposition rendered such a middle course impossible. A brief examination of the occupation policies in Belgium and Poland will reveal most of the major problems.

In his "September Program" Riezler had called for Belgium's political degradation to a vassal state and her economic degradation to a German province. There was little trace of indirect rule for Belgium in this program. However, it became clear to him in the fall of 1914 that the Belgian problem was not going to have a simple solution. On October 11 the chancellor asked him again to work out a solution to the Belgian problem; the "September Program" obviously had not expressed Bethmann Hollweg's last word on this question. Riezler answered that "the problem is terrible, much worse than the Polish, almost insoluble." He scoffed at the kaiser's and others' ideas to colonize annexed French and Belgian territory with deserving non-commissioned officers and enlisted men from the German army.[40]

One reason for the complexity of the problem was the bitter memories which the German invasion of Belgium had left in the minds of the Belgian population. In October 1914, Riezler mentioned a conversation with a cavalry officer who told of mass executions in small Belgian towns. In one town all men between the ages of sixteen and sixty years, approximately 1,000 in number, were shot in rows; the women were then forced to bury the bodies. "No one dares say anything against military necessity." Riezler feared that the damage could never be healed. "There remains no alternative to a military protective state." Riezler himself inspected much of the damage and spoke with Germany's military and civilian leaders in Belgium. He saw "artillery-scarred villages, fields covered with dead cows . . . plundered stores."[41]

Hatred against Germany convinced Riezler that "Belgium must be ruled entirely by appearances." Everything depended upon turning the hatred of the country against Britain, whose blockade of Germany made the feeding of the Belgian population by the Germans impossible. Bethmann Hollweg also saw indirect rule as the only possibility. On October 18 he established the guideline that Belgium should be a "German tributary state, which must remain as free as possible in form; but *de facto,* must be at our disposal in both military and economic respects."[42]

On February 15, 1915, Riezler wrote a memorandum on Belgium in which he proposed indirect rule: a "middle road between annexation and Belgian freedom." In fact, Riezler himself was not sure that such a middle road was possible in the case of Belgium. Nevertheless, he believed that such a solution must be sought. He proposed that the former dynasty be maintained under the condition that it assume responsibility for the military protection and diplomatic representation of Belgium. Economic control over Belgium would be guaranteed by German economic denizenship in Belgium, by a customs union, and by three German delegates in the Belgian customs office. Indirect taxes and, as a concession to Belgian workers, the more advanced German social welfare laws would be introduced. Germany's political wishes would be expressed by two ministers appointed by Germany to the Belgian cabinet.[43]

This was the most extensive German control which Riezler advocated for any country during the war except for Luxembourg. However, Riezler was prepared to draw on the imperial experience of Rome and Britain by suggesting a change of the German constitution which would perhaps allow Belgium to send representatives to the German customs office or to the Bundesrat. He even suggested the creation of some kind of federal arrangement for Belgium. Belgium's association with Germany would then serve as a model for other European states. While the type of German control over Belgium which Riezler sought was somewhat milder than that advocated by some representatives of the German military and industry, his proposal for constitutional change was unique and showed that his thinking went much further than a short-term, exploitative policy.[44]

By October 1915, no progress toward a solution to the Belgian problem had been made. Belgium was indeed "a hard nut." Nevertheless, Riezler's thinking on Belgium was always flexible and had changed considerably since the outbreak of war. He no longer saw any advantage to maintaining the Belgian state. He saw an opportunity for Germany to appear progressive by supporting the foundation of a predominantly Flemish state. Such a Flemish state would certainly have sought the protection of Germany. In order to tempt France to conclude a separate peace with Germany, Riezler was willing to consider offering France a piece of Walloon Belgium.[45]

It is uncertain whether Riezler influenced Bethmann Hollweg's thinking regarding the establishment of a Flemish state; it is much more likely that Bethmann Hollweg influenced Riezler in this matter. While Riezler did not mention Flemish independence in his "September Program," the chancellor pointed on September 2, 1914, to its significance for German political influence in Belgium. In December 1914, Bethmann Hollweg proposed a "German-Flemish policy" which would include remaking the University of Ghent into a purely Flemish university. In the next few months Bethmann Hollweg approved the Belgian language laws which introduced the Flemish language into Flemish elementary schools. On April 5, 1916, Bethmann Hollweg announced that it was German policy "not to surrender again the long-suppressed Flemish people to Frenchification."[46]

Riezler never disagreed with Bethmann Hollweg's ideas concerning Belgium, but he did criticize the chancellor's inability to put his ideas forcefully into effect, despite domestic opposition. Riezler found that the chancellor waited for problems to develop and then correctly dealt with them, but he did not confront matters before they became problems. He had "enormous passive energy but little active explosive power." From November 1915 to February 1916, German leaders negotiated with the Belgian king and almost succeeded in arranging a separate peace with Belgium. The price demanded of Belgium was military guarantees against France and Britain and an economic understanding with Germany. After the negotiations broke down, Riezler wanted to see the chancellor force radical changes in Belgium. He wrote in March 1916 that

one can conduct a policy of the armored plate and of the grenade; one must alternate according to the situation. Up to now the first was correct. There are two areas, however, where the second is needed: those are the occupied territories of Belgium and Poland. Here, time is short; here everything must be changed and be created anew. There must be Flemish officials in Flanders and a practically complete administrative separation.

Although the chancellor had ordered such administrative separation in January 1916, there was still resistance among German occupation authorities. Bethmann Hollweg seemed to tolerate such resistance, whereas Riezler wanted immediate action: "Immediately send all Flemish officials to Flanders and throw the Walloons there out!"[47]

The opportunity to establish a Flemish state sympathetic to Germany and thereby to appear as the liberator of European nationalities was lost through both delays and the tendency for German military and civilian occupation authorities to slip into what Riezler called "Germanization" and to preach "genuine inconsiderate Germanness."

The hope for Central European economic cooperation suffered a severe setback during the winter of 1916-17 when forced deportation of Belgian workers to Germany was ordered. These deportations proved to be an enormous political mistake which could never be corrected. From the beginning, the highest German occupation authority in Belgium, General Friedrich Wilhelm Freiherr von Bissing, had attempted to prevent the economic exploitation of Belgian industry, but in the first winter of the war the War Ministry and the Supreme Military Command ordered that all raw materials and machinery which could be used in the German arms industry be sent to Germany. Bissing protested unsuccessfully against such short-term exploitation, remarking sarcastically that "a squeezed-out lemon has no value and that a slaughtered cow gives no more milk."

115

Wayne C. Thompson

The plunder of Belgian industry led logically to high unemployment in Belgium. Important German military and industrial leaders, including Walter Rathenau, head of the war materials procurement office, began to press for forced deportation of labor from Belgium. They argued that this measure was necessary because the attempts to recruit voluntary labor from Belgium had failed. Bissing tried very hard to prevent this, arguing that the chancellor's Flemish policy and German plans for economic union would be ruined. His protests were ignored partly because Bethmann Hollweg failed to support him. The chancellor only expressed his preference for voluntary recruitment, but he had Foreign Office legal experts draw up a document supporting the legality of forced deportation. At this crucial moment even Bethmann Hollweg's "passive energy" was absent. As for Riezler's reaction, for some unexplainable reason, his diary does not reveal a single reference to this; his thoughts at this time appear to have been concentrated almost exclusively on Poland. Without a word of protest from his young adviser, the chancellor capitulated.

The mass deportations began on October 26, 1916, before careful preparations could be made. The execution of the policy was grotesque. Belgian officials refused to present lists of unemployed, and German countermeasures such as the arrest of mayors and other public officials did not have the desired results. Therefore, local German commanders were compelled to call together all Belgian males over sixteen years for "control assemblies." Those with proof of steady employment or with critical jobs, such as doctors, lawyers, teachers, and clergymen, were sent home. Those who remained were ordered to "volunteer" for labor service in Germany; the penalty for refusal was immediate transportation to Germany, often in open cattle trucks. The whole process looked, in the words of Gerhard Ritter, like a "slave market and slave transport." After arrival in Germany the Belgians often spent several months in reconverted prisoner-of-war camps waiting for employers, who often refused Belgian labor due to fear of sabotage.

The economic gain for Germany was minimal, but the political consequences were immeasurably great. Hatred in Belgium and in enemy nations against Germany reached a new high, and the test for a new kind of indirect German leadership was a total failure. German leadership had indeed proved to be offensive. The cruelties committed by German soldiers in Belgium, the inevitable attempt to "Germanize" the population, and the economic exploitation, shown most dramatically by the forced labor, helped confirm Riezler's growing doubts about Germany's lack of talent for world leadership. By June 1917, Riezler was willing to give up Belgium in return for a negotiated peace.[48]

116

While Riezler saw Belgium as an important step toward *Mitteleuropa*, he viewed Poland as the most crucial test. In the end there were two reasons why Riezler's idea of *Mitteleuropa* died in Poland. First, Germany's policy clearly gave the appearance of exploitation, rather than liberation of the Polish nation. Second, the disagreements between Germany and Austria-Hungary were so intense that relations between these two powers were strained almost irreparably. Thus, the foundation for *Mitteleuropa* was destroyed.

Riezler, like most Germans at the time, found that the Polish question was one "of entirely unimaginable complexity, . . . much more difficult that the Belgian problem." His earliest thoughts on Poland varied. In August 1914, Riezler complained that no thought had been given to Poland. In basic agreement with the military command, he favored an independent Poland. However, he was willing to consider an Austrian solution, which he saw as a prelude to a free Poland leaning toward Germany, especially in the event that the Austro-Hungarian Empire collapsed. By mid-October he seemed sure that the latter solution would be the best, but two weeks later he became convinced that the apparent disintegration of the Austro-Hungarian Empire made the Austrian solution unwise. After hearing of Austria's defeat at Ivangorod, his confidence in Austria was so low that he even wrote of the need at some point in the future to reach an understanding with Russia over the heads of the Austrians.[49]

Riezler's rejection of the Austrian solution to the Polish problem never changed again. Although he favored some form of German solution, he seemed until the summer of 1915 to agree with Bethmann Hollweg and the German Foreign Office that the Polish question should be postponed as long as possible. While the Austrians pressed Germany for a firm commitment on Poland, the German government had good reasons not to be bound to such a commitment. First, it was clear that an independent Poland or a Poland dependent upon either of the Central Powers would have incurred Russia's anger and would perhaps have made a separate peace with Russia impossible. Both Riezler and Bethmann Hollweg hoped that Russia could be lured out of the Entente. Second, the search for a solution to the Polish question would have inevitably brought the allies, Germany and Austria-Hungary, into conflict with each other and would unavoidably have weakened the Central Powers' war effort.[50]

By the summer of 1915 Riezler saw urgent reasons why a solution to the Polish problem could no longer be delayed. First, German troops were advancing steadily into Poland, and Warsaw was about to fall into German hands. Thus, the question of Poland's future ceased being a theoretical one and became a real one. Second, Riezler wanted to begin work on *Mitteleuropa* without delay. The publication in 1915 of Friedrich Naumann's exciting and idealistic book, *Mitteleuropa,* had brought this new organization of Europe back into public discussion; also, Bethmann Hollweg's interest was renewed. There was little time to lose, Riezler thought, before the application of "Germanization" caused irreparable damage.[51]

On July 16, 1915, Riezler wrote that he had advocated to the chancellor the proclamation of an autonomous Poland. Among other reasons such a proclamation would be "a gesture of freedom." Germany would appear to the other European peoples as a liberator. The chancellor wished to avoid this solution for a variety of reasons, including Prussian conservatives' fear of the effect an autonomous Poland between West and East Prussia would have on those Poles living under Prussian administration. He vacillated and hesitated to commit himself to any Polish policy. This indecision, as we have seen, was the characteristic which irritated Riezler most about Bethmann Hollweg: "Why always paint all the enormous difficulties on the wall, even if they are there? One does not need to solve the problems in an ideal way, especially if the solutions themselves do not weaken us."[52]

Riezler's advocacy of Polish autonomy can in no way be traced to a firm belief in national self-determination. He did not even argue to Bethmann Hollweg this principle's importance in the establishment of *Mitteleuropa.* In his conversations with the chancellor, Riezler stressed that even after granting Polish autonomy, Poland could always be divided or given to Russia if German interest required it. Poland, he argued, would be an "enormous object for negotiation or for a sellout." Riezler even suggested letting Austria-Hungary stand in the limelight when Poland is liberated and then communicating to the Russians that Germany was not pleased with such a settlement.[53] Germany's own national interests were uppermost in Riezler's mind. This difference of opinion between the chancellor and his young adviser with regard to the Polish question remained throughout Bethmann Hollweg's chancellorship. Though an independent Poland was proclaimed in November 1916, the driving force behind the proclamation was the Supreme Military Command, not Riezler, and the reasons for this were primarily military, not political.

On August 5, 1915, Warsaw was occupied by German troops; Riezler arrived in Warsaw almost immediately thereafter. During his stay in Poland, he spoke with Hindenburg, whom he found "a wonderful man," and with Ludendorff, whom he found politically "entirely uneducated."

Riezler was gathering information for his recommendations to the chancellor and to the Foreign Office. In a document he wrote on August 20, 1915, Riezler argued for an autonomous Poland dependent upon Germany. He found that the Poles themselves were hostile at the moment toward both Russia and Austria-Hungary and that Germany could win control of the Polish national movement by granting autonomy to a large part of Poland, which would include the capital. The only thing which Poles disliked about Germany was the insensitive treatment of Poles who lived under Prussian administration and the possibility of a Germanization policy in Poland. Riezler hoped that such treatment would cease. He concluded: "it would be a blessing if Germany can show the world that foreign peoples who join it are not oppressed."[54]

Bethmann Hollweg included one of Riezler's passages in a parliamentary speech calling for the beginning of a development which "eliminates the former conflicts between Germans and Poles" and which would allow Poles "to preserve the uniqueness of [their] national life." A few days later the chancellor asked Riezler about the political form which he envisaged for Poland. Riezler answered that Poland should be a protectorate with a constitution which granted agrarians the greatest power. A German prince should be named Duke of Warsaw. A military convention between Germany and the new Polish state should be drawn up, and a customs union should be formed. Finally, there should be no freedom of movement between Germany and Poland. Many in Germany, including the chancellor, feared that such freedom would lead to an unmanageable influx of Poles and Eastern Jews into Germany.

It is clear that Riezler's recommendations did not have a decisive influence on the chancellor's thinking on Poland at the time. For two weeks in September 1915, he did not talk to Riezler about Poland, and Riezler correctly surmised that the chancellor "coquettes more and more with the idea of turning the country over to Austria."[55]

Riezler never lost sight of the complexity of the Polish problem. His informational trip to Poland from October 26-29, 1915, merely confirmed the "hopelessness of the detailed local political questions and of the problem as a whole." He found Polish nationalism "without limits," but at the same time German occupation authorities, especially those under Governor-General Hans Hartwig von Beseler, showed no understanding for the local population. General Esch, chief of Beseler's staff, was the "prototype of the stupid *miles,* infuriated that the people speak Polish here, have theater performances in Polish *etc.*—opponents of the [Polish] university set up by us," and Major Richard von Heynitz, "who does not conduct war against Russia but against the civilian administration."

119

Despite the dismal impression which he gained from his trip, Riezler did not alter his recommendations to the chancellor. He argued that the experience gained in administering Poland in a new way would have great educational value for Germans. It would be

the most difficult and healthiest test, especially since it must be done by Prussians, and due to the necessity of accomplishing it, the entire Prussian essence will be reformed in the most favorable way possible. We will master the test; then all the small peoples will come to us, and our future will be saved.[56]

After Germany's failure in Belgium it is a wonder that Riezler remained optimistic. In Riezler's case, hope triumphed over experience.

Bethmann Hollweg was not convinced that Riezler's solution to the Polish problem was the best step toward the foundation of *Mitteleuropa*. The chancellor believed that only on a firm Austro-German foundation could *Mitteleuropa* become a reality, and unquestionably he was right. If the Central Powers grew farther apart, then the very heart of *Mitteleuropa* would be torn. Bethmann Hollweg did not want the Polish issue to stand between Germany and her only ally in the war. However, the crucial negotiations with the Austrians in November 1915, revealed that there was no desire on the part of the Austrians for a closer political or economic relationship with Germany. Bethmann Hollweg made an unfortunate reference to Austria as a "Germanic East March," a reference which gave the Austrians a true idea of what *Mitteleuropa* would really have been: an instrument for the maintenance and expansion of German power. Renewed German efforts to achieve a closer relationship with Austria-Hungary through negotiations in April 1916 failed; and with them ended any real chance for a *Mitteleuropa* as Riezler had envisaged it.

The failure to strengthen Austro-German bonds and the seemingly insoluble problems in Poland gave Riezler strong reason to doubt whether a new organization of Europe could ever emerge from the war. In December 1915, he even considered the possibility of crushing Poland in order to attain maximum short-term advantages from an occupation of the land.[57] However, such expressions were only temporary. In the long run, he clung to the hope that somehow Germany would suddenly change its style of ruling and that a successful administration of Poland could lead other European peoples to seek German leadership.

Riezler continued to advocate strongly an independent Poland in order to have a *fait accompli* before peace was made. In July 1916, Bethmann Hollweg finally agreed to the proclamation of Polish independence, but Riezler was not responsible for the chancellor's change of mind. The most significant pressures came from the German and Austrian military and from reports from Russia in July 1916 that Russia would soon proclaim an autonomous Poland. The danger of rising pro-Russian sympathies in Poland, which Riezler always feared, was thus increased.

The military's reason for an autonomous Poland was simple: a Polish army in the field on the side of the Central Powers was felt to be highly desirable. If Polish independence were proclaimed, then the preconditions would have been established for the raising of such an army. Bethmann Hollweg had always been skeptical about raising a volunteer Polish army and absolutely rejected any form of forced recruitment by an occupation power. Nevertheless, in light of the unfavorable military situation in July 1916, he consented. That he was not in sympathy with Polish autonomy was shown by his delay in ordering the proclamation and by his reserved support of it in the Prussian cabinet on August 19, 1916. His reserve was partly due to reports in early July of a possible separate peace with Russia; he clearly did not wish to lose an opportunity for such a peace. Riezler agreed that a separate peace with Russia was desirable, but, as we have seen, he felt that the proclamation of an autonomous Poland would present no basic problem: Poland could always be given to or divided with Russia if German interests required it.

Although there were strong domestic pressures in Germany against establishing a Polish kingdom, the military voice was the strongest. A few days after Hindenburg and Ludendorff were given supreme command of the German armed forces, Bethmann gave the final orders for the proclamation. The new military command had intervened in political affairs for the first significant time by means of direct influence on the kaiser. In an article written six years later Riezler confirmed Ludendorff's role as the driving force behind the proclamation. He wrote: "The General pushes, Bethmann hesitates."[58]

Unlike the chancellor, Riezler rejoiced at the sudden progress toward an autonomous Poland because he felt that Germany's entire future was at stake. "If the attempted solution fails, then it will lead to our downfall. If it is not tried, then we will probably also go under, perhaps after fifty years. . . ."

Last minute difficulties in determining the exact wording of the text provide insight into the complexity of government in Imperial Germany. As Riezler complained,

unity must be reached with the Supreme Military Command and with our allies; the federal states must be informed, and the ministers of state must be given a clear picture, On top of that, the press has to be dealt with, to say nothing of His

Majesty. An enormous apparatus which requires ninety percent of the steam; only ten percent is effective outside the apparatus.[59]

It is notable that Riezler did not mention the Parliament as a factor in this decision-making process. In fact, the inability to create a parliamentary majority behind the chancellor's policies was one important reason for Bethmann's fall one year later.

On November 5, 1916, Polish autonomy was proclaimed. The text itself was formulated in such a cautious and general way that the political effect which Riezler had hoped for could not possibly have been attained. There was no expression of the idea of Polish independence or unity, and the principle of self-determination of all peoples was not included. The ancient royal city of Cracow was not even included within the new autonomous Poland. There was no possibility for Poland to have her own executive. It will be remembered that Riezler did not want to see a truly independent Poland, at least for the time being, but he wanted her at least to seem independent. However, this appearance of independence was completely absent. The negative reaction outside of Germany to the proclamation showed that the image of Germany pursuing its own short-term self-interest remained. Riezler correctly feared at the time that the Polish affair had become a "half-measure."

Despite his own doubts about the effect of the proclamation, Riezler published a week and a half later an optimistic article supporting the proclamation and emphasizing the crucial importance of the Polish experiment for Germany's future. In this article Riezler argued that it was unavoidable that the newly proclaimed Poland contain only a part of the Polish nation. He argued that the borders of the ancient Polish kingdom would include many non-Polish people and that therefore the nationality principle would be violated.[60]

Riezler was placing decreasing emphasis on the nationality principle. Indeed, his general thinking on the concept of nation had changed considerably by the middle of the war, and at the end of the war he no longer viewed the nation as the path to "the highest." By that time, the tragedy of the war had discredited the entire concept of the nation. In an article entitled "Deutschtum und Europäertum" (Germanness and Europeanness), published in April 1916, the shift in his thinking on the nation, at least in his public writings, had already become clearly discernible. Here he stressed that which all nations have in common, namely the idea of humanity, instead of those characteristics which distinguish nations from one another. This idea of humanity had been the foundation for the earlier German national idea, and the great tasks which Germany had to accomplish required a renewed emphasis on the idea of humanity. He concluded:

We Germans cannot accomplish the political tasks before us, which arise from our most immediate vital necessities, if we allow ourselves to be robbed of the correlation between the idea of the nation and the idea of humanity.[61]

In his article on Poland Riezler devoted even more attention to this matter. He praised the former role of the national principle in furthering economic and technical advancement and more importantly in "deepening the uniqueness of national characteristics and thus in laying the foundation for a more secure and manifold development of the intellectual life of mankind." Nevertheless, he wrote that the "time for the unrestrained observance of the national principle is past." Nations would now probably find

their true possibility to be effective, with few exceptions, only in connection with the larger . . . groupings of peoples which are combined into state or supra-state organizations which observe the uniqueness and the certain measure of independence of their parts.

The cooperating nations would no longer have to fear attack from other nations: "No longer the unrestrained expansion of one *Volk*'s domination over the others, but a general guarantee of the different peoples' existence and cultural ideas alive within them against the storm of large leveling world empires." Though Riezler never advocated "the unrestrained expansion of one *Volk*'s domination over the others," he now denied this was even what a *Volk* "theoretically" wants to do. It was by no means clear, however, that Riezler had now found an "idea" which is above the specifically German idea of humanity. As we already know, Riezler's advocacy of *Mitteleuropa* was in part due to his concern to protect the "German idea," which would become the European idea. Despite his shift of emphasis to the idea of humanity, there is little doubt that Riezler continued to consider this idea and the "German idea" as one and the same. He wrote in November 1916: "Everywhere a fearful *[Götter]dämmerung* of nationalism will come, and Germany alone can replace it."

In Poland's case the end of the "unrestrained operation of the national principle" would have meant that the Central Powers would have had to "respect, to preserve, and to protect all of Poland's legitimate interests"; in return, Poland would have had to respect the interests of her Central European partners, to cooperate with them, and to avoid revolutionizing those Poles living within the borders of her partners.[62]

Riezler's high hopes for Poland, as well as for *Mitteleuropa,* were dashed by Germany's inability to rule indirectly and inoffensively. Even on the date that his optimistic article was published, he reported in his diary "confusion in Poland." A week later on November 22, 1916, Riezler lamented that "Poland is not going well." As to what went wrong in Poland, many errors were committed by Germany, but a few were particularly disastrous. Although a part of the Polish population, particularly the urban notables, the landowners, and higher clergy, showed some loyalty to the occupation powers, the Polish nationalist movement became more and more hostile to the German occupation regime. This hostility was nurtured by the regime, which became increasingly severe as Germany's fortunes of war sank lower. Requisitions of foodstuffs, raw materials, factory equipment, and forced deportation of workers helped insure the hatred of farmers and workers; support of Polish industrialists was lost through the forced severance of the Polish industry from its Russian markets. The Germans showed no understanding for Polish patriotism as the arrest of national hero and partisan leader, Joseph Pilsudski, on July 22, 1917, revealed. Nor were the Germans wise enough to make concessions to the Polish population within Germany's borders.

Germany's military policy was also extremely offensive to the Poles. On November 9, 1916, only four days after the proclamation of Polish autonomy, German plans for raising a Polish army were announced. Riezler was in favor of a Polish army fighting on the side of the Central Powers, but he opposed "the usual psychological errors" which the military committed in this matter. The almost immediate announcement of Polish recruitment was Ludendorff's decision. Since this was a military matter, the political authorities could not intervene, as Riezler would like to have done. The result was that the proclamation of Polish autonomy seemed to be merely a formal prerequisite for the exploitation of the Polish "human material." This was made even more obvious by Ludendorff's statement that he wanted to see results, that is, recruits, before any further political concessions could be made. Perhaps the greatest error, however, was Ludendorff's insistence that all Polish troops take an oath to the German kaiser! In Ludendorff's words, the Poles "must be shown once and for all that we give the orders here, not they." Riezler's disdain for this "military dilettante" was unreserved: "Ludendorff is too uneducated and, as all soldiers, without respect for the difficulty of political business. If given a completely free hand, he would plunge Germany into ruin in no time." Ludendorff, as indeed most Germans of his time, had no understanding of indirect rule. Riezler complained that in Poland "we raise them to the level of allies with the right hand, and with the left we peel the skin from their bodies like an absolute enemy."[63]

One wonders why the kind of compromise which Riezler advocated, in the form of indirect German rule of Central Europe and domestic reform within Germany, failed. Certainly the domestic obstacles to such policies proved to be insurmountable, but the policies themselves were to a considerable extent founded on illusions and wishful thinking.

First, the enemy coalition would never have allowed *Mitteleuropa* to be established. There was obviously too little sincerity in the German government's pronouncements concerning self-determination and too much open rejection of this principle by the chancellor's own domestic opponents. Bethmann's continuing inability to bring about peace negotiations with the enemy revealed that the Entente would rather continue the war than to accept a Central Europe controlled by Germany: Germany's enemies were clearly unwilling to tolerate even a moderately strengthened Germany.

Germany had insufficient military and economic strength simply to force the establishment of *Mitteleuropa*. Without the enthusiastic support of those nations which were designated to be a part of this international federation, German control, direct or indirect, would have been neither legitimate nor feasible. In any case, such voluntary support would never have materialized because of the fundamental flaw at the very heart of the entire concept of *Mitteleuropa:* The "German idea" was an undefined chimera unrelated to the aspirations of most Europeans, including most Germans themselves. German leaders easily confused this idea with the specific short-term needs of German policy. *Mitteleuropa* was too obviously an instrument to establish German domination rather than to provide for the material and spiritual well-being of all Europeans. The contradiction was too great between Germany's military and economic exploitation of conquered countries on the one hand, and the political necessity of creating sympathetic dependencies on the other. This is why firm Austro-German unity, the cornerstone for the new organization, was unattainable. There was simply nothing about the undefinable "German idea" to make the kind of *Mitteleuropa* which Riezler envisaged attractive or to serve as desirable compensation for the partners' loss of independence.

Aside from the "German idea's" lack of content and attractiveness was the visible fact that Germany was not capable of the kind of rule which such a new Europe would have required. Riezler suspected this throughout, but he clung to the hope, perhaps naively, that through experience Germany could learn the art of indirect rule. Toward the end of

125

the war, he knew that he had been wrong. He commented bitterly: "Never was a *Volk* more capable of conquering the world and more incapable of ruling it."[64]

The middle course which Riezler supported also foundered on the deadly rocks of a domestic political constellation entirely unable and unwilling to support such a compromising course. The military, the conservative and national parties, a large majority of the Prussian bureaucracy, an overwhelming majority of the educated elite, and many interest groups, including those of German heavy industry, sabotaged the policy internally. The policy never found a majority in the Reichstag, and Bethmann could not hope to gather enough support from the left to counteract his opponents on the right. Bethmann simply did not have enough supporters to enforce such a policy. In fact, Riezler noted in March 1916 that "if speech were free, then 100,000 would spontaneously assemble in front of the chancellor's palace."[65]

Of course, the opposition to the moderate course which Riezler advocated had existed before the war, but Bethmann had at least, albeit with great difficulty, been able to establish that course as official German policy, and there were encouraging signs that it would succeed. However, after the outbreak of war, the chancellor was faced with an increasing polarization between the advocates of far-reaching German annexations on the one hand and a growing number of Germans who, suffering from hunger due to the British blockade and from steadily growing war weariness, demanded more and more vociferously a peace which would return Europe to the *status quo ante bellum*. Thus, no consensus for his policy could be established.

A further problem, of course, was the familiar one of the German military's large degree of independence from civilian control, especially in the field. Riezler noted sarcastically that if he would only "don his officer's uniform and arrange to be stationed in an occupied area," he could "as a lieutenant playfully accomplish that which the Foreign Office is now unable to achieve." This problem was, to be sure, a long-standing structural problem in Prussia and in the German Empire. One calls to mind Frederick the Great's famous order of rank; "the oldest privy councillor behind the youngest ensign." The largely free-hand of the military exasperated Riezler, who spread no abuse for this "class of fools." In January 1917, he wrote that "the few perceptive persons in Germany secretly have one war aim: the destruction of Prussian militarism. . . . No one can say it, however, because it is also an English war aim." The particular dilemma was that in wartime there was an obviously increased reliance on physical force, thus on the military. Unfortunately, the influence of the military grew even more because of the official elevation of Hindenburg to the status of national hero in an attempt to strengthen domestic unity behind the war effort. This merely made it easier for the Supreme Command and those domestic groups which supported it to sabotage the government's policy of indirect rule and moderate war aims.[66]

Riezler's and the chancellor's domestic reforms proved to be equally unacceptable to most of Germany's ruling elite, who abhorred the idea of political concessions to the lower middle or working classes. Of course, Riezler's proposals, which fell short of a modern parliamentary system, were somewhat self-contradictory. He wrote in January 1917 that "it is clear that a truly great foreign policy in the sense of a European hegemony can be made only with the left." However, to shift the foundations of the state toward the left, without granting the working and lower middle classes an important part in the decision-making process was clearly unrealistic, to say nothing of the fact that Germany's traditional ruling elite would hardly have willingly abdicated its leadership. Riezler's remark also reveals another unsatisfactory feature of his reform thinking: domestic reform, especially in time of war, was justified almost exclusively on the grounds that it would increase Germany's external strength, not on the grounds that it was an indispensable step toward legitimate government. He made it clear that only on one condition would he support extensive concessions to the powerful working class: It would have to demonstrate "firm loyalty to the state and the system." His inclination to reform was thus excessively dictated by the war-time needs for domestic unity.[67]

Throughout the course of the war Riezler became increasingly dissatisfied that the necessary political realignment was not becoming a reality. On February 2, 1916, he wrote that the "most regrettable thing is how the *Volk* is falling apart." Pan-Germans "believe and propagate the most stupid trash, and except for their stupidity and lack of education, [they] have only a big mouth." Riezler clearly rejected the self-defeating, stubborn conservatism of the majority within the educated elite, many of whom staunchly supported the Pan-German League. In February 1916, he expressed amazement that the Pan-Germans did not already rule Germany; "it almost looks like the will of the nation is pushing into the abyss." In despair he wrote that "Germany must indeed undergo the domination of the Pan-Germans sometime" in order to see the disastrous consequences of such irrational politics.[68]

By March 1917, Bethmann Hollweg's "long battle against the dominant spirit" appeared to Riezler to be paying off, and even the chancellor, who tended to be more cautious than Riezler, was beginning to support his own plan of domestic reform more energetically. However, Riezler's hopes were dashed by the March Revolution in Russia and the outburst of socialist and worker discontent which followed in Germany. He wrote that this "revolutionary steam . . . naturally has had a negative effect on the military—the *Kreuzzeitung* exploits this thoroughly and in true German fashion gathers around the throne."[69]

Riezler criticized the left because it played into the hands of the right. "What stupidity [was] Scheidemann's threat of revolution. As is so often the case, the right will be saved by the left." The result was that "the right is in a rage—ancient Prussia is rearing up—the left does not want to wait any longer." Caught between these two poles, Bethmann could neither find an acceptable compromise, nor defend himself any longer. On July 13, 1917, he had to resign, and *de facto* political control passed for the duration of the war to the Supreme Military Command. After the chancellor had failed "to keep a society of madmen within the bounds of reason," Riezler saw the emergence in Germany of what seemed to him to be a "scarcely disguised military dictatorship."[70]

In retrospect, it can be said that part of the reason for the failure of Riezler's middle course between the political fronts during the war was that it was to some extent unrealistic, especially in view of the domestic constellation within Germany. This is not to suggest that any other course, domestic or international, would have been any less utopian or unrealistic. Indeed, given Germany's ruling elite, which Riezler criticized bitterly and perceptively, it is difficult to imagine that any other alternative would have had any greater likelihood of success. Nor is this to suggest that Riezler should have known all along that such a moderate reform and indirect rule policy would have inevitably failed. He certainly suspected that Germany would not develop the political maturity to see the wisdom of such a course, and the chancellor's pessimism was even greater. Nevertheless, Riezler was not inclined to capitulate to what he saw as a seriously misguided elite pursuing goals which he found "unattainable," "false," and "inappropriate." He had hoped that Germans could learn from their own experience. In the end, he realized that Germany had not yet come of age. He noted ruefully that the noble attempt to protect Germany by establishing indirect German hegemony over Central Europe "merely shows that an examination for a senior had been given to a sophomore."[71]

Chapter Five
RIEZLER AND THE REVOLUTION IN RUSSIA

In the case of Lenin's trip two opposite plans crossed at a definite point, and this point was a sealed car.

—Leon Trotsky

REVOLUTION AS A WEAPON OF WAR: THE LENIN TRIP

With the fall of Bethmann Hollweg, Riezler's activity in the "kitchen of Imperial Germany" came to an end. This changed Riezler's political activity in two basic ways: first, he no longer had the opportunity to deal with the variety of political problems as he had for the past eight years—peace moves, military-political problems, submarine warfare, construction of a new Europe, domestic reform, parliamentary liaison, press affairs, etc. Until shortly before the end of the war his attention became focused exclusively on Russia. Second, his influence on overall German policy and his opportunity to advocate innovative action were greatly reduced. His direct contact with the highest political leaders in Germany was severed, and his recommendations had to pass through his embassy superiors and the Foreign Office. Nevertheless, his new assignments were important ones, and he felt that he bore some responsibility for subsequent events in Russia; the Russian Revolution was the only aspect of his war-time political activity which he regretted in later life.[1]

Russia had always played an important role in Riezler's political thinking. He always had great respect for Russia's strength. Conscious of their enormous territory and their large population, the Russians "more than all other peoples in the present . . . have reason to believe in their eternity." This strength gave her great "explosive power" which presented a great long-term danger to Germany. Russia's entry into the war made this potential danger real and immediate.[2]

In the first three years of the war Riezler considered two basic ways of dealing with the immediate and long-range Russian danger to Germany. The first alternative was to erect a powerful *Mitteleuropa* through which Germany could protect itself from Britain and Russia. While he preferred

129

this alternative, he was privately pessimistic about Germany's ability to satisfy the prerequisites. Therefore, he always kept a second alternative in mind: coming to a political understanding with Russia at the expense of Germany's allies. As we saw, he first considered this briefly during the last two weeks before Germany and Russia had become locked in war. In January 1915, he again saw Austria and Turkey as objects which Germany could use to buy an understanding with Russia. Irritated a month later by Austria's unwillingness to make territorial concessions to Italy in order to prevent Italy from joining the Entente, he considered dealing with the inevitable dissolution of Austria-Hungary by partitioning the latter with Russia.[3]

Riezler continued to hope for some kind of Russo-German agreement while at the same time working for a strong *Mitteleuropa.* Indeed, his ideal solution to the strong Russia which he was sure would emerge from the war was the combination of both alternatives—a strong *Mitteleuropa,* as well as some kind of understanding with Russia. He feared that an understanding with Russia without strong backing from a German dominated Central Europe would inevitably lead Germany into the position of a Russian vassal state. He argued that only a Germany strong in the East could have good relations with Russia; Russia would have neither interest nor need for an understanding with a relatively weak and isolated Germany.[4]

Did Riezler consider revolution in Russia as an ultimate solution to the long-term Russian threat to Germany—in other words, as a third alternative? An examination of his revolutionary activity reveals that he did not. Throughout the war he viewed the revolutionizing of Russia, as well as a separate peace with Russia, as merely tactical means of weakening Russia temporarily in order to make her more receptive to the kind of relations with Germany which he sought. He had not abandoned his conviction, expressed earlier in *Grundzüge der Weltpolitik.* that Russia could never be weakened permanently. Nevertheless, a great power could disorient Russia, and Riezler was willing to help Germany do this in order to establish a temporarily favorable diplomatic situation for Germany.

Almost immediately after the outbreak of hostilities in 1914, the use of the revolutionary weapon against Germany's enemies had been discussed. Britain and France appeared most vulnerable, and Egypt, India, Ireland, and French Equitorial Africa all had been objects of German revolutionary activities. Russia, like Ireland, offered Germany a chance to point her revolutionary weapon almost directly at the heart of her enemy. Russia also offered Germany the opportunity to select either national or social revolution. Both national and social conflicts had erupted again during Russia's revolution in 1905-06 and were still latent dangers to the tsarist empire. As a result of the unsuccessful revolution, thousands of Russian emigrants had resettled in all parts of Europe. Many of the various dissident Russian emigrants could be used by Germany for whatever revolutionary assignments German interests required.

Bethmann Hollweg and Riezler were more interested in national revolutions within the Russian Empire than in a social revolution. Early in August 1914, Bethmann Hollweg had declared that the German goal in the East was the "liberation and protection of those races enslaved by Russia and the throwing back of Russian despotism to Moscow." In his "September Program" Riezler added that "Russia must if possible be pushed away from the German border, and her domination of non-Russian vassal peoples must be broken." Indeed, the Germans had information from many quarters that such a national revolution could be successful. The proclamation of such goals had been aimed not only at shortening the war and at expanding German influence or domination in the East, but also at achieving unity in the German war effort at home. The plans to dissolve the bonds which held peripheral peoples to Moscow and to decrease the powers of an autocratic tsar found enthusiastic support from Pan-Germans, German parties in the center, and Social Democrats.[5]

While the chancellor and Riezler preferred national revolution to social revolution, both dealt to a limited extent with the preparation of social revolution in Russia. The most important initial advocate of a social revolution in Russia was Alexander Parvus-Helphand, a Russian born German socialist with a wide network of commercial and political contacts throughout Europe. He had been referred to the Foreign Office on January 8, 1915, by Germany's ambassador in Constantinople, Freiherr Hans von Wangenheim. The German Foreign Office was interested in hearing Helphand's proposals, but it did not wish to appear to be in official contact with him. Since one of Riezler's duties was to speak to many unofficial persons who wished to convey advice to the chancellor, he was selected to meet discreetly with Helphand in Berlin on March 6, 1915. Riezler apparently showed no enthusiasm for the kinds of revolutionary enterprises which Helphand proposed. There is no record of what they actually discussed, but the substance of the talks was undoubtedly expressed in an important document which Helphand presented to the Germans early that same month. Helphand recommended deliveries of weapons to Russian national and social

131

revolutionaries inside Russia, organization of strikes, and establishment of contact with Bolsheviks, Mensheviks, and anti-tsarist Russian exiles in neutral countries.[6]

Estonian socialist, Alexander Keskküla, presented to the Germans an alternative to stronger support for Menshevik socialists. In September 1915, he delivered peace proposals from Lenin which opened the Germans' eyes to the possibility of supporting the Bolshevik socialists instead of the Menshevik socialists. In actuality contact was established and maintained with both groups, as well as with many other Russian dissident groups.[7]

Uppermost in Riezler's mind was still a separate peace with Russia. On January 10, 1915, he had expressed his irritation over "our clumsiness in preparing the Russian Revolution. Empty playing with the possibility of murdering Grand Duke Nikolai Nikolayevich." On March 5, 1915, he wrote about his intention "to convince the chancellor that here is a common German-Russian line, which can function with or without a separate peace." This common line could be made acceptable to Russia through German capital to replace the heavy French financial support and through "a slow sell-out of our eastern positions, first in Turkey, then in Austria." On March 7, 1915, he wrote again of such a "gradual sell-out in the East, Afghanistan, Persia, Turkey, and Austria in sequence, which would last one hundred years."[8]

Although Riezler gave only reserved support to the revolutionary effort, and then only to help bring about a separate peace, he was assigned to handle Germany's continuous contacts with Russian revolutionaries. He was liaison man between the two German organizations which dealt directly with Russian revolutionary activity—the German Foreign Office, which selected the seditious groups which should be supported, and the General Staff in Berlin, which handled the operational work. Thus, Riezler was extremely well-informed about Germany's support of Russian dissident activity. He occasionally noted in his diary that he had done "work on Russian revolutionizing"; in June 1915, he even speculated that a revolution was "the only possibility for a really good conclusion." Riezler was "one of the main organizers of the revolutionary policy," as George Katkov maintains.[9]

Riezler's own waivering between revolutionary activity and separate peace efforts was reflected on a larger scale in the German Foreign Office. The failure of insurrectionary efforts in Russia during the first two years of the war greatly strengthened the arguments by advocates of separate peace, who by September 1916 had clearly gained the upper hand within the Foreign Office. German financial support for many revolutionaries was cut or reduced, and efforts to reach a peace agreement with the tsar were stepped up. There is even some evidence that these efforts were beginning to bear fruit. The assignment of priority to achieving a separate peace in no way meant that the Foreign Office was unprepared for an eventual resumption of revolutionary activity. Germany was keeping the revolutionary alternative open.

The significance of keeping this option open became clear in the aftermath of momentous events in March 1917. Riezler later described to a parliamentary hearing the background of those events. He testified that the tsar's unbending opposition to reform had cost him the support of almost all elements of Russian society, including the aristocracy and the intelligensia. The temporary unity created by the outbreak of war had been destroyed completely by the tsar's extremely unwise decision in 1915 to assume personal command of the Russian army in the field. This decision was unwise because the tsar knew almost nothing about military matters, and because it left formal power in Petrograd in the hands of the tsarina, who was under the influence of Rasputin, the mystical peasant priest, who was widely reputed to be pro-German. Riezler observed that by 1916 the real power lay in the block of non-socialist progressive parties in the Duma, a parliament the creation of which the unwilling tsar had been forced to concede in 1906. This block fought bitterly with the government ministries over "questions concerning Rasputin, domestic policies and even the church." "One placed the other in check. The entire regime was unbelievably corroded and no longer capable of action."[10]

With the strains of war rapidly becoming unbearable for both Russian soldiers and civilians, the tsar quickly lost control of events. Early in March 1917, Petrograd and other Russian cities experienced strikes and bread riots. Not until after the strikes and demonstrations were in progress did a few revolutionary groups join in. On March 11 a military mutiny, incited largely by Mensheviks and Social Revolutionaries, broke out in Petrograd and spread rapidly. More and more regiments mutinied and placed themselves under the command of the Duma, which had become overnight a revolutionary command center. By late evening on March 12 the tsar's government ceased to exist, and on March 15 Tsar Nicholas followed the advice of his leading generals and abdicated. Trotsky observed: "There is no doubt that the fate of every revolution at a certain point is decided by a break in the disposition of the army."[11]

Riezler wrote that on March 15, 1917, the first reports of revolution in Petrograd arrived in Berlin. He noted that everyone in Berlin "considered the immediate victory of reaction as certain," but such a counterrevolution did not come. "Now our hopes are very high due to Russia . . . as far as one can judge, a revolutionary government cannot conduct such a complicated war."[12]

Bethmann Hollweg, as well as the kaiser, immediately recognized "the enormous significance of the event." Riezler wrote: "The Russian Revolution must be exploited in order to get peace." Perhaps still thinking of *Mitteleuropa,* Riezler continued: "We declare ourselves for freedom in Russia, declare our readiness not only for peace in general, but for an honorable peace."[13]

Riezler viewed peace with the new government in Russia as a matter of utmost urgency. The reasons are obvious considering the diplomatic and domestic dilemma which confronted Germany in the spring of 1917. A major aspect of that dilemma was that Germany's unrestricted submarine warfare was not only not working as planned, but it was almost certain to bring America into the war.[14] Riezler correctly saw that an American entry into the war would provide the Entente with a "new enormous moral boost" and would greatly strengthen the military pressure on Germany's western front. The continental blockade would be tightened. More German troops for the western front and food for Germany, where hunger riots had already become a constant problem, would have to be found. Both were to be found in Russia.

Another reason for peace with Russia was the domestic turmoil which the Russian Revolution caused in Germany itself. Not only was Social Democratic support of Bethmann Hollweg's government thrown into question, but there was danger that the German government would be by-passed by German socialists, who might attempt to sign a "peace of international socialism" with Russian socialists. Riezler was undoubtedly afraid that the German left would take seriously the Proclamation of the Petrograd Soviet "to the entire world," issued March 27, 1917, advocating revolution in all Western countries and a peace without annexations. Riezler was not yet ready to accept a peace which merely guaranteed the *status quo ante bellum.*[15]

The chancellor likewise viewed peace with Russia as a matter of utmost urgency, and he took immediate steps to indicate this both to the new Provisional government and to Russian emigrés in Switzerland who awaited the chance to use a peace with Germany for their own interests. Alexander Kerensky later recalled that as soon as the Russian monarchy fell, the German government established contact with the Provisional government through Copenhagen. However, the new government showed no interest in a separate peace with the German government and instead recommended to Britain and France the proclamation of war aims which would stimulate peace sentiment within Germany.[16]

Riezler thought of offering a temporary cease-fire as a means to tempt the new government to sign a separate peace with Germany, but he realized that such a peace would take too long to arrange. Reports from Russia indicated that the socialists wanted elections, the determination of a majority, and a constituent assembly before dealing with the question of peace. This would have required at least three months, and Germany's timetable would not have allowed such a delay. He realized the significance of America's entry into the war on April 4, 1917: "Time is again working against us. America!—... the war cannot be ended, to say nothing of being won." He noted: "It is difficult to conclude peace with democrats, especially with revolutionaries. These people act in committees and are hardly capable of action."[17]

Not only would arranging a peace with the Provisional government have required a longer time than Germany was willing to accept, but it would perhaps have enabled Russia to catch her breath and to regain her full military strength. Riezler had not lost his fear of Russian power. A peace which would weaken Russia could most likely be achieved from a determined band of revolutionaries under Vladimir Ilyich Lenin.[18] Without delay plans were made to transport Lenin from Switzerland through Germany to Russia.

It is known that Riezler felt a certain responsibility for this German policy. He told Hans Staudinger, Arnold Brecht, and Alvin Johnson many years later that he had conceived the idea for the trip.[19] There is no documentary evidence of this, but it is certain that he was informed on all aspects of that policy, and he certainly approved of it. He undoubtedly handled those aspects of the policy which fell under the responsibility of the chancellor. However, the decision and the execution of the policy to transport Lenin "like a plague bacillus from Switzerland to Russia," as Churchill described it, was the result of the combined efforts of German socialists, the kaiser, chancellor, Foreign Office, the Supreme Military Command, and the German trade unions. There seems to have been no responsible Germans who disapproved of the policy.

Before the German Foreign Office files were made available to the public, little was known about the conception and preparation of this trip. Few details were written in memoirs; Werner Hahlweg spoke of a "conspiracy of silence." Naturally Soviet scholars, who have access to Soviet party and government files, deemphasize this aspect of the successful Bolshevik Revolution which hardly fits neatly into a theory of in-

Wayne C. Thompson

evitable class revolution. Therefore, the purely documentary foundation for this important event remains weak. We must rely on the best available evidence.

Immediately after the outbreak of the March Revolution, Bethmann Hollweg directed Germany's ambassador in Bern, Gisbert von Romberg, "to establish contact with the political exiles from Russia living in Switzerland . . . for the purpose of their return to their homeland and to offer them transit through Germany." State Secretary for Foreign Affairs Arthur Zimmermann, the Supreme Military Command, and the kaiser all advocated the same. Thus, the period of stagnation in Germany's contacts with Russian revolutionary exiles since September 1916 ended as soon as the tsar's scepter fell from his hand.[20]

Naturally Lenin was willing to cooperate with the Germans. When he read the news of the tsar's abdication in the Swiss newspapers, he wrote: "I am beside myself with anger because I cannot travel to Scandinavia. I won't forgive myself for not risking going there in 1915." He remarked that he would even sign a contract with the devil if he could return to Russia.[21]

Lenin's name had first appeared in German Foreign Office files on November 30, 1914, and Bethmann Hollweg and Riezler knew of his aims at least since September 30, 1915. His special importance was recognized early, and all suggestions of employing Lenin in sabotage or courier operations in Russia or elsewhere were promptly rejected by Berlin. Lenin was being saved for something more important.[22]

Lenin was especially attractive to the Germans because by 1917 he demanded an immediate Russian withdrawal from the war. As early as June 1915, the Germans were aware through a report by Alexander Keskküla that Lenin, if he were able to assume control in Russia, was determined to make peace, without regard to France, in return for Germany's renunciation of annexations at Russia's expense. Given Germany's desperate military and domestic situation in the spring of 1917, it was logical from a strategic point of view to attempt to eliminate one enemy and one front by employing, in Churchill's words, "the most dreadful of all weapons"—revolution. In short, the Germans were forced to choose between revolutionaries who favored peace in 1917 and revolutionaries who did not.[23]

Lenin was of great value to Germany not only from the strategic point of view. In his pamphlet, *Socialism and War,* published in Geneva in 1915, Lenin supported "the right of oppressed nations to liberation, to secession from the big powers that oppress them." His reason for advocating self-determination at that time was clearly to weaken the tsarist regime, but self-determination would be equally effective in weakening the new Provisional government. The principle of self-determination was one which Riezler and Bethmann Hollweg also advocated during the war for a related reason—to weaken Germany's neighbors and thereby strengthen Germany. Thus, Lenin was seen as one who, if in control of the Russian government, would reduce Russia's power by permitting secessions. This, in Riezler's opinion, would have brought Germany two advantages; it would have eliminated the Russian danger which he perceived, and it would have created many small independent nations which would have been ideal objects for German indirect domination. Clearly, German policy vis-à-vis Russia was not based exclusively on tactical considerations. Moderate German war aims in the East appeared to be compatible with Lenin's program before April 1917.[24]

Finally, Lenin, with his narrow popular base and his long absence from Russia, appeared to be an ideal marionette for Germany; it was believed that without continued German support he would be unable to hold power more than a few weeks. Riezler and other Germans believed that one need not fear a Bolshevik regime because such a small, faction-ridden group would never be able to control the chaos in Russia and thus threaten Germany.[25]

Germans underestimated Lenin and misread him greatly. One must ask how such an immense miscalculation was possible. There are two basic reasons: first, no German who had a role in the transport of Lenin appears to have studied Lenin's writings and career well enough to have seen the opportunist character of his policies and writings. Nor did they have any appreciation of the determination, the ruthlessness, and the charisma of the man. Certainly there is no evidence that Riezler had sufficiently informed himself about the man and his writings before the transport. Not until November 1917 did Riezler report to German leaders in Berlin that Lenin was "a practical revolutionary of a grand style . . . a theoretician in his radical goals, but practical and concrete in the use of means." Second, Germany's policymaking at that point aimed excessively at immediate needs. As Lloyd George wrote, this is normal in wartime:

It is difficult to take long views in war. Victory is the only horizon. It is a lesson to the statesmanship which takes short-sighted views of a situation and seizes the chance of a temporary advantage without counting the certainty of future calamity.

Wayne C. Thompson

Neither the Germans nor Lenin had any concern for each others' interests. Self-interest was their guide. As Trotsky wrote in his memoirs: "In the case of Lenin's trip two opposite plans crossed at a definite point, and this point was a sealed car."[26]

The actual arrangements for the trip and the trip itself were completed within three weeks. The most difficult phase was during the first few days of April. Lenin was very concerned about being branded as a German agent. He therefore insisted that the Germans accept his terms that no German accompany the transport, that the train be extraterritorial, that the Russians pay their own fares, and that the selection of travelers be without regard to politics, especially insofar as the question of a separate peace was concerned. Because the Germans were in a great hurry, they accepted Lenin's terms on April 7.[27]

The German General Staff handled all of the technical details of the transport. The train, which departed from Zurich with thirty-two revolutionaries at 15:10 o'clock on April 9, was not sealed, as is often thought; the train was simply off limits to German officials of all kinds, and the Russians were segregated from the other passengers. As an "important diplomatic transport," such high traffic priority was given to the train that the German Crown Prince's own train was kept on a side track in Halle for two hours until Lenin's train had passed. Nevertheless, the train carrying the revolutionaries was delayed twice enroute. The first delay lasted two hours in Frankfurt am Main. The train was delayed again, perhaps intentionally, in Berlin. Unexplainably, the train had a twelve to twenty hour layover there. It has been suggested that Lenin talked to a German official, perhaps with Riezler, while the train was in Berlin, although there is no conclusive documentary evidence or diary entry to support this. Riezler was in fact in Berlin at the time,[28] and it cannot be excluded that Lenin left the train in disguise and met with Riezler or with other German officials. It is certainly unlikely that Riezler would have dared to board the train, however. Lenin was much too concerned about being compromised to meet with the known assistant to the German chancellor in a Berlin railway station. Riezler later indicated to a friend that he had sent a representative to meet with Lenin, but that the conversation had taken place on the ferry to Sweden, not on German soil.

Lenin held strictly to the agreed terms, which had been carefully designed to prevent Lenin's appearing to be a German agent. Indeed, it was the Germans' practice to make direct contacts with their revolutionary agents only very rarely. After the trip was completed, Lenin wrote that the Germans had "conducted themselves very correct-

138

ly" and that the terms had been "strictly observed."[29] The trip had not been a secret; on the morning of the departure from Zurich, the *Züricher Morgen Zeitung* published a short article reporting German permission for the transport through Germany of forty revolutionaries, all "convinced partisans of peace."

After a short stay in Stockholm, Lenin and his group proceeded through Sweden and Finland to Petrograd's Finland Station, where the group arrived at 10:30 P.M. on April 16 to be greeted by thousands of supporters. Before he entered the streets of Petrograd, Lenin announced that he had not come to strengthen the revolution which had taken place a month earlier. He now advocated a "second revolution." With satisfaction the Germans reported from Stockholm the following day: "Lenin's entry into Russia successful. He is working exactly as we would wish."[30]

BOLSHEVIK REVOLUTION AND BREST-LITOVSK

On August 5, 1917, Riezler officially returned to the Foreign Office where a very important assignment awaited him. The American entry into the war, the resultant increase in Entente morale, Austrian Kaiser Karl's widely known desire for a peace which would leave his empire intact, and Germany's own crumbling domestic unity had made a separate peace with Russia a matter of absolute necessity for Germany. Therefore, Germany needed "an especially well-informed political officer," who would be "our representative in Stockholm for Russia." Riezler was the ideal man to represent Germany in Stockholm, the crossroads between Russia and the outside world.[31]

Immediately after Riezler had assumed his new post on October 3, 1917, he resumed his work on revolution in Russia; he observed that peace on the eastern front could come only through "a wonder in the form of a single man," and he set out to make this wonder possible. He gave no information whatsoever in his diary to illuminate his activities in support of the Bolshevik Revolution. In fact, he made no diary entries at all from October 3, 1917, to January 14, 1918. Nor are there documents in the German Foreign Office archives which provide information on how he helped the Bolsheviks during the crucial month of October. It is certain, however, that he was charged with funding Bolshevik operations.

Without question, German financial assistance had been vital to the Bolsheviks during the first few weeks before the seizure of power in Petrograd on November 7, 1917. The Germans even provided large amounts of aid in the currency most desired in Russia, whose ruble had already disintegrated to a fraction of its former value. On October 25 one hundred thousand Swiss francs were sent by courier from Germany to the Bolsheviks in Russia. With this money, German agents were able to continue buying, almost publicly, rifles and machine guns from disaffected Russian soldiers for distribution to Bolshevik Red Guards. Also, the maintenance of Lettish and other non-Russian troops reliable to the Bolsheviks was largely financed by the Germans. Richard Kühlmann, who had replaced Zimmermann as state secretary for Foreign Affairs on August 5, 1917, later maintained that

it was not until the Bolsheviks had received from us a steady flow of funds through various channels and under different labels that they were in a position to be able to build up their main organ, *Pravda,* to conduct energetic propaganda, and appreciably to extend the originally narrow basis of their party.

A Foreign Office document dated November 10, 1917, three days after the Bolshevik Revolution, indicated that Riezler had dispensed millions of rubles for use in Russia.[32]

"Lenin is actually coming to power—another miracle to our rescue," Riezler exclaimed. On November 7, 1917, the Provisional government of Alexander Kerensky, which was already hopelessly paralyzed and powerless, was toppled by the small fragment of the Russian socialist movement which offered the war-weary Russians "peace and land." Peace on the eastern front was within reach; Germans and Bolsheviks had only to decide when and where to arrange the cease-fire and peace treaty and who should take part in the negotiations. As liaison man between Lenin and the German officials in Berlin, Riezler was responsible for arranging the peace negotiations. In addition, because he had the closest contact with the new Russian government, his reports on Russian tactics and internal political conditions were given careful attention by the official policymakers in Berlin.[33]

To accomplish the most important immediate goal of achieving and maintaining peace on the eastern front, Riezler advocated a policy which would prolong the chaos within Russia. In a document to the chancellor written five days after the Bolshevik Revolution Riezler reported that "even if the power of the Bolsheviks in Russia lasts only a few weeks, the country will almost certainly have to face terror such as even France under Marat hardly experienced. . . . The peasants will seize by force the land that has been promised them, and the soldiers will hurry home from the trenches in order not to be left out." If the Bolsheviks' plans to eliminate the existing administrative machinery and to place the executive into the hands of the local workers' and soldiers' councils were successful, then even if no cease-fire agreement should be reached, the country will cease to figure in military and economic calculations concerning the World War, and it will take the *ancien régime*, which would presumably be restored in this case, years to restore order among the chaos.

Riezler predicted that the slogan "peace and land," which had been "slid into the masses," would continue to plague subsequent Russian governments.[34]

Riezler believed that it was particularly important for Germany to take advantage of the chaos which the Bolsheviks were helping to maintain because their hold on power would only be temporary. In a report to Chancellor Georg Hertling on November 26 he warned that

one's joy at the courage and determination of the Bolshevik government must not lead one to put too much faith in the optimistic claims for the duration of their government being made by the Bolsheviks here. . . . For the moment, we are dealing with what is simply the forceful dictatorship of a handful of determined revolutionaries, whose domination is held in complete contempt by the rest of Russia and is only tolerated because these men promise immediate peace and, as is generally known, will bring it.

By any reasonable judgment, the supremacy of these people will shake the whole Russian state to its roots and, in all probability, in not more than a few months, when the *raison d'être* of the new government has ceased to exist, and the war against other nations has finally been brought to an end, it will then be swept away by a flood of violent hostility throughout the rest of Russia.[35]

Riezler was not sure how long Russia would be paralyzed. He was fairly certain that order would not be re-established immediately after the Bolsheviks were swept from power. One week later Riezler reported that "under the domination of the Bolsheviks the detachment of alien peoples from Russia will unquestionably make great progress." He stressed, however, that this disintegration would be only temporary; after a while, economic interest and traditional loyalties would lead the prodigal peoples back to Moscow. Riezler never lost his conviction, which he had expressed in *Grundzüge der Weltpolitik,* that Russia was indestructible. Nevertheless, the temporary disintegration of the Russian state due to Bolshevik rule was ideal for Germany because the independence of such peripheral nations as Finland, the Ukraine, and Estonia would be a consequence of Bolshevik theory, not of German demands. Also, the independence of these peoples would not have to be written into a peace treaty. Thus, neither *Mitteleuropa* nor future German-Russian relations would have been burdened by the peace settlement.[36]

In the meantime, a cease-fire had to be arranged with the "temporary" leaders of Russia. The immediate problem was the Second All-Russian

Congress's appeal on November 8 to all belligerent nations for a peace without annexations or reparations.[37]

Riezler and the German government wanted to avoid such a peace at all costs, and it is not difficult to see why. First, as the appeal itself indicated, the peace would have been one without annexations. Although Riezler was not interested in permanent German annexations of Russian territory, he wanted to be certain that Russia would remain weak for the duration of the war and that Germany would have temporary access to important resources within the borders of the Russian Empire. Both of these goals could best be guaranteed by temporary German control over wide areas within the Russian Empire. Such control could then be relinquished as soon as a more permanent government had been established in Russia. Thus, there would be no danger that future Russian-German relations could be poisoned. Second, his diaries reveal his worry that revolution in Russia would spread to Germany. Revolutionary activity had already been reported in Vienna, and Riezler wanted to seal off the Bolsheviks from all further unofficial contacts with German or Austrian citizens.

Riezler's concern about the introduction of Bolshevik revolutionary ideas into Germany was apparent almost immediately. On November 8 he warned the Foreign Office against "all public manifestations of friendly understanding with Russia." At the same time he attempted to convince his chief Bolshevik contact in Stockholm, V. V. Vorovsky, that there was no likelihood of a revolution in Germany. Also, Riezler requested that the German Social Democratic newspaper, *Vorwärts*, state openly that the German proletariat would not consider bringing about the "victory of the bloodthirsty English-American capitalism through strikes" and that "our Social Democracy . . . help block the way to an international socialist understanding." The majority SPD certainly had no taste for the kind of revolution which had taken place in Russia on November 7. Nevertheless, SPD leaders, Friedrich Ebert and Philipp Scheidemann, had agreed to a declaration of mutual sympathy and to a "demand for an immediate cease-fire in preparation for a democratic peace." This declaration and a response from the Bolsheviks were to be read at mass socialist rallies in Dresden and Bremen. However, because Riezler delayed the transmission of the Bolshevik message, no response to the SPD declaration could be read at the rallies.[38]

Much more serious than the exchange of sympathy declarations were the attempts by Matthias Erzberger, representative of the majority parties in Parliament, and by Scheidemann to deal directly with the

Bolshevik representatives in Stockholm. Riezler and the German Foreign Office wished to prevent such contacts at all costs.

The first attempt at direct negotiations had been made by Erzberger several months earlier. On behalf of the majority parties, which on July 19, 1917, had adopted a "peace resolution" calling for peace without annexations, Erzberger sent Paul Wucherpfennig and Hermann Goldberg to meet with the Bolsheviks in Stockholm. Riezler was irritated that Erzberger "had to trample between things here like an elephant." Erzberger's peace offer was actually presented to Vorovsky on November 23, but Riezler did everything possible to convince the Bolsheviks "that only the conclusion of an immediate cease-fire and subsequent direct peace negotiations" had any chance of success. Riezler was instructed by Kühlmann to convince Erzberger's representatives of the same, but Wucherpfennig and Goldberg were not easily persuaded. Riezler was, of course, operating under specific instructions from the Foreign Office; nevertheless, he was personally convinced that such unorthodox diplomatic moves were wholly inappropriate. On November 26 he repeated what he had written to the Foreign Office the day before. One must not be tempted

to adopt the idea that a *rapprochement* between the German people and the Russian people—in the sense of friendship between peoples—should be initiated through negotiations between the majority parties and delegates of those now in power in Russia. It is this idea that Goldberg has thrust into the foreground. It would probably be a grave political error even to seem to bind the future of Russo-German relations to the fortunes of the men now in power in Russia. The duration of their government will bring no more than a cease-fire and possibly a formal peace. Under the circumstances, and in view of the violent shocks which are probably still facing Russia, we shall not be able to take up proper peaceful communications and resume a friendly, neighborly relationship until some considerable time has elapsed and a start has been made in the gradual restoration of order. That will be the time to begin working for the kinds of agreements with the Russian people and with another Russian government which Goldberg has in mind. Until then, only a cautious handling of commercial issues by representatives of the actual government will be possible or to the point, and only action of this kind will enable us to achieve a transition to good relations, even with a new government and a Russia which is not Bolshevik.

The initiative of Erzberger became quickly outdated. Before Vorovsky could receive from Petrograd a response to Erzberger's peace offer, Goldberg had left Stockholm in order to continue work on the plan in Berlin. At Riezler's suggestion, Goldberg was prevented from returning to Stockholm. Therefore, the Bolsheviks, who needed peace desperately, decided to enter cease-fire negotiations with German government representatives beginning December 3 at Brest-Litovsk, a Russian city located behind the German lines.[39]

After the cease-fire negotiations had already begun in Brest, a second threat to the desired government-to-government talks developed. On December 9, 1917, Riezler received information from Kühlmann that the Social Democrat, Philipp Scheidemann, had departed for Stockholm in order to persuade the Bolsheviks to conduct peace negotiations with either the majority socialists or Reichstag majority instead of with the German government. Kühlmann instructed Riezler to stop Scheidemann immediately upon arrival in Stockholm in order to convince him that his actions were a mistake. Therefore, after arriving in Stockholm Scheidemann was met by Riezler, who convinced him "that every socialist conference must delay and endanger the only promising negotiations." Thus, the danger of a "socialist peace" was averted.[40]

After having blocked attempts by German socialists and Reichstag majority, Riezler was successful in persuading the Bolsheviks that only a resumption of direct peace negotiations between the German and Bolshevik governments could be advantageous. He knew how to exploit Lenin's and Trotsky's aversion to German Social Democrats. Riezler himself conducted the crucial negotiations with Vorovsky in the Stockholm apartment of journalist Alfons Paquet on December 8, 10, and 14, 1917. Riezler negotiated skillfully and got along very well with Vorovsky. "The Bolsheviks are fantastic fellows and did everything very well and nicely." The results were an agreement on December 15 for a cease-fire on the eastern front and for peace negotiations at the German military headquarters in Brest-Litovsk, not in a neutral country, as the Bolsheviks had wished.[41]

Lenin consented to send a delegation headed by Leon Trotsky to the peace negotiations, which opened in Brest-Litovsk on December 22, 1917. This did not mean, however, that the Bolsheviks were convinced that they would ultimately have to sign a peace treaty with Russia's former enemies. As Lenin's biographer, Louis Fischer, wrote: "At Brest-Litovsk . . . the Soviets conferred with the foreign diplomats and scanned the western horizon for red flames. Bolshevik eyes were in double focus." Gerhard Ritter added that "seldom have peace negotiations commenced with so much insincerity as at Brest-Litovsk."[42]

Riezler was not a member of the delegation and did not play a major role in the formulation of German policy applied in the peace negotiations, as he had in the cease-fire negotiations. Nevertheless, a brief look at Riezler's general position on the negotiations and at the basic problems which developed in the course of the talks is helpful for understanding Riezler's assignment in Moscow from April to August 1918.

Initially the Bolsheviks were optimistic. Their optimism was buoyed by the Central Powers' formal acceptance on Christmas Day of the Bolsheviks' formula: "no annexations, no indemnities." Thus, there seemed to be common ground; Lenin's April Theses and the Reichstag's peace resolution of July 1917 had called for a peace without annexations. Both parties officially recognized self-determination as the guiding principle. However, it soon became obvious that the negotiators were not standing on common ground after all. When the Bolsheviks' military attaché at Brest asked his German counterpart, General Max Hoffmann, on December 27 how much German-annexed Russian territory would be evacuated, he received the reply: "Not one millimeter."[43]

Clearly, the principle of self-determination had been interpreted in different ways. The Bolsheviks demanded that elections be held after the withdrawal of German troops. Such withdrawal would have put the Bolsheviks in a position to influence the elections. The Germans wanted elections to be held while their troops were still occupying the Russian territory. This would have meant that the elections would have been held under German influence. In fact, neither side was truly interested in seeing the peoples on the periphery of the Russian Empire determine their own destinies. The Bolshevik proclamation of self-determination had already been significantly modified by an earlier All-Russian Party Congress which on May 12, 1917, had accepted Stalin's proposal:

The question of the right of nations to voluntary separation must not be confused with the question of the right or the expediency of the separation of this or that nation at this or that moment. The last question must be solved in each individual case completely independently by the party of the proletariat and indeed from the standpoint of the interests of the entire social development and of the proletariat's class struggle for socialism.[44]

In practice, therefore, secession was not open to non-Bolshevik nations.[44]

The German negotiators were equally uninterested in the principle of self-determination. Ludendorff bluntly stated his view as follows: "To evacuate the country was a military absurdity; we needed it for our existence and had no mind to deliver it up to unscrupulous Bolshevism." Kühlmann, who led the German delegation at Brest, actually engaged in long theoretical debates with Trotsky on the principle of self-determination, but his motive was not to defend the principle itself. As he wrote in his memoirs,

145

my plan was to tie up Trotsky in a purely academic discussion about the right of peoples to self-determination and about its practical implementation, and on the basis of the right of self-determination of peoples to get whatever we really needed in the way of territorial concessions.

Riezler concurred entirely in the opposition to self-determination. Although he never wished to disavow the principle publicly, he did not wish to see it applied in Russia at this time. Observing the appeal of this principle among many influential Germans and Austrians, he wrote on January 29, 1918, that "one has absolutely no idea what Russia is today; one races blindly after a long outdated idea." He saw the weakness of self-determination in that it would not have justified temporary German control of such important territories as Lithuania and Courland, which later would perhaps be crucial to Germany's defense against a strong Russia. Also, he correctly recognized that the principle of self-determination was subordinate to Bolshevik party interests. A naive belief in self-determination would have delivered to Bolshevism those peoples "from the Finnish Gulf to the Adriatic Sea."[45]

By January 18 Trotsky saw that he had successfully delayed the signing of the peace but had not budged the Germans from their occupation of more than 170,000 square kilometers of Russian territory. Without declaring a formal recess he left to consult his party comrades in Petrograd, where a bitter party debate ensued. Lenin was in a difficult dilemma: on the one hand, he had come to power on the strength of his call for peace, and he now needed that peace in order to bring the domestic chaos under control. On the other hand, he was trapped between ideological purists who wanted to "prepare for and wage a revolutionary war," as he himself had vowed in 1915, and those elements extending from rightist social revolutionaries to monarchists who would not have accepted a peace with Germany under any circumstances.[46]

During this recess in the discussions Chancellor Hertling asked Riezler, who expected to be sent to Brest-Litovsk for the next round of negotiations, both to submit a written recommendation on the tactic to be followed at Brest and to report his views personally in Berlin. Riezler had already expressed dissatisfaction with Kühlmann's forensics with Trotsky. Although he knew that Kühlmann did not really believe that Germany could reach and understanding with the Bolsheviks, he noted that one should "not be too Machiavellian with ideologues." Riezler thought that the time had come to speak forcefully with the Bolsheviks.[47]

In his report to the chancellor, Riezler wrote that certain points must be kept in mind. First, the Bolshevik goal is neither the salvation of the Russian future nor understanding and reconciliation of peoples. The thought of an understanding with the not yet Bolshevized Central Powers is entirely non-Bolshevistic. They came to Brest, not because they are in principle for peace, but because they were aided to power by the people's longing for peace; [they] are forced at least to appear to make great exertions in order to achieve the preempted chief demand of the Russian people. . . . They have used Brest as an agitation tribune for Europe, especially for the revolutionizing of Central Europe.

Riezler found that Bolshevik demands were presented only for agitational purposes and that the talks had been delayed only in order to further the revolution in Central Europe, not in order to gain concessions, which they would not have accepted anyway. While the Bolshevists needed peace badly,

they can justify the conclusion of a peace with bourgeois states only by having no alternatives. . . . Under these circumstances there appears to me to be no other alternative than to present the concessions by the Central Powers as the final ones, to maintain this position for a short time, and to make it clear to them that in the event of a rejection the negotiations and, as a logical consequence, the cease-fire would be terminated.[48]

In the midst of this hectic diplomatic activity, Riezler revealed increasing pessimism concerning man's ability to exert any control over the chaos around him:

One searches in vain for a meaning to the catastrophe all around—it has none or only that which each individual gives it. Mankind's ludicrous belief in a meaning for the world! The undergrowth of hypocrisy, uncertainty, monetary interests, delusion of the *Volk*, heroism and idealism. Impossible to judge as a contemporary—the only thing is to act blindly. However, that action is not action in the former sense: nowhere a stone which offers the chisel firm contours, an enormous muddy mass in movement, which cannot be held onto by the human grip, too large, too unattainable—only to try to stay on top of the rushing avalanche.[49]

Riezler was probing the limits of statesmanship in time of crisis. The German statesmen were stumbling down a dark alley plagued by a crumbling domestic and military situation, by a situation in Russia which they could neither understand nor control, by conflicts of interests, dreams, and emotions which could find neither national nor international common denominator, and by an inability to see the necessity of cutting losses and seeking a general peace which would reestablish the *status quo ante bellum*. Riezler sensed that this was no time for either hubris or naiveté, but he did not know how to free his nation of them. Indeed, he himself continued to be touched by both, although to a decreasing extent.

Riezler's recommendation was in basic agreement with Kühlmann's: one had to speak much more forcefully with the Bolsheviks. However, Trotsky had no mind to capitulate quickly to German threats. When he returned to Brest on January 26, he brought no authority to sign a peace treaty. His instructions were unmistakably to protract the negotiations as long as possible. He was able to do this until February 8, when Germany chose to sign a separate treaty with a moderately socialist Ukrainian government, dependent upon the Central Powers. Trotsky's answer to this separate treaty took the Germans completely by surprise. On February 10 he proclaimed "no war, no peace": "We no longer wish to participate in this purely imperialistic war . . . we are equally unreconciled to the imperialism of both camps."[50]

Trotsky's statement led to an intense dispute in Brest and Berlin. Did the cease-fire still apply? The Supreme Military Command, the kaiser, and Chancellor Hertling argued that it no longer was in force and advocated not only renewed military activity but the forceful removal of the Bolsheviks from power. Kühlmann, on the other hand, argued unsuccessfully that the cease-fire was still in effect and that the Bolsheviks should be kept in power. On February 18 the German Supreme Military Command announced that the state of war had been renewed.

Riezler's position in this dispute was indicated rather clearly in a letter he wrote to the Foreign Office on February 21. Germany had "no alternative than to fight step by step for areas which are important for us." Defensive considerations were paramount: "We must, I believe, prepare ourselves for the possibility that suddenly everything in the East will stand against us." While he favored the resumption of military activity, he did not yet advocate the overthrow of the Bolsheviks, because only Bolsheviks would tolerate a "forced peace."[51]

In Russia most Bolsheviks prepared to fight in order to defend "the red fortress of the world revolution." Only Lenin argued for signing the peace on Germany's harsh terms. The pragmatist Lenin argued that

the revolutionary phrase is a repetition of revolutionary slogans without considering objective circumstances . . . we must fight the revolutionary phrase, we must fight it, absolutely fight it, lest some day they tell the bitter truth about us: 'The revolutionary phrase about a revolutionary war killed the revolution.'

By February 23 Lenin had won support for the treaty despite the extremely unfavorable terms for Russia. He convinced his comrades that Russia needed time in order to save the revolution and that although the anticipated German socialist revolution was late, "it will come."[52]

148

How desperately the Bolsheviks needed peace was revealed by the terms which they accepted on March 3. Courland, Lithuania, and Poland were separated completely from the Russian state. Germany was granted occupation rights in Estonia and Livonia, and Russia recognized the independence of the Ukraine and agreed to evacuate Finland. Finally, the Armenian areas—Ardahan, Kars, and Batum—were given to Turkey.[53]

Riezler favored what he himself admitted was a "forced peace," despite the fact that the Treaty of Brest-Litovsk could hardly have cast Germany in the light of a champion of freedom and "everything progressive." However, he saw the peace only as a temporary expedient. His opinion of the treaty and the policy which he advocated from Moscow shortly thereafter were revealed in a letter he wrote to the chancellor on March 8:

If we operate on the assumption that a counterrevolution will win . . . even without our help, then an early understanding with this movement, which would operate with us rather than against us, would unquestionably be the best. However, we must be ready to regard the peace of Brest-Litovsk, which a Russia liberated from the Bolsheviks will never forget, as something which can later be liquidated.[54]

This treaty, along with the reparations demanded of Russia in August, set a most unfortunate precedent. It established a new standard for the visible divergence of publicly proclaimed ideals, such as self-determination of all nations, and the naked national interests which underlay them. This treaty merely stimulated the Entente's will to resist and reinforced the enemy's moral self-confidence to impose on the Germans nine months later a peace no less Draconian than this one. The predominance of national interest as a guide in international politics was, of course, as characteristic of diplomacy at that time as it is now. However, German leaders shared in the failure of many European statesmen during the war and its tragic aftermath to recognize that a nation's long-term interests are best served in an international setting in which the legitimate aspirations of all nations are mutually recognized and accommodated.

MISSION IN MOSCOW

Because of his reputation as an expert on Russian affairs, Riezler was assigned as legation counselor to the first German mission in Bolshevik Moscow. Lenin had decided on March 12, 1918, to move the capital from Petrograd to Moscow in order to protect the fragile government as much

Wayne C. Thompson

as possible from foreign military interference. On April 18, 1918, Riezler left Berlin for his new assignment. "A fantastic trip! Railroad stations with people in military coats, children, refugees, filth, broken-down passenger and baggage cars stuffed with people." Riezler's party was given an official reception at the railroad station in Moscow. "An enormous line of people—Never was such a conqueror received with such joy."[55]

Riezler could see chaos everywhere. Moscow, as well as most Russian cities, suffered acute food shortages, which Lenin had unsuccessfully tried to remedy through requisitions in the countryside. Labor discipline and productivity were declining rapidly, and a black market was growing. Inflation had also become uncontrollable, so that despite nominal wage boosts real wages had declined drastically.

The work which lay ahead of the German diplomats in Moscow bore little resemblance to that of a conqueror." Our *Ostpolitik* without a unified plan, entirely disjointed—an expanse of ruins, a hardly describable confusion." His first reaction to what he encountered in Moscow was that "devils could not have confused the entire capitalist world more completely and irremediably than the Bolsheviks."[56] A confused and divided "conqueror" groped for a way to deal with a chaotic land.

German policy was split basically along three lines: (1) the Supreme Military Command pursued an annexationist, anti-Bolshevik interventionist policy, (2) the Foreign Office favored continued support of the Bolsheviks on the basis of the Brest-Litovsk Treaty, (3) Riezler and Count Mirbach, German ambassador to Moscow, favored a termination of the Brest-Litovsk Treaty, a recognition of Russian territorial unity, and active German support of the monarchist and bourgeois counterrevolution.[57]

On September 12, 1918, Riezler retrospectively summarized his Russian policy as it had developed from April to August 1918. Basically he sought to give "coherent direction to the disjointed half-measures." Initially he supported the Foreign Office in its efforts to maintain the Bolsheviks in power and to halt the unauthorized military advance into Russian territory. By June 4, however, while overtly supporting the Bolsheviks, as his instructions required him to do, he secretly made preparations for a counterrevolution. Riezler wanted anti-Bolshevik Russians to know that the Brest-Litovsk Treaty was applicable only to a Bolshevik government and could therefore be revised or revoked later. While he was authorized to establish contact with counterrevolutionary groups, he never succeeded in persuading the Foreign Office to adopt a policy of counterrevolution. Instead, the Foreign Office chose to seek sup-

150

plementary treaties with the Bolsheviks. Riezler's efforts to give "coherent direction" to German policy in revolutionary Russia remained fruitless.[58]

During his service in Moscow, Riezler made only three entries in his diary. However, German Foreign Office files contain countless documents written by Riezler which confirm his claim to have advocated unsuccessfully an alternative to the conflicting policies of the Foreign Office and the Supreme Military Command.

On March 8 Riezler maintained that it was not in Germany's interest to depose the Bolsheviks until a general peace had been reached. Germany needed both chaos in Russia and the Brest-Litovsk Treaty. Thus, at the time of his appointment to the Moscow mission, Riezler was in full agreement with the policy of the Foreign Office. On the other hand, his differences with the military command were apparent from April 22, the day he arrived in Moscow. Since Mirbach did not arrive in Moscow until a few days later, Riezler was immediately escorted to Commissar for Foreign Affairs Georgi Chicherin for a briefing. This briefing proved to be very embarrassing for Riezler, who reported that Germany was in

a bad moral position because our military advance has long since crossed the borders of the Ukraine. We are standing close to Briansk. In other words, a direct predatory incursion after the conclusion of peace. Chicherin and Karakhan showed the situation on the map without the slightest reproach, with muted but effective accusation. I can only listen and express doubt about the accuracy of their reports.

Not only did the military disregard the provisions of the Brest-Litovsk Treaty, but by May 8 Ludendorff was already exploring the possibility of counterrevolution.[59]

In May Riezler noted that the Bolsheviks were still able to maintain themselves in power: "The counterrevolution certainly sits all around them, even in the Bolsheviks' own offices, but has neither pluck nor power." The Bolsheviks' success was due largely to the talents of their leader. "Lenin does everything, personally completely unpretentious . . . a conspirator of the first order." The chaos was no great threat to the regime because of the character of the Russian people. "Every other land would have collapsed long ago, but Russia can bear an indescribable chaos while the cart continues more or less to roll on."[60]

Mirbach did not share Riezler's growing confidence in Lenin's ability to stay in power. On May 16 he reported a meeting with Lenin, who

trusts his lucky star with the utmost conviction and repeatedly expresses the most boundless optimism in an almost overpowering way. However, he does admit that even though his system is still standing firm, the number of his opponents has increased and the situation 'demands more intense vigilance than it did a month ago.'

Although his enemies showed an inability to unify against him, Lenin found an increasing number of them in his own camp, where the left wing had never been able to accept the Brest-Litovsk Treaty. Four days later Mirbach reported that the Bolsheviks' influence on the people had indeed weakened considerably in the past few weeks.[61]

The first indication that Riezler had begun to question the Foreign Office's basic policy of supporting the Bolsheviks can be found in a document he wrote on June 4. Riezler confirmed what Mirbach had reported: the Bolsheviks had been greatly weakened by the worsening hunger, the hatred resulting from the Bolshevik terror, and the increasingly questionable loyalty of the Latvian soldiers, who had played a crucial role in keeping the Bolsheviks in power since the October Revolution. "The Bolsheviks are very nervous, feel their end approaching, for which reason the rats are everywhere beginning to abandon the ship." Germany, Riezler argued, had to confront the possibility that bourgeois Russia would seize power with the help of the Entente. Therefore, Germany should prepare herself

to revise the Brest peace in favor of an economic hegemony in entire Russia. . . . Not a very attractive prospect to facilitate the reemergence of a Russia which would again be imperialist, but perhaps unavoidable, since . . . despite everything the vitality of the one Russian soul is enormous.

Riezler was much more direct in a diary entry four days later:

The great question—to allow the Bolshevik collapse to develop into an Entente-oriented chaos . . .—or to sponsor the reemergence of a Russia which we ourselves crushed and to have an alliance and economic hegemony as a reward for the complete reunification of the Ukraine with Greater Russia.[62]

Riezler by no means thought that the right course of action was obvious: "If politics were ever a voyage in uncharted seas, then so it is now." His policy preference was expressed in the way he presented what he believed to be the only possible alternatives: "the restoration of Russia sooner or later or a high wire dance from moment to moment, at which one could break his neck at any time."[63] Thus, Riezler and Ludendorff now agreed that perhaps the Bolsheviks should be overthrown. However, their thinking differed in one decisive respect: Riezler was con-

vinced that prerevolutionary Russia should be reunited, whereas Ludendorff consistently refused to recognize the fact that a non-Bolshevik
government would never accept the permanent loss of that Russian
territory under German occupation in the summer of 1918.

By the end of June there was no longer any question in Riezler's mind
concerning the correct German policy for Russia. "We stand at the
crossroads." The key consideration was that "we gain nothing from the
chaos—and there is practically nothing . . . one can gain from the
Bolsheviks." Since it was not possible to "maintain peace in the East
purely by bayonets," it was necessary to offer the "reemerging Russia"
national unity, including the Ukraine. Then some counterrevolutionary
combination should be supported which would depose the Bolsheviks
"through its own power if possible, with the least amount of help possible
if necessary, and collaborate with us *de facto* against the Entente."
Riezler took a firm stand in favor of counterrevolution, and Mirbach was
in complete agreement. Nevertheless, Kühlmann ordered the mission "to
support the Bolsheviks and only to be in touch with the others." His ex-
planation was that "Bolshevik rule means the weakness of Russia, and
we still have a great interest in that."[64] From June on, Riezler's position
was distinctly in variance with those of the Supreme Military Command
and the Foreign Office.

Riezler's conviction that the utility of the Brest-Litovsk Treaty had
come to an end was reinforced by his experience during and after the
Fifth All-Russian Soviet Congress, which opened on July 4 in the Bolshoi
Theater. At this Congress, Lenin's foreign policy was strongly criticized
by many of the delegates, especially by the Left Social Revolutionaries,
who had never favored the Brest-Litovsk Treaty because it allegedly
harmed the world revolution, and who believed that the dictatorship of
the proletariat had become a "dictatorship of Mirbach." The Left Social
Revolutionaries delivered particularly inflammatory speeches, often
pointing directly to the diplomatic loge where Riezler was sitting. "Down
with Mirbach. Away with the German butchers. Away with the
hangman's noose of Brest!" Such cries were enthusiastically received by
many of the delegates at the Congress. The tumult in the Bolshoi
Theater was only a prelude to an event on July 6 which brought German-
Russian relations to an open and intense crisis.[65]

Shortly after 2:30 P.M., two Russians, Jacob G. Blyumkin and N. An-
dreyev, appeared at the German embassy on Denezhyi Pereulok in
Moscow. Showing identification signed by the head of the secret police
(CHEKA), Felix Dzerzhinski, the two men asked to see Mirbach.
Because of numerous threats to assassinate the ambassador, Riezler had

been ordered to see all visitors to the embassy. The two men informed Riezler that they had been sent in connection with an espionage case involving a Hungarian officer with the same name as the ambassador. Soon after opening the conversation, Blyumkin insisted upon seeing the ambassador personally since the matter possibly involved a member of his family. When Mirbach was informed of this, he appeared to speak with the two men.

Mirbach took a seat at the head of a heavy marble table, and Riezler and the translator, a Lieutenant Müller, sat on a couch behind the marble table directly opposite Blyumkin. Andreyev stood by the door. When Blyumkin repeated the charge against the alleged relative of Count Mirbach, Riezler advised Mirbach not to discuss the matter with Blyumkin, but instead to direct a personal query to Chicherin. As soon as Riezler had said this, Blyumkin exclaimed: "For Count Mirbach it is a question of life and death!" This exclamation apparently was a prearranged signal for both Russians to draw pistols from their brief cases and to fire point blank at Mirbach, Riezler, and Müller. Miraculously none of the Germans was hit in the room where the conversation had taken place. Riezler recalled a paralyzing surprise and leaned backward while Müller fell to the floor. After a few seconds Mirbach stood up and ran from the room. Riezler remembered Mirbach's distorted features and his own tortured feeling of not being able to help him. The assassins had positioned themselves cleverly so that Riezler and Müller, who were trapped behind the heavy marble table, could not come to Mirbach's aid.

After escaping from the room, Mirbach had almost reached safety when Andreyev stopped firing at Riezler and Müller and fired the fatal shot at Mirbach hitting him in the back of the neck. Andreyev then threw a hand grenade into the middle of the room where Mirbach lay. The explosion was so powerful that Riezler was thrown to the floor; through the heavy clouds of smoke he could see Blyumkin and Andreyev escape via an open window into the front yard to a waiting vehicle. Embassy guards fired at the assassins, but Blyumkin and Andreyev managed to escape. Riezler remembered the entire incident as "so terrible that I could not even think about it for weeks."[66]

It appeared to Riezler that the assassination had been planned and executed by the Left Social Revolutionaries, who on June 24 had decided to conduct terrorist actions against prominent "representatives of German imperialism." In fact, actual guilt for the murder remains far from clear. Although there were scattered insurrections in such cities as Petrograd, Yaroslave, Rybinsk, and Murom, it remains uncertain whether "the assassination of the Count [Mirbach was] . . . obviously the signal for the overthrow of the Bolsheviks," as Riezler maintained on July 7. A small uprising in Moscow was crushed immediately by Lenin, and Lenin took this opportunity to liquidate some of his opponents within the party. However, the Bolsheviks did not meet Riezler's demand that the leaders of the Left Social Revolutionaries be shot and that the case be clarified. Although a few of the insurrectionists were subsequently brought to trial, only light sentences were pronounced. Riezler wrote that "a thick veil of mendacity" hung over the entire affair. It is true that the most important Bolshevik leaders, Radek, Chicherin, Karakhan, and Lenin came to the German mission to express official regrets, but these regrets, especially Lenin's, appeared to Riezler to be insincere and "an ice-cold pardon."[67]

After the assassination Riezler became the chief of the German mission. Alfons Paquet, the mission's highest press official, compared the new mission chief with the assassinated Mirbach:

Mirbach too much a man of the court. Riezler on the other hand is entirely absorbed in the affairs of the mission, lets himself be overwhelmed by them. Wants to see all incoming messages, to take care of all details. At the same time is terribly distracted, cannot pursue one thought. Incomprehensible how he disappears from the embassy for hours at a time. Friday morning I see him with an approximately eighteen-year-old Russian lad . . . (his language teacher), who accompanies him on a stroll. . . . What is the meaning of all this? . . . I warn him . . . against leaving the embassy alone; he is the one responsible for the mission.

The strain on Riezler was great. Paquet wrote on June 28 that "Riezler swallows one medicine after the other, his face daily becomes more wrinkled and bitter, the intellectual—intriguer due to helplessness."[68]

Under Riezler's responsibility were also soldiers who either represented the Supreme Military Command or who provided protection for the embassy. It is not surprising that Riezler's rapport with the military personnel was not good. Riezler and Major Freiherr von Bothmer, the mission's highest ranking representative of the Supreme Military Command, bore mutual hatred for each other. Riezler saw Bothmer as the prototypical "stupid and uneducated officer," who gave the entire mission an "officers' club atmosphere," which Riezler disliked. The anti-Semitic Bothmer found Riezler

politically liberal, insufficiently well-groomed, jealous and full of fear that we soldiers could be mingling in politics. . . . In any event all the diplomats are just like one imagines them. Only Riezler is an exception in that he lacks the absolutely necessary life style and physical culture. One could imagine him as anything but a secret legation counselor. Journalist, mediocre salesman etc. could fit him much better. . . . The man is in any case very unpleasant and so very unappetizing.[69]

155

As chief of mission, Riezler argued even more energetically for the overthrow of the Bolsheviks, and he intensified his dealings with counterrevolutionary groups. These dealings were known to the Bolsheviks even before the assassination of Mirbach. On July 5 Karakhan had informed Riezler that the Bolsheviks were aware of German contacts with counterrevolutionary groups. Riezler replied that it was entirely normal for a diplomatic mission to maintain such contacts. The Bolsheviks had every reason to be thankful "if we were helpful in dividing the bourgeois elements and in preventing a unified counterrevolutionary front which could become a danger for them [Bolsheviks]." In reality, Riezler had no intention of attempting to split the bourgeois elements but to aid them in unifying against the Bolsheviks. To do his work, Riezler was appropriated extraordinarily large sums of money; for example, on June 8 he was granted forty million marks. However, despite the events of the first week in July and despite Kühlmann's replacement on July 9 by Admiral Paul von Hintze, the Foreign Office's policy of supporting the Bolsheviks remained unchanged.[70]

This official policy became increasingly out of touch with the confused political conditions in Russia, and Riezler's reports and recommendations became more and more forceful. On July 19 he declared:

The Bolsheviks are dead. Their corpse continues to live only because the grave-diggers could not agree upon who should bury it. The struggle which is today being conducted on Russian soil between us and the Entente is no longer a struggle for the favor of the corpse; it has now become a struggle over the successor, over the orientation of the future Russia.

Riezler was attempting to combat the thinking in the Foreign Office that a chaotic situation in Russia was still to Germany's advantage; he believed that chaos now opened the door to the Entente, which could exploit the unpopular Brest-Litovsk Treaty and use the Czechoslovakian division, Czech patriots who, though trapped in Russia, composed perhaps the most effective military force within Russia. On the other hand, Germany had only one crucial advantage: "the deep need of the Russian people for peace." Bourgeois and monarchist Russians know that peace could come only from cooperation with the Germans, whereas cooperation with the Entente would bring Russia back into the war. Riezler argued that Germany must utilize this advantage in its favor. Specifically, a German-oriented, bourgeois-monarchist government should be helped to power in Moscow and Petrograd. By promising peace and order, such a government could upset the entire counterrevolutionary hopes of the Entente. In order to counter the arguments of the Supreme Military Command, Riezler argued explicitly that only a bourgeois Russia which controlled all her prewar territories could provide the raw materials and economic advantages which Germany needed. Certainly Germany should "visibly withdraw her protective hand from the Bolsheviks through some kind of act and lend her prestige to the new order." Numerous telegrams from Riezler indicate exactly which visible act he had in mind—the severance of diplomatic relations allegedly due to unsatisfactory clarification of the Mirbach murder. Though security of the mission was not unimportant to him, he was seeking a dramatic signal for a change of policy.[71]

Within one week Riezler reported in detail the contacts he had established so that the Foreign Office could have a much clearer idea of how counterrevolution could succeed. Foreign Minister Hintze summarized Riezler's recommendations on July 26: Due to internal pressure from the Left Social Revolutionaries and to external pressure from the Entente, who had begun large-scale landings of troops at Murmansk on the first of July, "the power of the Bolsheviks is at an end." Therefore, Germany must consider which successors would best serve her interests, and Riezler identified four: (1) the Moscow Kadets (Constitutional Democrats), (2) monarchists, whose base was in Petrograd, (3) the Siberian government in Omsk, (4) the Cossacks in the Don area.[72]

Riezler concluded that if Germany chose to lead the counterrevolution in Russia, then she could count on support from all four groups. The Entente could expect support only from the Czechoslovakians within Russia, Right Social Revolutionaries, Mensheviks, leftist Kadets, and a few officer organizations. Success in Moscow would depend primarily on the disposition of the Latvian troops, whose loyalty Riezler thought could be won if Germany offered them enough money and promised them safe passage back to Latvia. Complete success could be expected only if a well-timed and organized simultaneous uprising in Moscow and Petrograd linked with military advances from the Ukraine, the Don area, and Siberia were to take place. A successful transfer of power in Moscow would be crucial, but a change of regime for entire Russia could not be expected until a definite German decision on the revision or renunciation of the Brest-Litovsk Treaty had been made. Riezler repeatedly emphasized that a revision of the Brest-Litovsk Treaty was the *sine qua non* for a successful German policy in Russia. If the Treaty were revised, then an anti-Entente "colorless coalition with a program of order, peace and liberation from the Bolsheviks" could be kept in power. Such a coalition would definitely serve Germany's interests, he argued.[73]

157

Riezler's recommendations to the Foreign Office were not only rejected, but they obviously irritated Germany's foreign policy makers in Berlin, who were bracing themselves for the ominous consequences of the collapsing final German offensive on the western front. Not only was Riezler kept uninformed about many matters important to him as Germany's diplomatic representative in Moscow, but a plan was being considered in the Foreign Office to employ German military force to put the Bolsheviks back into power in case a successful uprising against them occurred. Tension between the Foreign Office and the Moscow mission had become almost unbearable. In the deadlock Riezler rejoiced that Karl Helfferich was appointed on July 20 as Mirbach's successor "because if I remain alone, there will be trouble with Berlin. . . . The bigger the cannon, the better."[74]

Since the assassination of Mirbach, security was so strictly observed by all but Riezler that life at the embassy was similar to internment. In fact, security for German personnel was such a problem that Helfferich was taken to Moscow in a heavily armed Russian train, which stopped suddenly fourteen kilometers outside of Moscow. Riezler and the Bolshevik Karl Radek appeared immediately to take Helfferich inconspicuously by car to the embassy.[75]

Riezler found it obvious that Helfferich had been sent to Moscow "in order to switch off my reporting, which is not convenient in Berlin's eyes." Very quickly, however, Riezler convinced Helfferich that the position which the Moscow mission had taken was correct. Indeed, it was not difficult for newcomers in Moscow to see how untenable the situation for the Germans was. Since the new chief of mission left the German mission only once during the ten days he was in Moscow, his picture of the actual Russian political situation was painted mainly by Riezler. "With his precision and trenchancy and his confidence in his influence on the Supreme Military Command and His Majesty," Helfferich began sending reports and recommendations which were exactly in line with Riezler's thinking: severence of diplomatic relations or at least removal of the German mission from Moscow, revision of the Brest-Litovsk Treaty, negotiations with bourgeois and monarchist groups, and military support of counterrevolutionary groups.[76]

One recommendation of Helfferich particularly bears the stamp of Riezler's thinking. A few days after Helfferich arrived in Moscow, Chicherin visited him and proposed a strange plan for German military action on Russian soil. First, German troops would advance from Finland, avoiding Russian cities, to intercept the Anglo-French interventionist forces moving down from Murmansk and Archangel. Second, using her troops in the Ukraine, Germany would attack anti-Bolshevik forces in the Don Cossack region. Years later Chicherin revealed the true intentions behind this plan both to Louis Fischer and to the Soviet press. Lenin, Chicherin reported, "made an attempt to exploit the antagonism of the two belligerent imperialist coalitions in order to weaken the Entente offensive." Thus, in desperation Lenin attempted to direct Germany's and the Entente's hostilities against one another.

Because he depended on Riezler's assessment of the political situation, Helfferich's recommendation was in all likelihood conceived by Riezler. The Moscow mission recommended that Germany ostensibly agree to the Bolshevik plan and make the necessary military preparations. Germany should, however, "in the last minute join the Cossack leaders against the Bolsheviks." Duplicity was indeed a game which Riezler could play as well as Lenin.[77]

Hintze was not persuaded by Helfferich's recommendations and merely repeated his earlier instructions to continue supporting the Bolsheviks. He argued that the mission's departure from Moscow would mean severance of diplomatic relations with Russia, and such severance would not be in Germany's interest. Thus, the mission should remain unless the lives of the German diplomatic personnel in Moscow were seriously threatened. Riezler concluded that Berlin was only interested in signing more treaties with the Bolsheviks; Germany's relations with the "future Russia" had not been considered.[78]

Riezler and the members of the mission were indignant that the decision concerning removal of the mission had been left to them; such an important political decision should only be made in Berlin. Helfferich had demanded from the kaiser and the Foreign Office a clear decision on the policy which Germany should pursue in Russia. Instead of making such a decision, Hintze and the kaiser ordered Helfferich to return to Berlin immediately for consultations. On August 6, the day he departed from Moscow, Helfferich transferred the mission to Petrograd and returned responsibility for the mission to Riezler.[79]

From Petrograd Riezler hoped to continue work on the counterrevolution, and on August 9 he reported that he had received confirmation of the "German orientation" within the Siberian Provisional government. However, the Foreign Office was definitely not interested in counterrevolution and ordered the German mission to be withdrawn from Petrograd to behind the German lines. When Riezler informed the Bolsheviks of the departure, he understandably met with distrust; Lenin thought that Riezler had panicked, and Radek was positive that Riezler would never return to Russia. Lenin was wrong, but Radek was right.

159

Wayne C. Thompson

Riezler took the mission on a circuitous journey over Helsinki to Reval, from where he left for a vacation in Oberstdorf. His responsibility for Russian affairs had ended.[80]

During his holiday in Oberstdorf Riezler reflected on some of the problems of Germany's fragmented *Ostpolitik*. First, the establishment of an independent Ukraine might have worked if one had allowed Ukrainians to rule. Instead, men were put into power who were both Kadets and non-Ukrainians, people who "have to try very hard to speak the Ukrainian language, which they tried to cram into their heads quickly. . . . We saw immediately in Moscow that one cannot be 'Kadetish' in Kiev and pro-Bolshevik in Moscow."[81]

Second, the German military was permitted to continue its advance beyond the lines established at Brest-Litovsk. As a result, not only were Russian nationalists and Left Social Revolutionaries incensed, but the Bolsheviks were greatly weakened because they were cut off from Baku and their grain supplies in Kuban.

If one wishes to support the Bolsheviks, to use them to purge the Russians' hatred toward us, then one must allow the Bolsheviks to live; one must not deprive them of one vital necessity after another, disorient and cheat them every week through a new ultimatum: Kursk, Rostov, Novorossisk.

Hunger had led to rebellions and assassinations, and the Bolsheviks felt compelled to respond with terror.[82]

Riezler initially criticized the Foreign Office not so much because it continued to support the Bolsheviks, but because it was unable to restrain the military. Once the Bolsheviks had been dangerously weakened, he believed that counterrevolution and a revision of the Brest-Litovsk Treaty were essential. Not only was such revision a precondition for cooperation with counterrevolutionary groups, but the deteriorating military situation in the West made the annexation of entire provinces in the East impossible. Nevertheless, the Foreign Office failed to perceive the need for a radical change of policy. By not joining the counterrevolution soon enough, Germany played into the hands of the Entente:

Now England will again be able to liberate Russia from Germany and to win Russia for herself. What a game is lost here! The ignorance and despotism of the Supreme Military Command, the errors of the Foreign Office . . . the disconnectedness of both authorities—what an opportunity and what charlatanism. And that *Volk* wants to be a world *Volk* and conquer England. What mockery![83]

160

Riezler's analysis of Germany's unsuccessful Russian policy is quite perceptive, but it leaves some very important questions unanswered: was there really a good chance for the counterrevolution, which Riezler wanted, to have succeeded? Of course, the Germans could always have withdrawn their financial support from the Bolsheviks. Perhaps Hintze was correct, however, in considering "the collection of several groups for a unified action as impossible"; with regard to a German military intervention in Russia, Hintze was of the opinion "that any military support on our part would soon require forces which could in no way be provided by the Supreme Military Command." Also, based on Germany's negative wartime experience in applying methods of indirect rule to establish *Mitteleuropa,* could it have been expected that the German military, the kaiser, and the German public would have accepted the voluntary restraint on their claims to Russian territory, which was the precondition for cooperation with bourgeois and monarchist groups? Indeed, the absence of any effective domestic pressure within Germany for a moderate policy toward the East strengthened the hand of those who saw Russia only as an object of short-term exploitation.[84]

The extremely dismal prospects for the Bolsheviks' retention of power led Riezler to discount the difficulties of his proposed counterrevolution. The Bolsheviks were indeed in serious trouble; the regime was shaken by hunger revolts and threatened from the east, west and south by counterrevolution and Entente intervention. It was also threatened within its own camp by the bitter hostility between Bolsheviks and Social Revolutionaries. Discouragement shone through the official optimism of the Bolsheviks; it has even been reported that Lenin suggested that the Bolsheviks leave Moscow because all was lost.[85] Riezler asked: if the Bolsheviks were going to fall, why should German interests suffer with them?

What a post-Bolshevik Russia would have looked like is a question which Riezler appears not to have taken seriously at the time. Could the counterrevolutionary groups with which Riezler had contact have worked together after a successful uprising? For example, could monarchists in Petrograd have worked together with those from the Siberian government, who, like the Kerensky government, demanded a constituent assembly? Given the social and economic conditions in post-tsarist Russia, which group or groups might have had the best long-range chance of establishing order in Russia? Was it realistic to expect a new non-Bolshevik coalition, whatever its composition, to support the German war effort against the Entente, especially given Germany's decreasing military strength on the western front? There is no evidence that Riezler paid sufficient attention to such questions. His analysis and recommendations were perhaps inevitably dictated to an excessive degree by purely short-term tactical calculation. He realized sooner than most German leaders that there was no possibility of lasting cooperation between two so different political and social systems as the Bolshevik and German; nevertheless, he, like other German leaders at the time, was never able to resolve the problem of short versus long range German objectives in the East. In the final analysis, Riezler offered no feasible alternative to the Russian policy of the German Foreign Office or military.

Finally, the rapid deterioration of the military situation in the West eliminated the basis for any German-conceived solution in Russia, including Riezler's. Ultimately, Germany's *Ostpolitik* was a factor dependent upon events on the western front. On August 8 the German front in the West broke for the first time, and this "black day" was the prelude to the German military collapse. Even Ludendorff admitted that "the war must be ended." Germany's collapse placed the burden for counterrevolution in Russia on the shoulders of the Entente, which abandoned the enterprise a few years later. The Bolsheviks were able to consolidate their power and ironically were eventually led out of international isolation by the newly-founded German republic.[86] But the new Russia was by no means the "future Russia" which Riezler had envisaged at the time of Lenin's transport to Russia or at the time of the signing of the Brest-Litovsk Treaty. Political calculation which completely disregarded ideology had exacted a severe penalty. The marionettes which were to serve Germany's short-term interests became giant figures in world politics.

Chapter Six
REVOLUTION IN GERMANY

All around [us are] Workers' and Soldiers' Councils which [are] more or less Bolshevik republics. Berlin falls like a ripe piece of fruit; the troops desert. . . .

—Kurt Riezler

PEACE

The autumn peace and beauty which Riezler shared in the Alpine resort of Oberstdorf stood in sharp contrast to the country which was collapsing around him. Riezler was not able to get his mind off Germany's desperate situation, which had by no means come suddenly. Early in 1918 Hamburg, Leipzig, Cologne, Munich and the heavily industrialized Ruhr area had experienced serious strikes, and in Berlin 200,000 munitions workers had struck. These strikes were in large part due to hunger stemming from the effective British blockade of Germany; by January 1918, the average rations for German civilians had been cut to only one thousand calories per day.

The tension was greatly increased by a worsening of the military situation. The cease-fire on the eastern front had not led to large-scale transfers of German troops from the eastern to the western front, which would have enhanced prospects for a German victory in France. These troops were especially needed to match the numbers of American troops which began arriving in France in the spring of 1918. At the time when Germany's last great offensive was launched on March 21, 1918, Germany had only a slight superiority in numbers, whereas success in frontal assaults was possible only by overwhelming superiority. Despite initial successes, no breakthrough was made, and by June the offensive was clearly a failure. The exhausted Germans were unable to cope with the Allied counteroffensive, which began July 18 and which was supported by more than one million well-equipped American troops. On August 8, known to Germans as "black Friday," British infantry, supported by tanks, broke through the German lines at Amiens. The German troops in

163

France could only retreat. On August 14 Ludendorff was forced to admit in the Crown Council that the war could no longer be won militarily.

The effect of these setbacks was obvious and shocking to Riezler, who had returned to Berlin from the Soviet Union in August. He observed a changed atmosphere in Berlin:

Nearly everything has changed. . . . Revolution and defeat, the dual fear of the bourgeoisie. All talk about the former, with the exception of the Social Democrats; no one dares to speak of the latter, and even the most sober do not know what it [defeat] means. It is all terribly sad.

He also saw ominous parallels with prerevolutionary Russia: "the same weariness and fatalism on the part of the ones who know; the incipient lawlessness and anarchy from below, and blindness pervades everything so that everything stumbles into ruin."[1]

Riezler's vacation was interrupted by a telegram from Diego von Bergen, director of the political section of the Foreign Office, who asked Riezler to aid in the effort to replace the aged, incompetent, and indecisive chancellor, Count Georg Hertling. Upon returning to Berlin the evening of September 22, Riezler found an "unbelievable mess." The loyalty of Vienna was doubted by all, and Hertling's government was not respected by anyone, especially not by the enemy. For Riezler the latter problem was particularly serious because, to him, the crucial matter at this point was to have a government which could negotiate successfully with the Allies:

To make every effort to avoid the complete collapse and at least to be able to negotiate. The prospects are slim. If it comes to negotiations, then the inability of Russia to negotiate, the common interest of all against the Bolsheviks will be significant; the same applies to the partition of Turkey. But where is the statesman?[2]

Riezler was not alone in believing that Bethmann Hollweg was the only man who could perform the difficult tasks which lay immediately ahead. Bethmann was the statesman whom the hour demanded "because of his *savoir faire,* authority and force—because the potential negotiators trust him, and the enemy would have confidence that he would hold the German people together." Riezler was asked to broach the subject with the former chancellor, but he was uncomfortable about his assignment; it was difficult to ask a man whom he admired to assume responsibility for the desperate situation, to negotiate a bad peace, or even to preside over a disintegrating Germany where nothing could be saved. This would be a very cruel fate for a man who had already suffered so much indignity.

Riezler spoke with Bethmann Hollweg at Hohenfinow about the possibility, but the former chancellor rejected it "openly and very angrily." Bethmann Hollweg could not forget what had happened during his chancellorship. Riezler was disappointed, but he was not without hope that after the peace had been achieved Bethmann Hollweg could assume the role of pulling the German Empire back together.

In Riezler's opinion, the only other acceptable choice was Friedrich Ebert, Bebel's successor as leader of the Social Democratic Party of Germany; Ebert was "concrete, sturdy and calm." However, it was clear that Germany was not quite ready to accept a Social Democrat as chancellor; in fact, Riezler sensed that "the right wanted to set up a dictatorship without delay. This cannot bring about a peace, and only peace can rescue us from revolution."[3]

On September 30, 1918, Hertling finally resigned and was replaced three days later by Prince Max von Baden, the crown prince of the southern German state of Baden. Riezler found Prince Max a decent person, though "naturally an utter dilettante, who allows himself to be advised by numerous outsiders, [and] believes everyone." For the first time in German history, a new government was formed with the participation of Parliament. The same three majority parties which, to Riezler's great displeasure, had voted for the Peace Resolution of July 1917 had representatives in the new cabinet. For the first time, a Social Democrat, Philipp Scheidemann, had assumed a position of responsibility in the German central government. Though this was a significant step in the direction of parliamentary government, Riezler was not pleased by the innovation. Not only had men been appointed to cabinet positions for reasons of party loyalty and not of ability, a democratic necessity which Riezler had difficulty accepting, but the need to have three parties' approval for all major decisions led to endless haggling. This condition ultimately contributed to an almost complete inability to cope with the many demands which were flooding the ministries in Berlin.[4]

On October 6, Riezler was named cabinet chief for Wilhelm Solf, newly-appointed state secretary for foreign affairs. Until the end of the war, Riezler's attention would be directed exclusively to the peace terms to be negotiated with the enemy. The road to a cease-fire was cluttered with problems. Among the most serious problems facing Germany were the collapse of Austria, pressure from the German Supreme Military Command for an immediate cease-fire, and revolutionary activity within Germany herself. On September 29, Ludendorff had communicated to the Supreme Headquarters that "the present condition of our army demands an immediate cease-fire in order to avoid catastrophe." On October 3, the day Prince Max took office, Hindenburg responded in the negative to the chancellor's question whether the army could hold on a little longer in order to enable better political preparation for the armistice to be made. Hindenburg referred to the situation on the front which was daily growing worse and judged that "under these circumstances it is necessary to break off the fight in order to spare the German people and its allies needless victims. Every lost day costs thousands of brave soldiers their lives."[5]

Riezler was irritated that Ludendorff "had lost his nerve" at such a critical time and that the general was so naive as to think that a peace could be made overnight. Riezler noted repeated attempts by political leaders to stiffen the spine of the military so that a somewhat less desperate appeal for favorable terms could be made to President Wilson. At the same time, Riezler saw clearly the outlines of an emerging "stab in the back" theory from the military. He wrote on October 13: "The Supreme Military Command is very broken, but the word is still disseminated that the civilian government which has lost its nerve bears the full responsibility for the peace move, etc., etc. One is neither able nor permitted to contradict this."[6]

Germany's negotiating position was further weakened by the dissolution of the Austro-Hungarian Empire. Riezler was convinced that Germany could not ignore events in Austria. Some actions, such as feeding Vienna or aiding in the foundation of a new Austrian state and in the occupation of German Bohemia, appeared to him to be necessary in order to prevent hunger and despair from leading to strikes and revolution; he was sure that such events would inevitably spill over into Germany. He also advocated a step from which he never turned throughout the Weimar Republic: "We must absorb German-Austria. Everyone talks about that, but no one realizes that that means reordering the Empire and remodeling the Bismarckian constitution from the bottom up."[7]

Germany's moves to establish peace with the Entente were opened by a note to President Wilson on October 3, 1918, invoking the president's Fourteen Points and requesting the "immediate arrangement of a ceasefire on land, at sea, and in the air." Wilson's answers to this letter on October 8 and 14 were received in Berlin with indignation. In the second letter Wilson's demands included guarantees for the continuation of the Entente's military superiority and the destruction of Germany's military power, "which up to now has determined the fate of the German nation." Wilson later demanded the abdication of the kaiser as a precondition for negotiations.[8]

Riezler was not pleased with Wilson's demands, but he was not astonished by them, unlike many of those around him, for whom the defeat was just beginning to seem like a real possibility. "All of them are red in the face. Each gives answers in which proud retorts are directed toward the fool Wilson. Then one throws the answers in the waste paper basket and remembers that one is defeated and that the defeated accomplish nothing with the best arguments." Riezler clearly favored acceptance of Wilson's terms, including the kaiser's abdication, because he saw no alternative. "Should one partially capitulate or answer proudly now, only to have to capitulate entirely in two months? Better the former and save a part of the army in order that resistance can be made later."[9] He was undoubtedly right that Germany had to accept the terms.

Riezler actively participated in the drafting of the notes in answer to President Wilson, although the exact extent of his participation is unknown. He was greatly discouraged by both the way the work had to be accomplished and by the general uncertainty into which Germany was moving. He complained of "session after session" to discuss the wording and the terms; "everyone adds his own two cents' worth—that will not work at all." Others who worked with Riezler regarded his general pessimism and apparent indecision as a problem. Kurt Hahn, a close associate of Prince Max at the time, described Riezler as a "sleeping poison." Indeed, Riezler was quite dejected about the effect of the defeat on Germany's uncertain future. Early in October he wrote in his diary that

I stare continually into the darkness. That one cannot howl like a little palace dog. . . . The Germans? What will they represent? A sneer at so much stupidity. And to think that victory could have been ours with a little less *hubris*.[10]

No amount of careful drafting of notes could change the reality which the defeated Germany had to face. Her armies were retreating, her allies crumbling, her people starving. Out of an atmosphere of "deepest disheartenment," a German delegation departed from Berlin on November 7, 1918, to seek peace with the Entente. They left behind a Germany shaken by strikes and revolution.

In such a chaotic time, the German delegation met General Foch in the famous rail car at Compiègne on November 8, 1918. When the leader of the delegation, Matthias Erzberger, asked for Foch's suggestions for a cease-fire, Foch stated icely that "I have no suggestions to make." Foch delivered only undiscussable conditions which Germany could either take or leave. Riezler had predicted severe terms, but the conditions were more severe than anyone had believed possible: the thirty-four articles included the withdrawal of the German army to the eastern bank of the Rhine, withdrawal from Belgium, France and Alsace-Lorraine, Entente occupation of the left bank of the Rhine and delivery to the Entente of all German submarines and heavy military and transport materials. Germany was given until 11:00 A.M., November 11, to accept or reject the terms. Responsible Germans, including Riezler, saw no alternative but to accept the terms and to end the war, which had already cost Germany more than two million lives.[11]

REVOLUTION

Before the German delegation could sign the cease-fire on November 11, the empire had ceased to exist. The critical day had been November 9. When the majority Social Democrats learned that the kaiser had decided not to abdicate, Philipp Scheidemann announced that the Social Democrats were withdrawing from the government. Under increasing pressure from striking workers waving red flags outside the Chancellery, and unable to reestablish contact with the kaiser's villa in Spa, Prince Max simply announced the abdication of the kaiser and ordered his aides to begin phoning the newspapers.

A short time later, Scheidemann, who was having lunch in the Reichstag building, was informed by a group of workers that Karl Liebknecht was speaking from the balcony of the royal palace and was about to proclaim the Soviet Republic. Scheidemann recounted later:

Now I clearly saw what was afoot. I knew his slogan—supreme authority for the workers' and soldiers' councils. Germany to be therefore a Russian province, a branch of the Soviet. No, no, a thousand times no! . . . I [went to the window of the Reichstag and] said a few words, which were received with tremendous cheering. 'Workers and soldiers . . . the cursed war is at an end. . . . The Emperor has abdicated . . . Long live the new! Long live the German Republic![12]

Scheidemann's fears foreshadowed the bloody disputes over the question which was to wrack Germany for several years—what kind of republic should take the place of the fallen monarchy?

Riezler was now convinced that the kind of republic which Scheidemann had called to life and helped to lead was the best form of government for a highly industrialized society such as Germany. It alone could overcome the deep social divisions and attract enough popular support to maintain order and to protect the nation from the extremes of right and left, of mindless reaction and anarchy. It alone could undercut the separatist movements which threatened the nation and provide the firm domestic backing for the difficult diplomatic road ahead. The old regime had clearly failed in these tasks. A more modern approach was needed. This did not mean that he had become a thorough-going democrat at heart, but he saw correctly that public support of the Republic was the most practical and realistic course. He was a *Vernunftrepublikaner* (common-sense republican), who denounced all metaphysical, speculative, romantic, abstract, nationalistic, and mystical politics. In the fourteen years until Hitler's assumption of power, Riezler never ceased publicly to support the Republic and to oppose the communist and conservative revolutions which undermined it.[13]

The events which immediately followed the declaration of the Republic involved, by comparison with later convulsions in Weimar Germany, relatively little violence. At no time was streetcar, telegraph, electric, gas, and water service interrupted. Nevertheless, there were about fifteen deaths and considerable confusion in Berlin, and in his final diary entry, Riezler decribed the chaos which had befallen Germany;

All around [us are] workers' and soldiers' councils which [are] more or less Bolshevist republics. Berlin falls like a ripe piece of fruit; the troops desert; while the front disintegrates, the severest cease-fire which was ever made is signed and must be signed. Meanwhile chaos in Berlin; the garrison is dissolved, and the only remaining question is which workers' and soldiers' council maintains the upper hand and whether Liebknecht can take over the scarcely guarded strategic positions [in the city] with a handful of fanatics. This danger seems less acute now, . . . but to make things worse, the new army formed from the disintegrated armies east and west is arriving, returning without work or provisions. While we hold on to occupied territory as far as Rostow, everything collapses even to the point that the Poles are marching today against Upper Silesia and Posen. The bourgeoisie seems to have disappeared, and the president and members of the Parliament have gone home. A miserable sight—out of fear the press is silent.[14]

No sooner had the Republic been declared on November 9 than demands began to be made for a "second revolution." Upon assuming the chancellorship of the new German Republic, Friedrich Ebert proclaimed certain reforms including eventual socialization of basic industries. However, he made no secret about the fact that his emphasis, as well as the emphasis of the majorities within the three parties which composed the governing "Weimar Coalition," was upon the establishment of order and of a parliamentary-democratic political structure in the shaken country. Ebert, the pragmatist, was not interested in the kind of social revolution which would have brought radical and far-reaching social changes to German society.

169

Some people held Ebert's position to be nothing less than "counter-revolution" and betrayal. Rosa Luxemburg remarked sarcastically: "Oh how German this German Revolution is! How proper, how pedantic, how lacking in verve and in grandeur." It was not long before some groups chose force against Ebert's government as the only key of effecting the "second revolution." The rallying cry was that power be transferred to the workers' and soldiers' councils, which had sprung up in numerous cities throughout Germany.[15]

No one was more sensitive about the rise of such workers' and soldiers' councils than Riezler. He saw that the councils represented a radical decentralization and, in some instances, could become instruments through which foreign powers, especially the Soviet Union, could exert damaging influence over German internal affairs. He had watched with horror as the Bolsheviks, whom he had helped place on stage temporarily in order to serve Germany's short-term interests, had consolidated their rule and now appeared to be exporting revolution westward. Indeed, many Bolsheviks were convinced that only by revolutionizing the rest of Europe and the world could the fledgling Soviet Republic be preserved. Riezler saw great danger presented by this development; the possible results of such a revolution could be observed only too clearly in chaotic Russia: Russia had been so weakened by civil war that for several years she was hardly able to function as a state and was almost completely disregarded in world affairs. Also, she was ruled by what he saw as a small group of fanatical ideologues, who in no way ruled in the interest of all the citizens. Council rule was, in Riezler's view, nothing but a prelude to seizure and control of the state by a small, ruthless minority.

Thus, Riezler strongly opposed the "second revolution" as it was taking shape. Berlin was full of rumors that Karl Liebknecht and his radical following would stage a putsch against the Social Democratic government. Ebert was entirely uncertain about what to do in the event of such a putsch. In a meeting in the Chancellery on December 26, Riezler gave a report on the revolutionary situation and recommended that since there were so few reliable troops, the best thing to do under the circumstances was to move the German government to another city, preferably Weimar. According to Count Harry Kessler, all the men present at that meeting expected to be arrested that night or the next morning by putschists led by Liebknecht. After the meeting Riezler went with others to the royal palace, which had been stormed by workers two days earlier, in order to witness the declaration of Liebknecht as head of a new radical government. Kessler remembered that an "intellectual" was arguing that the German people were not ready for political power and therefore needed not a national assembly, but workers' and soldiers' councils. Riezler, after attempting to argue with the man, reportedly "ran into trouble, got scared, wanted to leave and was scornfully pursued by the mob."[16]

Indeed, the next three weeks witnessed significant events which threatened the Republic in its infancy. On December 29 the Independent Social Democrats left the governing coalition, and on December 30 the Communist Party of Germany (KPD) was formed. On the same day, Franz Seldte founded the *Stahlhelm* (Steel Helmet) League, a right-wing para-military organization of disenchanted war veterans. The fatal split in German society which would paralyze and ultimately destroy the young Republic continued to widen. The new German Republic clearly found itself in a crisis from which it would never be able to extricate itself.

The Communists made two unsuccessful violent attempts to seize power in Berlin. The first occurred from January 6-12, 1919, and more than a thousand lives were lost in putting it down. The second erupted during the first two weeks of March 1919. After two thousand deaths and considerable destruction to the city of Berlin, the rebellion was quelled. Riezler favored the suppression of the uprisings by *Freikorps* (Free Corps) units, despite the heavy loss of lives. Clearly, he wanted at all costs to defend the first revolution, the one which had occurred November 9. This became unmistakably evident as a result of his part in the ruthless suppression of the Bavarian Soviet Republic.[17]

Riezler's native city of Munich was the site of the first republic to be proclaimed in twentieth-century Germany. Two days before Scheidemann proclaimed the German Republic, Kurt Eisner, a journalist and pacifist Independent Socialist, launched an attempt to lead Bavaria into socialism. He advocated immediate "democratization and socialization of the economy and administration by means of a Council Republic." A Workers', Soldiers' and Peasants' Council assumed all power, and command of the hastily formed "Red Army" was given to the sailor Rudolf Egelhofer. Eisner faced the immediate problems of managing the revolution he had declared.

On January 12, 1919, the final day of the Spartacist uprising in Berlin, Eisner suffered a serious setback in the state parliamentary election. Convinced that he had been rejected by the people, Eisner decided to resign. However, on February 20 while he was on his way to the State Parliament Building to arrange a transfer of power, a young student, Count Anton Arco-Valley, fired two bullets into Eisner's head. Arco's action, far from restoring the authority of the State Parliament, as he had intended, was a miraculous reprieve for the socialist revolution, which

171

had already died out in most other parts of Germany; the assassination sparked a second and far more radical revolution in Munich. Determined revolutionaries declared the dictatorship of the "Central Council of Workers', Peasants' and Soldiers' Councils," took hostages and armed the workers "for the security of the revolution."[18]

Within a few days the lawlessness died down, and the revolution took a more moderate turn. The fifty hostages who had been taken a few days earlier were released, and plans for the establishment of a "Workers' Army" and a socialist soviet republic in Bavaria were abandoned. In mid-March the State Parliament met without incident, and after feverish negotiations full authority was granted to a cabinet under Majority Social Democrat, Johannes Hoffmann, who promised a broad program of socialization and who appeared to be determined to lead the revolution between the extremes of left and right. Bavarian political leaders seemed to be recognizing the political and legal predominance of parliamentary government. Nevertheless, the Central Council, an organ composed of representatives of various workers' councils in Munich and other Bavarian cities, not only continued to exist, but had been granted on March 8 the right to demand a referendum on any action of the State Parliament.[19]

Riezler feared an untenable dualism in Munich and remained skeptical that the moderates, especially the Majority Social Democrats, could restrain the radicals and retain control. For a Bavarian, Riezler showed a surprising disdain for other Bavarians at this time. In early April 1919, he said in private to Count Kessler that the Bavarian people were a "people of sows *(Sauvolk),*" who were "emotional and unstable." Publicly, he wrote that he, "a Bavarian, can say it: Bavaria has shamed itself right down to its bones."[20] He was referring to Bavaria's continued refusal to pattern its political life according to the republican model accepted and advocated by the German central government. Not without reason, Riezler considered that model to be the only one which could protect Germans from the dangers of dictatorship or helplessness in the face of the European powers.

In the first week of March, Riezler was sent by the Foreign Office to Munich in order to evaluate political developments in that city. On March 9, he sent a report to Berlin strongly condemning the actions of the Central Council and especially the provision to grant the councils the right to call a referendum on any parliamentary act. He stressed that the "situation cannot be taken seriously enough." He described the dilemma as follows:

The State Parliament is confronted with the choice between committing suicide by accepting the demands [for the continuing existence of the councils and for the right to demand a referendum] or rejecting them with the support of the bourgeois votes. In the first case, the return to democracy is as good as blocked, at least because the State Parliament would lose its entire prestige; in the second case commences the complete division of the land into a socialist camp resting on the council system and a bourgeois camp resting on democracy, a development which cannot persist without repercussions on the Reich as a whole, especially in light of the fact that the completely leaderless and spineless [Bavarian] Majority Socialists would then slide completely into the train of the radicals. In our opinion social democracy would disintegrate if it left the democratic basis.

In this document Riezler clearly expressed his preference for a democracy which functions through parliament; in his opinion, there was no democracy at all in the council system. This judgment was certainly based on his experience with the Russian Revolution where the councils had been perverted by becoming mere tools in the hands of a minority.[21]

To counter what he saw to be a dangerous trend, Riezler proposed what became generally known in Berlin as "the Riezler plan," which had two parts. He advocated, first, that Berlin dispatch to Bavaria not only telegrams, but also respected Social Democratic parliamentarians in order personally to dissuade "local Majority Socialists from leaving the foundation of democracy; and if they momentarily are forced to give in to the council thinking, that they at least specify certain conditions which would keep their hands untied." The second recommendation dealt with the danger that a soviet republic might be declared: "Once the Bavarian *Freikorps* has grown to sufficient strength, the State Parliament and Prime Minister [should] declare its own sovereignty and assemble in northern Bavaria, from where it, with the political support of the Reich government, could then very quickly bring the entire state behind it and watch the local [Munich] economy collapse on its own." Riezler closed this message with the observation that "the revolution must maintain the same tempo in the larger federal states. A variation in tempo toward left and then toward right would inevitably rip the Reich apart, given the present foreign political situation." Clearly, Riezler was greatly concerned not only with the threats to democracy in Germany but also with Germany's ability to face the threat posed by Germany's European neighbors. Riezler's plan was accepted by the Foreign Office in Berlin and was put into action immediately.[22]

Within a couple of weeks Riezler's fears that radicals would gain the upper hand in Munich proved to be well-founded. An ominous signal had come from Budapest, where a Hungarian Soviet Republic had been proclaimed on March 22, under the leadership of Bela Kun. Lenin sent greetings in the name of the Third International to that new soviet republic.

The idea of a council republic also appeared to be gaining more and more strength in Bavaria. On April 3, a council assembly in Augsburg adopted by a large majority a "resolution in favor of a Bavarian Soviet Republic, an alliance with the soviet governments of Russia and Hungary, and a program of full socialization." When delegates from Augsburg arrived in Munich to present the resolution to the cabinet, Hoffmann had already left for consultations in Berlin. Without their leader, the Social Democrats were unwilling to take a stand on the resolution. The Central Council also refused to make a decision on the resolution, but took the dangerous step of postponing the convocation of the State Parliament which had been scheduled for April 8.[23]

This refusal to take an immediate and negative position on the resolution appeared to leave the question of the soviet republic open. Munich suddenly became again "a city of public meetings, protests, plots, resolutions—and confusion." On April 4 an assembly of soldiers declared that in the event of a general strike in Munich, their "sympathies will lie on the side of the workers." On the same evening a resolution was proposed to a mass meeting in Munich's Löwenbräu Beer Cellar demanding, among other things, the "elimination of parties, union of the entire proletariat, proclamation of a soviet republic and brotherhood with the Russian and Hungarian proletariat." Clearly, Minister President Hoffmann's policy of attempting to pacify radical council leaders while maintaining the legal authority of the State Parliament had failed; Riezler's suspicions were confirmed. A daring move was about to be made to end the deadlock between the parliamentary and council systems. On Sunday, April 6, a rump session of the Central Council was convened in the Wittelsbach Palace in Munich and drafted the text of a proclamation. The next morning, April 7, Munich's streetcorners were decorated with signs reading: "Bavaria is a Soviet Republic."[24]

Significantly, the new republic was supported neither by the Majority Social Democrats, whose leader was in Berlin, nor by the Communist Party. Though Riezler feared that Munich would become a mere stepping stone for the advance of Bolshevik Communism from the east, the Bavarian Communist Party refused to take part in a putsch "proclaimed from the green table" by undisciplined idealists. Indeed, the Bavarian citizenry was either indifferent to the events, as Riezler saw it, or bewildered by them, as the new leaders quickly realized. A notice to the Munich population was aimed at a confused citizenry: "Comrades! You do not know what a Soviet Republic means. You will tell it now by its work. The Soviet Republic will bring the new order." The new regime then proceeded as expected to socialize press and mines, to introduce special revolutionary tribunals to replace the existing judicial system, to establish a Red Army, and to express support for the "International for the World Revolution."[25]

On April 5, 1919, Riezler had informed a group of his friends that he was to be sent to Munich the next day "with a suitcase full of money" to activate his plan to evacuate the Majority Social Democratic government to northern Bavaria as soon as the council republic was declared. In accordance with the "Riezler plan," the Hoffmann government immediately moved its temporary seat to the northern Bavarian city of Bamberg and declared its determination to "remain the SINGLE possessor of power in Bavaria" and to be the sole authority "qualified to release legal regulations and to issue orders. . . ."[26] Of course, Hoffmann's major problem was to enforce that authority. Below the Danube in a triangle formed by the cities of Augsburg, Rosenheim, and Garmisch, the Bavarian Soviet Republic exercised full power. The legitimate Bavarian government had far too few troops to be confident that it could dislodge the revolutionary government in Munich without the help of the Reich. Hoffmann wanted to handle the Munich situation without outside intervention, if possible, in order to maintain the autonomy of Bavaria.

In Berlin the final decision was made on April 11 not to tolerate the Bavarian Soviet Republic any longer. After the French government had offered to send in troops and had threatened to cut off food supplies to Germany unless order were re-established everywhere in Germany, a policy which Riezler thought would have been disastrous for Germany, Ebert reacted rapidly by announcing that if the radical republic did not die of economic causes "in short order, a military procedure seems to be the only possible solution. Experience in other places has taught that the more quickly and the more thoroughly this is accomplished, the less resistance and bloodshed are to be expected." Correspondence from the Reich office in Bamberg indicates that Riezler supported this policy.[27] Perhaps the Reich government's policy of acting quickly was not always the wisest. In some cases, such as in Bremen a few weeks earlier, the council republics, if left alone, would have died on the vine because of their own incompetence and lack of popular support. In times of chaos and crisis, however, patience and far-sightedness are never in large supply.

Before the Reich could intervene in a serious way, the Hoffmann government attempted a desperate move in Munich against the

175

Bavarian Soviets. Before dawn on April 13, Palm Sunday, a detachment of troops loyal to the Hoffmann government stormed the Wittelsbach Palace and captured several members of the Central Council. A few hours later, posters were displayed in the city announcing that the Central Council had been deposed and the Hoffmann government restored. In the afternoon of the same day, however, supporters of the Bavarian Soviet government successfully counterattacked. The Bavarian Soviet Republic had been saved, but only temporarily.[28]

It was Hoffmann's unsuccessful attempt to regain authority in Munich which prompted the Communists to assume control of the Bavarian Soviet Republic. In the evening of April 13, while the battle was still raging, a meeting was convened in the downstairs of the Hofbräuhaus by Russian-born Eugen Leviné. He and the others present declared themselves to be the Factory and Soldiers' Councils of Munich and announced themselves as the *de facto* legislature of the Bavarian Soviet Republic. The Hofbräuhaus was made the parliament building of the Soviet regime. As the new chief executive, Leviné proclaimed the "genuine rule of the proletariat." This action was in open defiance of orders from Communist Party headquarters in Berlin, which had instructed the Bavarian organization to avoid violent action "even when a local or momentary success might be possible." Nevertheless, Leviné saw a Communist duty to "stand in the vanguard of the defenders" of the Soviet regime.[29]

The rise of Leviné to power merely confirmed Riezler's conviction that events in Bavaria would not only fatally weaken the Reich in this time of crisis, but that one was dealing with a Bolshevist revolution on the Russian model. In both the Bavarian and Russian cases, a few fanatics, profiting from the destructive consequences of war, supported by only a small fraction of the population, seized power in a large city in a desperate situation while all other political parties and groups were disunited and while a sufficient number of disciplined troops could not be massed against them. In both cases the aim was not only to seize power, but to destroy the existing state and social order. "The bourgeoisie must disappear completely," Leviné announced. Both established "Red Armies," did not hesitate to use terrorist actions, such as the taking of hostages, and proclaimed themselves to be a stage in the imminent world revolution. Riezler constantly referred to the Bavarian Communist leaders as "Russians," and to their methods as the "Russian technique." He deeply regretted that this "most un-Bavarian, most uncharacteristic of all revolutions" could happen in his native Bavaria and that Bavarians did so little to prevent the "foreign *literati* and adolescent blabbermouths" from seizing and holding power.[30]

176

The rhetoric which the new leaders used further strengthened Riezler's conviction that he was dealing with an expansion of Russian Bolshevism, which he himself had helped place in the saddle. Leviné's pronouncements had an understandably disturbing effect in Bamberg and Berlin: "Long live the Russian Soviet Republic"; "the proletarian revolution has come from the East"; "Communism is on the march." The Hoffmann and Berlin governments emphasized these pronouncements in order to strengthen the Bavarians' will to resist the Bavarian Soviet Republic. In actual fact, contacts between Moscow and the Bavarian Communists were very limited. Although Lenin had reportedly been elated about the November Revolution, he gave no more than perfunctory support for the Bavarian Revolution.[31] The precise nature of Moscow-Munich ties could not be known clearly at the time, however, and Riezler was only too aware of how the Bolsheviks had seized power in Moscow not to be sensitive of possible parallels in Germany. In any case, the threat which such uprisings presented to the first German Republic was very great, whether they were directed by Moscow or not.

As the chief representative of the Reich in Bamberg, where the Hoffmann government was temporarily located, Riezler helped bring about the fall of the Bavarian Soviet Republic. Indeed, the revolutionary regime found itself in a highly unfavorable situation: It could expect no help from the outside. Rumanian troops had invaded Hungary on April 10, and Russia was embroiled in a civil war which occupied Lenin's full attention. The Austrian Civil Guard *(Volkswehr)* had effectively quelled a Communist uprising in Vienna; thus Leviné could expect no assistance from the south. Northern Germany was already firmly under the control of the Reich government, and the other southern German states were unanimous in their support of the Hoffmann government in Bamberg.

In a flurry of reports and recommendations from Riezler to the Foreign Office in Berlin during the month of April 1919, Riezler's recommended tactic became clear. First, an effective siege had to be thrown around Munich. Riezler had recommended an embargo on deliveries of coal and oil into Munich which was so effective that within Munich every use of coal had to be approved by the highest administrative organ of the Soviet regime, the *Vollzugsrat*. The farmers of northern Bavaria, who had been disgusted by the Munich events, had already stopped most food deliveries to that city; as an indication of the food shortage, it became an act of "sabotage against the Soviet Republic" to churn milk into cheese or butter. Farmers had also cut the rail lines leading into Munich by destroying the tracks.[32]

177

Second, Riezler recommended that economic collapse be brought about by ordering the Reichsbank director in Munich not only to close all banks in the city, but also to lock up the gold and note reserves and to remove all keys from Munich. Riezler remembered that before and after seizing power, Lenin had derived considerable benefit from confiscating financial resources wherever he could in order to finance his activities. Indeed, Leviné soon found his regime in serious financial difficulty. To maintain the "Red Army" and to meet the most urgent expenses, the Soviet regime did what many financially desperate regimes do: it printed several million marks in emergency notes which were declared to be legal tender in Munich. This action was tantamount to a declaration of financial bankruptcy.[33]

Third, Riezler advocated dispatching national SPD leaders to Munich to encourage Bavarian Social Democrats to assert their leadership more forcefully in order to undercut Communist and radical strength. He distrusted what he called "the Bavarian method" of compromising with the radicals instead of facing them openly.[34] He obviously wanted the Bavarian Soviet Republic to collapse, rather than to be coaxed back into a power sharing arrangement in Bavaria.

Fourth and finally, Riezler wanted Hoffmann to use national troops in suppressing the Bavarian Soviet Republic in the event that it did not succumb soon. He not only wanted to ensure that the action against the Soviets would succeed, but he wanted to show that Bavaria was dependent upon the Reich and that Bavarian autonomy was an outdated fiction. It was Riezler's job to persuade Hoffmann to accept the Reich's aid.

Although Hoffmann opposed any Bavarian move away from the Reich, he wished to deal with the situation without Berlin's aid. He particularly did not want non-Bavarian troops to be used against Munich. However, despite all his efforts, he was unable to raise more than 8,000 Bavarian troops by mid-April. These troops, whose reliability was highly questionable, would have had to face a rumored (falsely, as it turned out) 25,000 troops of the "Red Army." Hoffmann therefore had no alternative to accepting Riezler's offer of troops from the Reich. On April 23 the Reich Defense Minister Gustav Noske, known to German radical revolutionaries as "Butcher Noske," authorized 20,000 *Freikorps* and *Reichswehr* troops to move into Bavaria. Due to recruitment and logistical problems, only 7,500 actually arrived in time to play a role in the events. In return, Hoffmann was forced to place supreme command of all troops into the hands of a Prussian, General von Oven. Although Riezler had a few reservations, especially concerning the quality of the newly recruited *Freikorps* troops, he felt by the end of April that enough force had been assembled to crush the Soviet regime in Munich.[35]

Before the last act of the Bavarian drama could open, however, Leviné and his followers were forced to resign. At a meeting at the Hofbräuhaus on April 26, one of the commanders of the "Red Army," Ernst Toller, and a young bank clerk who had been appointed commissioner of finance, Emil Männer, challenged the Communist leadership on three counts. First, Leviné had refused to consider negotiations with Hoffmann at such a hopelessly desperate time. Second, the Communists had withheld from the people information concerning the military and economic situation. Third, and most interestingly, the Leviné group was accused of being too Russian. Toller charged that "the great feat of the Russian Revolution lends to these men a magic luster. Experienced German Communists stare at them as if dazzled. Because Lenin is a Russian, they are assumed to have his ability. 'In Russia we did it differently'—this phrase upsets every decision." A few hours later a more explicit statement of Toller's allegation was set to print:

> With each action it is not questioned whether it suits the situation of our special circumstances, the views of the great mass of our working people, the cares for our present and future; but only whether it conforms to the teachings of Russian Bolshevism, whether Lenin and Trotsky in a similar instance would react thus or thus. . . . We Bavarians are not Russians! . . .

Riezler's impression that "Russians" and "the best known international Communists" were calling the shots in Munich was thus shared by some of the Bavarian Soviet leaders themselves and by the majority in the highest Bavarian Soviet organ, the Executive Council *(Vollzugsrat)*, which returned a vote of no-confidence against Leviné on April 27.[36]

The removal of Leviné as leader of the Bavarian Soviet Republic ultimately had no influence on the events which followed. Though Riezler would certainly have liked to have seen a voluntary capitulation of the Soviet regime, thereby avoiding unnecessary bloodshed, he was undoubtedly pleased that neither side had been able to compromise with each other, thereby delaying even further Bavaria's complete return to the overall authority of the Reich. The stage was set for the fatal blow against the Soviet Republic.

In anticipation of the show-down to come, Lenin sent a message to the Bavarian Soviet Republic on April 27: "Best greetings and wishes for success." On May 1 he announced to a huge crowd assembled in Red Square:

In all nations the workers have set foot on the path of struggle with imperialism. The liberated working class is celebrating its anniversary freely and openly not only in Soviet Russia, but also in Soviet Hungary and Soviet Bavaria.[37]

Events in Munich on that same day showed that the "wheel of history" did not move only in one direction. General von Oven's troops were poised around Munich for an attack to begin at noon, May 2, presumably hoping not to create Communist martyrs on May Day. However, the patience of the commander and his troops ended with the news that ten hostages had been murdered by the Soviets inside Munich at Riezler's former school, the Luitpold-Gymnasium. This was an extremely unwise act which transformed what would have been a skirmish into a cruel slaughter. Elements of the *Freikorps* began moving into the city in early evening of May 1, shooting anyone caught with a weapon and brutally silencing any resistance whatsoever. By the afternoon of May 3, after a bitter struggle claiming six hundred casualties the city was under the full control of the *Freikorps* and the Hoffmann government.[38]

On May 6, 1919, in the wake of considerable criticism against the brutal "white terror," Riezler telegraphed to Berlin:

The Munich Spartacists fought resolutely and insidiously. In spite of the *Reichswehr's* discipline and calm, innocent persons could have been and must have been victims of the necessary and numerous summary executions. One must expect an exaggeration and exploitation of such cases, as well as indignation. The leaderless . . . workers were surprised to see the socialist government put down the 'proletariat' with the aid of the 'bourgeois army' and officers' troops.

Riezler concluded that under the circumstances "the behavior of the Prussian commandos was fitting and expedient"; Bavaria's "shame" had come to an end, and the unity of the Reich had been preserved.[39]

Riezler's official report that the behavior of the troops in Munich had been "fitting" and characterized by "discipline and calm" was exaggerated and inaccurate. The violence used to suppress the uprising was largely uncontrolled and far exceeded that used by the rebels themselves. Riezler undoubtedly knew this. His private thoughts on this matter are unknown; only his official reports are available. He, as well as the leaders of the central government, might well have privately felt some regret, even remorse. Their private feelings would have varied, no doubt, and certainly emotions might have mingled in. For instance, the facts that Riezler felt a certain guilt about his role in revolutionizing Russia, that Munich was the city of his birth, and that the hostages had been shot in his former *Gymnasium* probably influenced his reaction to the events.

Nevertheless, despite large differences in educational, social and political background, all leaders in the central government shared a strong common political motive: the unwillingness to watch helplessly the dissolution and demise of Germany's first democracy.[40] The preservation of the Republic was to them the overriding concern of the moment; too little thought was given to the precedence which the methods used would have on the future.

One might suspect that German leaders, including Riezler, were blind in the right eye. In fact, the government and Riezler showed in March 1920 that they were equally unwilling to submit to attacks from the right. But at this time, in the spring of 1919, the direct attacks on the Republic were coming from the left, not the right. That later right-wing strikes against the Republic were not suppressed with equal brutality stemmed from the fact that the *Reichswehr* and *Freikorps* troops were, on the whole, anti-republican and far more sympathetic toward the right; they were never successfully transformed into reliable instruments of the Weimar Republic. The new regime found itself in the predicament of having no alternative to using troops which were, in the main, unruly, disillusioned freebooters who had become far too accustomed to violence during a war which had severely shaken their sense of values and proportion. Such troops were extremely difficult to control. Nevertheless, it can certainly be said that the leaders of the central government made far too little effort to control them. Thus, the blemish of partiality toward the right was placed, in the minds of many Germans, not only on the unruly troops, but on the new Republic itself.

In the critical six months since October 1918, Riezler had devoted his full attention toward reestablishing unity and stability in a greatly changed German Reich. He had helped persuade German leaders that there was no reasonable alternative to accepting the enemies' terms for cease-fire. He had supported the German Revolution of November 9, which had established a Republic with a coalition government committed to parliamentary democracy. He took a leading role in defending that Republic from all assaults by those who wished to take power from a popularly elected assembly and head of state and to deposit that power nominally in workers' and soldiers' councils throughout Germany.

However, Germany was still a nation plagued by grave internal and external crises. Its relations with the rest of the world had to be greatly revised and improved. A workable and democratic constitution had to be adopted, and the dangerous division within German society had to be overcome. Riezler directed his attention toward solving these crises.

181

Chapter Seven
THE CRISES OF WEIMAR

*He protects the Republic best who strives to gain recognition of its faults
and who pursues the paths of improvement continually.*

—Kurt Riezler

The Weimar Republic was born out of crisis and lived in crisis until the
end. There was no general agreement among Germans on what kind of
republic Germany should have, or whether she should even have a
republic at all. Nor was there agreement on what kind of constitution
Germany should adopt. Germans' opinions widely differed on the nature
of Germany's foreign political dilemma and how that dilemma should be
solved. Finally, German society had lost much of its unity and stability.

Riezler not only observed from a particularly favorable vantage point
the crises of Weimar, but he also took an active hand in attempting to
cope with these crises. Immediately following the end of the war, Riezler
was made adviser for German affairs in the political section of the
Foreign Office. In this role, Riezler became the Foreign Office's representative to those commissions which prepared the draft constitution, later
enacted by the National Assembly in Weimar. He was also responsible
for formulating the Foreign Office's recommendations concerning the
suppression of domestic uprisings. On November 15, 1919, he was
assigned with the rank of ambassador as chief adviser to President
Friedrich Ebert, a position which he held until April 11, 1920.

Also, for the first time in his life, Riezler became an active member of a
political party, the *Deutsche Demokratische Partei* (German Democratic
Party—DDP). This party, which sought to preserve in Germany the
liberal tradition established in Frankfurt's Paulskirche in 1848, attracted
most of the academics in Germany who advocated a democratic republic.
Among its leading members were Naumann, Hugo Preuss, and Max
Weber, who worked out the democratic framework for the Weimar Constitution. The DDP, the SPD, and the Catholic Center Party formed the
"Weimar Coalition," which immediately declared support for the new

Republic. At one time Riezler even considered running for a seat in the Reichstag.

Finally, Riezler devoted a great deal of his time to journalism. His service in the Imperial Chancellery had convinced him of the potentially great impact journalism could have on a nation's thinking. What was needed, he felt, was intelligent and responsible journalism, and he intended to provide that. The significance of his writings on the Weimar crises is considerably enhanced by the fact that Riezler assumed political responsibilities and took an active part in the attempt to overcome those crises.

After leaving public service in April 1920, for reasons which we shall see, Riezler published a postscript to the new edition of *Grundzüge der Weltpolitik*. This postscript, which at the request of the publisher was also published as a separate book, had no other goal, in the words of Riezler, than "to stimulate reflection, to warn, and to bring the unthinking to their senses both in the divided and tortured homeland and . . . in the rest of the world."[1] In this work, entitled *The Three Crises*, Riezler examined the major crises which confronted Weimar Germany: the crisis of foreign politics, the crisis of the state, and the crisis of society.

CRISIS OF FOREIGN POLICY

The new constellation of powers which emerged from the war had the potential for benefiting the world, Riezler thought. The war left the United States and Britain as the predominant world powers, and he believed that these two Anglo-Saxon powers could have offered stability and a sober, pragmatic character to world politics. However, on the European continent they were either unable or unwilling to restrain that power which had not been cured of the desire for continental hegemony—France. They tolerated a French policy which was apparently designed

to keep Germany disarmed in the middle of Europe, to destroy Germany economically, to foster chaos in order to bring about its [Germany's] political fragmentation, to keep alive the points of friction on its [Germany's] eastern border, to turn the new states on its [Germany's] borders into military states until they suffer social collapse due to the financial burdens.

Riezler saw this French "Balkanization" or fragmentation policy as merely a continuation of French policy from the seventeenth century: French continental hegemony through German fragmentation; French strength "among weak neighbors."[2]

183

French policy was, in Riezler's opinion, embodied in the Versailles Treaty, which Riezler and most other Germans bitterly opposed. Riezler saw this treaty as a strange mixture of French hatred toward Germany and the idealism and naiveté of President Wilson's Fourteen Points. This unhealthy mixture resulted in such hypocrisy that in Germany cynicism was stimulated toward both the treaty and toward any German government which would sign it. Of course, Germany's Draconian policy toward a collapsing Russia at Brest-Litovsk had provided a disastrous precedent for the later peace treaty. Nevertheless, Germany's short-sightedness in 1918 could not reasonably be invoked to justify an equally short-sighted policy a year later. As Chancellor Scheidemann said to the National Assembly on May 12, 1919, five days after the Entente had announced the terms of the treaty: "Which hand would not wither up which put itself and us into these bonds?"[3]

The Versailles Treaty not only helped create a deep division in German society, but it seriously hampered the normalization of Germany's relations with the outside world. Riezler thus viewed the treaty as a failure from the point of view of the proper function of any treaty: to provide a reliable foundation for the coexistence of peoples. Riezler clearly foresaw the dangerous consequences of a policy of dismembering Germany in order to diminish the German nation-state *(Volksstaat)*. Germans were forced to assume citizenship in states which surrounded Germany, including Belgium and Poland:

The delivery of three million German Bohemians [Sudeten Germans] to Czechoslovakia; the rejection of German-Austrian *Anschluss;* the creation of as many points of friction and hostility all around Germany as possible; and additionally the real purpose of the occupation of the area left of the Rhine: to attempt to accomplish by means of occupation pressure those transfers of territory which could not be accomplished through the peace treaty . . . . While Germany should disarm herself, the new state creations on her eastern border are with French assistance and leadership being artificially armed with old war material and are being provided with new affiliates of the French armaments industry.[4]

The solution to the collapsed Austro-Hungarian Empire was another example of Europe's "complete disorganization." Riezler described the newly constructed southern Europe as follows:

On the one hand, Hungary and German Austria, former enemies of the victors, pruned down on all sides to the point of being unable to survive. On the other hand, Czechoslovakia, Poland, Yugoslavia and Rumania, far beyond their capacity to be allies, each one well supplied with minorities of foreign race and language, in part patched together with disparate parts, all burdened with the hatred and hostility of their neighbors. Whoever can arm himself does so; . . . what the Allies and their associated powers call peace is nothing more than latent war.

Riezler found that France's policy of "dominating a fragmented Germany, maintaining hegemony over Poland, Czechoslovakia, Yugoslavia, and the Balkans, her reassertion of claims to her former predominance in Turkey and, in addition to all that, the dominance of a gigantic colonial empire—all that with a land of pensioners *(Rentnervolk)*" was wholly unrealistic, could only be maintained by force and would eventually lead to war. In Riezler's opinion, the settlement at Versailes left Europe "tired," "disorganized," and full of "untenable situations." Prophetically, he saw that it contained "tiny solutions and great postponements."[5]

Riezler realized that the prostrate Germany could do very little about the unfavorable foreign political position in which she found herself. He was especially aware by 1920 that Germany could do nothing militarily to change the situation. The time was past, he thought, when modern, industrialized states could gain anything positive through use of arms against other states. Further, Riezler realized before many of his countrymen that more than any other power Germany, "due to her geographic location and her military weakness, would only serve as the battlefield, whether she participated in the conflict or not: [Germany] has little to gain from a possible conflict and much evil to fear from such [a conflict]."[6]

Nevertheless, Riezler was not resigned to the situation. He sacrificed much time and effort, as well as his position in the Foreign Office, to try to establish a more tolerable, less explosive constellation. He believed that the first step toward correcting the dangerous constellation was to oppose the signing of the Versailles Treaty. He tried to persuade the German Democratic Party to leave the government if either of the other two coalition parties chose to sign the treaty. On June 22, 1919, faced with a threat on the part of the victorious Allies to invade Germany if the treaty were not signed, a majority of the National Assembly in Weimar voted to accept it. Riezler's response to the decision came the next day. He resigned from the Foreign Office in protest against Germany's signing "unconditionally and without protest despite the fact that the most extreme military pressure visible to the entire world" had not yet been applied against Germany. Clearly, he believed that Germany should have threatened to use its remaining military power against the Allies in order to resist signing the document. Under the circumstances, however, this

185

course was entirely unrealistic and would certainly have been futile. In his letter of resignation he also protested the government's inability to formulate a foreign policy concept which "could bring us salvation from the chaotic situation of contemporary Europe," but Riezler did not advocate a policy himself to accomplish this. At this point, he was better at identifying the problems than in prescribing solutions to them, but it must be remembered that most Europeans did not even understand the problems. Riezler's party also withdrew from the coalition government, and Chancellor Philipp Scheidemann was forced to resign.[7]

Not until October 1, 1919, was Riezler officially released from his duties at the Foreign Office, and within a month and a half he was appointed as chief adviser to President Ebert, a post which he held until April 11, 1920. Nevertheless, even after leaving his final political post, Riezler continued to advocate through the medium of journalism not only specific steps toward decreasing the number of conflict areas and points of friction within Europe, but also a new way of approaching foreign affairs. The journal to which he contributed most frequently was *Die Deutsche Nation,* which had been cofounded by his friend and now party colleague, Conrad Haussmann. The aims of this journal were "to preserve German national unity, and above all to create understanding for the great political tasks of the present." It promised to "conduct a campaign against the Paris alliance and in support of the true alliance of peoples, against the servitude of the Versailles Treaty and in support of Germany's national rights and economic freedom." According to Haussmann, Riezler, who used his pseudonym of J. J. Ruedorffer, was the "intellectual center" of the journal.[8]

Riezler consistently pleaded for a revision of the Versailles Treaty, especially with regard to the German reparations and to the League of Nations. He demanded that German reparations be scaled down to a level which Germany could actually pay and which left some incentive for Germans to continue to work. "There is no one who can force the German worker to work only for France." Further, paragraph five of the League of Nations Covenant, which required unanimity for all decisions, turned the entire League into "a dispensable decoration." Riezler felt that such a clumsy and unworkable League should be replaced by a summit council composed of the leading European statesmen from the victorious, defeated, and neutral nations.

Riezler attempted not only to expose the short-sightedness of France's desired hegemony over Europe, but he also proposed far-sighted steps which could slowly lead to a reconciliation between France and Germany, steps which other Europeans were unwilling to take until three generations later. He recommended practical measures such as mutually beneficial Franco-German agreements to share coal, coke, and steel. In general, he thought that commerce and the free movement of labor should be stimulated among nations. Such small steps could, he believed, smooth the way toward more significant international agreements which could in turn lead to a reduction of the bitter hostility toward Germany which found expression in the Versailles Treaty.[9] Europe was clearly not ready for such bold and imaginative steps.

Riezler was genuinely convinced that no diplomatic steps would lead to any lasting solution to Europe's problems unless Europeans adopted an entirely new way of thinking about international politics. Europeans had to learn the lessons of the war which had just devastated Europe. Men had to move away from "the stupid belief in sheer power and, still more, in its empty gestures," but also had to resist the "childish delusion of international kindness." The only possible standard for "objective and consistent foreign politics in all states" should be the "standard of reason." Riezler admitted that human beings disagree on what is rational and that it is exceedingly difficult to know what is rational. Nevertheless, it was possible for European nations to examine rationally their mutual interest and to act on the basis of that mutual interest. It was clear to him that the three crises which confronted Europe had been produced by a neglect of reason and were soluble only by the application of reason. *"Vernunft oder Untergang"* (Reason or Destruction)—these were the alternatives which he saw, and his preference was clearly the former.[10]

Riezler admitted that his prewar analysis of international politics had in some respects revealed that "the author had not been protected through his youth from many mistakes to which older, more experienced and wiser statesmen and writers were also subject." For instance, Riezler had argued before the war that armaments were important contributors to peace because they greatly complicated the computation of chances for winning a modern war. He was now convinced of the opposite: armaments foster war, not peace. The war, he believed, had displayed the "tragedy of technical progress," and now "the peace has inherited the discoveries of the war." However, "the political leaders hesitate to recognize that their accustomed way of thinking has been made obsolete by these new facts." New weapons would surely lead to war unless political solutions were found to the problems facing a troubled Europe.

While Riezler found it illogical that bankrupt states continued to arm themselves, he found armament inevitable "as long as the states and nations faced each other lurkingly and distrustfully as beasts of prey." Everywhere he looked, he noted a "nervous unrest." Riezler's view of the nation had obviously changed markedly. Before the war Riezler had seen nations as "paths to God" and to human perfection. Enmity among nations was, he had thought, both natural and good because it was a necessary stimulus to a *Volk*'s self-realization. He now believed that while the nation still exists and could still help individual human beings understand the world, it could in no way elevate them toward perfection and could actually do great harm. Referring to nations' striving toward perfection: "the ascent of the one is the descent of the other."[11]

History, Riezler was now convinced, had absolutely no overall meaning *(Gesamtsinn)* and no inevitable directionality.

It does not lead slowly upwards to any kind of apex of humanity along a straight, if rocky, road. It is a constant battle among many goals, and it incessantly thwarts its own intentions and gets tangled up in its own ropes, cannot find its way, and starts all over again, continually appointing new actors and again goes astray.

"Progress is a moral requirement, not an historical fact. All meaning is man's work and man's task."

In the absence of any overall meaning in world history, theories of politics and ideologies had become entirely dispensable, and statemen should not let themselves be guided by them. "Theories . . . only confuse the already sufficiently confused events." The mature Riezler, as all who knew him recall, had no use for slogans or ideologies of any kind, for he had become convinced that they only stand in the way of understanding a changing world.[12]

One such slogan—"Germany was stabbed in the back"—was particularly destructive in Germany. This slogan implied that the war had been lost because of political and revolutionary events in Germany, not because of Germany's failure on the battlefield. This misconception helped to divide Germans into those who wanted to learn from the war and those who wanted to refight it. Riezler, along with such leaders as Gustav Stresemann, was a German who wished to learn from the war. This did not mean that he did not want Germany to assert itself in European politics. Indeed, he criticised the Social Democratic Party in 1922 for not being assertive enough and for following "the line of the least risk." Such a policy, he feared, would only stimulate "scorn and contempt" toward Germany. However, he correctly saw that the time had come for nations to put dangerous national jealousies aside and to join together to find rational solutions to the world's problems. The nation alone could not solve the problems facing all Europeans. For that, a true

Pan-European sentiment had to be developed. "European interests are common interests because the misery is mutual and can only be dealt with through common effort."[13]

Riezler had no illusions that Europeans would definitely learn the lessons of the war or be able to eliminate the points of friction quickly. Nevertheless, he did not lose hope, and in 1928 he asserted in an article entitled *"Gefahren und Hoffnungen"* ("Dangers and Hopes") that "Germany is patient."[14] Tragically, Riezler was wrong about this. The following decade showed just how little patience Germany actually had.

CRISIS OF THE STATE

It was unfortunate that national humiliation coincided with the birth of the first democracy in Germany. When at last Germany had adopted the political organization extolled by the victorious Allies, she became an international outcast. This unfortunate coincidence contributed heavily to the second crisis which Riezler analyzed: the crisis of the state.

Riezler had always believed that a properly organized state could perform the highly desirable function of enabling "the interests of the entire nation to be served rationally according to plan and purpose"; it could be the efficient arm of the nation. However, in the first few months following the end of the war, Riezler was torn over the question of whether the state in its previous form was even usable anymore. He recognized that Germany had always had a crisis of state; the Prussian state had been, in his opinion, a "military state," not a people's state *(Volksstaat),* and the German Empire which had been built on the foundations of the Prussian state had been devoid of all spirit and was only an external display of arrogance and hubris.

On April 1, 1919, Riezler gave a speech in which he described the "bankruptcy of the idea of the state in the entire world . . . which is irreversible because the world war had carried this idea *ad absurdum.*" Riezler considered the continued existence of the state to be incompatible with the continued existence of humanity because as long as states remain as powerful as they are, they will fight with one another time and time again. Therefore, humanity or at least culture will be eradicated, especially since military technology has become so advanced.[15]

However, Riezler's initial pessimism about the modern state did not manifest itself in resignation or cynicism. He had no illusions about the fact that the world would continue to be divided into states which would retain their own sovereignty. He certainly had no illusions about the problems which all Germans could observe at the time. The German peo-

189

ple were badly divided, and emotions were so high and narrow self-interest so strong in all European states that rational solutions to the great problems often seemed impossible. Nevertheless, recognizing that Germany must adopt some kind of statehood, Riezler wanted to help his nation create a state and a constitution which could serve the interests of the entire nation. To this end, he not only aided in the drafting of a new constitution, but he also turned his official and journalistic attention to protecting and improving the new Republic.[16]

As early as November 9, 1918, Riezler favored the immediate convocation of a constitutional assembly, and in mid-December, 1918, he wrote to Conrad Haussmann: "I am remaining in office only for the purpose of collaborating in the constitutional work and would even like to be a candidate for a seat in the Constitutional Assembly in order to be able to pursue that [work] further." However, because he had no rapport with the leaders of his party in Munich, whom he would presumably have had to represent, he never succeeded in getting such a mandate. Besides, his friend, Theodor Heuss, doubted that Riezler would have trusted his own talent "to court the people directly."[17]

Riezler was very clear about the kind of state he did not think was appropriate for Germany. To begin with, Riezler thought that Germany no longer had any use for monarchy. Before and during the war he had found little to admire in the kaiser, whose saber rattling and love of naval things had been obstacles to Bethmann Hollweg's policy of establishing good relations with Britain and a secure continental position for Germany. During the war the kaiser had proved himself to be "blindly oblivious" concerning the aims and conduct of the war. On April 15, 1918, he noted: "His Majesty is all wrapped up in the soldiers' beating of tam tam drums and in the distribution of medals which his forebears founded." In the closing days of the war, Riezler had recommended that the kaiser and the crown prince abdicate voluntarily so that at least the dynasty could be saved.[18] Riezler, as well as other German leaders such as Friedrich Ebert, had believed initially that the monarchy would be indispensable in maintaining both general order and the loyalty of German conservatives. Indeed, restoration of the monarchy later became a rallying cry for many of the Republic's enemies.

Once the dynasty had fallen, Riezler believed that Germany should concentrate on becoming a functioning republic. Not only had the victorious Allies insisted upon the abolition of the monarchy, but many Germans had opposed the monarchy entirely. Nevertheless, Riezler could see that for some Germans

the monarchy remains a commitment, but no political plan. . . . One knows that
Germany will never unify itself around a kaiser and that the twenty-one princes
cannot be restored; one sees no possibility for that. Such a commitment is a
means of agitation. The road to its realization leads over the rubble of the Reich.
. . . The goal is not the introduction of the monarchy, but the sabotage of the
Republic. Where is the national objective?[19]

Riezler wanted a republican constitution in which all adult citizens
elected representatives who determined policies and laws. Above all, he
believed that the purpose of any constitution was to enable the "will of
all" *(Gesamtwille)*, based on the interests of all citizens, to
predominate.[20] Unlike Rousseau, Riezler believed that this "will of all"
could be expressed through representatives elected directly by the people. To insure that this would not be choked by particularist interests,
Germans should reject any republic which perverted the "will of all." In
practical terms, this meant that Bolshevist or council republics were to
be eliminated. This also meant that Germany should not adopt a
strongly federal constitution. Like most traditional German liberals,
Riezler favored a centralized state.

The future relationship between the Reich government and the individual German states was one of the most critical questions which the
framers of the Weimar Constitution had to settle. Riezler ultimately
came to oppose any significant degree of federalism, but very early he
realized that it was unrealistic merely to eliminate the German states, as
State Secretary of the Interior Hugo Preuss wished to do. In conversations with experts in the Ministry of the Interior arranged by Preuss from
December 9 to 12, 1918, Riezler, who represented the Foreign Office, supported Max Weber in arguing that Preuss's idea of unitary government
for the Reich was unrealistic at the time. Riezler particularly pointed to
the inevitable opposition of the South German states to unitary government.

Riezler's warnings proved to be correct. In the Commission of the
States *(Staatenausschuss)*, in which Riezler represented the Foreign Office, he witnessed determined South German (especially Bavarian) insistence that no unified German army be created and that "financial
supremacy" and control of postal services be granted to the states.
Riezler was only too aware that Kurt Eisner's Bavarian regime, the
Bavarian bureaucracy, and most Bavarian legal experts all denied absolutely the sovereignty of the National Assembly to proclaim a new constitution for all of Germany. He was convinced of the impossibility of
achieving anything through attempts to drown Bavaria in majority rule.

Wayne C. Thompson

Seeing that compromise would be difficult to achieve in large gatherings composed of both national and state officials, Riezler proposed small commissions wherein the states could work out among themselves the reserve rights which they wished to retain or relinquish. Riezler hoped that the most far-reaching South German demands could be moderated by other state officials. Thus, the differences in views between South German and national leaders could be narrowed considerably.

While Riezler the negotiator appeared compromising, Riezler the journalist was far more direct on the question of federalism. In an article which he published in *Die Deutsche Nation* in February 1919, under the pseudonym of "Gajus," Riezler argued forcefully for a unitary republic. He began by reminding his readers of the historical difficulty of combining federalism with a workable parliamentary system on both the national and state level. To combine federalism and parliamentary government successfully would require the highest level of "political talent and will"; however, Germany was the land in which "this political talent is most lacking and less developed than anywhere else in the world." Thus, he asked, how could one expect this combination to be possible in Germany?

Further, Riezler pointed to the problem of coordinating national and state parliaments. He recalled the serious problems which had developed earlier when the policies of the Prussian State Parliament and the Reichstag diverged. This problem could arise again, especially in Bavaria, which he accurately predicted would become an assembly point for anti-republican and anti-democratic tendencies. In view of the fact that there would be no way of guaranteeing that the same party coalitions would rule in Berlin and the states, the possibility of any coordinated German policy would, in his opinion, have been very slight.[21]

Even if all the problems of federalism could have been solved satisfactorily, Riezler was skeptical that the politically inexperienced Germans could express their national will effectively through many parties in a single parliamentary body at the Reich level. During the war he had spoken very condescendingly of the parliamentarians with whom he had to work. Throughout his diary he used such terms as "vain bubbles" to describe parliamentary leaders. He hated the time which had to be spent with the "miserable parliamentarians":

It is awful—we waste all our energy on unnecessary babble with uneducated parliamentarians, some of whom are dependent upon slogans and others upon heavy industry and other interests.

192

Riezler was loathe to consider the Parliament as representing the *Volk* or the nation. He disagreed with Bethmann Hollweg, "who slides into the temptation to consider them [the parliamentarians] as the *Volk*"; "the party leaders are not the *Volk* but a miserable rabble which squeaks when the government calls for the *Volk*." In January 1916, he wrote that it was somewhat tragic "that if blunders are made here, we, who offered the antiquated nineteenth century new (incidentally in the long run unbearable) ideas about the state and individualism, we, the only moderns, will succumb to the same errors of the West, to parliamentarianism etc., which has become a machine, and indeed a bad one long ago." He never forgot that a majority in the Reichstag had actually supported the disastrous demands of Generals Ludendorff and Hindenburg to remove Bethmann Hollweg from the chancellorship in July 1917.[22] Riezler could not shed these biases overnight. Nevertheless, his skepticism about the Weimar Parliament proved in the end to be correct.

Riezler believed that the only legitimate parliament was one whose policies represent the entire nation's interests, and not those of certain influential groups. He found to his regret, however, that parliaments in his time, which had originated as protectors against the dominance of the particularist concerns of dynasties and upper classes, were themselves now in the process of sliding into control by particularist interests: "Numerous interlocking organizations and special interests have inserted themselves between the individual and the state." Riezler became convinced that private interest groups are the "string pullers" of parliamentarians and therefore of most governmental leaders. In fact, this is what Riezler saw as the modern crisis of the state: it made no difference what political leaders might decide was in the long-term national interest based on a rational appraisal of the situation; these leaders would always be prevented from acting according to that appraisal. The domestic "machinery" of interest groups which demand attention to their concerns would always prevail.

Riezler's view was, of course, influenced by his political experience before and during the war. He recalled that many crucial German mistakes, such as the acquiescence in demands for a navy which could threaten Britain, for an exaggerated colonial empire at the expense of other powers, for prestige coups in Morocco, for unreasonable war aims, for unrestricted submarine warfare, and for the maintenance of an unreformed Prussian electoral system had been due to some extent to domestic pressures. Riezler found it particularly regrettable in times of crisis that foreign and domestic policies were at the mercy of particular

193

Wayne C. Thompson

interests and that governments were reduced almost to helplessness against demagoguery. Demagogues, he argued, often with newspaper giants and trusts behind them, threw a net over the helpless statesmen.[23]

In Imperial Germany this domestic pressure could be exerted at many points, such as at the Reichstag, the Prussian State Parliament, the Federal Council, the Chancellery, the military and, of course, the kaiser. In the Weimar Republic Riezler expected such special interests to concentrate their attention increasingly upon the parties in the Reichstag. This attention would strengthen the "oligarchies" within those parties. Also, the number of access points within the Parliament was greatly increased by the numerous parties, most of which owed their seats to the proportional representation system, an electoral system which Riezler came to oppose strongly. The large number of parties in Parliament made it necessary that governments be built on coalitions of parties, some of which represented only a small fraction of the nation's voters. This dependence on coalitions made the governments "slaves of the party oligarchs." According to Riezler, since party leaders had to spend "at least three-quarters of their time" consolidating and protecting their own positions within their parties, governments would be dependent on leaders who paid only part-time attention to the concerns of the nation. Although at first Riezler saw no alternative to establishing the "Weimar coalition," composed of the Social Democratic, German Democratic, and Center parties, he believed that coalition government ultimately presented great dangers to Germany.[24] The need to build governments on coalitions of several parties, none of which even approached having a majority because of proportional representation, did introduce a strong and continuous element of parliamentary instability into the Weimar experiment.

To avoid the potential instability of a purely parliamentary system, Riezler advocated a unitary state in which a powerful president would be elected directly by the people. He believed that such a directly elected president, not the Parliament, should be the major democratic element in the state. Only such a president could, he believed, protect the whole nation against strong particularist groups and class warfare. To ensure that this democratically elected president would not be paralyzed by party squabbles in Parliament, the chancellor should be selected by the president, not by the Parliament. The chancellor would then select the cabinet members exclusively on the grounds of their talent for statesmanship, with no regard to their party standing or affiliation. In May 1922, he advocated that Parliament be reformed by abolishing the proportional representation system. Riezler believed that the consequent

194

reduction in the number of parliamentary parties would have streamlined the Parliament and thereby enabled it to fulfill its proper role of aiding the president in serving the interests of the entire nation.

In order to reduce the power of the special interests even further, Riezler renewed his advocacy of the nationalization of all major industry. Through the "subjugation of capital to the aims of the state," the political power of the "plutocrats," i.e., the magnates of news, steel, electricity, etc., which had allegedly increased their power since the revolution, could be eliminated. Although such a nationalization program was the officially proclaimed policy of the Ebert government, Riezler did not think that the SPD was moving energetically enough in the direction of weakening the "economic barons." For example, he criticised the SPD's proposed tax policy in October 1922 on the grounds that it hit the small property owner hardest and barely affected the large owners. Such a policy, he thought, merely served the financially strong.[25]

A properly reformed republic, Riezler believed, would be one guided by a directly elected president, capable of acting rapidly and decisively in order to cope with the crises which confronted Weimar Germany. Necessary reforms would protect the fledgling democracy from its "childhood illnesses" and thus save it. Germany would then have a "true democracy," one in which the government would be able to act effectively according to the will of its people; it would not have a "false democracy," one in which the government served only party and group interests.

There can be little question that Riezler's reforms would have provided greater parliamentary stability. The rapid succession of governments made the cabinet crisis the unfortunate symbol of the new regime in the eyes of many Germans. These cabinet crises merely stimulated cynicism against the Republic. After several years of existence, Riezler remarked in an editorial conference of *Die Deutsche Nation* that "false parliamentarianism has made itself so despised in our country that even today a single lieutenant and ten men could put an end to it all. The danger is very great."[26]

While it is true that Riezler had pinpointed some of the basic problems of parliamentary government in the Weimar Republic, there is good reason to doubt that Riezler's medicine would have cured the "childhood illnesses" of the new Republic. For example, the accumulation of more powers in an already strong presidency would not necessarily have been a solution to an enfeebled democracy. He himself alluded to this possible problem in 1925 at the time of the presidential election following Ebert's death. Referring to the likelihood that Hindenburg would be elected to replace Ebert, Riezler wrote that "nothing is politically so stupid that it could not happen in Germany." Only eight years later, Hitler ascended to the presidency. Clearly the advantages of a strong president increase or decrease according to the person who occupies the office and to how that person uses presidential powers.

Further, his conception of the presidency would have deprived Parliament of any significant political function. In 1917 he had written that he had been converted to parliamentary government "because nothing can be worse than the prevailing system."[27] However, one must ask what function a parliament could have played in a system in which the president chose the chancellor and cabinet, with no regard for party affiliation. How could such a weakened parliament have aided the president in serving the interests of the entire nation? It is doubtful that it could have.

Although Riezler joined a political party and spoke much about democracy, he was uneasy about the implications of democracy and at times appeared to misunderstand democratic practice. No democracy can function without the possibility that "domestic pressure" be exerted on political leaders. He never really accepted the legitimacy of political parties as they inevitably are in democratic societies: either representatives of particular interests or coalitions of particular interests which compete for control of the government. Riezler, who in August 1914 had coined the expression, "I know no parties; I know only Germans!" considered, like many Germans, the activity of accommodating diverse interests through compromise and trading of advantages as undignified *"Kuhhandel"* (shady business) which left the interest of the people behind. He knew that pluralism had to be maintained in a society, but he was impatient about its consequences in politics. Actually, in the Weimar Republic the problem lay not in the fact of pluralism, but in the difficulty which German groups and parties had in compromising and cooperating with each other. Indeed in some extreme cases, groups and parties could not even tolerate each other's very existence.[28]

Riezler's acceptance of democracy had been based on the absence of any real alternative to it. He was a common-sense democrat. The empire had collapsed because of its own incompetence, and his hatred of Ludendorff and others of similar anti-republican political leanings in postwar Germany helped incline him in the opposite direction, toward democracy. In 1915 when Chancellor Bethmann Hollweg claimed that Riezler was not a democrat at all, Riezler wrote in his diary:

Strange man. Of course, he is basically right. The new development is for me . . . an abomination. The time for the beauty of the masses is coming. The individual is now only possible as the bearer or leader of mass feeling. Nothing more of the splendor of the singular.

In August 1919, in a letter to Conrad Haussmann, Riezler emphasized that he "did not need a revolution in order to become a democrat." However, the democracy which he meant was one in which well-educated persons who were elected for long terms by the people made rational policies which served the interest of the entire nation. He certainly had no taste for a democrary where the masses of citizens, who too often appeared to be prisoners of clichés and emotions, actually guided the political affairs of the nation. More than a quarter of a century later Riezler's colleague and dean at the New School for Social Research, Hans Staudinger, noticed that for Riezler democracy meant "leading the masses."[29] In short, Riezler envisaged a regime legitimized by the people, but not bothered by the people.

The difficulty which Riezler had in accepting the new-styled democratic leadership was shown during his service in Ebert's office from November 15, 1919, until April 11, 1920. It might seem surprising that Riezler was selected by Ebert to be the chief presidential adviser in the first place. Of course, the two men had several things in common: both were Southern Germans with a long-standing distaste for Prussianism in any form. Both tended to approach politics in a more or less pragmatic way. Both wished to preserve German unity and to defend the young Republic against extremists on the left as well as on the right. Although each belonged to different political parties, neither believed that party interests should take priority over the interests of the entire nation. Both had always been patriotic Germans. Indeed, as his diary testifies, Riezler had considerable respect for Ebert during the war, and after the war he admired Ebert's sharp intelligence and his "skill and experience in knowing how to intervene in matters quietly in order to avoid conflicts."

On the other hand, the two men came from greatly different backgrounds. In contrast to the highly-cultured, refined, and superbly educated Riezler, Ebert had been born into poverty, the son of a Heidelberg tailor. His profession was saddle making, and he had also worked in his earlier years as a bartender. As he had announced to the National Assembly on the occasion of his election to the office of president of the Reich on February 11, 1919: "I must confess that I am a son of the working class and grew up in the world of socialist thought and that I am inclined to deny neither my origin nor my convictions."[30]

Wayne C. Thompson

A person who was able to observe their collaboration very closely was Arnold Brecht, who at the time was an official in the Chancellery. Brecht and Riezler regularly saw each other in cabinet meetings, where Riezler represented Ebert, and they frequently discussed their views on the events and personalities of the day. In his autobiography, Brecht described his conversations with Riezler at the time:

His fundamental views were primarily culturally and philosophically determined. They manifested themselves in ways sometimes aristocratic, sometimes liberal and often unrestrained Bohemiam. . . . He could hardly bear the intellectual-cultural mediocrity of the Social Democratic and left bourgeois party representatives in the government. . . . As much as I felt myself attracted to him philosophically and culturally, I was equally doubtful of his suitability as a political adviser in that kind of circumstance. I countered his impatient and sharp criticism with, as I referred to it at the time, a more good-natured attitude, and I attempted to win him to my view. The new men were aristocrats neither by birth nor by intelligence, but no one expected that. The Social Democratic leaders were representatives of a new social stratum, and their solid, cool weighing of workers' problems by rule of thumb from their own personal familiarity brings a new and valuable element into the German government. We could help them, of course, by advising, warning and formulating, but we could not assume the leadership ourselves nor transform their character. Riezler had neither inclination nor patience for this view. He irritated Ebert through his complicated way of presenting things and through his critical attitude, and Ebert irritated him through his simple, uncomplicated way of thinking, which was too simplistic for Riezler.[31]

Riezler's complicated way of briefing was also noted by his friend and critic, Count Harry Kessler, who gave a highly exaggerated description of Riezler:

Riezler is an incorrigible theoretician. Instead of seizing the practical, he constructs a definition. Gradually I understand the fateful sterility of the Bethmann policy, whose major representative Riezler was. It stood there like a Christmas tree, decorated all over with ideas, which, however, were all without sap and force. For Riezler the idea is always a pretext for not doing something. . . . He has the least capable mind for politics as organized action which I ever encountered. His entire thinking by nature flows into organized inaction, organized impotence, which iridescently and seductively claims to be supreme wisdom. That Bethmann put up with this trickery for years proves also his own faulty competence. Bismarck and Napoleon would have driven Riezler to the devil after the first briefing.[32]

Although Kessler's description of Riezler is incorrect with regard to Riezler's ability to act and to the alleged "trickery" and emptiness of Riezler's theoretical approach, it does point to Ebert's and Riezler's different means of expression and different ways of examining problems. Also, the two men's style and background were too different, and Riezler was not able tactfully to overcome that. For example, on occasion, "the elegant Riezler," as one of his contemporaries described him, gave Ebert advice concerning the kind of suits he should wear at receptions or ceremonies, and he even had Mrs. Riezler give the same sort of advice to Mrs. Ebert. Such advice was undoubtedly intended to help Ebert gain more authority in the eyes of a people which, in general, expected its leaders to dress and behave in a traditionally dignified way. Riezler saw that the new leaders had power, but little authority. Nevertheless, such advice was bound to irritate a sturdy and proud working class family such as the Eberts. As we shall see, on April 11, 1920, the intellectual and the saddle maker terminated their working relationship.[33]

Riezler publicly supported the new Republic and offered his assistance to its leaders. Never did he publicly malign the new regime, nor did he openly speak condescendingly toward it. Such support by members of Germany's educated elite was desperately needed by the new democracy, but only a minority within that elite gave it. Riezler differed greatly from those who could not adjust to the needs of the time and who wished to bring the Republic to its knees. In short, he played no part whatsoever in the "conservative revolution" which helped to corrode and to undermine the Republic and which ultimately brought Germany's experiment in democracy to an end.[34]

Nevertheless, Riezler privately had little emotional attachment to liberal democracy. He knew that democracy was the only alternative under the circumstances; but he had not yet been able to free himself completely from an intellectual tradition in which the commitment to popular government was very weak and in which the conviction that the wisest should rule was very strong. Also, the tradition of German idealism, which Riezler had inherited, made it more difficult for highly-educated Germans, such as Riezler, to communicate and to work easily with intelligent, but far less educated, Germans such as Ebert. That is, the gilded edge of German educational elitism became an obstacle to the high degree of unity among German realists which would have been crucial in surmounting successfully the problems of reaction, anarchy, national humiliation, and economic disaster.

Perhaps it was because Riezler did not embrace democracy with strong personal conviction that he placed excessive demands on it. He wrote in 1920 that democracy must insure that "in all states objective and consistent foreign policy can again be made. . . . Democracy must firmly convince all Europeans of the mutual distress of Europe. [That conviction

199

must be] free of all chauvinism and [be] a cool, objective perception of the political situation. . . . In addition to that, it must so reorder the state that reason, which was dethroned by coincidence, can guide human affairs freely and objectively. . . ."[35] Nowhere in the world can democracy meet those standards.

It frequently but incorrectly has been said that the Weimar Republic was a democracy without democrats. Although Germany had had only a feeble tradition of democracy, there were many Germans who, like Riezler, considered themselves democrats and who worked to establish a democratic Germany after the First World War. However, there was little consensus about what a democracy should look like and how it should function in Germany. Many democrats had much to learn about democracy. Also, the critical problems which plagued Germany allowed very little time for experimentation and transition, and after a disastrously short probationary period, large numbers of Germans impatiently dismissed democracy as inadequate.[36]

The problems of federalism proved not to be nearly so great as Riezler had anticipated, partly because the Weimar Constitution tended to be interpreted in most instances in favor of the Reich, but also, as we shall see, because the problems of Weimar lay much deeper than in a mere institutional flaw. Also, Riezler's proposed nationalization of major industries would certainly have been an unacceptable economic gamble at a time of desperate economic problems. Ebert had also proclaimed the goal of nationalization, but he, as well as most other responsible political leaders, saw that economic recovery, not economic experimentation, was the order of the day. Indeed, it was the fragile economic condition which ultimately proved to be the Achilles heel of the Republic and which enabled her enemies to destroy her.

In a letter written on February 1, 1924, to his friend Carl Petersen, mayor of Hamburg, Riezler expressed such great concern about the dangers which faced the new Republic that he was willing even to broach the subject of a preventive putsch to rectify the situation. Riezler was certainly not the kind of person who normally sought to find solutions in such strikes against the state; however, in view of the tragic assassinations of defenders of the Republic, of devastating inflation, and of renewed foreign occupation of the Ruhr area, the domestic political situation appeared to be reaching a breaking point. Riezler asked what might await Germany if domestic collapse actually came about. "Since Weimar this question just won't leave my mind. It becomes more urgent from month to month." He feared that such collapse would be a prelude to a putsch by the extreme left or right. At the very least, such a collapse would open the door to French occupation of Germany's western provinces and consequently increase the weight of Prussia within the Reich. This would elevate "the most dangerous of all particularisms: the East Elbian," and in general deliver the Republic into the hands of reactionary political forces.

Riezler did not think that the defenders of the Republic (or "the middle," as he called them) should stand idly by and watch such a development take shape. Realizing that the reforms which he had proposed could never be effected through Parliament, Riezler concluded that only a dissolution of both the Reich and Prussian Parliaments, a powerful and unmistakable demand from the people themselves, a plebiscite, or even a putsch would be required. Nevertheless, he recognized the impossibility of such a putsch; "today practically no one is prepared for actions of this scope and intensity." Thus, he saw no need to consider how such a putsch should be organized and against whom it should be directed. Riezler would have approved of such a putsch only in the last resort, and the fact that he mentioned it to a friend in such a casual, unelaborated way indicated that he was not convinced that such a last resort was now imperative. However, that he would even mention in a letter to the mayor of Hamburg a putsch against the Republic in order to save it indicated that his political critique, as well as his journalistic writing, had become sharper, less patient, less conciliatory, and somewhat more desperate in the few years following the founding of the Republic.[37] It also showed that by this time his faith in democracy's future in Germany was anything but unshakable and that he foresaw no immediate solution to the crisis of the state.

Even before the Weimar Constitution had been adopted by the National Assembly, Riezler had expressed through official channels his doubts that the document which was being prepared could serve Germany well. On June 17, 1919, in a message to the Foreign Office, he had urged emphatically that an amending clause be inserted into the Constitution which would permit amendments to be adopted in the first five years by a simple majority vote in the Reichstag. Such an amending procedure would have provided the document with the "character which it actually has, namely that of a temporary emergency expedient which was hammered together in haste at a time and under circumstances in which no *Volk* had ever attempted or could ever succeed in providing itself with a new constitution."[38]

Riezler never ceased to regard the Weimar Constitution as transitional. However, unlike many Germans, he did not advocate a transition away from the idea of a workable, democratic republic. He never

201

gave up hope that the illness of the Republic could be healed. As he wrote in 1922: "He protects the Republic best who strives to gain recognition of its faults and who pursues the paths of improvement continually."[39]

Serious problems plagued the new Republic from the very beginning. It faced humiliation abroad, reduction of its territory and a very critical economic situation at home. The political institutions which it had devised for itself were not functioning well. The crises of foreign affairs and of the state remained unsolved, and these crises were closely linked to a third crisis: the crisis of society. The most visible aspect of this crisis of society in Germany was the division of her people. Despite foreign pressure on Germany and the Germans' common suffering during and after the war, Riezler saw no signs that this wound was healing. On the contrary, he noted in August 1922, that "the rip is becoming deeper, passions are becoming more heated, the speech of one is becoming more and more incomprehensible to the other, the masses are turning toward the extremes, and the role of reason . . . is becoming less and less significant."[40]

Riezler thought that those on the political right who had learned nothing from the war were perhaps most responsible for this continued division within German society. At the forefront of those who had learned nothing stood the retired General Ludendorff, who in books and articles argued that "Jews, socialists and democrats had turned against the splendid Reich and an unbroken army." Despite the gross inaccuracy of these charges, this "policy of former officers, who have read nothing but Karl May, continues, and no one on the right has the courage to call these men what they are: fools and traitors." Riezler demanded that someone who had occupied high governmental positions at the time, such as Karl Helfferich, speak out against the lies which were being spread. When Riezler once publicly charged that Ludendorff was lying, the *München-Augsburger Abendzeitung,* a newspaper friendly to Ludendorff, refused to respond directly to Riezler's charges. Instead, it accused Riezler of maintaining intimate connections with the French envoy in Munich, whom Riezler had never met. For the most part, Ludendorff's statements went unchecked.

The real tragedy, Riezler thought, was that these extremists were not alone. The "fools" would have been harmless if only they had not been "in basic agreement with a large part of that German elite who have learned to consider themselves the only ones who are truly national." Many of the most educated and intelligent Germans actually believed

202

Ludendorff. After all, "how should the boys [the impressionable students] be expected to know that Ludendorff is no authority? Don't universities still celebrate this man, not only as a commander, but as a political leader and a national hero? Should not the boys and youngsters honor the professors and the rectors of the universities, the guardians of education and intelligence?" This infection of a large part of the elite was truly dangerous, for "the basic attitudes of the elites transform the stupidity of the individual into the fate of the nation."[41]

This unthinking negativism and the harking back to the former Prussianized Germany, which had already thoroughly proved its inadequacy, led the elite to engage in the *Katastrophenpolitik* (policy of catastrophy) of attacking and irritating the ruling Social Democrats at every opportunity. Riezler argued that one could not expect miracles from the Social Democratic Party, a party which had been excluded from political responsibility for decades. Although, as we have seen, Riezler experienced difficulty in working together with Social Democrats, he argued publicly that no one should make it impossible for the Social Democrats to rule; "all the defects of the present state in no way justify efforts to sabotage this state, instead of to improve it." In 1922 he wrote:

Thus the state rocks in the struggle of exasperations; a few more deeds of insanity or stupidity and the civil war will have arrived. . . . Poor trampled land; a sick spirit and confused mind! And certainly your fate is also the fate of the countless hearty and decent persons who today, paying attention only to their own affairs, stand on the sideline, their hands in their laps.[42]

A wide-spread malaise had settled over a humiliated Germany. The new political and social situation, in which that child of industrialization—the working class—was playing such an important role, was perceived by many Germans as the worst manifestation of modernity. This impression of modernity was reinforced by a complex of aversions to what appeared to be excessive materialism, bourgeois hypocrisy, and spiritual impoverishment. It was also reinforced by a longing for a sense of community, for a new faith, and for "wholeness." There were many voices, including many respected ones, which denigrated reason and elevated feeling. As Fritz Stern argues, such feelings and moods are latent in all modern industrialized societies. However, they were particularly fatal to Germany after the First World War because they came to a head at a time when Germany was faced with genuine economic, domestic, and diplomatic crises. The widespread "cultural despair" was bound to have serious political consequences in Weimar Germany.[43]

Wayne C. Thompson

As could be expected, the irresponsible propaganda from such widely respected men as Ludendorff could not fail to inspire action from impressionable followers. Reactionary putsch attempts and assassinations of two of its ministers were seriously to jolt the fledgling Republic. In March 1920, while Riezler was still chief adviser to President Ebert, an event occurred which revealed not only the fragility of the Republic, but the serious division within German society. During the night of March 12-13, *Freikorps* troops marched on Berlin. The object of the march was not to suppress a Spartacist uprising, as had been the case on several occasions in 1919, but to displace the national government of Germany.

The immediate issue was the government's order to disband a *Freikorps* unit garrisoned at Döberitz, fifteen miles west of Berlin. However, determined opponents of the Republic decided to utilize the crisis to put an end to the new regime. Ludendorff, who had returned from exile in Sweden and who was living in Berlin under the cover name of "Karl Neumann," certainly supported the conspiracy, but he refused to lead it. Therefore, the conspirators chose as their leader Wolfgang Kapp, who had been born and raised in New York, where his father had sought exile following the unsuccessful German revolution of 1848. Wolfgang Kapp returned to Germany and during the First World War became the cofounder of the short-lived Fatherland Party and was one of the foremost advocates of far-reaching territorial war aims.

The spark which actually ignited the putsch was Defense Minister Noske's dismissal on March 11 of the Commandant of Berlin, General Walther Freiherr von Lüttwitz, who had refused to obey the order to disband the unit. At the same time, Noske ordered the arrest of Kapp and other conspirators. The following night, the Ehrhardt Brigade marched toward Berlin, singing military songs and flying the black-red-white flag of Imperial Germany. On their helmets was a popular *Freikorps* symbol: the swastika. The brigade faced no armed resistance since the majority of generals in Berlin refused to allow their soldiers to fire on former comrades from the front. Despite Noske's efforts, the German army had not been made into a reliable instrument of the Republic. Under these circumstances, the government was able to use force only against the radical left, never against the radical right. By noon of March 13, Ehrhardt's troops controlled all of Berlin, and Kapp was installed as chancellor.

The government had been forced to flee the city that morning at 5:00 A.M. Before departing, however, the government had called a general strike, which was observed by virtually all groups in Berlin: socialist labor unions, radical leftist militants, shopkeepers, and the government

204

ministries. Factories, schools, banks, and stores closed. Streetcars and buses ceased running, and water, electricity, and gas were shut off. Crowds gathered in the streets, some arrests were made by the putschists, and gunfire was occasionally heard.

Almost all government officials, civil servants and military personnel refused to obey the putschists. Several of Riezler's later colleagues at the New School for Social Research in New York contributed to the governmental standstill. Arnold Brecht, a top counselor in the Chancellery, ordered all telephone operators in the Chancellery to take a week's vacation and then left the building with all the governmental stamps and seals in his coat pockets. Hans Staudinger, a counselor in the Economics Ministry, issued the order that no ministry document was to be official without the approval of the Economics Minister, who had naturally accompanied the government to Stuttgart. The economist, Adolf Lowe, who was in bed with the Spanish flu and a temperature of 104, was asked by Ludendorff's brother-in-law, who had been sent by the general, about the possibility of labor union support for Kapp. Lowe answered: "He is quite right to be worried about this strike. I think this is one time when there will be some truth in the Socialist slogans about the strength of the united workers."

The highest government official who remained in Berlin was Kurt Riezler. He was later supported by Vice-Chancellor Eugen Schiffer and Ministers Schmidt and Schlicke, who had returned to Berlin the evening of March 13. Riezler's job was to report by means of courier and, when possible, by telephone what was happening in Berlin. As he put it, he was directly involved with "unraveling the situation." He was also charged with representing the government in meetings with the putschists to persuade them of the futility of their adventure and to arrange for the resignation of the Kapp "government." Indeed, almost immediately the futility of the putsch attempt became manifest to all observers and participants.[44]

On March 16, Riezler met with leaders of the putsch. This meeting was important not only because it helped lead to the collapse of the putsch, but because it revealed Riezler's basic conviction that the Republic had to be defended from attacks from both left and right extremes. Reports (which later proved to be false) had been received by the putschists that a Spartacist uprising was about to be ordered and that a new radical government had been formed with the Independent Social Democrats, Ernst Däumig and Oskar Cohn, at the head. In the face of this dual threat to the Republic, Riezler recommended to President Ebert and Chancellor Bauer in Stuttgart that while no compromise of any kind

205

should be made with Kapp, Lüttwitz should be permitted to retain command for twenty-four hours over the troops controlling Berlin since those troops would obey no other general. Those troops could then be used against a Spartacist uprising in Berlin. He stressed that he was not suggesting that Lüttwitz be pardoned for his treasonous activity against the Republic. "He will put a bullet through his head anyway." Although the cabinet in Stuttgart was by no means resolutely united against Riezler's recommendation, Ebert and Bauer absolutely rejected it. Riezler had hoped to direct one putschist group against another in order to allow both extremes to destroy each other. On the other hand, the president and chancellor correctly saw that such a plan was unrealistic and that working class support for the government would have been irretrievably lost if the government had turned troops under Lüttwitz against rebelling workers at this particular time. Far from destroying the extremes, Riezler's proposal would have widened the gap between them and isolated the middle even further.[45]

Completely unable to maintain control any longer, Kapp and Lüttwitz were forced to flee to Sweden on March 17. On the same day, the *Freikorps* retreated in military formation down Unter den Linden and through the Brandenburg Gate on their way out of Berlin. On March 18 Riezler reported to Ebert: "Situation quiet in Berlin. Insignificant exchanges of fire throughout the night." Finally, on March 20 Ebert and the German government were able to return to Berlin.[46]

The suppression of the Kapp Putsch enabled the beleaguered Republic to survive only thirteen more years, years of political and economic turmoil. On August 21, 1921, former Finance Minister Matthias Erzberger was assassinated by members of the right radical "Organization Consul." This organization collected money from those who were scared of Communism, but who, as Riezler wrote, were not wise enough to know that "if the Communists still have the slightest hope, it lies today in the deeds of the Organization C, as it once lay in the Kapp Putsch." The following year, Foreign Minister Walther Rathenau was felled by assassins' bullets. The next day, Chancellor Josef Wirth declared in the Reichstag, where Rathenau's body lay in state: "The enemy is on the right!" Riezler agreed completely.[47]

The year 1923 saw unsuccessful putsches by Communists in Hamburg and by National Socialists in Munich. Though unsuccessful in 1923, these two parties of the extreme left and right continued to grow throughout the next decade; by 1932 they were able to win more than half of all votes cast in Reichstag elections. Those parties which supported the Republic finally suffocated between the extremes. By March 24, 1933, the Weimar Republic was dead.

More than a decade later, after he had already left Germany, Riezler looked back on the crisis of German society and on the revolution which had taken place within that society. His analysis of the rise of Hitler is incomplete, and his terms are somewhat imprecise. He did not pretend that this was an exhaustive evaluation of that tragic process. Nevertheless, his psychological analysis reveals some important elements of that victory of irrationalism on January 30, 1933.

That which Riezler called the Fascist revolution was a granddaughter, not a daughter of the war; the desperate economic situation, resulting from ruinous inflation in the early years and from severe unemployment in the later years, had led to a widespread "fear of the unknown." That economic catastrophe was the "parent" of the Fascist revolution. "Insofar as economic development, as in early capitalism, or a total war and defeat means an atomization of the masses, uproots and disperses the individuals, destroys ties and natural groups, it prepares the potential herd and the way for the dictatorial leader of modern times." He argued that this danger is particularly great considering two "hard facts" of the industrial age. That age creates elaborate central machinery, whose control offers great potential power. Also, the industrial age multiplies and refines the technical instruments of power which can be used to "misuse the masses": centralized propaganda and news organs, as well as great concentration of military and police power which can make opposition to even a minority in power impossible.[48]

Riezler described in 1943 the psychological process of the Fascist revolution in Germany. He noted that in such a badly divided society, as Germany was, chiefly because of her extremely rapid industrialization, certain groups, especially capitalists and workers, suspiciously watch each other, blind to everything else. Seeing nothing but their supposed enemies on the other side of the chasm, and bewildered and paralyzed by fear, both become vulnerable to a "flank attack" by determined revolutionaries who recruit the discontented from all classes.

This flank attack receives the unwitting cooperation of three "psychological classes." The first such class is that of the "outcasts," those who have lost their standing in the society and resent this fact bitterly. This class includes both the "economically uprooted," and the "intellectually uprooted." The former refers especially to the German lower middle classes, who had been ravaged by the twin evils of inflation and unemployment. The latter refers to those whose ideals had been crushed

207

by the fall of the Empire and the loss of the war. The most important part of the "intellectually uprooted" were the disillusioned military officers returning from war and defeat. However, the immense popularity of battle-front novels, written by such authors as Ernst Jünger, Werner Beumelburg, and Edwin Erich Dwinger, indicates that this category included far more than the officers. It also included many intellectuals, especially the "intellectual nihilists." These relativists, who had learned that "values are only valuations and arbitrary," had a special role in the development of the "outcast mentality." "When the social order begins to question itself, the intellectual nihilist has the function of providing the outcast with a good conscience, of breaking down his last inhibitions and preparing him mentally for his future role. The new power either puts the intellectual nihilist into a concentration camp or employs him on the staff of a Goebbels or a Himmler."

This "social scrap of all classes" is always the best raw material for a revolution. Such "social scrap" has a great need to renew its sense of success and importance, and it flocks to any party or to any well-organized emotional movement, even to a "shabby provincial and nonsensical ideology," to regain its sense of importance. It "clubs together," and the sense of togetherness soon becomes stronger than former social class differences.[49]

This outcast class would, however, have no chance of conquering a state without the aid of another psychological class: the "fools." Every age, of course, has its fools, but Riezler had a special kind of fool in mind: the kind who are the "natural offspring of the industrial age." The industrial age, Riezler argued, had led to "an enormous complexity of social, economic, political factors, whose ramifications fewer and fewer men are able to master." In normal times these people are ordinary "decent" citizens, but in times of crisis, they become easily frightened and bewildered, and they are unable to understand what is happening. They are gripped by "collective insecurity," the source of which they cannot understand. Their reaction is to simplify and to accuse; they need scapegoats, and they raise a passionate demand for change, no matter what kind. These "fools" become easy prey for emotional leaders and for great simplifiers. Riezler included both Marxists and German industrialists in this class.

The third class is the least numerous class and is also an offspring of the industrial age: "the experts." According to Riezler, the experts respond to the increasing complexity of the industrial age by becoming narrow specialists, who feel helpless outside their fields. Their knowledge concerns means, not ends; they assume that dealing with ends is the job of another expert. However, because of the rise in the number and prestige of the experts for means, those persons with the wisdom to be experts for ends decline in number and prestige. Ultimately, there are no longer truly wise and respected individuals who can serve as experts for ends. A major problem with the expert for means is that he will serve any regime. Whether in the state bureaucracy or outside of it, he stands ever ready to pull out blueprints and straighten out the files. Riezler noted that "if the world perishes, files and accounts will be in perfect order."

Observing the German example, Riezler described the cooperation of these three psychological classes in the following way:

The fool hires an outcast to handle the masses. The outcast, supported by the fool, rides into power on the crest of an emotional movement. When in power, he fools the fool. The fooled fool sees his economic power taken over by the holder of political power. The popular movement, which was the vehicle of success, is dismissed—after the purges. There is a . . . struggle between the popular movement as such—the "party" or the revolutionary forces—and an authoritarian organization centered in the secret police. This struggle ends with the victory of the police. The expert, given his chance by the new power, rushes into service. The desks full of blueprints are searched for projects that the new power can use for its own ends. The service of the expert makes the new power efficient.

From this description, four things need to be noted. First, Riezler laid heavy blame on the "well-to-do, commanding iron, steel or coal" who, he thought, had played a crucial role in Hitler's acquisition of power. These "fools" assumed falsely that the man "who pays the piper calls the tune." There is at least some truth in this. However, while Hitler received aid at crucial moments from the German industrialist Fritz Thyssen and the Dutch oil magnate Henry Deterding, the role of German industry in Hitler's rise to power is frequently greatly exaggerated. Second, while National Socialism appeared to be a popular movement in the last stage before its take-over, Hitler soon thereafter eliminated the popular element of the revolution. With all the instruments of state control firmly in his hands, he had no further need of the popular element. Riezler observed that "in this point the Fascist revolution follows the example of other revolutions." Third, the old stratification of society merely gave way to a new stratification. "The elite of the outcasts, the selection of many purges, would form the new upper class, enjoying all sorts of privileges and the better part of the wealth. The experts would form the new middle class, with higher salaries and a certain amount of economic security. The fools, with all the rest of the population, would be enslaved and live in the hope that their sons might rise into the class of experts and their daughters marry into the new elite."

209

Fourth, the National Socialists were able to tap a deep well of malcontent stemming in part from economic and spiritual shocks since 1918. These shocks magnified the fear of modernity to its irrational limits. Such malcontent nourished, in Fritz Stern's words, a "descent from idealism to nihilism," which easily merged with the tide of Hitler's movement. Riezler recognized this important reason for the resentful rejection of the Weimar Republic, which, again in Stern's words, "had little to do with objective grievances and everything with a disdain that was compounded of loneliness and embittered expectations of the unattainable."[50]

Riezler admitted that the crisis of society, which had culminated in the Fascist revolution, was the most difficult crisis with which to cope, and it cannot be said that he offered any facile solutions to that crisis. He could only suggest a few remedies. Of course, he saw that solutions to the first two crises, those of foreign policy and the state, would have greatly alleviated the crisis of society. Also, if the severe economic difficulties could have been overcome, then the paralyzing fear, as well as the numbers of "social scrap," could have been reduced. After the Second World War he pointed to the need for a kind of "civic virtue" to help prevent a divided society from sliding into crisis. Greatly impressed with Alexis de Tocqueville, Riezler argued for a civic virtue which would not only permit, but encourage a "lively spirit of debate" and "two-way communication" between the government and the citizens, as well as among the citizens themselves. A free press and responsible journalism would be indispensable in fostering such civic virtue. However, Riezler knew that a nation can develop civic virtue only over a long period of time. It is certainly most difficult or impossible to develop in time of crisis, when the emotion of fear converts the spirit of debate into a spirit of struggle and converts sober reasoning into an irrational call for change of any kind and at any cost. The Weimar Republic had neither the time nor the calm which would have permitted civic virtue to have developed.

Riezler also believed that the crisis of society could be solved if governments would try to be guided by reason. This frequently voiced demand of Riezler was indeed a large order which, as he later recognized, is burdened with the difficulty that reasonable persons can disagree greatly on what a reasonable course of action might be. While one cannot hope that governments start conducting their affairs according to agreed upon standards of reason, one can, as he suggested and demonstrated, help government leaders and citizens through thoughtful journalism to make more deliberate and informed decisions. Indeed, despite his lack at the time of a powerful inner attachment to liberal democracy, Riezler's out-

210

ward behavior was a kind without which no republican experiment can ever succeed: the visible willingness to break with at least a part of tradition, the unswerving public commitment to the new democratic order, and, above all, the continuous appeal to reason, not to a flight into irrationality.

Responsible journalism can help citizens and leaders understand the causes of crises and thereby avoid unacceptable solutions to those crises. It is clear that the intelligent journalist can have a positive impact if he is given enough time. However, the Weimar Republic had precious little time. It was quickly overcome by its crises.[51]

UNIVERSITY OF FRANKFURT

As we have already indicated, Riezler departed from public service in April 1920. Several years later, Theodor Heuss half seriously remarked that it was a pity that Riezler had left active political life. Riezler replied that such a person as himself was apparently "good for such a life only in times of revolution." Actually, he never cut himself off completely from politics. For a few years he continued to perform party work, traveling to conferences and congresses and delivering speeches. He also continued to write numerous political articles under pseudonyms as well as his own name. In addition, Riezler regularly participated in political clubs, such as the November Club, and editorial gatherings in Berlin. After the failure of *Die Deutsche Nation* in 1925, Riezler attended the weekly editorial staff meetings of the *Deutscher Volkswirt,* a journal edited by Gustav Stolper and devoted to the linkage of economic and foreign policy. Mrs. Toni Stolper described Riezler as a "spark of the discussions" and as the major contributor to the "intellectual stature" of the journal. Riezler, she remembered, was "a philosophical author with the knowledge of an insider and the liberty of a statesman out of office."[52]

However, his primary interest began to change noticeably. His attention became increasingly redirected toward philosophy. By 1923 his philosophical writings began to appear with greater frequency than his political writings. Of course, Riezler had never ceased being philosophically inclined. Indeed, this inclination had been the basic reason why Bethmann Hollweg had been attracted to him and why Ebert had not. By 1927 Riezler was recognized in Germany as a man of considerable philosophical stature. Combined with his great political experience and his high connections in Berlin, this reputation opened the door to a fortunate opportunity.

211

In the fall of 1927, the Kurator of the University of Frankfurt, Kurt Gerlach, died unexpectedly. Riezler was immediately recommended for the post by the Frankfurt City Councilman, Dr. Michel, and by Ministerial Director Richter, who described Riezler as "an exceptional philosophical mind, who could even be considered for a professorship in philosophy if he so desired." Richter commented further that although Riezler was greatly experienced in administration, he nevertheless "is one of those people who have no ambition and who are striving toward nothing at the moment. As far as I see, he would without question meet our demands politically. You would gain for Frankfurt the opposite of a bureaucrat—an intellectual person about whom one could better ask: will he muster the necessary enthusiasm for the day-to-day bureaucratic obligations?"[53]

In an exchange of letters with the mayor of Frankfurt, Riezler made clear his intention, if appointed, to take a hand not only in the administrative, but also in the academic life of the institution. Also, he made his acceptance conditional on his appointment both as *Kurator* and as professor of philosophy. On April 5, 1928, after much delay, his terms were accepted. With Riezler's appointment began "the great years of the young university in which the most intensive intellectual discussions of all contemporary trends took place. From approximately 1928 until 1933 Frankfurt University was able to assume a leading role among all the German universities."[54]

In sharp contrast to most bureaucrats and professors during the Weimar period, Riezler did not shy away from publicly supporting the existing political order. A few months after his inauguration, Riezler delivered an address in the Paulskirche, Germany's cradle of liberalism, to mark the anniversary of the enactment of the Weimar Constitution. In this address, he argued for the legitimacy of organized interests and parties as the inevitable mediators between citizens and the state as a whole, but he advised that such mediators must attempt daily to balance special interests and common interests. He recognized that this mediating role presented both dangers and great opportunities for a parliamentary regime. However, his most important message to the individual citizen was that each person's development as a human being was not dependent upon the state, but upon himself. "The most essential thing" *(das Wesentliche)* for man lay beyond politics; it was "in being and becoming a person, in becoming conscious of himself and in becoming and being introspective." Although the first part of Riezler's message was understood, in the words of the *Frankfurter Zeitung,* as a "manly commitment to the republican-democratic national state," Riezler had the impression that the more important message—to "be oneself"—had not been understood.[55]

This speech revealed the extent to which Riezler was still touched by his own education which stressed the independent value of cultural self-fulfillment. Of course, there can be no doubt that man's greatest enrichment involves activities of the mind which are more than instrumentalities for a better material existence on earth. However, no person can divorce himself from social responsibilities. Riezler had distinguished himself from those within the educated elite who believed that the cultivated man should always flee from politics into a higher world. From the beginning of his political career he had advocated responsible and rational political engagement by Germany's academically trained leaders. Therefore, one would have expected him to have gone one step further in his Frankfurt speech. Modern democratic political thought no longer assigns to the regime the role of guiding man to perfection. Nevertheless, it clearly posits the necessity of a regime which can establish and maintain the preconditions for man's striving toward his own perfection or happiness. As he learned only five years later, this striving can never be possible in a regime which does not recognize inviolable human rights and human freedom. Therefore, instead of divorcing, even theoretically, the regime from man's highest aspirations, his message would have been far more constructive if it had shown the indispensability of a liberal democratic regime for those ultimate human aims.

Riezler's service in Frankfurt was distinguished in every way. He proved himself to be competent in both attracting financial resources to the university and in managing the university's finances. He was extremely effective in dealing with officials from the city and from the Prussian Ministry of Culture in Berlin. His many highly placed connections in Berlin, as well as his commanding personality, enabled him to block any inappropriate intervention in the academic affairs of the university.

The shrewdness and negotiating skill which he displayed in dealing with Prussian officials in Berlin were also shown in his dealings with the faculty, which normally made academic appointments. In fact, he was responsible for initiating many new appointments, and in no case was an appointment ever made without his approval. His great negotiating skill was coupled with his high standing as a scholar and as an honorary professor, which made his judgment on appointment matters highly valued by the faculty. As a scholar, he was regarded as "one of them." Among his successful appointments were those of Max Wertheimer, the father of *Gestalt* theory, the sociologist Karl Mannheim, the philosopher

213

Max Horkheimer, the historian Ernst Kantorowicz, the theologian Paul Tillich, and the economist Adolf Lowe. These appointments, along with some of the professors who had been appointed earlier, provided Frankfurt with a diverse and highly distinguished faculty.

Riezler's positive influence on the faculty went beyond the matter of new appointments. He managed to keep exceptionally well informed about faculty affairs through a circle of friends whom he gathered around him. This circle, which met for discussions on a regular basis, was drawn from a variety of disciplines and included only scholars whose interests and insights went far beyond their specialties. Through this circle, Riezler was able to inform himself thoroughly of faculty problems, to extend his own influence over the faculty, and in a friendly and informal way to make his own views and wishes known.[56]

Riezler also participated in a number of collective seminars with faculty members of widely different disciplines at the university. For example, he took part in one such seminar dealing with the concept of truth in the various academic disciplines in which such colleagues as Wertheimer, Tillich, Mannheim, the theoretical physicist Madelung, and the jurists Hermann Heller and de Boor, also participated. These "Wisdom Seminars," as they were known to the students, often lasted until late in the night. Riezler also participated as a guest lecturer and discussant at the Academy of Work, which had been founded in 1920 in order to further the education of the common people. Although he wanted to stimulate the research effort of the university's faculty, he no longer shared the view that higher education should be only impractical and reserved for the very few. He also lectured and discussed at the famed, if highly controversial, *Institut für Sozialforschung* (Institute for Social Research). In addition, he gave courses on such topics as the "Dynamics of Metaphysical Problems." He devoted an increasingly large amount of his time to his lectures and seminars, and for the summer semester of 1933 he had announced lectures on philosophical anthropology and a seminar on the doctrine of emotions.[57] However, Riezler's academic activities were interrupted by radical political developments.

After the National Socialist assumption of power on January 30, 1933, Riezler was bound to have difficulties. His disdain for National Socialists had scarcely been concealed, and he had gained a reputation for defending students who had gotten into political difficulties with the new leaders. Also, his private thoughts could not have been unknown to the Nazis. Adolf Lowe related that Riezler had been a frequent guest in his Frankfurt home and that both had learned after many visits that Lowe's maid was the girlfriend of Riezler's male secretary, who was a member of the National Socialist party. Once the maid was caught listening in on their conversations, which often ranged into politics.

Shortly after January 1933, a Nazi commissar was sent to the Frankfurt University to investigate Riezler, who was under suspicion for having shown sympathy for Communists and pacifists. Challenged to defend himself, Riezler reminded the Prussian Ministry of Culture that he had actively worked against the Communists in Moscow and Bamberg and had opposed the signing of the Versailles Treaty. The investigation revealed no negligence of duty on Riezler's part, but he had hardly eliminated the suspicion toward him.

As the new political leaders prepared to include the universities in their program of *Gleichschaltung* (in effect, "elimination of opponents"), the unrest at German universities grew. Adolf Lowe recalled a division which developed within the faculty between those professors who declared loyalty to Hitler and those who did not. At the end of March 1933, violent student disruptions occurred: the university was boycotted by Nazi sympathizers, and clashes between student groups erupted. On April 1, 1933, the university was occupied by an SA unit in order to purge it of "Jews and Marxists." Riezler, who was delivering a lecture at the time of the occupation, was driven from the podium by uniformed troops. The only audible protest against this act of violence was that of Dr. Kövendi, a Hungarian who had come to Frankfurt to study classical philology. Karl Reinhardt reported that Kövendi screamed: "How is such a thing possible in the land of Schiller and Goethe!" Reinhardt noted that "as a stupid foreigner, one let him [Kövendi] go."[58]

Riezler was put into jail under "protective custody," and he was able to gain his release only by consenting to a temporary resignation from his duties as *Kurator*. His permanent separation from all university duties came with the proclamation on April 7, 1933, of the "Law for the Restoration of the Professional Civil Service," which was directed against those who, "judged by their previous political activity, cannot offer the guarantee that they stand up unconditionally for the national state at all times." The "leadership principle" was introduced into the universities by granting to the Reich Ministry of Culture the right to appoint the rectors and leaders of student associations, hitherto appointed by the faculties and students themselves. Also, Nazi party affiliation was introduced into the admission procedure. Clearly, such a university had no use for Kurt Riezler. Accused of "national unreliability," Riezler entered forced retirement, as the Nazis moved to destroy the "Riezler clique" at the University of Frankfurt.

215

A few weeks later Riezler described the intellectual shambles left at the university:

> When the student body can determine on its own authority who will be admitted to examinations; when students are encouraged to control the lectures of the professors for politically revealing utterances or even assume to be qualified to judge the German or un-German spirit of books or teachers based on their conceptions of the day; when pressure can be exercised on the teachers through the threat of disrupting lectures or on students through the threat of exclusion from examinations; when such miserable slogans as 'the fundamental principles of the student body against the un-German spirit' can even be proclaimed, even if only temporarily—then the freedom to teach is practically destroyed and every *pro forma* recognition [of that freedom to teach] is an empty word.[59]

Of course, many of Germany's academics had contributed at least indirectly to the successful Fascist overthrow of the Republic. By publicly attacking the Republic at every opportunity, by speaking so often and convincingly of the need for "national rebirth" and "spiritual revival," and by openly discrediting any social or cultural adjustment to modernity, they provided a rationalization and a good conscience to those who were willing to risk a "leap from despair to utopia across all existing reality."[60] Riezler certainly was not among those German academics who in any way had encouraged Germans to make that leap.

Riezler spent the next five years in Berlin, living from his pension as a retired diplomat. He devoted his full attention to philosophy. During that time he produced what is perhaps his greatest philosophical work: his interpretation of the pre-Socratic thinker, Parmenides. However, it was not possible, as he well knew, to escape the political turmoil of the day. Riezler had good reason to fear it: his wife was Jewish, and his daughter was naturally also categorized by the Nazis as a Jew.

During the First World War, Riezler had written that Germany would someday have to undergo rule by the Pan-Germans before being able ever to achieve political maturity. That rule had now come, and Riezler had no desire to live under it. Instead, he chose to emigrate to the United States, where a teaching post at the graduate faculty of political and social science of the New School in New York awaited him.

Chapter Eight
EXILE

The happiest man is he who is able to integrate the end of his life with its beginning.

—Goethe

In December 1938, Riezler and his family journeyed to the United States. Due to some of his highly placed personal connections, Riezler was able to leave with his family's most valuable possessions: Max Liebermann's priceless private art collection, as well as Liebermann's rare furniture.[1]

It is indeed ironic that Riezler sought exile in one of those countries which he had admired least. In his *Grundzüge der Weltpolitik,* written a quarter of a century earlier, Riezler had presented the United States as a land of materialism, trusts, and political corruption. After the First World War he resented the political naiveté, represented by Woodrow Wilson, whose idealism merely masked the power hunger and the uncompromising vindictiveness of France. Perhaps more significant to Riezler, the United States appeared to be a land without culture or manners. For Riezler, these were serious weaknesses. In his opinion, the culture of a nation was to a great extent reflected in its art, and he found that the United States had accomplished little in this respect. Also, he had witnessed too many unruly American travelers to be able to escape the generalization that Americans were an unrefined people. Although he would eventually come to admire certain American characteristics, he never truly became a part of his new environment. He always remained a European.

It is not surprising that Riezler's move to the United States was not a final move away from politics. The world was on the brink of disaster, and the political Riezler could not shut his eyes to the danger. Indeed, Hans Staudinger, former dean at the New School, remembered him as always "unbelievably interested in politics." His political thoughts were not expressed in smug cynicism about what the political situation in the world had come to. As always, his political thoughts were directed toward the ways in which he could help guide political events into a more rational direction.

217

Riezler in Exile

His political activity soon after arrival in the United States indicated that he had not been indifferent to the momentous political events which had occurred since his removal from the University of Frankfurt in April 1933. While in retirement in Berlin, Riezler had established contacts with various resistance groups. One of these groups was the Kreisau Circle led by Count Helmut James von Moltke. This group was devoted to the establishment of a sort of "co-operative society" of European states and ultimately of a European government, which would reduce the significance of the individual European states.[2] Both of these ideas had appeared in Riezler's writings as early as 1920.

Riezler's contact with anti-Hitler resistance groups became especially useful in the crucial period immediately following the German attack on Poland on September 1, 1939. This was a time particularly favorable for resistance efforts because many high officials in both the German military and the German Foreign Office were committed to the resistance effort. Within the Foreign Office a state secretary, Baron Ernst von Weizsäcker, had formed a cohesive anti-Ribbentrop group, which was attempting to establish and maintain contact with Britain, the United States, and other major powers. Weizsäcker was regularly able to send high level messengers to these powers in an attempt to achieve the twin objectives of restoring peace and overthrowing the Hitler regime, objectives which Weizsäcker regarded as inseparably linked.[3] Riezler played a minor role in one of the many ill-fated attempts to establish contact between German resistance groups and high officials of the major enemy and neutral powers.

Adam von Trott zu Solz had established himself as a respected expert on Asian affairs. He was a German whose principles and dignity stamped him, in the opinion of his many British friends, as a symbol of commitment to all that remained decent in Germany. Trott, who had made three trips to Britain in the eight months before the war, was in close contact in Germany with the resistance leaders General Ludwig Beck and Carl Goerdeler and with the followers of Ernst von Weizsäcker.

Through Weizsäcker, Trott was able to accept an invitation to attend a convention of the Institute of Pacific Relations to be held in Virginia Beach, Virginia, during the month of November 1939. Inevitably, the fact that Trott had the official permission of the German Foreign Office to attend the conference in the United States aroused great suspicion in the United States which he was never able to dispel. He nevertheless made the journey in order to seek support for a plan to end the war by means of an anti-Hitler uprising within Germany. Such an uprising needed the strong encouragement of the governments of Britain and neutral America in the form of a definition of war aims which would not antagonize most Germans. It was believed that unreasonable war aims would have made the work of the German resistance impossible.

It is unknown when Riezler had first met Trott, but Riezler was one of the first people Trott called on after arriving in the United States in October 1939, and Riezler was also one of the few compatriots to whom Trott confided the names of those in Germany who were ready to risk their lives in a violent uprising against Hitler. Among those with whom Trott also met were former German Chancellor Heinrich Brüning, John Wheeler-Bennet, Hans Simons, and Paul Scheffer. The product of all these meetings was a memorandum containing their views on the prospects and the necessary preconditions for an uprising against Hitler.[4]

Most of the memorandum was written by Paul Scheffer, a former Berlin editor who was serving as the American correspondent of the *Deutsche Allgemeine Zeitung.* Trott himself wrote the conclusion. The memorandum called for American diplomatic pressure on those governments at war with Germany to declare peace aims which could help rally the German people against Hitler. Germany's part would lie "first and foremost in the abandonment of her present political leadership." The result would be a rapid termination of the war, a generous negotiated peace, and the establishment by "constructive elements" everywhere of machinery for European cooperation, in which the anti-Nazi opposition forces in Germany would also participate.[5] Riezler's exact contribution to this program cannot be documented, but he undoubtedly supported it. This support derived from his own experience during the First World War with the negative effect of excessive war aims on attempts to establish peace, from his recognition of long-term damage done by the Draconian peace terms dictated at Versailles, and from his conviction that sovereign states were obsolete and had to be replaced by supranational political units.

This memorandum rapidly found its way to the highest official circles in the United States. Through Heinrich Brüning the memorandum was delivered to Assistant Secretary of State George S. Messersmith, the department's acknowledged expert on Central European affairs. Messersmith was very enthusiastic about the document, and he not only gave a copy to Secretary of State Cordell Hull and Under-Secretary of State Sumner Welles, but he also indiscreetly had twenty-four copies distributed. The White House had not only received a copy, but had reportedly shown "lively interest" in the memorandum. Apparently President Roosevelt had at least been briefed on its contents.[6]

While Trott had succeeded in familiarizing the president of the United States with certain needs of the German resistance against Hitler, the skepticism of Justice Felix Frankfurter, a leading Zionist and a man greatly respected by the president, as well as a series of indiscretions on Trott's part caused his overall mission to fail.

He spoke far too openly with far too many people about his goals. To observers, this openness revealed either extreme carelessness on Trott's part or approval of his mission by highly placed Nazis. Unaware of the actual split within the German Foreign Office, too many people in the United States, including many German emigres, found in Trott's way of operating proof that he was a Gestapo agent, a spy, or a loyal servant of Hitler, and that he wished at a minimum to revive the policy of appeasement. Riezler was moved to complain to Scheffer about Trott, who was actually being followed everywhere by the FBI. Riezler found such behavior "hair-raising" as Trott's telling more than a hundred people in one gathering about the aims of the opposition regarding the formation of a post-Nazi government.[7]

Despite the wide distribution of the memorandum, which extended to the Canadian and British governments, Trott's mission failed to influence official policy in the Allied countries as he and his supporters inside and outside of Germany had hoped. It was merely one of many examples of how little Allied support was ever given to the German resistance. This episode was quickly forgotten, and few took note of Trott's unfortunate fate. On August 26, 1944, he was hanged by the Nazis for his prominent role in the anti-Hitler resistance.

Riezler never talked with his colleagues or acquaintances about his resistance activities. In fact, he discussed politics only with a few of his colleagues. He certainly had no ambition to hold political office, either in the United States or in Germany. However, he remained interested in the question of how the scholar could aid the statesman, and his later writings are an important reflection of what he had learned during a long political life. In 1946 he delivered a lecture on this subject at a meeting of the American Philosophical Association, held at the University of Chicago. In this lecture, entitled "The Philosopher of History and the Modern Statesman," he noted that "in actual life the philosopher of history and the statesman are not too willing to listen to each other—now less than ever, as ours is a time in which action tends to be thoughtless and thought inactive."[8]

Riezler found two kinds of scholars particularly unsuited to instruct the statesman: the "methodologist of scientific historiography" and the

221

"metaphysician of history." The "methodologist," who attempts to apply the methods of natural science to the study of history and politics, is "a modest fellow" who does not claim to be listened to by any statesman. Nevertheless, as we shall see, Riezler regretted that such methodologists, known as behaviorists, had become so prominent in American social science because he believed that they made the social science alien to actual political decision-making.[9]

The second kind of scholar, the "metaphysician of history," is , according to Riezler, as arrogant as the methodologist is humble. The "metaphysician of history," whether he be a Marxist or simply a believer in the inevitability of human progress, interprets universal history as "unity of a plot." "Though his respect for evidence is but small, he can be a forceful mind of great speculative power and he many lay his hands on the thought of a century."

The work of the "metaphysician of history" is a response to a deeply felt need in the soul of modern man:

Man, the ephemeral being, craves to think of the sweat and sorrow of his few days as imbedded in a process that carries the past into the future upwards toward a goal of ultimate meaning by an inherent necessity. As the power of religion fades and (in the mass society of our own days) God and Providence evaporate behind a thin veil of words, the metaphysician of history fills a void: his constructions of the historical process become the raw material of the secularized religions we call ideologies.

Ideologies, like religion, offer hope and belief. They therefore become ideal instruments in the hands of those who seek power to serve their own ends. Those power seekers reshape the ideologies into "systems of magic formulas of dubious meaning, to be waved as flags fitting the political purpose of the revolutionary movements." Whenever acts or policies are necessary which do not fit into the ideological scheme, then revolutionary leaders speak of "transition periods," which would temporarily justify those acts or policies. However, "the revolutionary leader, unable to renounce those means or to fulfill those promises, goes on forever acting in a period of transition." History, which Riezler was now convinced had no meaning or plan whatsoever, remains indifferent to such power seekers: "It shoves aside the real Hegel and the real Marx, without pity or respect, and upholds Stalin for a while at the top of the world."[10]

Riezler was no less critical of another kind of metaphysician of history in "a still free society," the one who preaches the "philosophy of progress." This philosophy is the belief in "an automatic progress as a law of the historical process as such, brought about not by man's actions and intentions but by a law of evolution." This "mostly half-conscious assumption . . . implies an increasing power of reason over man—a wrong conclusion contradicted by more and more evidence, yet suggested by wishful thinking." Riezler certainly believed in the possibility of human progress and in the possibility of the increasing power of reason in man; indeed, he hoped that man, through his own efforts, would transform these possibilities into reality. Nevertheless, he denied that these developments were inevitable.[11]

The acting statesman "is called upon not to interpret history but to make it." He acts, and "some of his decisions decide the future of his nation one way or the other." He orients his actions according to the actual political situation, not according to "the meaning of a universal process." He regards the future "as not only unknown but still undecided." Of course, the statesman is limited to one degree or the other by domestic pressures, by limited resources, and by conflicting interests of other states. Thus, much of the situation within which he can operate is "predecided"; his flexibility is sometimes great, sometimes limited. Certainly, the past can greatly influence the choices which are available to the statesman. Nevertheless, Riezler was convinced that despite the inevitable constraints which are always placed on the statesman, "the future is still open; it is to be decided."

Riezler saw a further dimension to statesmanship. The statesman considers not only the possible, but also the desirable; in fact, "he looks at the one under the aspect of the other." Thus, the statesman tries to pursue a policy which serves not only his nation's interests, but which serves his own values as well. "His eyes are cold and hard yet the flame burns in his heart as he opposes his specific virtue to the play that necessity and chance play with each other." As he wrote seven years later, man "stands and acts in between a must, a can, a want to, and an ought. . . . Man in political action is man in his totality. . . ."

The scholar who can provide useful assistance to the statesman is one who correctly understands the circumstances and the context within which the statesman must act. He is one who understands the real world, which Riezler compared to a play:

It is a strange play; there is no audience. The actors themselves are its sole observers. No actor, not even a community of actors, stays through the play from beginning to end. Even any hero drops out after hardly more than half a scene. Most of us are poor actors, playing merely ourselves. There are no rehearsals, no script. We do not know our lines, though we have only a few to say. We must be satisfied if the two lines we improvise make sense to ourselves or to our nearest co-actors for some time or seem worth being remembered. It may not be a play at all, as it lacks the unity of a play. If there is to be a meaning, the actors must provide it during the play. This is the core of their acting.[12]

The analysis of the mature Riezler obviously differed considerably from that of the German chancellor's young assistant prior to the First World War. The young Riezler had seen powerful "tendencies" at work in the world, and he had viewed nations as organisms which naturally strive to develop and to perfect themselves. These tendencies and this national development gave meaning to the world and to world politics, and they greatly restricted the field in which the statesman operated. Indeed, a "theory of politics" was necessary in order to elucidate them. The mature Riezler no longer believed in either the idea that nations strive toward perfection or in the importance of "tendencies" or "trends." "Many a belief in a trend is but a convenient excuse." Most trends spring from "the blindness and stupidity of past actions and decisions. We shrug our shoulders and point to a trend. Yet the guilt is still man's."

Riezler's later analysis no longer had such an optimistic and exuberant tone which had characterized his *Grundzüge der Weltpolitik*. His experience had dampened that optimism. Nevertheless, his diminished optimism did not lead him to conclude that human existence was necessarily meaningless. Indeed, he was convinced that human existence could have meaning; however, "man—the present man—gives the meaning or fails to give the meaning."

Riezler recognized that the global political situation after the Second World War was far too complex for one man to master. In order to cope with the new and unprecedented situation, statesmen needed to be supported "by the statesmanship of a whole nation."

Look at the present scene: the aftermath of a total war, a half devastated world; shattered, dislocated or confused are minds, souls and bodies, the moral standards of both victors and vanquished, traditions, loyalties, hopes, ideas and interests; blind passions, held down but by hunger; a thick fog of old and new lies—this is the situation in which humanity gropes its way along the abyss of its technological advance, frightened yet still dreaming. But even this situation has not pre-decided the future. Man—in this case the equivalent of the statesman or the politician is the nation as a whole and thus in each of us in particular—man himself will decide it.[13]

One of the major decisions facing the nations of the "half devastated world" concerned the treatment of that country which, Riezler admitted, had been responsible for starting "the first total war"—Germany. In 1947 he wrote a lengthy comment on an article written by Hans Speier concerning the survival of German nationalism. Riezler's predictions proved to be extremely accurate. He went beyond the future of German nationalism and treated the future of Germany itself in a world radically changed from the one in which Riezler had begun his political activity almost a half century earlier.

He considered the circumstances in which Germany found herself to be almost unprecedented in history: shrunken, divided, impoverished, occupied, and without a government or a voice as a nation. In the face of this unique situation, Riezler admitted to the difficulty of making any accurate predictions concerning what would happen; "we cannot foresee the balance of the mistakes that the occupying powers are bound to make." He shied away from making any specific legal recommendations. However, he drew on his own experience to recommend certain ways of approaching the unique situation in which Germany found herself.

He basically warned against the assumption that Germans were completely unique people who would react to circumstances in a wholly unpredictable way. He argued that "it would be wiser to assume that the Germans, as a whole, will react to future conditions as would any other people. It is always wise to put oneself in another's place and at least to try to take on his role. If people did that, they would make fewer mistakes of judgment and action." Germans, he argued, "will hardly behave differently from the people of Vermont or Maine under similar conditions."

In direct response to Speier's warnings about the dangers of emerging nationalism in postwar Germany, Riezler argued that the nationalism which survived the holocaust of the Second World War would, for the most part, be of a totally different character than the loud, aggressively extensive nationalism which tended to predominate in Germany's past. It would be a kind of healthy patriotism which "will be no mere survival of any nationalistic longing for the sweetness of power," and would be based on "the existing reality and not on romantic dreams." This new nationalism would not be "immoral" and would be unrelated to the "master race" notion, which, according to Riezler, always had in it more of a sense of inferiority than of pride. Certainly, all persons or peoples need some form of pride, and the basic question was whether the Germans would be able to develop some kind of, or reasons for, a constructive pride, which would not be dangerous to other peoples. Only two years after the end of the Second World War, Riezler was optimistic that this would be possible, as well as necessary:

225

Wayne C. Thompson

Even the Germans may be able to do this if they are given some opportunity to do constructive work on a transnational basis, without, however, being constantly reminded of a sense of shame that they should not only feel but show. No human being and certainly no nation can be expected to perpetuate the feeling of shame without developing an always repulsive and sometimes aggressive defense mechanism, an attitude that rabble-rousers of the future would not fail to exploit.

Riezler anticipated that the former, harmful form of nationalism would linger on for awhile in the minds of some Germans. Indeed, he even foresaw danger in purging the minds of those few "old German nationalists" too suddenly. He feared that a person who abandoned strong nationalist ideas too quickly would perhaps believe in nothing and "become a nihilist before he becomes anything else"; this would be no less dangerous than the ideas he too rapidly abandoned. In any case, he correctly foresaw that "the old German nationalists will have no role to play" in the new Germany. "They are a poor sort, and none of their old power tricks will serve." Generally, German "rabble-rousers" will have few opportunities in the new Germany; the shock of the terrible defeat and the disastrous consequences of the past two decades had made Germans extremely hesitant to trust anybody.

Riezler granted that the Germans had started the Second World War and that they had no right to complain about the plight of their nation. However, he rejected the notion of "collective guilt," and he maintained that the moral argument about who was right and who was wrong had little bearing on the actual situation and offered in itself no guidance as to what policy toward Germany should be adopted. Moral arguments "can convince the victor that he is morally right, but not that he is clever or wise. Righteousness can be used to excuse many a major stupidity."

Further, no one should be surprised if the millions of unwelcomed Germans who were uprooted from their homes in Czechoslovakia or Poland and who were forced to disperse throughout the western zones of Germany wished to regain their homelands and possessions. People from Maine or Vermont, he reminded the reader, would hardly feel different. Even the word, *"Lebensraum,"* which in the past had been "a mere romantic swindle with no reality behind it," could now perhaps be used to mean "something very real, natural, and only human" for the millions of uprooted people forced to try to live in the western zones.

Riezler was convinced that now "the Germans, like any other people, will submit to a necessity that they can neither change nor escape." They would accept partition, at least for awhile, and accept the predominance of the United States and the Soviet Union in Europe and in the world.

Nor would Germany attempt to improve her situation through war, which would most likely pit the United States against the Soviet Union. "Whoever might survive in such a war, Germany, whether neutral or not, will not survive—no house, no industrial plant, nothing that resembles a people . . . all Germans are mortally afraid of such a war."

It was not difficult for Riezler or anyone else to see that Germany would play an important role in the emerging political and military confrontation between the East and the West. However, he was sure that the major potential problem was not that German nationalists would play on this antagonism in order to elevate the new Germany into the ranks of the superpowers. On the contrary, the major problem would be how the two great powers, seeing the potential of Germany to tip the scales in the balance of power, might attempt to serve their own interests by using or antagonizing the emergent German patriotism and the Germans' ardent desire to end the division of Germany.

Although Riezler's view proved in most cases to be remarkably accurate when seen a quarter of a century later, he did not pretend to predict exactly what would happen to Germany in the decades to come. He pleaded for the application of imagination and wisdom to the solution of the German problem so that one could not look back afterward and say, as Thucydides did, that "the concatenation of events by no means proceeds less stupidly than the thoughts of man."[14]

Riezler had no desire to return to Germany in order to take a direct hand in solving the difficult, unprecedented political and economic problems facing that country. He was already beyond sixty-five years of age and had long since turned his primary attention to philosophy. He looked back on his early political career, in the words of his brother, "as a detour which distracted him from the actual center of his being."[15] His sentiments are understandable given his past inability to help Germany successfully to steer a moderate reform course and thereby to avoid the disaster which befell her. His teaching and writing at the New School for Social Research in New York appeared to him to be of far greater significance than new political responsibilities in Germany.

The Graduate Faculty of Political and Social Science had been founded as the "University in Exile" in 1933 by the farsighted Alvin Johnson. The fact that 1,145 German university professors had been dismissed for political and racial reasons from 1933-34 in a country with the academic preeminence of Germany had not escaped Johnson's attention. He saw a potentially great gain for the United States in creating in New York an assembly point for scholars forbidden for political and racial reasons from working in their own countries. The New School for Social

Research, an institution of experimentation and of great freedom for students and teachers, was a natural place for such a "University in Exile," and eventually one hundred seventy-three European scholars were attracted there.[16]

Riezler contributed to the diverse and stimulating intellectual life of the New School. In addition to his own seminars on the classics, Riezler participated in many joint seminars with such scholars as Karen Horney, Hans Speier, and Max Wertheimer, Riezler's former colleague at the University of Frankfurt and the founder of *Gestalt* theory. He also participated in joint seminars on Aristotle and Plato with his good friend Kurt von Fritz at Columbia University. In addition, he was an active participant in the weekly "General Seminars" at the New School, where papers delivered by colleagues were discussed by faculty and students.

Riezler was not completely satisfied with the New School. He frequently argued with the dean, Hans Staudinger, about appointments to the faculty. Riezler wanted only supreme intellects who knew far more than their specialties to be appointed to the faculty, and he often believed that some inferior scholars were being appointed. Riezler was, as Staudinger described him, *"ein philosophischer Herr,"* who demanded excellence not only in himself, but in his colleagues.

Riezler had been brought to the New School as a professor of philosophy, but he greatly missed not being a part of a larger philosophy department. He, of course, had colleagues such as Leo Strauss with whom he shared many philosophical interests, but he found himself more intellectually at home at the University of Chicago, where Robert Hutchins had assembled a large philosophy department, which included Paul Tillich. Riezler spent long periods of time in Chicago, a practice which caused considerable resentment on the part of some of his colleagues in New York. He even spoke to Staudinger once about moving permanently to Chicago, although he decided against leaving the New School only a few years before his retirement.

Riezler made a very distinct impression on both his colleagues and students. With his own family, he was "always friendly and ready to help, calm and controlled," his brother Walter recalled. On the other hand, many outside his family found him an impatient, aloof, and unsentimental man. Nevertheless, he inspired great respect from some of his colleagues. Perhaps the most revealing description of Riezler was given by Leo Strauss:

Riezler represented to me, more than anyone else among my acquaintances, the virtue of humanity. I believe he was formed by Goethe more than by any

228

other master. His interests and sympathies extended to all fields of worthy human endeavor. . . . The activity of his mind had the character of noble and serious employment of leisure, not of harried labor. And his wide ranging interests and sympathies were never divorced from his sense of human responsibility. Nothing human was alien to him unless we reckon the sordid, the mean, the vulgar and the fanatical among the human. He could become angry but he never felt moral indignation. He could despise causes and even human beings but his contempt was never cut off from pity. He was a man of great warmth and tenderness but he was utterly unsentimental. He disliked words like duty and fatherland but he was singularly free from levity and he retained until his end a certain Bavarian sturdiness that had become transfigured into an unpretentious strength and greatness of soul. In his long and varied career he could not help hurting other human beings but there was no trace of cruelty in him. . . . In company he was altogether pleasant: neither heavy or moody nor frivolous or half absent. He was a man of rare intelligence but only a crude man could call him an intellectual. . . . He did not derive pleasure from winning arguments. When I try to see vividly what distinguishes wisdom from cleverness, I think of Riezler.[17]

His students remember Riezler as a very imposing figure; all remember Riezler as a tall, handsome, dignified, and erudite person, and all had a certain awe of him. Some admired him immensely and were greatly influenced by him. Richard Kennington was one of Riezler's closest students and lived with Riezler during the last month before the latter's departure from the United States. Kennington recalled his immense bearing and poise. Riezler was a warm person with a "soul of complete courtesy," who exhibited a unique combination of alertness and good humor. He also displayed an extraordinary loftiness of mind and humaneness. This latter quality was apparent in the wide range of Riezler's knowledge and in his sympathy for all kinds of human cultivation. This is why, Kennington explained, Riezler admired Goethe so much. Because of his education, wisdom, and striving for "fullness," Goethe was a model for mankind, Riezler thought.[18] The humanism which the mature Riezler displayed was of a thoroughly admirable kind in the eyes of those who knew him in the United States. The reason is that that humanism no longer stood in opposition to the western view of man. Riezler had reconciled the cultivation of man's highest aspirations with liberal democracy.

Some students found Riezler gruff, impatient, and aloof, and were somewhat afraid of him. In any case, it cannot be said that he had a large student following in the United States. His philosophical work, which we shall examine briefly, was not widely and enthusiastically received in America. In a letter to Heuss he wrote: "Teaching in such a totally different environment has its difficulties if one is true to himself. . . . The country is large and almost everything echoes in emptiness."[19]

There were certain things which Riezler liked about his American students and about Americans in general. He was impressed with their politeness, good nature, human warmth and directness, although he noted that "they are all busy and in a hurry." He read many works about American history in order to understand better the land in which he was living. He was particularly impressed with Alexis de Tocqueville's *Democracy in America.* Occasionally he even wished he were younger and "less burdened with the past," so that he could feel more at home in such a young and dynamic land; "when I mention that I had once heard Bismarck speak . . . , all look at me in disbelief that I am not long since dead."

Riezler never entirely adjusted to life in the United States; perhaps Hans Speier is correct in noting that "philosophers do not adjust . . . to this or that condition. They live and work." In any case Riezler's letters to his friends in Europe, as well as to his European friends in the United States, revealed a certain loneliness in his new country. In his first letter to Karl Reinhardt after arriving in New York, he wrote:

I am sitting again at my old desk, the one which has wandered around so much, and I look from a twelfth story over the next building, across the Hudson and to the fog-enveloped lights on the other side . . . and would feel very content, if a few people were not so far away.

To his friend Theodor Heuss he wrote:

We are doing well. I lead a quiet, but very hard-working life, fully concentrated on my philosophy teaching, which is not touched by the events of the time or by the controversies over the present; an island to which one can withdraw from the occasional commotion of wildly differing opinions.[20]

Of course, the sum of Riezler's past political engagement offers ample evidence that he was not a person who in critical moments fled to philosophy.

Riezler's move to the United States had hardly interrupted his philosophical work, and exile did not destroy his creativity and talent. Scarcely more than a year after his arrival, he published his first book in English. This book, with the revealing title, *Physics and Reality,* was written in the form of lectures given by Aristotle to an international assembly of modern physicists and is a treatment of the two predominant themes of his post-World War I philosophical thinking.

The first major theme of his work is the establishment of the possibility of man's free will by showing the limits of natural science. In a

230

book written in 1924, *Gestalt und Gesetz, Entwurf einer Metaphysik der Freiheit (Form and Law, Project of a Metaphysics of Freedom)*, Riezler had discussed the dualism of that part of reality which can be explained in terms of causal determination and that which cannot. Riezler found that there are many cause and effect relationships which natural scientists can describe, measure, and use. Riezler did not belittle this achievement, and in *Physics and Reality* he praised the modern scientists' ability to accomplish such things as making airplanes fly. However, Riezler warned against the proposition that that segment of reality which can be explained in terms of cause and effect relationships is in fact the whole of reality. Such a proposition would be no more than a mere hypothesis which could never be proved because no human being would ever be capable of comprehending all of reality. Certainly, natural science is incapable of such comprehension. "Neither our physical-chemical nor biological knowledge put us in a position today to look into the essence *(das Innere)* of nature or at least to deny such an essence." Riezler argued that it is the task of philosophy to attempt to grasp the whole of reality, although he had to admit that the breadth of the task far outstripped the philosopher's means.

The limitation of natural science when applied to the study of man was also a subject of his final book, *Man Mutable and Immutable, The Fundamental Structure of Social Life,* published in 1950. He described the problem as follows:

We have discarded eternal man and cut mutable man into pieces to be inquired into by different sciences, each of which claims autonomy. The pieces fit into one another less and less. A relatively immutable remnant, called human nature, is left to the care of a biology that speaks the language of physics and chemistry. In this language the mammal we call man is meaningless to himself.[21]

The second major theme of Riezler's writings from the late 1920s is that philosophy is ontology. That is, philosophy involves the investigation of "being," or "the essence of things in so far as they 'are'." The philosopher, he believed, should not concentrate exclusively on individual beings or things or on specific causal relationships such as those dealt with in aerodynamics; instead he should seek to understand that in which all things share if they are to exist at all. In short, the philosopher must focus on "being" as a whole.

To find an adequate treatment of the philosophical problem of "being," Riezler recommended a return to the pre-Socratics, especially to Parmenides, who argued the existence of an unchanging, unified "be-

231

ing." Referring to pre-Socratic thought, Riezler found that "compared with this gold of philosophy which is covered by dust, everything else for centuries has been only dust covered by gold."

Riezler recognized the difficulty of expressing the concept of "being" by means of words. Of course, the first step is for man to look deeply into himself and to reflect on his own experience. He suggested in a book written in 1935 that the philosopher could perhaps see the expression of "being" most clearly in a work of art. Riezler was himself a connoisseur of art with a large personal collection. In art, the expression is also the expressed, and the human soul can find expression in a work of art. "In the work of art beingness itself, the mystery of life, comes to sight or into appearance."

Riezler's conviction of the central importance of "being" for the philosopher and the way he expressed the problems were unquestionably strongly influenced by Martin Heidegger. According to Riezler's colleague at the New School, Leo Strauss, "it would be an understatement to say that Heidegger was the greatest contemporary power which Riezler ever encountered. . . . As soon as he [Heidegger] appeared on the scene, he stood in its center and he began to dominate it . . . philosophizing seems to have been transformed into listening with reverence to the incipient *mythoi* of Heidegger's philosophical influence on Riezler's thinking was not diminished by Heidegger's initial support of the National Socialist regime although, according to his colleagues, Riezler considered Heidegger's action a grave political blunder.[22]

Riezler's philosophical approach raises the crucial question of how man can derive values which are valid for all men at all times. In none of his writings did he ever argue that ethical standards should be derived from divine revelation, and he frequently noted the decline of religion's power over men. By turning from Socratic thought he denied that universal laws of nature, which man could comprehend through reason, could serve as such standards. Pre-Socratic thought, including Parmenides' focus on "being" is a dubious starting point for discovering universally valid standards. Still, a man needs a standard greater than himself. As one of Riezler's students, Harry V. Jaffa, observed many years later: "An empty soul turned inward finds: nothing." Of course, Riezler shared with most modern men this philosophical dilemma of insecurely anchored moral standards.

In 1952 Riezler retired from the New School and received the title of professor emeritus. He remained very busy with his work in New York and Chicago. In February of that year he wrote to Hans Speier that "I am so terribly far behind of what I wanted to be . . . time outruns me."[23]

In 1953 he was selected to deliver the Charles R. Walgreen lectures at the University of Chicago. These lectures, which he published a year later under the title, "Political Decisions in Modern Society," were his last public works and were devoted to the subject of how democracy can be preserved. These lectures dealt with the context within which modern political decisions are made and were full of political remembrances and insights which the seventy-one year old Riezler had accumulated over a lifetime. He touched upon the pre-1914 diplomatic constellation, the outbreak of war in August 1914, the Russian Revolution, the weaknesses of the Weimar Republic, and the reasons for Hitler's rise to power in Germany. A half-century of political events and political mistakes passed in review.

The lectures were given in a highly emotional time in the United States, characterized, in his words, by the "hunting of Communist witches." Riezler worried that a "collective fear" was being created by the charges made by Senator Joseph McCarthy and others against any persons deemed by them to be sympathetic to what was perceived as a dangerous advance of Communism into the United States. "We seem to live in general fear of Russia, Russian spies, Russian infiltration." Riezler was by no means sympathetic to Communism, nor was he naive about the objectives or actions of the Soviet Union. With confidence he could say that "from personal experience, I know something about Russian methods." Nevertheless, he was appalled by the proportions the attacks and fears were taking:

It seems to me utterly ridiculous that the most powerful nation in the world is in the grip of fear, confesses its helplessness by demanding loyalty oaths from everyone, and develops the concept of loyalty risk—a typical police concept—on the basis of vague suspicion and denunciation.

Riezler was convinced that most of the people who were suspected, fired, or declared bad loyalty risks were not, in fact, loyalty risks. Among the least dangerous were those who refused to take loyalty oaths:

The dangerous ones take any oath and do not belong to any organization on which we can lay our hands. They are organized in secret cells and sometimes even ordered to attack others with pro-Communist connections.[24]

Further, Riezler dared to suggest that the assumption upon which the hysteria was based—that there existed an impressive multitude of seven to eight hundred million Russian, Eastern European, and Chinese Communists aligned against the United States—was perhaps false. Riezler speculated about the great benefit which the Soviet Union could derive from a war between the United States and China "in which a hundred million Chinese would be killed by bombs or starved to death." He asserted that the benefit to the Soviet Union could have been very great indeed because "in the long run China will become Russia's biggest danger"; it had always been Russia's policy in the past to keep China weak and divided. Recalling his own rail journey to China in 1914 as a diplomatic courier Riezler explained:

Some basic and unalterable facts of political geography favor China, not Russia. . . . For thousands and thousands of miles, the Siberian railway, so far the only one connecting eastern Siberia with Russia, runs along the northern border of China through practically empty country; then, further east, it branches out, crosses the Manchurian border, and turns south again for thousands and thousands of miles. There the country is bursting with life. Everywhere people, whose number no one has ever counted,work in the fields. It is another world, as alien to the Russians as it is to us, and when China is industrialized and organized, Russia's domination of Siberia will be a thing of the past, and the few Siberians will be no match for the four hundred million hard working, enduring, modest people of China. This may mean looking far ahead, but is very real in the Russian mind, accustomed as it is to thinking in longer streches of time that we do. . . . I frankly do not know who actually helps the cause of Russia more—those who advocate war with China or those who warn against being swept by emotion step and step into irreparable mistakes.[25]

Riezler's major concern was that the "collective fear" which can grip the mass of citizens could be skillfully exploited by the enemies of democracy. He had already witnessed successful manipulation of mass hysteria in Germany in the midst of economic catastrophe, and he was sure that the pattern could be followed in other countries as well. In all modern societies, thanks to technological progress, the atomized masses can through fear or emotion behave as a "crowd" in an unpredictable and an uncontrollable way. Riezler cited the reactions in the United States to Orson Welles's radio story about the invasion from Mars and to President Truman's dismissal of the war hero, General Douglas MacArthur, as examples of how such mass hysteria can lead to the formation of crowds.

Crowds exist only for short periods, and once the emotion which unified the crowd dies away, the crowd disperses, and the persons "go home and wonder how they had ever gotten into that crowd mind." However, a skillful leader or group of leaders can sometimes activate crowds for political purposes. To do this, leaders must "perpetuate" the emotion or arouse new ones, one after the other, or make them apparently consistent and embody them in fictions, convictions and principles, called "ideologies." If the leader is successful in organizing the crowd, then the crowd becomes a "herd," which is then "regimented and put into uniforms" in order to serve the political objectives of the leader.

Riezler turned to the question of how herds could be prevented from forming. He indicated that a useful function could be performed by certain intelligent newspapers, commentators, or other conscientious people, who could help to bring reasoned arguments to millions of groups and individuals in the society. However, on the whole, Riezler feared that the mass media would not aid in this process of making the masses accessible to reasoned arguments. The desire to sell newspapers and journals prompts the leaders of the mass media to search for and to focus on anything which has "news value." Thus, Riezler feared that the commercial interests of these media would incline them to intensify emotions, rather than to counter them with reasoned arguments. Of course, government control of the media would perhaps be even more dangerous because of the possibility that governments would misuse them in order to mislead the people. In either case, communication becomes a "one-way process of communication." A large and unknown audience listens to the radio or reads a newspaper. The content of the reports has been geared toward the largest possible audience. Most significantly, the listener or reader "cannot talk back, he is not addressed personally, and he cannot ask questions. He may, of course, stop reading or turn off the radio, but he must be quick about it."

Riezler argued that the crucial question was whether another kind of communication, a "two-way communication," could exist side-by-side with the one-way. Two-way communication is a process by which "people talk to someone about something. . . . The people talked to listen and respond, ask questions, doubt, and finally agree or do not agree. Arguments and something we call reasoning go back and forth; doubts are voiced and dispelled. The speaker must listen, defend his facts with some kind of apparent evidence and his reasons with some kind of apparent reason. . . . They want to reach the other fellow's mind, his perspective, his reasons for differing, and they try to understand with the help of the other fellow the something about which they talk."

This two-way communication is fired by the "spirit of debate," although each side does not think exclusively of winning an argument. It is dialogue, not propaganda. Although Riezler was aware that this spirit would not be able completely to replace the "spirit of propaganda" or always to "pierce through the noise of sales talk," he believed that this dialogue could and must take place in private homes, in schools, in clubs, at work, in the journalist's study, and in the government. A "silent dialogue" should even take place in the mind of each individual when that individual is trying to make up his mind about something. This kind of dialogue should take place, of course, within the government and in the minds of government leaders. Above all, government leaders should act on the conclusions reached through that dialogue with others and within their own minds. Riezler was not unaware of the extreme pressure placed by constitutents on political leaders who must face regular elections. However, he feared that if political leaders took their bearings from emotions, clichés and stereotypes which are often repeated in the land, then not only would extremely unwise decisions be made, but democracy would be perverted to a "pseudo-democracy." He was by no means confident that the tools of demagoguery used so successfully by such non-democratic leaders as Napoleon III, Bismarck, and Hitler could not be applied in the United States. He emphasized that rational decisions in a democracy must emerge from dialogue.

Democracy lives and has all its strength in the vigor and intensity of the process of mutual response within which the talkers listen and the listeners talk back. Without this process, the holy word 'democracy' loses its content.

In the healthy society, Riezler believed that the spirit of debate and dialogue is so pervasive that what Tocqueville called "manners" develop. Such manners can, in turn, powerfully reinforce that spirit, but they remain fragile and can break down, as he feared was happening in the United States. On the other hand, in that society where they retain their power, "the one-way process of communication meets . . . the other process, the two-way kind of communication. The spirit of propaganda meets the spirit of debate. Emotion meets reason. . . . As long as it [emotion] does not overcome this resistance, and the spirit corresponding to the two-way process of communication prevails, democracy is fairly safe. But only fairly."[26]

In this last political statement Riezler asserted that "mass tastes" could under certain circumstances present great dangers. However, the dangers are not that they compete with or crush the loftier values of an educated elite, but that they could be manipulated by persons who wish to undermine democracy itself. A healthy democracy requires both widespread, continual and rational discussion and the willingness of the political leadership to listen. Above all, democracy requires the alert and active participation of all citizens. He wrote:

The daily work and its worries of each single individual may suggest to many an escape into wishful thinking—confidence in the political strength of the nation, in its efficiency, skill, and superiority of production and invention, or indulgence in a kind of self-adoration of the nation which is the vice of all great modern nations and now is spreading even in this country, though it is not part of the American tradition. No such escape will help.[27]

After his retirement his desire to remain in the United States began to diminish very quickly. His attachment to his country of exile had never been strong, and it was loosened even further as a result of his wife's death during a trip to Europe in 1952.

He began to feel a strong pull to move permanently to Rome and Greece, lands which he had loved since childhood although he had seldom visited them. His decision to move was prompted by a love of these lands and also by the realization that his life was approaching an end. In 1953 he wrote to his friend Karl Reinhardt: "The time has come; the sand in the clock will very soon have run through."[28]

In 1954 he occupied an apartment overlooking the former imperial city of Rome. Though he maintained contact with his acquaintances in the United States and Germany, he turned the greater part of his attention away from the contemporary world, which had changed so much during his lifetime. Riezler had returned home. His long-time close friend and admirer, Theodor Heuss, reflected:

At times, when I summoned into my mind Kurt Riezler's presence—the beautiful landscape of his features, with their spirited and commanding intellectuality, though overcast perhaps with resignation—I would say to our friends: Can you see it? He is on leave in our midst from the court of Lorenzo de'Medici. For in Riezler humanism rediscovered itself in a new affirmation of the human, a radiant upsurge of the free mind over against Savonarola, terrifying image of dark fanaticism. Where, where are our sustaining forces in the uncertain balance of insecure values? Hark Lorenzo's voice, now in encouragement for today, now in forewarning of things to come—"Di Doman' non e certezza. . . ."[29]

Unfortunately, his return was to be very brief. In July 1955, while in Greece, Riezler collapsed, his body stricken with cancer. He was flown to a clinic in Munich although it was soon apparent that he had no chance of survival. There he was visited by his remaining family and by many acquaintances and colleagues.

Riezler lay dying in the city of his birth. There, as a young man, he had been given a classical education and a love for philosophy and the fine arts. Within a few years after leaving his city, he had risen to the heart of political power in a restless Germany. From those heights he watched his country drift into war and proceed toward defeat. Defeat in war had brought revolution to Europe. In Russia he had helped foment it; to

Munich he had returned to suppress it. He had endeavored to save the infant German Republic from ruin, but he eventually became one of the many victims of those who destroyed it. Gradually, he withdrew from political affairs and returned to philosophy and to teaching, in order to help man understand himself.

After a lifetime of philosophical searching, of high level political involvement in times of war, revolution, and peace, and of resistance and exile in the United States, Riezler came to rest. On September 5, 1955, in the early morning hours, he died in Munich, where his life had begun nearly three-quarters of a century earlier.

NOTES

CHAPTER ONE

[1] A few miles south of Oberstdorf in the Walsertal is a small village named Riezlern. The biographical information in this chapter is drawn chiefly from conversations with Riezler's daughter, Mrs. Howard White, from Riezler's military records, Personalakt Nr. 47102, Bayerisches Hauptstaats-Archiv München, Abt. IV: Kriegsarchiv, and from the introduction to *Kurt Riezler, Tagebücher, Aufsätze, Dokumente (Diaries)*, ed. by Karl Dietrich Erdmann, Deutsche Geschichtsquellen des 19. und 20. Jahrhunderts, Bd. 48 (Göttingen: Vandenhoeck & Ruprecht, 1972). Leo Strauss, "Kurt Riezler," in *What is Political Philosophy* (Glencoe, Ill.: Free Press, 1959), p. 234.

[2] Riezler married Käthe Liebermann May 11, 1915. Arnold Brecht recalled that Käthe Liebermann had assumed the name, Camille Desmoulins, from the years 1906-09 and had been "the center of all attention." Arnold Brecht, *Aus nächster Nähe: Lebenserinnerungen 1884-1927* (Stuttgart: Deutsche Verlags-Anstalt, 1966), p. 76. See Kurt Riezler, *Traktat vom Schönen: Zur Ontologie der Kunst* (Frankfurt am Main: Vittorio Klostermann, 1935). Riezler also had a sister, Getraud.

[3] Karl Alexander von Müller, ed., *Riezler Festschrift: Beiträge zur Bayerischen Geschichte* (Gotha: Friedrich Andreas Perthes A.-G., 1913).

[4] Riezler's military records.

[5] Kurt Riezler, *Gestalt und Gesetz, Entwurf einer Metaphysik der Freiheit* (Munich: Musarion-Verlag, 1924), pp. 4-5. See also Kurt Riezler, *Parmenides*. Quellen der Philosophie 12, 2d ed. (Frankfurt am Main: Vittorio Klostermann, 1970). Karl Alexander von Müller, *Aus Gärten der Vergangenheit: Erinnerungen 1882-1914* (Stuttgart: Gustav Kilpper Verlag, 1951), pp. 415-16.

[6] Fritz K. Ringer, *The Decline of the German Mandarins: The German Academic Community, 1890-1933* (Cambridge: Harvard University Press, 1969), pp. 5, 19-20. Ludwig Curtius, *Deutsche und Antike Welt: Lebenserinnerungen* (Stuttgart: Deutsche Verlags–Anstalt, 1950), p. 455. Fritz Stern, *The Politics of Cultural Despair: A Study in the Rise of the Germanic Ideology* (Berkeley and Los Angeles: University of California Press, 1974), pp. xxiv, 279. Walter Horace Bruford, *The German Tradition of Self-Cultivation: Bildung from Humboldt to Thomas*

Mann (London: Cambridge University Press, 1975). For an attempt to classify sociologically the German *Bildungsbürgertum,* see Klaus Vondung, ed., *Das wilhelmische Bildungsbürgertum: Zur Sozialgeschichte seiner Ideen* (Göttingen: Vandenhoeck & Ruprecht, 1976), esp. pp. 22-28. Greek thought reflects a rich and varied tradition which can be used either to enrich the modern age or to attack it. Robert Anchor noted that many Germans "used the Greeks as a stick with which to beat modern society." Anchor, *Germany Confronts Modernization: German Culture and Society, 1790-1890,* Civilization and Society: Studies in Social Economic and Cultural History (Lexington, Mass.: Heath, 1972), pp. 9-10, 16, 22-27, 139.

[7] Friedrich Meinecke, *The German Catastrophe: The Social and Historical Influences which Led to the Rise and Ruin of Hitler and Germany* (Boston: Beacon Press, 1963), p. 54. Hajo Holborn, "German Idealism in the Light of Social History," in *Germany and Europe: Historical Essays* (Garden City, N.Y.: Doubleday, 1971), p. 24. Riezler, *Diaries,* Dec. 4, 1915, p. 318. In literature and art the term, "German Idealism," often refers collectively to both classicism and romanticism despite the fact that these movements differ from each other. In philosophy the term refers to a wide variety of views which usually include the notion that "idea," "mind," or "spirit" are, in fact, the fundamental metaphysical reality of the universe and that the universe presents an ordered whole in which each manifestation of the mind finds its proper place. In this work the term is used in a broad sense which encompasses all the meanings above. See H. Stuart Hughes, *Consciousness and Society: The Reorientation of European Social Thought 1890-1930* (New York: Vintage, 1958), pp. 183-91, 229-48. Also, Anchor, *Germany Confronts Modernization,* chaps. 2, 3, 4.

[8] "Western countries" and the "West" refer primarily to Britain, France, the United States, and the Netherlands. Leonard Krieger, *The German Idea of Freedom: History of a Political Tradition from the Reformation to 1871* (Chicago: University of Chicago Press, 1957), pp. 36-37, 86. Stern, *Cultural Despair,* p. xxiv. Ringer, *German Mandarins,* pp. 102, 106, 117, 119, 121. Meinecke, *German Catastrophe,* p. 14.

[9] Fritz Stern, "The Political Consequences of the Unpolitical German," in *The Failure of Illiberalism: Essays on the Political Culture of Modern Germany* (New York: Knopf, 1972), pp. 5-7. Ringer, *German Mandarins,* p. 11. Meinecke, *German Catastrophe,* p. 10. For the link between culture and German nationalism, see Anchor, *Germany Confronts Modernization,* pp. 11, 144-45.

[10] The best book on the development of natural right doctrine is by Leo Strauss, *Natural Right and History* (Chicago: University of Chicago Press, 1953). Harry V. Jaffa, "What is Equality," in *The Conditions of Freedom: Essays in Political Philosophy* (Baltimore: Johns Hopkins

University Press, 1975), pp. 154-55. Leonard Krieger carefully describes how throughout the nineteenth century Germans were able to minimize the anti-absolutist implications of modern natural rights and contract theory by means of a process of theoretical integration and reconciliation which allowed the state to appear as the indispensable guardian of individual liberties, rather than as the potential enemy of them. *German Idea of Freedom,* pp. 3, 50-51, 140, 146. Ringer, *German Mandarins,* p. 10. Treitschke quote in Stern, "Unpolitical German," p. 18. See also p. 11. Fontane quote in Joachim Remak, *The Gentle Critic: Theodor Fontane and German Politics, 1848-1898* (Syracuse: Syracuse University Press, 1964), p. 9. Riezler found Fichte's formulation of freedom the best: "Realization of freedom through the state." Riezler preferred a kind of freedom "in which everyone should be judged according to his strengths, thus not equally. Freedom through order." *Diaries,* Dec. 4, 1915, pp. 317-18. For Germany's break with the West and for the concept of *Rechtsstaat,* see Hughes, *Consciousness and Society,* pp. 27, 184, 245-46, 334; and Anchor, *Germany Confronts Modernization,* pp. 3-5, 69, 73, 94-96.

[11] Krieger, *German Ideal of Freedom,* pp. 206-08. Ringer, *German Mandarins,* pp. 114-15, 212. Stern, "Unpolitical German," pp. 10, 18. Holborn, "German Idealism," pp. 4, 25, 31. Hughes, *Consciousness and Society,* pp. 183-85; and Anchor, *Germany Confronts Modernization,* pp. 8, 112.

[12] Stern, *Cultural Despair,* pp. xx, xxv, 280. Stern, "Unpolitical German," p. 9. Ringer, *German Mandarins,* p. 121.

[13] Between 1816 and 1913 German population almost tripled from 24.8 millions to 66.9 millions. In 1830, four-fifths of the population lived outside of towns and engaged in agriculture; in 1895 barely one-fifth did so. Total German industrial production overtook that of France in the 1870s, equalled that of the British around 1900, and was well ahead of British industrial production by 1910. By that year Germany was second only to the U.S.A. in terms of industrial production. Golo Mann, *Deutsche Geschichte des neunzehnten und zwanzigsten Jahrhunderts* (Frankfurt/M.: S. Fischer Verlag, 1958), p. 394. Fritz Fischer, *Krieg der Illusionen: Die deutsche Politik von 1911 bis 1914* (Düsseldorf: Droste Verlag, 1969), p. 18. J. J. Ruedorffer [Kurt Riezler], *Grundzüge der Weltpolitik in der Gegenwart* (Stuttgart: Deutsche Verlags-Anstalt, 1914), p. 102. See Kenneth D. Barkin, *The Controversy over German Industrialization* (Chicago: University of Chicago Press, 1970). Educated Germans' reactions to changes wrought by industrialization were not entirely unlike the reactions of other educated Europeans. See Barkin's review article of Ringer's *German Mandarins* in the *Journal of Modern History,* 43 (June 1971), 284-86. Konrad H. Jarausch, *The Enigmatic Chancellor: Bethmann Hollweg and the Hubris of Imperial Germany* (New Haven: Yale University Press, 1973), pp. 10, 106-07, 403. Stern, *Cultural Despair,* p. xxvii.

¹⁴ Stern, *Cultural Despair*, pp. xxvi, xxviii.

¹⁵ Klaus Wernecke, *Der Wille Zur Weltgeltung: Aussenpolitik und Öffentlichkeit im Kaiserreich am Vorabend des Ersten Weltkrieges* (Düsseldorf: Droste Verlag, 1970), p. 20.

¹⁶ Riezler's military records, evaluation of Aug. 18, 1908. Kurt Riezler, "Der Reichstag und die Presse," *Die Grenzboten*, 65 (1906). See Riezler, *Diaries*, pp. 28, 31. The press office of the German Foreign Office served all of the ministries in Berlin, as well as the Imperial Chancellery. This provided unity to the government's press policy. For Riezler's recommendation on how Germany could gain influence over the French press, see PA Bonn, Deutschland 126a secr., Bd. 2, Nov. 4, 1909. For German Press Office dealings with the press, see Riezler, "Political Decisions in Modern Society," *Ethics* (January 1954), 14-17. He commented on the small size of the Press Office (four civil servants) and the shortage of funds. He, for example, had only $1,000 per year "to bribe the Egyptian press."

¹⁷ Riezler, *Diaries*, p. 29. Bülow was Imperial Chancellor 1900-09, and German ambassador to Rome 1914-16.

¹⁸ Bernhard Fürst von Bülow, *Denkwürdigkeiten*, 3 vols. (Berlin: Im Verlag Ullstein, 1930-31), 3, pp. 24-25. For Riezler's later criticism of Bülow, see J. J. Ruedorffer, *Die drei Krisen: Eine Untersuchung über den gegenwärtigen politischen Weltzustand* (Stuttgart: Deutsche Verlags-Anstalt, 1920), pp. 32-33. Riezler later told a colleague in New York an anecdote about flattery. Riezler had been instructed by Bülow to write a highly exaggerated letter of praise to an author of a mediocre book on art. When Riezler reminded Bülow of the book's truly modest quality, Bülow responded to his young assistant that "flattery, even when detected, always works." Author's interview with Hans Speier, New York, April 1976.

¹⁹ Theodor Heuss, "A Word in Memory of Kurt Riezler," *Social Research*, 23 (1956).

CHAPTER TWO

¹ Kurt Riezler, *Das Zweite Buch der pseudoaristotelischen Ökonomik* (Berlin: Norddeutsche Buchdruckerei und Verlagsanstalt, 1906). This was published one year later as Kurt Riezler, *Über Finanzen und Monopole im alten Griechenland: Zur Theorie und Geschichte der antiken Stadtwirtschaft* (Berlin: Puttkammer & Mühlbrecht, 1907), p. 48.

² *Ibid.*, pp. 70, 93. Riezler used the words *polis* and state interchangeably.

³ *Ibid.*, p. 76.

⁴ *Ibid.*, pp. 48, 71. Imanuel Geiss, "Zur Beurteilung der deutschen Reichspolitik im ersten Weltkrieg," in H. Pogge-V. Strandmann and Imanuel Geiss, *Die Erforderlichkeit des Unmöglichen: Deutschland am Vorabend des ersten Weltkrieges,* Hamburger Studien zur neueren Geschichte, Bd. 2 (Hamburg: Europäische Verlagsanstalt, 1965), p. 56.

⁵ Otto Graf zu Stolberg-Wernigerode, *Die unentschiedene Generation: Deutschlands konservative Führungsschichten am Vorabend des Ersten Weltkrieges* (Munich: R. Oldenbourg, 1968), p. 22. George W. F. Hallgarten, *Imperialismus vor 1914: Die soziologischen Grundlagen der Aussenpolitik europäischer Grossmächte vor dem Ersten Weltkrieg,* Erster Band (Munich: C. H. Beck'sche Verlagsbuchhandlung, 1963), p. 20. Barbara W. Tuchman, *The Proud Tower: A Portrait of the World Before the War* (New York: Bantam Books, 1967), pp. 290-91. David Friedrich Strauss, *Der alte und der neue Glaube,* 3d ed. (Leipzig: Verlag von S. Hirzel, 1872), pp. 179-80. Eberhard v. Vietsch, *Bethmann Hollweg: Staatsmann zwischen Macht und Ethos,* Schriften des Bundesarchivs 18 (Boppard am Rhein: Harold Boldt Verlag, 1969), pp. 36-38. Hans-Günter Zmarzlik, "Der Sozialdarwinismus als geschichtliches Problem," in *Vierteljahrshefte für Zeitgeschichte,* 3d Heft (July 1963). Heinrich von Treitschke, *Politik,* ed. by Max Cornicelius, 1 (Leipzig: Verlag von S. Hirzel, 1897), p. 50. Gerhard Ritter, *Das deutsche Problem: Grundfragen deutschen Staatslebens gestern und heute* (Munich: R. Oldenbourg, 1962), pp. 103-04. Geiss, "Beurteilung," p. 56. Ruedorffer, *Grundzüge der Weltpolitik,* pp. 25-26, 119. Hans Kohn, *The Mind of Germany: The Education of a Nation* (New York: Harper & Row, Harper Torchbooks, 1960), pp. 204-05. Wolfgang J. Mommsen, *Das Zeitalter des Imperialismus,* Fischer Weltgeschichte, Bd. 28 (Frankfurt am Main: Fischer Bücherei GmbH, 1969), p. 20. Fischer, *Krieg der Illusionen,* pp. 66, 77-84, 243-45. Leo Strauss, "Kurt Riezler," p. 235. Wolfgang J. Mommsen, *Max Weber und die deutsche Politik 1890-1920* (Tübingen: J. C. B. Mohr, Paul Siebert, 1959), p. 75. Richard Hofstadter, *Social Darwinism in American Thought* (Boston: Beacon, 1972), p. 292.

⁶ Riezler, *Finanzen und Monopole,* p. 82.

⁷ *Ibid.*, pp. 80-84, 87-88, 91. See also Thucydides, *The Peloponnesian War.* Riezler, "Political Decisions," 6-12.

⁸ Riezler, "Die Weltpolitik im Jahre 1906," *Die Weltwirtschaft,* 2 (1907), 7. Vietsch, *Bethmann Hollweg,* p. 116.

⁹ Riezler, "Weltpolitik," 3-4.

¹⁰ Ruedorffer, *Grundzüge der Weltpolitik,* pp. 135-38, 219. Riezler, "Weltpolitik," 13.

¹¹ *Ibid.*

¹² Wernecke, *Wille zur Weltgeltung,* p. 20. Riezler, *Diaries,* Feb. 2, 1910, p. 167. Vietsch, *Bethmann Hollweg,* pp. 29-60. See also Jarausch, *Enigmatic Chancellor,* and Willibald Gutsche, *Aufstieg und Fall eines kaiserlichen Reichskanzler: Theobald von Bethmann Hollweg 1856-1921* (Berlin: Akademie-Verlag GmbH, 1973).

¹³ Theobald von Bethmann Hollweg, *Betrachtungen zum Weltkriege,* 2 vols. (Berlin: Verlag von Reimar Hobbing, 1919, 1921), 1, p. 3. Vietsch, *Bethmann Hollweg,* pp. 116-18. Konrad H. Jarausch, "The Illusion of Limited War: Chancellor Bethmann Hollweg's Calculated Risk, July, 1914," *Central European History,* 2 (March 1969), 51: "According to Bethmann's son, Felix, the relationship was that of a bright young man and skeptical elder statesman whose difference in age, temperament and responsibility made for scintillating discussions while riding in the Tiergarten. But Riezler's liberal imperialist writings cannot simply be taken to express the Chancellor's more cautious foreign policy."

¹⁴ Hans Plehn, *Deutsche Weltpolitik und kein Krieg* (Berlin: Verlag von Puttkammer & Mühlbrecht, 1913), p. 1. Riezler, "Political Decisions." Ruedorffer, *Grundzüge der Weltpolitik,* p. 224.

¹⁵ Kurt Riezler, *Die Erforderlichkeit des Unmöglichen: Prolegomena zu einer Theorie der Politik und zu anderen Theorien* (Munich: Müller Verlag, 1913), p. 6. Riezler, *Gestalt und Gesetz.* Strauss, "Kurt Riezler," p. 241.

¹⁶ Riezler, *Erforderlichkeit des Unmöglichen,* p. 196, and Ruedorffer, *Grundzüge der Weltpolitik,* p. 198.

¹⁷ Riezler dealt with this matter in great detail. See *Physics and Reality* (New Haven: Yale University Press, 1940).

¹⁸ Riezler, *Erforderlichkeit des Unmöglichen,* p. 315. Gerhard Ritter, *Staatskunst und Kriegshandwerk: Das Problem des Militarismus in Deutschland,* 4 vols. (Munich: Verlag R. Oldenbourg, 1965), 2, p. 29. Mommsen, *Imperialismus,* p. 25.

¹⁹ Geiss, "Beurteilung," p. 64. Riezler, *Erforderlichkeit des Unmöglichen,* p. 250.

²⁰ Ruedorffer, *Grundzüge der Weltpolitik,* p. 7. The German word *Volk* is used instead of "people" because the idea of unity is more inherent in the German word.

[21] Riezler, *Erforderlichkeit des Unmöglichen*, pp. 201-03. Kohn, *Mind of Germany*, p. 77. Strauss, "Kurt Riezler," p. 237. Ruedorffer, *Grundzüge der Weltpolitik*, pp. 8-9, 12, 14.

[22] Riezler, *Erforderlichkeit des Unmöglichen*, pp. 204-06. Hans Freiherr von Liebig, *Die Politik von Bethmann Hollweg* (n.p., 1915), p. 84. For race thinking in Imperial Germany see Fischer, *Krieg der Illusionen*, pp. 64-68, 243-45. Mann, *Deutsche Geschichte*, pp. 500-01.

[23] Riezler, *Erforderlichkeit des Unmöglichen*, pp. 204, 207-09, 213-14. *Diaries*, p. 560. See Riezler, *Traktat vom Schönen*. Ruedorffer, *Grundzüge der Weltpolitik*, pp. 19, 84.

[24] Ruedorffer, *Grundzüge der Weltpolitik*, pp. 11, 18, 20. *Erforderlichkeit des Unmöglichen*, pp. 209-10. Strauss, "Kurt Riezler," p. 237.

[25] Riezler, *Erforderlichkeit des Unmöglichen*, pp. 177-78, 198-99, 218. He agreed with Hegel that special rules apply to the genius. *Grundzüge der Weltpolitik*, pp. 5, 16, 26. Mommsen, *Max Weber*, p. 56.

[26] Riezler, *Erforderlichkeit des Unmöglichen*, pp. 83-84, 181-83. On pp. 203-04 he wrote that the source of tragedy is "constant effort and never complete attainment." See also Strauss, "Kurt Riezler," p. 242.

[27] Ruedorffer, *Grundzüge der Weltpolitik*, pp. 3, 9, 12, 47, 152, 224. Riezler, *Erforderlichkeit des Unmöglichen*, pp. 227-29. Ludwig Dehio, *Deutschland und die Weltpolitik im 20. Jahrhundert* (Munich: Verlag R. Oldenbourg, 1955), p. 82. Ruedorffer, *Drei Krisen*, pp. 10-11. Riezler, *Finanzen und Monopole*, p. 73. Treitschke, *Politik*, p. 29. Mommsen, *Max Weber*, pp. 45, 54.

[28] Geiss, "Beurteilung," p. 58.

[29] Ruedorffer, *Grundzüge der Weltpolitik*, p. 12. Riezler was very concerned about the transformation of German nationalism in the course of the nineteenth century away from idealism and the view of nations as bearers of ideas toward the exclusively materialist-biological view of "Germanness." For more on this development see Ritter, *Das Deutsche Problem*. Theodor Heuss, *Die Deutsche Nationalidee im Wandel der Geschichte* (Stuttgart: Franz Mittelbach, 1946). Friedrich Meinecke, *The German Catastrophe*, p. 21, and Meinecke, *Politische Schriften und Reden*, 2d ed. (Darmstadt: Siegfried Toeche-Mittler Verlag, 1966), p. 81. See Kohn, *Mind of Germany*. Also Kohn, *The Idea of Nationalism: A Study in its Origins and Background* (New York: Collier Books, 1969), pp. 328-451. Also Stolberg-Wernigerode, *Unentschiedene Generation*, pp. 21-28.

³⁰ Ruedorffer, *Grundzüge der Weltpolitik*, pp. 31, 111, 113, 115. Riezler was greatly influenced by Basel historian Jacob Burckhardt to whom he owed his interest in history. See Riezler, *Das Zweite Buch der pseudoaristotelischen Ökonomik*, p. 3. From Burckhardt Riezler learned to emphasize cultural history as opposed to "the development of events and their connections." Cultural decline and the coming of the age of "mass-men" horrified both men. Riezler, like Burckhardt, disliked great schemes of historical interpretation such as Hegel's. Finally, Burckhardt influenced Riezler's thinking regarding the great importance of historical tendencies and the relative unimportance of men in history.

³¹ Ruedorffer, *Grundzüge der Weltpolitik*, p. 21. Mann, *Deutsche Geschichte*, p. 502. Vietsch, *Bethmann Hollweg*, p. 143. Heuss, *Deutsche Nationalidee*, p. 27. Stolberg-Wernigerode was not correct in asserting that the main mistake was that "Pan-Germans were not taken seriously enough by the government." *Unentschiedene Generation*, p. 385. For Riezler's opposition to the Pan-Germans, see Konrad H. Jarausch, "Die Alldeutschen und die Regierung Bethmann Hollweg, Eine Denkschrift Kurt Riezlers vom Herbst 1916," *Vierteljahrshefte für Zeitgeschichte*, 4 Heft (October 1973), 435-68. Vietsch, *Bethmann Hollweg*, p. 178.

³² Ruedorffer, *Grundzüge der Weltpolitik*, p. 115.

³³ For Riezler's perceptive discussion of China, see *Grundzüge der Weltpolitik*, pp. 138-42.

³⁴ *Ibid.*, pp. 151-52. See Treitschke, *Politik*, p. 97. Despite Riezler's criticism of pacifism, Dietrich Schäfer called him a "protagonist of feeble pacifism." Walter Laqueur and George L. Mosse, eds., *1914: The Coming of the First World War* (New York: Harper & Row, Harper Torchbooks, 1966), p. 61.

³⁵ Ruedorffer, *Grundzüge der Weltpolitik*, pp. 152-54. Riezler believed that a nation like Britain could expertly manipulate international pity in her own interest. See Treitschke, *Politik*, p. 67, and Tuchman, *Proud Tower*, p. 319.

³⁶ Ruedorffer, *Grundzüge der Weltpolitik*, pp. 155-56, 162. Treitschke, *Politik*, p. 77. Tuchman, *Proud Tower*, p. 275.

³⁷ Ruedorffer, *Grundzüge der Weltpolitik*, pp. 165-67, 171. Treitschke, *Politik*, pp. 38, 102. Riezler distinguished between genuine cosmopolitanism, which was not politically relevant, and superficial cosmopolitanism, which affected only political form, not substance. We saw earlier that Riezler did not think that only nations could reach "the highest"; individuals of many nations can all strive for the "highest," and a genius who emerges from a *Volk* belongs not to that *Volk* alone,

but to mankind. "But this genuine cosmopolitanism does not affect the fundamental relation among the nations." Strauss, "Kurt Riezler," p. 240.

[38] Ruedorffer, *Grundzüge der Weltpolitik,* pp. 108-09.

[39] Riezler, *Diaries,* May 29, July 29, 30, Aug. 1, 1911, pp. 177-81. Ruedorffer, *Grundzüge der Weltpolitik,* p. 109. For more details on the crisis, see Jarausch, *Enigmatic Chancellor,* pp. 119-26. Fritz Fischer, *Griff nach der Weltmacht: Die Kriegszielpolitik des kaiserlichen Deutschland 1914-18* (Düsseldorf: Droste Verlag, 1961), p. 32. *Krieg der Illusionen,* pp. 137, 326. Note Lloyd George's Mansion House Speech of July 21 in Winston S. Churchill, *The World Crisis,* 6 vols. (New York: Scribner's, 1951), 1, pp. 43-44. See also p. 65. For Bethmann Hollweg's reaction to this speech, see his *Betrachtungen,* 1, p. 47. Bethmann Hollweg stated during the crisis: "Our prestige is ruined; in the extreme case we must fight." He also made public statements indicating that he did not want war. See Vietsch, *Bethmann Hollweg,* pp. 131, 134, 136.

[40] Riezler, *Diaries,* July 30, 1911, pp. 179-80. Geiss, "Beurteilung," p. 53. That Bethmann did not want war is revealed by two statements he made in November 1911. On the ninth he stated publicly: "For me, who had to bear the responsibility today, it is an obligation to conduct politics in such a way that a war which can be avoided and which the honor of Germany does not require will also be avoided." In a private letter to his friend, Eisendecher, he wrote that a war over Morocco "would have been a crime. . . . But the German *Volk* played with war very frivolously this summer. That bothers me greatly; I had to oppose that even at the risk of incurring the displeasure of the *Volk.*" Vietsch, *Bethmann Hollweg,* p. 134.

[41] Riezler, *Diaries,* May 29, 1911, p. 177.

[42] Ruedorffer, *Grundzüge der Weltpolitik,* pp. 112-13.

[43] Bethmann Hollweg, *Betrachtungen,* 1, pp. 30, 34. Fischer, *Krieg der Illusionen,* p. 132. A. J. P. Taylor, *The Course of German History: A Survey of the Development of Germany Since 1815,* 6th ed. (New York: Capricorn Books, 1962), p. 161. Churchill, *World Crisis,* 1, p. 65. Ruedorffer, *Grundzüge der Weltpolitik,* p. 109. Fritz R. Stern, *Bethmann Hollweg und der Krieg: Die Grenzen der Verantwortung* (Tübingen: J. C. B. Mohr, 1968), p. 15.

[44] Ritter, *Das Deutsche Problem,* pp. 148-49. Bethmann Hollweg's thinking on war was well expressed in 1912: "If a war is thrust upon us, then we will fight it and with God's help will not perish in the process. To cause a war on our account, without our honor or our vital interests being touched, would be a sin against the fate of Germany, even if, according to all human prediction, we could hope for a complete victory."

Fischer, *Krieg der Illusionen,* pp. 189, 232-45. See also Fischer, *Griff nach der Weltmacht,* pp. 41, 43. Bethmann Hollweg, *Betrachtungen,* 1, pp. 12-13.

[45] Friedrich von Bernhardi, *Germany and the Next War,* auth. Amer. ed. (New York: J. J. Little & Ives, 1912), pp. iii, 18, 20-21, 23, 26, 38, 40, 53, 106. Mommsen, *Imperialismus,* p. 269. Tuchman, *Proud Tower,* p. 388. Ritter, *Staatskunst,* 2, p. 143. *Das Deutsche Problem,* p. 149. Hans Herzfeld, *Der Erste Weltkrieg,* Weltgeschichte des 20. Jahrhunderts, Bd. 1 (Munich: Deutscher Taschenbuch Verlag GmbH, 1968), p. 26.

[46] Fischer, *Krieg der Illusionen,* p. 142.

[47] Vietsch, *Bethmann Hollweg,* p. 155. Jarausch, *The Enigmatic Chancellor,* pp. 143, 465. Fischer, *Krieg der Illusionen,* pp. 369-70. Ritter, *Staatskunst,* 2, p. 126.

[48] Geiss, "Beurteilung," pp. 58, 63-64.

[49] Ruedorffer, *Grundzüge der Weltpolitik,* pp. 160, 183. Riezler's stress on tendencies directly contradicted Treitschke's view that men make history, and his stress on the constellation can be seen as a refutation of Bernhardi, who argued that war was natural, but who failed to consider sufficiently the environment in which such war should take place. Meinecke applied a similar analysis to "power politics," which has two sides: The "timeless" *(Zeitlos),* which is "state egoism striving toward unconditional self-determination and recognition of its interests with all power means at its disposal," and the "time-bound" *(Zeitgeschichtlich),* which places limits on their manifestations, their means and their goals." *Politische Schriften,* p. 80.

[50] Ruedorffer, *Grundzüge der Weltpolitik,* p. 184. Riezler preferred the term "world politics" to "imperialism," which was used in his time to refer only to the activity of extensive expansion of a nation's power. See Klaus Schwabe, *Wissenschaft und Kriegsmoral: Die deutschen Hochschullehrer und die politischen Grundfragen des Ersten Weltkrieges* (Göttingen: Musterschmidt-Verlag, 1969), p. 13. Mommsen, *Imperialismus,* pp. 152, 167. Mommsen, *Max Weber,* p. 59. Max Weber said in his acceptance speech in Freiburg shortly before the turn of the century: "The establishment of the German Empire would be a boyish trick if a new foundation allowing world politics were not given to her." Herzfeld, *Der Erste Weltkrieg,* p. 19. Hans-Ulrich Wehler argues that Germany's foreign policy, including the arms race and imperialism, was chiefly a defensive strategy on the part of Germany's elites to divert or check the domestic challenge of the working and entrepreneurial classes which grew out of industrialization. *Das Deutsche Kaiserreich 1871-1918* (Göttingen: Vandenhoeck & Ruprecht, 1973). See Konrad H. Jarausch's review of this book in the *Journal of Modern History,* 48 (December 1976), 728-32. As the reader will see, Riezler's work will not support Wehler's thesis of "social imperialism."

[51] Ruedorffer, *Grundzüge der Weltpolitik,* pp. 184, 186-87.

[52] *Ibid.,* pp. 188-96, 213. Riezler, "Political Decisions," 14. In fact, such interpenetration could also increase hostility as Germany's "pénétration pacifique" in France since 1900 indicated. See Fischer, *Krieg der Illusionen,* pp. 34, 462, 471-73.

[53] *Ibid.,* pp. 102-23, 106, 203. Expansion was not so easy as Riezler wrote. Russia's eastern expansion was blocked by Japan, and her western expansion by Austria-Hungary. Austria's expansion in the Balkans was blocked by Russia and Italy, and French expansion in Northern Africa was opposed by Germany. Also, it must not be overlooked that Germany had accumulated a few colonies outside Europe and was negotiating with some optimism the eventual acquisition of the Portuguese colonies.

[54] *Ibid.,* pp. 106-07. See Bethmann Hollweg's speech to Parliament, November 9, 1911, in Vietsch, *Bethmann Hollweg,* pp. 137-38. Stolberg-Wernigerode, *Unentschiedene Generation,* p. 114.

[55] Geiss, "Beurteilung," p. 56.

[56] Ruedorffer, *Grundzüge der Weltpolitik,* pp. 91-92. Riezler, *Diaries,* p. 47. Wernecke, *Wille zur Weltgeltung,* p. 159. Churchill, *World Crisis,* 1, pp. 101-05, 113. Richard B. Haldane, *Before the War* (London: Cassell, 1920), p. 88. Fischer, *Krieg der Illusionen,* pp. 171-72, 181-82. Bethmann Hollweg did succeed in getting an increase in the land army in 1913.

[57] Ruedorffer, *Grundzüge der Weltpolitik,* pp. 89-91, 95-101. Geiss, "Beurteilung," p. 56. Churchill, *World Crisis,* 1, p. 185. Lichnowsky, *My Mission to London 1912-1914* (New York: Doran, 1916). Mommsen, *Imperialismus,* p. 19.

[58] Fischer, *Griff nach der Weltmacht,* p. 33.

[59] Churchill, *World Crisis,* 1, p. 8. Fischer, *Krieg der Illusionen,* p. 143.

[60] Churchill, *World Crisis,* 1, pp. 104-05, 188. One cannot maintain, as Fischer did, that Germany's bid for neutrality was an aggressive step to enable her to win hegemony over Europe. The breaking up of threatening coalitions is the permanent goal of any country's foreign policy. Fischer, *Griff nach der Weltmacht,* p. 34. Bethmann Hollweg, *Betrachtungen,* 1, pp. 57, 61-62. Ritter, *Staatskunst,* 2, pp. 209-38. Fischer, *Krieg der Illusionen,* pp. 181-190. Haldane, *Before the War,* pp. 46-70. Vietsch, *Bethmann Hollweg,* pp. 137, 141. Ruedorffer, *Grundzüge der Weltpolitik,* p. 193. Plehn, *Deutsche Weltpolitik,* pp. 14-15, 18, 49-52, 60, 95.

[61] Riezler's political conception as related to "pre-fascist ideology" is the unsubstantiated conclusion to an otherwise highly intelligent article by Wolfgang J. Mommsen, "Kurt Riezler, ein Intellektueller im Dienste Wilhelmischer Machtpolitik," *Geschichte in Wissenschaft und Unterricht,* 25 (April 1974), 193-209. This conclusion was repeated uncritically in a less perceptive study by Eike-Wolfgang Kornhass, "Zwischen Kulturkritik und Machtverherrlichung: Kurt Riezler," in Vondung, *Das wilhelmische Bildungsbürgertum,* pp. 99, 104-05.

[62] Hermann Oncken, *Weltwirtschaftliches Archiv* 5, Teil 1 (1915), p. 432. Dietrich Schäfer, *Mein Leben* (Berlin: Verlag von K. F. Kochler, 1926), p. 169. *26. Versammlung deutscher Historiker in Berlin 1964, Beiheft zur Zeitschrift Geschichte in Wissenschaft und Unterricht* (Stuttgart: Ernst Klett Verlag, 1965), p. 72.

[63] Hans Herzfeld, *Die Deutsche Rüstungspolitik vor dem Weltkrieg* (Bonn and Leipzig: Kurt Schroeder, 1923), p. 147. Müller, *Aus Gärten der Vergangenheit,* p. 542. Wolfgang Schumann, Ernst Neukamp, *Zeitschrift für Politik,* 9 (1916), 296-311.

[64] Franz Sontag, "Grundzüge der Weltpolitik," *Alldeutsche Blätter,* 51 (December 19, 1914), pp. 445-47, and 3 (January 16, 1915), pp. 17-19. Junius Alter [Franz Sontag], *Das Deutsche Reich auf dem Wege zur geschichtlichen Episode: Eine Studie Bethmann Hollweg'scher Politik in Skizzen und Umrissen* (Munich: J. F. Lehmanns Verlag, 1919), p. 20. Klaus-Peter Reiss, *Von Bassermann zu Stresemann, Die Sitzungen des nationalliberalen Zentralvorstandes 1912-1917* (Düsseldorf: Droste Verlag, 1967), p. 263. Liebig, *Politik von Bethmann Hollweg,* pp. 53-55. Riezler, *Diaries,* pp. 49-51.

CHAPTER THREE

[1] Karl Alexander von Müller, *Mars und Venus: Erinnerungen 1914-1919* (Stuttgart: Gustav Kilpper Verlag, 1954), p. 33.

[2] Ruedorffer, *Grundzüge der Weltpolitik,* pp. 214-16. Riezler repeated his arguments on armaments in an article, published under his pseudonym of J. J. Ruedorffer, entitled "Die Rüstungen," in *Die Grenzboten,* 1 (March 1914). Barbara Tuchman, *The Guns of August* (New York: Dell, 1963), p. 24.

[3] Ruedorffer, *Grundzüge der Weltpolitik,* pp. 217-19.

[4] *Ibid.*, p. 219.

[5] *Ibid.*, p. 220. See also Churchill, *World Crisis*, 1, p. 3.

[6] *Ibid.*, p. 221.

[7] *Ibid.*, p. 222.

[8] Ruedorffer, *Grundzüge der Weltpolitik*, pp. 223, 225.

[9] *Ibid.*, pp. 226-27. For Riezler, the status quo was theoretically impossible; "Development presses on; becoming knows no end."

[10] *Ibid.*, pp. 227-28.

[11] *Ibid.*, pp. 229-30.

[12] *Ibid.*, p. 232.

[13] *Ibid.*, pp. 241-42.

[14] Churchill, *World Crisis*, 1, p. 207. June 28 was a Serbian holiday commemorating the assassination of the Turkish Sultan in 1389 by a Serbian patriot. However, the major significance of the date, June 28, 1389, was the defeat of an independent Serbia later that day. See Georg Ostrogorsky, *Geschichte des Bysantinischen Staates* (Munich: Beck'sche, n.d.), pp. 433ff. Riezler quote on "rational considerations" in a letter to Prof. Eduard Meyer, Jan. 10, 1917, ZStA Potsdam, Reichskanzlei, nr. 2410.

[15] Many years later Riezler described the prewar diplomatic constellation in "Political Decisions," 13-16.

[16] Fischer, *Krieg der Illusionen*, pp. 613-26. Stefan T. Possony, *Zur Bewältigung der Kriegsschuldfrage: Völkerrecht und Strategie bei der Auslösung zweier Weltkriege*, Demokratie und Frieden, Bd. 5 (Opladen: Westdeutscher Verlag, 1968), pp. 202-04, 212.

[17] Riezler, *Diaries*, July 7, 1914, pp. 181-83. Fischer, *Krieg der Illusionen*, pp. 627-35. Egmont Zechlin, "Deutschland zwischen Kabinettskrieg und Wirtschaftskrieg. Politik und Kriegführung in den ersten Monaten des Weltkriegs 1914," *Historische Zeitschrift*, 199 (1964), 347ff. Zechlin, "Probleme des Kriegskalküls," in Schieder, *Erster Weltkrieg*, pp. 151-52. Many years later, Riezler explained some of the factors which had brought Britain and Russia together. See Riezler, "Political Decisions," 31. See Erwin Hölzle, *Der Geheim-*

nisverrat und der Kriegsausbruch 1914, Historisch-Politische Hefte der Ranke-Gesellschaft, Heft 23 (Göttingen: Musterschmidt, 1973), and Hölzle, *Die Selbstentmachtung Europas: Das Experiment des Friedens vor und im Ersten Weltkrieg* (Göttingen: Musterschmidt, 1975), pp. 308-10.

[18] Laurence Lafore, *The Long Fuse: An Interpretation of the Origins of World War I,* Critical Periods of History, 2d ed. (New York: Lippincott, 1971), pp. 188-89. See L. L. Farrar, Jr., *The Short-War Illusion: German Policy, Strategy & Domestic Affairs August-December 1914,* Twentieth Century Series (Santa Barbara: Clio Press, 1973). L. C. F. Turner, *Origins of the First World War* (London: Edward Arnold, 1970), p. 5. ZStA Potsdam, Reichskanzlei, nr. 2410.

[19] The literature on the "war guilt question" is immense. Perhaps the best summary in English is edited by Dwight E. Lee, *The Outbreak of the First World War: Causes and Responsibilities,* Problems in European Civilization, 4th ed. (Lexington, Mass.: Heath, 1975). The 3d edition was published in 1970. See also Wolfgang J. Mommsen, "The Debate on German War Aims," and Imanuel Geiss, "The Outbreak of the First World War and German War Aims," in *Coming of the First World War,* ed. by Laqueur and Mosse. See Wolfgang Schieder, ed., *Erster Weltkrieg Ursachen und Kriegsziele,* Neue Wissenschaftliche Bibliothek (Cologne, Berlin: Kiepenheuer & Witsch, 1969), and Joachim Remak, ed., *The First World War: Causes, Conduct, Consequences,* Major Issues in History (New York: Wiley, 1971). Also Fischer, *Griff nach der Weltmacht,* the book which helped unleash the fury and emotion associated with the entire question. He added more depth to his treatment in *Krieg der Illusionen.* A respected response was provided by Ritter, *Staatskunst,* 3. Not surprisingly, Riezler has been brought into the controversy, not only because his diaries offer the closest look at German decision-making which now exists, but also because of the possible role which he himself played as one of the closest advisers of the German chancellor. One respected German historian, Andreas Hillgruber, suggested that there was a relationship between Riezler's theories about war and the calculated risk on the one hand and the German government's policy during the "July crisis" on the other hand. Andreas Hillgruber, "Riezlers Theorie des kalkulierten Risikos und Bethmann Hollwegs politische Konzeption in der Julikrise 1914," *Historische Zeitschrift,* 202 (1966). Hillgruber's essay is the only attempt to show Riezler as an important figure in the events of July 1914. Imanuel Geiss argued that even Riezler himself must have known that his ideas could only be realized by war, but he failed to show concretely how Riezler's prewar ideas contributed to the outbreak of war. In his published collection of documents, he produced no document indicating Riezler's influence on German decision making during the July crisis, although he pointed to Riezler as "perhaps the most sophisticated of German thinkers and politicians in the age of *Weltpolitik,*" whose "historical relevance cannot be ignored or belittled." Imanuel Geiss,

Julikrise und Kriegsausbruch 1914, 2 vols. (Hannover: Verlag für Literatur und Zeitgeschichte GmbH, 1963-64), is by far the most complete and best edited collection of documents in print on the outbreak of war. The English edition is considerably shorter: *July 1914* (New York: Schribner's, 1967). The Geiss quotations above are taken from pp. 33 and 369. Jarausch, "Illusion of Limited War," 51. This study is included in *Enigmatic Chancellor,* pp. 148-84. For impressions of Riezler's role in the events of July 1914, see Gottlieb Jagow, *Ursachen und Ausbruch des Weltkrieges* (Berlin: Verlag von Reimar Hobbing, 1919), p. 55, and *Die Ursachen des Deutschen Zusammenbruchs im Jahre 1918. Vierte Reihe,* ed. Dr. Albrecht Philipp (Berlin: Deutsche Verlagsgesellschaft für Politik und Geschichte, 1925), 1, p. 393. In the parliamentary hearings, Riezler was quite misleading concerning his role in the Chancellery. Riezler's answer to the question whether "the widespread impression is true that you were the right hand and confidant of Herr von Bethmann Hollweg," was: "No, especially not in questions of foreign policy." NA Washington, Parlamentarischer Untersuchungsausschuss, Dec. 21, 1921, T120, Roll 1130.

[20] Conrad Haussmann, *Schlaglichter, Reichstagsbriefe und Aufzeichnungen* (Frankfurt/M.: Frankfurter Societäts-Druckerei, GmbH, 1924), p. 26. Vietsch, *Bethmann Hollweg,* p. 157. Jarausch, *Enigmatic Chancellor,* pp. 105, 187. Riezler, *Diaries,* p. 55. Gordon A. Craig, *The Politics of the Prussian Army 1640-1945* (Oxford: Clarendon Press, 1955), pp. 327-29. John G. Williamson, *Karl Helfferich 1874-1924: Economist, Financier, Politician* (Princeton: Princeton University Press, 1971), and Rudolf von Valentini, *Kaiser und Kabinettschef* (Oldenbourg: Gerhard Stalling, 1931).

[21] Geiss, *Julikrise,* 1, nos. 12, 15. In order to aid the reader interested in referring to the original documents, all documents used in this study which are published in collections of documents, regardless of origin, are cited by the document publication numbers. See Konrad H. Jarausch, "Statesmen versus Structures: Germany's Role in the Outbreak of World War One Reexamined," *Laurentian University Review, Aspects of Imperial Germany,* 5 (June 1973), pp. 136-37.

[22] Geiss, *Julikrise,* 1, nos. 9, 21, and p. 56. Geiss interpreted Franz Joseph's letter as not indicating firm Austrian determination for war with Serbia. See also Fischer, *Krieg der Illusionen,* pp. 689-90.

[23] Bethmann Hollweg, *Betrachtungen,* 1, pp. 135-36.

[24] Geiss, *Julikrise,* 1, no. 24a-c.

[25] *Ibid.,* no. 21. Geiss argues that the German decisions made at this "Crown Council" placed the major responsibility for the world war on Germany. *Julikrise,* 2, p. 722. Fritz Kern attempted a psychological study of the "Crown Council" in *Skizzen zum Kriegsausbruch im Jahre*

1914 (Darmstadt: Wissenschaftliche Buchgesellschaft, 1968), pp. 58-76. For Bethmann's description, see *Betrachtungen,* 1, pp. 134-36. It should be remembered that France and Russia were also issuing "blank checks" to their allies at this time. See Joachim Remak, "The Third Balkan War," in Lee, *Outbreak,* pp. 134-47.

[26] Jarausch, "Statesmen versus Structures," 148. Falkenhayn was Prussian Minister of War.

[27] Fischer, *Krieg der Illusionen,* p. 688. Gutsche, *Aufstieg und Fall,* pp. 115-17.

[28] Hillgruber, "Riezlers Theorie," 335, 341. Jarausch, "Statesmen versus Structures," 138, 148-49. Remak, "Third Balkan War," pp. 141-42. John Röhl, *1914: Delusion or Design* (London: Elek Books, 1973), pp. 22-27.

[29] Riezler, *Diaries,* July 7, 1914, pp. 181-83. See Harry F. Young, *Prince Lichnowsky and the Great War* (Athens: University of Georgia Press, 1977).

[30] Ruedorffer, *Grundzüge der Weltpolitik,* p. 64. Riezler, *Diaries,* July 23, 1914, pp. 188-89. Vietsch, *Bethmann Hollweg,* pp. 146-55. Mommsen, *Imperialismus,* pp. 255-62. Fischer, *Krieg der Illusionen,* pp. 289, 600. Ritter, *Staatskunst,* 3, p. 18.

[31] Zechlin, "Kabinettskrieg und Wirtschaftskrieg," p. 400. Jagow found the conflict between Slavs and Germans as the underlying cause of the war. *Ursachen und Ausbruch,* p. 193. For Riezler's evaluation of the Russian nation, see *Grundzüge der Weltpolitik,* pp. 69-73.

[32] Riezler, *Diaries,* July 11, 1914, p. 185. The realization from the beginning that a world war could result stands at variance with Riezler's theory of the calculated risk, which because of modern weapon technology practically excluded war. Riezler did allow for the possibility that in a specific crisis war could become unavoidable. In order not to have to bear the responsibility for starting the war, the final decision to make war would always be left to the enemy. However, the awareness that there was danger of a war would come in the course of the crisis, not in the beginning of the crisis, as was the case in July 1914. Fritz Fischer mistakenly views Riezler's remarks of July 8 as indicating that Riezler wanted war and that only if it were impossible to have it would a peace with "the prospect of maneuvering the Entente apart over this matter" have been acceptable to Germany. He writes that "with this statement Bethmann Hollweg calculated unmistakably the European war as the first alternative of his policy, and only as a second, less desirable [alternative], a mere diplomatic success." Fischer, *Krieg der Illusionen,* p. 693. To read Riezler's entire diary and to see such remarks in context indicates why such an interpretation is mistaken. It must be remembered

that Fischer had not had the opportunity to read Riezler's diary before the publication of *Krieg der Illusionen.* Zechlin, "Probleme des Kriegskalküls," 154. Hillgruber, "Riezlers Theorie," 346.

[33] Geiss, *Julikrise,* 1, nos. 39, 52. Sidney Bradshaw Fay, "Origins of the World War," in Lee, *Outbreak,* p. 12. Ruedorffer, *Grundzüge der Weltpolitik,* p. 226. George Peabody Gooch, "Why the War in 1914?" in Lee, *Outbreak,* p. 26. For documents in English concerning the free hand given to Berchtold, see Geiss, *July 1914,* nos. 26, 30, 33. In the latter document, dated July 18, Zimmermann summarized the contents of the ultimatum and also noted "that it is almost embarrassing to the always timid and undecided authorities at Vienna not to be admonished by Germany to caution and self-restraint." The lack of control over Austrian policy renders Hillgruber's argument highly questionable. It is entirely impossible for statesmen in a particular country to engineer a small realignment, which should not be perceived until "it has already succeeded," if control over the situation has been given to another country. Riezler quotations in *Diaries,* July 11, 1914, pp. 184-85.

[34] Riezler, *Diaries,* July 14, 1914, p. 185. For Riezler's desire to see the Entente broken up, see *Diaries,* July 20, 23, 1914, pp. 187-89. In 1920 and 1953, Riezler looked back on the helplessness which seemed to characterize the feelings of Europe's statesmen at that critical time. See Ruedorffer, *Drei Krisen,* pp. 8-10, and Riezler, "Political Decisions," p. 5.

[35] Riezler, *Diaries,* July 20, 1914, p. 186. Geiss, *Julikrise,* 1, no. 123. The critical documents can be found in English in Geiss, *July 1914,* nos. 33, 20-29, especially no. 21. The latter document indicates that Bethmann Hollweg was immediately informed of the Austrian decision concerning the unacceptable ultimatum, that he favored it, but that he was opposed to the delay of its delivery until after the French president, Poincaré, had departed from St. Petersburg on July 25. The Germans were aware of the general demands to Serbia which were to be contained in the Austrian ultimatum. See Geiss, *July 1914,* nos. 20-27.

[36] Riezler, *Diaries,* July 20, 1914, p. 187. Because of the nature of their relationship, it can be assumed that Riezler would have told the chancellor all his thoughts bearing on German policy which he recorded in his diaries.

[37] Geiss, *Julikrise,* 1, nos. 62, 188. *The German White-Book: How Russia and her Ruler Betrayed Germany's Confidence and Thereby Caused the European War* (Berlin: Liebheit & Thiesen, 1914).

[38] Riezler, *Diaries,* July 20, 1914, p. 187.

[39] *Ibid.,* July 23, 1914, p. 188.

[40] *Ibid.*, pp. 188-89. Sazonov's statement is translated: "If Germany drops Austria, I will drop France immediately thereafter." Ruedorffer, *Drei Krisen*, p. 9.

[41] Riezler, *Diaries*, p. 190.

[42] Geiss, *Julikrise*, 1, nos. 259, 261-62, 276, 310, 327, 359. Copy of text of ultimatum in Hans Dollinger, *Der Erste Weltkrieg in Bildern und Dokumenten*, 3 vols. (Munich, Vienna, Basel: Verlag Kurt Desch, 1969), 1, p. 33.

[43] Riezler, *Diaries*, July 25, 1914, p. 191. Rudolf Havenstein was president of the Reichsbank board of directors. It was still hoped in Berlin that the war could be localized. However, the realization of the increasing likelihood that a general war could erupt from such a localized war and the fact that a realignment could not be quietly engineered without being perceived by the other powers gave this tactic little resemblance to Riezler's earlier theory of the calculated risk.

[44] *Ibid.*, July 23, 25, and 27, 1914, pp. 190-192. Wilhelm II thought that the Serbian answer to the ultimatum eliminated all cause for war. Geiss, *Julikrise*, 1, no. 350. See also nos. 271, 275, 276, 278, 280, 281, 283. Churchill, *World Crisis*, 1, pp. 5-6.

[45] Geiss, *Julikrise*, 1, nos. 286, 361, and 2, 416-17, 429, 441-42, 496. Riezler, *Diaries*, July 27, 1914, p. 192.

[46] *Ibid.* See also Geiss, *Julikrise*, 2, nos. 432, 481, 495, 497-98.

[47] Riezler, *Diaries*, July 27 and Aug. 14, 1914, pp. 192-93.

[48] Geiss, *Julikrise*, 2, no. 784. The documents in the Politisches Archiv des Auswärtigen Amts, Bonn (hereafter referred to as PA Bonn) relating to the outbreak of war, especially Akten des Auswärtigen Amts im Grossen Hauptquartier, 1914-1916, 1, Europäischer Krieg, vols. 1-5, which cover the time during which Riezler was assigned to the Grosses Hauptquartier, revealed that Riezler signed no significant documents. He signed only those documents relating to press affairs. He did initial most of the documents written after August 1914, indicating that he was well-informed.

[49] As his diary entry of Aug. 15, 1914, indicated, Riezler worked on the problem of mediation, but there is no indication of his position on this matter. See Geiss, *Julikrise*, 2, pp. 79-85, and nos. 476, 482, 496.

[50] *Ibid.*, nos. 503, 575.

[51] *Ibid.*, no. 425. Fay, "Origins of the War," pp. 13-14, and Bernadotte E. Schmitt, "The Origins of the First World War," in Lee, *Outbreak*, 3d ed., p. 72. Remak, "Third Balkan War," p. 139.

[52] Geiss, *Julikrise*, 2, p. 166, and nos. 835, 883. There is insufficient evidence to support Geiss's argument that by July 28 German concern was "not primarily a question of preventing a war against Serbia, which had necessarily to lead to a world war, but of attributing the overwhelming guilt [for this war] to Russia," and that Bethmann Hollweg was guided by the motive of convicting the Russians of the guilt for a general war which he himself wanted. See also Vietsch, *Bethmann Hollweg*, p. 198.

[53] Riezler, *Diaries*, Aug. 15, 1914, pp. 194-95.

[54] *Ibid.*, Geiss, *Julikrise*, 2, no. 684.

[55] *Ibid.*, nos. 695-96. Jarausch, "Illusion of Limited War," 69.

[56] Geiss, *Julikrise*, 2, nos. 678, 696.

[57] *Ibid.*, nos. 793, 797-98. Jarausch, "Illusion of Limited War," 68-69.

[58] Geiss, *Julikrise*, 2, p. 338, and nos. 801, 820.

[59] *Ibid.*, pp. 166, 341, and nos. 809, 835, 883.

[60] *Ibid.*, nos. 875, 892-94, 1053.

[61] Churchill, *World Crisis*, 1, pp. 211, 215. Bethmann Hollweg, *Betrachtungen*, 1, p. 192. Tuchman, *Guns of August*, pp. 33-34. Geiss, *Julikrise*, 2, no. 1053.

[62] B. H. Lidell Hart, *Strategy*, 2d rev. ed. (New York: Praeger, 1968), pp. 168-72. Ritter, *Staatskunst*, 2, pp. 239-55. Bethmann Hollweg, *Betrachtungen*, 1, p. 167. Vietsch, *Bethmann Hollweg*, pp. 170-71. Riezler, *Diaries*, Sept. 20, 1914, p. 207. Only Jagow and Bülow were known to have expressed objections about the general concept of the Schlieffen Plan. Tuchman, *Guns of August*, p. 39. Fischer, *Krieg der Illusionen*, p. 679.

[63] Geiss, *Julikrise*, 2, p. 612, and nos. 1000, 1068. Riezler, *Diaries*, Aug. 15, 1914, p. 194. Churchill admitted that it would have been better if Britain had made its support of the Entente unmistakably clear from the beginning. *World Crisis*, 1, p. 217.

[64] Geiss, *Julikrise*, 2, no. 1146. Bethmann Hollweg retracted his confession of guilt against Belgium on December 2, 1914. See Ritter, *Staatskunst*, 3, p. 47. Riezler, *Diaries*, Aug. 15, 1914, p. 195. Ruedorffer, *Drei Krisen*, p. 10.

[65] Bethmann Hollweg thought that he was speaking off the record. *Betrachtungen*, 1, p. 180. Geiss, "Beurteilung," p. 58.

The allegation that the chancellor accepted the risk of war with nonchalance was made by Bernadotte Schmitt in Lee, *Outbreak,* p. 71. German willingness to accept the risk of war from the beginning was clearly admitted in the German White Book, *Outbreak of the European War,* 3d ed., p. 406.

[67] Fischer, *Krieg der Illusionen,* p. 738. Mommsen, "The Debate on German War Aims," and Geiss, "The Crisis of July 1914," in Laqueur & Mosse, *Coming of the First World War,* pp. 53, 60, 78. See also "Report Presented to the Preliminary Peace Conference (1919)," and Taylor, "The Outbreak of War," in Lee, *Outbreak,* 3d ed., pp. 4, 57. Geiss wrote that "German policy in the July crisis was the missing link between *Weltpolitik* and the war aims." *Julikrise,* 2, p. 731.

[68] Fischer maintains that the dominant view of historians in 1969 was that Germany had risked a preventive war. *Krieg der Illusionen,* p. 663. Hillgruber argues that the ideas of a preventive war were only in the minds of the German military. Andreas Hillgruber, *Kontinuität und Diskontinuität in der deutschen Aussenpolitik von Bismarck bis Hitler* (Düsseldorf: Droste Verlag, 1969), p. 3. Of course, the kaiser also spoke occasionally of the need for a preventive war against Russia. See Churchill's statement on the favorable time for the war in *World Crisis,* 1, p. 245.

[69] Fischer, "Weltmacht oder Niedergang, Deutschland im Ersten Weltkrieg," in Schieder, *Erster Weltkrieg,* p. 88, and *Krieg der Illusionen,* p. 682. See also Dehio, *Deutschland und die Weltpolitik im 20. Jahrhundert.*

[70] Willibald Gutsche, *Die Beziehungen zwischen der Regierung Bethmann Hollweg und dem Monopolkapital in den ersten Monaten des ersten Weltkrieges,* unpublished Habilitationsschrift, Humboldtuniversität, Berlin, 1967, and *Aufstieg und Fall,* p. 136. K. Zilliacus, "Economic and Social Causes of the War," in Lee, *Outbreak,* 3d ed., p. 47. Pierre Renouvin, "Background of the War: General Conclusions," in Lee, *Outbreak,* p. 41.

[71] Graf Pourtalès, *Am Scheidewege zwischen Krieg und Frieden. Meine letzten Verhandlungen in Petersburg Ende Juli 1914* (Berlin: Deutsche Verlagsgesellschaft für Politik und Geschichte, 1919), pp. 10, 93. Gerhard Ritter, "A New War-Guilt Thesis?" in Lee, *Outbreak,* p. 105. Zechlin, "Probleme des Kriegskalküls," and "Bethmann Hollweg, Kriegsrisiko und SPD 1914," in Schieder, *Erster Weltkrieg,* pp. 153, 166. Geiss, *Julikrise,* 1, no. 327. James Joll suggested that "unspoken assumptions" were more likely constraints on German leaders than domestic pressure. In moments of crisis when political leaders cannot foresee the outcome of their decisions, they often fall back on certain traditions, beliefs, rules or objectives which they take for granted. See Joll, *1914 The Unspoken Assumption* (London and Southhampton:

Camelot Press, 1968), pp. 6-7. Riezler's reference in *Grundzüge der Weltpolitik,* pp. 241-42, that "the power of the government in general operates in the broad or narrow limits which parliaments and public opinion allow" is far more accurate in reference to the situation in Germany before the July crisis and during the war than during the actual July crisis itself. Certainly, many crucial German mistakes before and during the war can be traced to domestic pressures, but Riezler's diaries contain little evidence of such pressure at the time of the outbreak of war in 1914.

[72] Riezler, *Diaries,* Aug. 15, 1914, p. 195. Forty years later, Riezler wrote about the excuse frequently heard from statesmen that "I did not have any choice—there was no alternative." He wrote that "the trouble is that no one can ever disprove such a statement since we cannot, as in natural science, make an experiment, restore the original situation, change a factor, and see what happens. In some cases the impasse in which there is no choice is of the statesman's own making." Riezler, "Political Decisions," pp. 5-6.

CHAPTER FOUR

[1] Riezler, *Diaries,* Aug. 14, 1914, p. 193.

[2] Bethmann Hollweg, *Betrachtungen,* 2, pp. 5, 30. Schwabe, *Wissenschaft und Kriegsmoral,* p. 21. Karl Lamprecht, *Krieg und Kultur* (Leipzig: Verlag S. Hirzel, 1914), pp. 14-15. Hermann Luebbe, "Die philosophischen Ideen von 1914," in *Politische Philosophie in Deutschland: Studien zu ihrer Geschichte* (Stuttgart: 1963), pp. 173-238.

[3] Riezler, *Diaries,* Sept. 30, 1914, and May 16, 1915, pp. 210, 271. For Riezler's comparison of German and non-German freedom see *Diaries,* Dec. 4, 1915, p. 317. See also Ringer, *German Mandarins,* pp. 181-87, and Meinecke, *German Catastrophe,* p. 19. The argument that the war was justified because it was a struggle against "mechanistic" philosophies for which France and Britain stood was made not only by most conservative German intellectuals, but also by respected persons in the accommodationist camp, such as Thomas Mann, Ernst Troeltsch, and Friedrich Meinecke. See Hughes, *Consciousness and Society,* pp. 237-38, 370; and Nigel Hamilton, *The Brothers Mann* (London: Secker & Warburg, 1978), pp. 161-70.

⁴ *Ibid.*, Aug. 14, 1914, p. 193. Schwabe, *Wissenschaft und Kriegsmoral*, p. 39. Fischer, *Griff nach der Weltmacht*, p. 185.

⁵ Riezler was in charge of preparing war aims in the Grosses Hauptquartier, and a coordinating office for war aims was set up in the Imperial Department of the Interior under Freiherr von Rechenberg. For Riezler's influence on war aims, see Jarausch, *Enigmatic Chancellor*, p. 479, n. 12. On August 16, 1914, the Supreme Headquarters, composed of the kaiser, the Supreme Military Command and other high military staff officers, the chancellor, the state secretary for foreign affairs, the Prussian war minister and parts of their staffs, moved to Coblenz. On August 30, 1914, it moved again to Luxembourg. On August 19, 1914, Riezler wrote to Hammann that "one does not hear much more military information here than in Berlin." Riezler suspected that his telephone conversations were being tapped by the military, so in a letter to Hammann on August 22 he suggested that they work out a code so that their conversations would be more difficult to understand. "August" would signify "the soldiers, who have gone mad." ZStA Potsdam, nr. 34, Nachlass Hammann.

⁶ Riezler, *Diaries*, Aug. 22, 1914, p. 201. Jarausch, *Enigmatic Chancellor*, p. 186. Riezler to Hammann, Aug. 29, 1914, SZtA Potsdam, nr. 34, Nachlass Hammann. Zechlin, "Weltkriegsrisiko und defensive Kriegsziele," in Schieder, *Erster Weltkrieg*, p. 201. For war aims of various German political parties, see Dollinger, *Der Erste Weltkrieg*, 2, pp. 85-88. Gutsche, *Monopolkapital*, pp. 33-39, 48, 94.

⁷ Fischer, *Griff nach der Weltmacht*, p. 112. Fischer's basic argument is that there was no essential difference between the two camps traditionally seen in German historiography as annexationists and antiannexationists. Ritter, *Staatskunst*, 3, pp. 299-318. Jarausch, *Enigmatic Chancellor*, pp. 196-98. Gutsche, *Monopolkapital*, pp. 110-12. Bethmann Hollweg wrote in a letter to General von Kessel on Oct. 11, 1914, that "the goal of this war is not the re-establishment of the European balance of power." ZStA Potsdam, Reichskanzlei, nr. 2476. Mann, *Deutsche Geschichte*, pp. 590-91.

⁸ Pflanze, *Bismarck*, p. 479. Riezler, *Diaries*, Aug. 22, 1914, pp. 201-02. This harsh peace for France was in contradiction to the conciliatory tone of the proclamation to the French people written by Riezler in the event of an early French surrender. The invasion was, he wrote on Sept. 6, 1914, a "nécessité cruelle." ZStA Potsdam, Rkz, nr. 2465/1. Also Zechlin, "Kabinettskrieg," 376-81. See *Diaries*, Oct. 11, 1914, p. 216. By 1916, Riezler wrote optimistically of reconciliation with France. See his article, "Wo stehen wir?" in *Europäische Staats- und Wirtschafts-Zeitung* (Hereafter referred to as *ESWZ*), March 11, 1916, reprinted in Riezler, *Diaries*, pp. 514-15.

⁹ Fischer, *Griff nach der Weltmacht,* pp. 116-18. A translation of Riezler's entire document can be found in Gerald D. Feldman, *German Imperialism 1914-1918: The Development of a Historical Debate* (New York: Wiley, 1972), pp. 125-26.

¹⁰ *Ibid.,* p. 118. Gutsche, *Monopolkapital,* p. 92.

¹¹ Vietsch, *Bethmann Hollweg,* p. 209. Ringer, *German Mandarins,* pp. 190-91.

¹² Riezler, *Diaries,* Sept. 20, 1914, Oct. 6, 1914, Nov. 2, 1914, Nov. 11, 1916, pp. 208, 212, 223, 380. See also Ritter, *Staatskunst,* 3, p. 42, and Lamprecht, *Krieg und Kultur,* p. 60.

¹³ Letters Riezler to Hammann, Aug. 29 and Sept. 5, 1914, ZStA Potsdam, nr. 34, Nachlass Hammann. References to "imminent victory over France" on p. 116, and to "war aims program" on p. 113 of Fischer, *Griff nach der Weltmacht.*

¹⁴ Fischer, *Krieg der Illusionen,* pp. 762-63, 767, and *Griff nach der Weltmacht,* p. 113, and "Weltmacht oder Niedergang," in Schieder, *Erster Weltkrieg,* p. 95. Zechlin, "Kriegskalkül," in Schieder, *Erster Weltkrieg,* pp. 155-57. Letter Zimmermann to Delbrück, Sept. 9, 1914, ZStA Potsdam, Reichskanzlei, nr. 2476. In the ZStA Potsdam, where Fischer found Riezler's "September Program," there are several documents which confirm that among political leaders at the German Supreme Headquarters there was no expectation of sudden victory, as Fischer maintained in *Griff nach der Weltmacht,* p. 116. Further, the documents make clear that there was no unanimity within the chancellor's circle concerning the exact demands which Germany should make. In a letter from Riezler in the Supreme Headquarters to Otto Hammann in Berlin, dated Aug. 29, 1914, the chancellor's instructions regarding the "annexation fever" in Berlin were given: ". . . Due both to Belgium and Poland, certainly two very difficult problems, no final decisions have yet been made and, according to the chancellor, cannot be made at this time since it is improbable that we are on the brink of an impending peace with France; it is completely uncertain whether we can really dictate conditions to England. You can well imagine that here there are the strongest currents among the incoming nobles with the rabble of soldiers for the entirely impossible *out-and-out* [Riezler's emphasis] annexation. On the other hand, one cannot allow the entirely devastated France to emerge in the old form; [we] may perhaps have to lay a hand on Antwerp. All well and good; however, everything is still up in the air. The same applies to Poland. An annexation of the Champagne, Burgundy, Franche-Comté is out of the question. It is a different story with the mining area *(Erzgebiet).* The purpose of the war is to secure ourselves in the East and West for all imaginable time through the weakening of our enemies. This weakening does not necessarily have

to come through annexations. Annexations can become the source of our own weakness. The weakening of our enemies can be economic and financial, through trade agreements *etc.*" On Sept. 5, 1914, Riezler again wrote Hammann that Bethmann "requests that the campaign of the intellectuals against the annexation fever be continued, but that the government not be exposed or placed into a vulnerable position." Both letters above from ZStA Potsdam, nr. 34, Nachlass Hammann. We shall see that most intellectuals actually fueled the "annexation fever."

[15] Letter Imperial Chancellor to Delbrück, Sept. 19, 1914, ZStA Potsdam, Reichskanzlei, nr. 2476.

[16] *26. Versammlung deutscher Historiker,* pp. 63-65. Riezler, *Diaries,* pp. 58-59. Ritter, *Staatskunst,* 3, pp. 43-44. Text of letter to Hammann in Vietsch, *Bethmann Hollweg,* pp. 326-27. See also pp. 205-06. Riezler never mentioned the "September Program" in his *Diaries,* nor did he or the chancellor ever refer to this document as a "program." Final Bethmann quote from letter Lerchenfeld to Hertling, May 29, 1916, in Jarausch, *Enigmatic Chancellor,* p. 198. For Bethmann's interpretation of the "September Program," see his letter to Count von Hertling, Jan. 26, 1918, in Feldman, *German Imperialism,* pp. 129-31.

[17] Telegramm des Legationsrats Riezler an das Auswärtige Amt. Entwurf von Leitsätzen für die Handhabung der Zensur in Kriegszielfragen. Oct. 19, 1914, Gr. Hauptquartier, nr. 284, PA Bonn, Weltkrieg nr. 8, vol. 42. Text reprinted in full in Wilhelm Deist, *Militär und Innenpolitik im Weltkrieg 1914-1918.* Quellen zur Geschichte des Parlamentarismus und der politischen Parteien, 2 vols. (Düsseldorf: Droste Verlag, 1970), pp. 78-80. Alter, *Deutsches Reich auf dem Wege,* p. 5. Müller, *Mars und Venus,* p. 75.

[18] For Riezler and the war aims discussion, see *Diaries,* Apr. 28, 1915, p. 269, and Dec. 2, 1915, p. 317. For war aims movement, see Fischer, *Griff nach der Weltmacht,* pp. 198-216. See also Gutsche, *Monopolkapital,* pp. 100-01, and Werner Baseler, *Deutschlands Annexionspolitik in Polen und im Baltikum, 1914-1918* (Berlin: Rütten und Loening, 1962), pp. 16, 348-49.

[19] Theodor Heuss, *Friedrich Naumann und die deutsche Demokratie* (Wiesbaden: Im Insel Verlag, 1960), pp. 47, 336. Ritter, *Staatskunst,* 3, pp. 117-18. See also Schwabe, *Wissenschaft und Kriegsmoral,* pp. 63-68, and Henry Cord Meyer, *Mitteleuropa in German Thought and Action 1815-1945,* International Scholars Forum, 4 (The Hague: Martinus Nijhoff, 1955), pp. 194-215. Heuss and Naumann were known to have been good friends and very close collaborators.

[20] Riezler, *Diaries,* June 1, 1917, p. 391, and "Innere und äussere Politik," *ESWZ,* reprinted in *Diaries,* pp. 538-39. In his October

Memorandum Riezler had advocated state-owned monopolies. ZStA Potsdam, Reichskanzlei, nr. 2476.

²¹ Riezler, *Diaries,* pp. 547, 580, 513, 604, and Nov. 8, 1914, p. 226.

²² Riezler, "Deutsche Mission," *ESWZ,* reprinted in *Diaries,* pp. 554-56, 559-60.

²³ Riezler, *Diaries,* pp. 603, 561. Bethmann Hollweg expressed ideas very similar to these in *Betrachtungen,* 2, pp. 57-60.

²⁴ Riezler, *Diaries,* pp. 563-64.

²⁵ *Ibid.,* p. 551, and July 6, 1916, Oct. 11, 23, 1915, Feb. 19, 1916, pp. 365, 305, 309, 333.

²⁶ *Ibid.,* Oct. 30, 1914, p. 222. Bethmann Hollweg said same in *Betrachtungen,* 2, p. 17. See also Mann, *Deutsche Geschichte,* p. 591.

²⁷ Riezler, *Diaries,* pp. 538, 550. Fischer, *Griff nach der Weltmacht,* p. 317.

²⁸ Ruedorffer, *Grundzüge der Weltpolitik,* p. 138. Also, *Diaries,* Feb. 22, 1916, p. 335. For an example of the "intoxication of the violent method," see Erich Ludendorff, *Kriegführung und Politik* (Berlin: Verlag von E. S. Mittler & Sohn, 1922) in which he wrote that because of their cosmopolitanism, many Germans had failed to see that "in the life of peoples *(Völkerleben)* might means right." p. vii.

²⁹ Riezler, *Diaries,* pp. 550, 523, and Dec. 29, 1916, p. 390.

³⁰ *Ibid.,* Apr. 18, 1915, pp. 268-69.

³¹ *Ibid.,* July 6 and Nov. 11, 1916, pp. 364-65, 380. Kohn, *Mind of Germany,* pp. 275-78.

³² *Ibid.,* Feb. 12, 1916, Feb. 27, 1915, pp. 386, 253. See Fritz Klein, "Bemerkungen zum Riezler Tagebuch," *Zeitschrift für Geschichtswissenschaft,* 21 (1973), 675-76.

³³ Ruedorffer, *Grundzüge der Weltpolitik,* p. 95. Riezler, *Diaries,* May 31 and July 28, 1915, pp. 276, 289. See Jarausch, *Enigmatic Chancellor,* p. 193.

³⁴ Riezler, *Diaries,* Sept. 20, Dec. 13, 1914, May 22, 1915, pp. 208, 234, 274.

³⁵ Fontane quote in Remak, *Fontane,* p. 75. Ringer, *German Mandarins,* pp. 132-35, 189, 192-93, 210.

[36] The document is located in the ZStA Potsdam, Reichskanzlei, nr. 2476, and bears the unmistakable stamp of Riezler. Outline of document printed in *Deutschland im Ersten Weltkrieg,* von einem Autorenkollektiv unter Leitung von Fritz Klein, 3 vols. (Berlin: Akademie-Verlag, 1968), 1, pp. 426-29. Jarausch, *Enigmatic Chancellor,* p. 313. The first Member of Parliament to be killed in the war (September 3, 1914) was Dr. Ludwig Franck, a Social Democrat. On September 12, Riezler wrote to Hammann from the Supreme Headquarters: "Naturally the reactionary prophets of doom are beginning to work on the kaiser because of the Social Democratic danger. . . . How stupid these people are can be seen by the fact that one of the aides-de-camp wishes to perceive the death of Franck as a propaganda ploy." ZStA Potsdam, nr. 34, Nachlass Hammann. Riezler, *Diaries,* Sept. 25, 1914, p. 209.

[37] Riezler, *Diaries,* July 27, 1914, p. 193. Zechlin, "Bethmann Hollweg, Kriegsrisiko und SPD 1914," in Schieder, *Erster Weltkrieg,* pp. 174-82. Zmarzlik, *Bethmann Hollweg,* p. 143. In the document Riezler recommended that labor union leaders be drawn into the government so that the "dogmatists of the Social Democrats" will not be able to lead the workers against the state. Jarausch, *Enigmatic Chancellor,* p. 208.

[38] Riezler, "Deutsches Programm," *ESWZ,* June 17, 1916; in *Diaries,* pp. 579-81.

[39] Klein, *Deutschland im Ersten Weltkrieg,* 1, p. 428. Riezler, *Diaries,* Aug. 22, Oct. 11, 1914, pp. 201, 216.

[40] Riezler, *Diaries,* Aug. 22, Oct. 6 and 11, 1914, pp. 201,213, 216. Bethmann Hollweg, *Betrachtungen,* 1, pp. 70-74.

[41] Riezler, *Diaries,* Oct. 11, 19, 1914, pp. 216-18. Hans W. Gatzke, *Germany's Drive to the West. A Study of Germany's Western War Aims During the First World War* (Baltimore: Johns Hopkins Press, 1950), pp. 84-91.

[42] Riezler, *Diaries,* Oct. 19, 1914, p. 218. Fischer, *Griff nach der Weltmacht,* pp. 125-26.

[43] The memorandum is summarized in Riezler, *Diaries,* p. 679. See also *Diaries,* Feb. 6, 1915, p. 246. Friedrich Payer wrote that few Germans wanted the direct annexation of Belgium. See *Von Bethmann Hollweg bis Ebert, Erinnerungen und Bilder* (Frankfurt am Main: Frankfurter Societäts-Druckerei, GmbH, 1923), p. 273.

[44] Riezler, *Diaries,* p. 679. The Bundesrat was the federal council in which the various German states were represented.

[45] *Ibid.*, Oct. 16, 1915, p. 308. Vietsch, *Bethmann Hollweg,* p. 206.

[46] Fischer, *Griff nach der Weltmacht,* pp. 126, 265, 343-45.

[47]*Ibid.*, pp. 268-80. Riezler, *Diaries,* May 10 and 26, 1916, pp. 340, 344-45.

[48] Riezler, *Diaries,* June 14, 1917, pp. 438, 550. The military did not agree to give up Belgium until the end of August 1918. For conservative demands with regard to Belgium in March 1917, see Nachlass Conrad Haussmann, Hauptstaatsarchiv Stuttgart, Büschel 27, Letter Riezler to Haussmann, Mar. 7, 1917. For Entente use of German atrocities for propaganda purposes, see Joseph Bédier, *German Atrocities from German Evidence,* Studies and Documents on the War, 3 (Paris: Colon, 1915). Ritter, *Staatskunst,* 3, pp. 433-50. Jarausch, *Enigmatic Chancellor,* pp. 411-12.

[49] Riezler, *Diaries,* Aug. 18, Oct. 12 and 27, 1914, and Feb. 20, 1915, pp. 197, 218, 221, 250-51. Bethmann Hollweg, *Betrachtungen,* 2, pp. 87-98.

[50] Vietsch, *Bethmann Hollweg,* p. 237. Ritter, *Staatskunst,* 3, pp. 124-44. Baseler, *Deutschlands Annexionspolitik,* p. 15.

[51] Riezler, *Diaries,* June 10, 1915, p. 278.

[52] *Ibid.*, July 16, 1915, p. 285. Bülow, *Denkwürdigkeiten,* 2, p. 464; 3, pp. 249, 562-63.

[53] Riezler, *Diaries,* July 21, 1915, pp. 286-87.

[54] *Ibid.*, Aug. 15, 1915, pp. 290-91, and Oct. 26, 1915, p. 310. Werner Conze, *Polnische Nation und deutsche Politik im Ersten Weltkrieg* (Cologne: Böhlau Verlag, 1958), p. 83. Further, *Diaries,* pp. 680-82, and Sept. 23, 1915, p. 300.

[55] *Ibid.*, Aug. 19, and Sept. 23, 1915, pp. 293-94, 300. Conze, *Polnische Nation,* p. 141. Baseler, *Deutschlands Annexionspolitik,* pp. 123-24.

[56] Riezler, *Diaries,* Oct. 26, 27, 29, 1915, pp. 309-12.

[57] *Ibid.*, Nov. 2, Dec. 21, 1915, pp. 313, 319. Fischer, *Griff nach der Weltmacht,* pp. 254-64.

[58] Riezler, *Diaries,* Oct. 29, 1915, pp. 313, 259, 261, 264, 268. Ritter, *Staatskunst,* 3, p. 261. Vietsch, *Bethmann Hollweg,* pp. 240-41.

[59] Riezler, *Diaries,* Aug. 1 and 8, Nov. 3, 1916, pp. 367, 369, 377-78.

⁶⁰ *Ibid.,* Nov. 3 and 11, 1916, pp. 378-79, 605-06, 610, 614-15. Ritter, *Staatskunst,* 3, pp. 276-77. Vietsch, *Bethmann Hollweg,* pp. 242-43. The text of the proclamation is in Dollinger, *Der Erste Weltkrieg,* 2, p. 156.

⁶¹ Riezler, *Diaries,* pp. 550-52. Harry Graf Kessler, *Tagebücher 1918-1937* (Frankfurt/M.: Im Insel Verlag, 1961), p. 167. See also Ruedorffer, *Drei Krisen,* pp. 13, 41-43, 60, 67, 71 for Riezler's recanting of many of his prewar ideas on the nation and state.

⁶² Riezler, *Diaries,* Mar. 22, Nov. 22, 1916, pp. 343, 382, 616-19. Riezler did not indicate when the *Götterdämmerung* (twilight of the gods) would come.

⁶³ *Ibid.,* Nov. 11, 16, and 22, 1916, Jan. 21, Feb. 14, 1917, pp. 379-81, 383-84, 400-01, 404. Conze, *Polnische Nation,* pp. 264-65. Payer, *Erinnerungen,* pp. 229-31.

⁶⁴ Riezler, *Diaries,* Apr. 15, 1918, p. 461.

⁶⁵ *Ibid.,* Mar. 26, 1916, p. 344. Jarausch, *Enigmatic Chancellor,* pp. 204-05, 349. Ringer, *German Mandarins,* p. 139.

⁶⁶ Riezler's quote on lieutenant's uniform from Philipp Scheidemann, *Memoiren eines Sozialdemokraten* (Dresden: Carl Reissner Verlag, 1928), p. 159. Riezler, *Diaries,* Jan. 12, 1917, p. 398. Remak, *Fontane,* p. 63. Jarausch, *Enigmatic Chancellor,* p. 229.

⁶⁷ Riezler, *Diaries,* Jan. 25, 1917, pp. 63, 401.

⁶⁸ *Ibid.,* Mar. 4, 1915, Feb. 22 and July 4, 1916, pp. 254, 334, 363. Jarausch, "All-deutschen," 441-42.

⁶⁹ *Ibid.,* Mar. 25, 1917, pp. 419-20. Haussmann, *Schlaglichter,* p. 92. Bethmann Hollweg, *Betrachtungen,* 2, pp. 174, 182. Scheidemann, *Der Zusammenbruch,* pp. 39-42, 148.

⁷⁰ Riezler, *Diaries,* May 9, 19, 1917, Apr. 15, 1918, pp. 432, 434, 459. Bethmann Hollweg, *Betrachtungen,* 2, pp. 175-80, 219-38. Vietsch, *Bethmann Hollweg,* pp. 262-76. Nachlass Haussmann and *Schlaglichter,* p. 129. Payer, *Erinnerungen,* pp. 23, 177. Jarausch, *Enigmatic Chancellor,* pp. 379-80.

⁷¹ Riezler, *Diaries,* Jan. 21, 1917, p. 401. Unsigned letter Riezler to von Loebell, Mar. 6, 1916, in ZStA Potsdam, Reichskanzlei, nr. 2410. Mommsen, "Kurt Riezler," pp. 201-09.

CHAPTER FIVE

[1] Reference to "kitchen" in Riezler, "Political Decisions," p. 13. For Riezler's sensitiveness on the Russian Revolution, see *Diaries,* p. 84 n. 40.

[2] Ruedorffer, *Grundzüge der Weltpolitik,* p. 68.

[3] Riezler, *Diaries,* July 23, 1914, Jan. 7 and Feb. 20, 1915, pp. 188-89, 240, 250-51.

[4] Riezler, *Diaries,* Sept. 27, 1915, pp. 301, 610-13.

[5] Stefan T. Possony, *Lenin: The Compulsive Revolutionary* (Chicago: Regnery, 1964), pp. 156-57. George Katkov, "German Political Intervention in Russia during World War I," in Richard Pipes, *Revolutionary Russia* (Cambridge: Harvard University Press, 1968), pp. 66-69.

[6] *Germany and the Revolution in Russia 1915-1918: Documents from the Archives of the German Foreign Ministry,* ed. by Z. A. B. Zeman (London: Oxford University Press, 1958), docs. 1, 2. Helphand document reprinted in Winfried B. Scharlau and Z. A. B. Zeman, *Freibeuter der Revolution: Parvus-Helphand Eine politische Biographie* (Cologne: Verlag Wissenschaft und Politik, 1964), pp. 361-74.

[7] Alan Moorehead, *The Russian Revolution* (New York: Harper & Row, 1965), pp. 115-16. Possony, *Lenin,* p. 179. For Lenin's peace proposals delivered by Keskuela, see *Lenins Rückkehr nach Russland 1917: Die Deutschen Akten,* ed. by Werner Hahlweg (Leiden: E. J. Brill, 1957), doc. 3, and Riezler, *Diaries,* p. 85.

[8] Riezler, *Diaries,* Jan. 11 and 20, and Mar. 7, 1915, pp. 241, 243, 256.

[9] *Ibid.,* June 4, 1915, p. 277. Katkov, "German Political Intervention," p. 71.

[10] National Archives (NA) Washington microfilm, Zweiter Unterausschuss der Parlamentarischen Untersuchung, July 6, 1921, T120, Roll 1130.

[11] Leon Trotsky, *The History of the Russian Revolution* (Ann Arbor: 1932), pp. 120-25, in Louis Fischer, *Lenin,* p. 127. See also Karl Radek, *In den Reihen der Deutschen Revolution* (Munich: Kurt Wolff Verlag, 1921), pp. 437-39.

¹² Riezler, *Diaries,* Mar. 18, 1917, p. 419. See Ritter, *Staatkunst,* 3, pp. 482-502. Friedrich Meinecke, *Autobiographische Schriften* (Stuttgart: K. F. Koehler Verlag, 1969), pp. 278-79. Bethmann Hollweg, *Betrachtungen,* 2, pp. 174, 181.

¹³ Hahlweg, *Lenins Rückkehr,* p. 11. Riezler, *Diaries,* Mar. 28, 1917, p. 420. Bethmann Hollweg, *Betrachtungen,* 2, pp. 173-74.

¹⁴ The most detailed statements of Riezler's views on submarine warfare can be found in the files of the Zentrales Staatarchiv in Potsdam, Reichskanzlei, nr. 2410, 2410/1.

¹⁵ Riezler, *Diaries,* Mar. 28, 1917, p. 421. Ritter, *Staatskunst,* 3, p. 490. Scheidemann, *Zusammenbruch,* pp. 148-50.

¹⁶ Fischer, *Lenin,* p. 109. Katkov, "German Political Intervention," pp. 82-83.

¹⁷ Riezler, *Diaries,* April 1, 3, and 6, 1917, pp. 423-24, and doc. 3, pp. 682-84, and Beilage 4, pp. 500-01.

¹⁸ *Ibid.,* Apr. 1, 11, 13, 1917, pp. 424-26.

¹⁹ Author's interviews with Hans Staudinger and Erich Hula in New York, April 1975. In his memoirs Arnold Brecht wrote that Riezler "was not the father of this plan, but only carried out a job which was assigned to him." See *Aus nächster Nähe,* p. 325.

²⁰ Riezler, *Diaries,* p. 84, n. 40. Hahlweg, *Lenins Rückkehr,* docs. 54, 55, and p. 3. Zeman, *Germany and the Revolution,* docs. 15, 16. For German financial assistance to the Bolsheviks and for German links with Lenin, see Possony, *Lenin,* pp. 179-80, 182-83, 192, 212, 230. Of course, the destruction in 1945 of all military files makes the exact tracing of links difficult.

²¹ Fischer, *Lenin,* p. 108. Scharlau-Zeman, *Freibeuter,* p. 248.

²² Hahlweg, *Lenins Rückkehr,* pp. 8-9. Katkov, "German Political Intervention," p. 75.

²³ Hahlweg, *Lenins Rückkehr,* pp. 8-9. Fischer, *Lenin,* pp. 124-37. Kennan argued that Germany's decision was logical. See "Discussion of Katkov" in Pipes, *Revolutionary Russia,* p. 95. Churchill, *World Crisis,* 6, p. 72. Riezler spoke later of the total change of thinking regarding the use of revolution in warfare. Before 1914 "none dreamed of overthrowing the government of another power, let alone changing its regime or undermining its social order." Riezler, "Political Decisions," p. 13.

²⁴ Fischer, *Lenin,* pp. 86-89. Ritter, *Staatkunst,* 4, p. 93. Fischer, *Griff*

nach der Weltmacht, p. 174. Riezler, *Diaries,* Apr. 1 and 16, 1917, pp. 422 and 427.

[25] The narrowness of the Bolsheviks' base was shown in the election held shortly after the Bolshevik takeover.The Bolsheviks won only twenty-four percent of the votes cast. They showed their greatest electoral strength in the military units around Petrograd and on the front which faced the German army. Possony, *Lenin,* p. 259.

[26] Hahlweg, *Lenins Rückkehr,* pp. 4, 23, 25. Riezler, *Diaries,* doc. 3. David Lloyd George, *War Memoirs,* 2 vols. (London: Odhams Press, n.d.), 2, p. 1519. Heuss, *Erinnerungen,* p. 213.

[27] Hahlweg, *Lenins Rückkehr,* p. 19. Zeman, *Germany and the Revolution,* docs. 14-42.

[28] Possony, *Lenin,* pp. 166, 213. Riezler, *Diaries,* Apr. 10 and 11, 1917, pp. 424-25.

[29] Hahlweg, *Lenins Rückkehr,* p. 19 and docs. 70, 79. PA Bonn, Wk 2, secr. vols. 31-34. Riezler, *Diaries,* Apr. 10 and 11, 1917, pp. 424-25.

[30] Hahlweg, *Lenins Rückkehr,* doc. 68. Zeman, *Germany and the Revolution,* doc. 43. Possony, *Lenin,* pp. 213-16. Scharlau-Zeman, *Freibeuter,* pp. 248-66. See Alexander Solzhenitsyn, *Lenin in Zurich* (New York: Farrar, Straus and Giroux, 1976).

[31] Nadolny to Lucius, Oct. 5, 1917, in PA Bonn, Deutschland 135, vol. 18/1. Zeman, *Germany and the Revolution,* doc. 13. For the significance of Stockholm, see Michael Futrell, *Northern Underground* (New York: Praeger, 1963), pp. 18-20. Fischer, *Lenin,* pp. 172-73.

[32] Riezler, *Diaries,* Oct. 3, 1917, Jan. 14, 1918, pp. 453-54. Zeman, *Germany and the Revolution,* docs. 72, 75, 78-79, 94. Docs. 72 and 75 indicate Riezler's expenditures. Possony, *Lenin,* pp. 192, 241-42, 248, 255.

[33] Riezler, *Diaries,* Jan. 14, 1918, p. 454. Leonard Schapiro, "The Political Thought of the First Provisionnal Government," in Pipes, *Revolutionary Russia.* See also *The Russian Revolution and Bolshevik Victory,* ed. Arthur E. Adams, Problems in European Civilization (Lexington, Mass.: Heath, 1960), pp. 78-107.

[34] Fischer, *Lenin,* p. 132. Riezler, *Diaries,* Mar. 28, 1917, pp. 420-21, and doc. 3. Zeman, *Germany and the Revolution,* doc. 81. Leon Trotsky, *Von der Oktober Revolution bis zum Brester Friedensvertrag* (Belp-Bern: Promachos-Verlag, 1918), pp. 70-71, 78-80, 87. Alexander Kerensky, *Russia and History's Turning Point* (New York: Duell, Sloan and Pearce, 1965), p. 479.

[35] Riezler, *Diaries,* doc. 5. Zeman, *Germany and the Revolution,* doc. 89.

[36] Riezler, *Diaries,* doc. 6.

[37] Ritter, *Staatskunst,* 4, p. 90. Fischer, *Lenin,* pp. 151-53.

[38] Riezler to Foreign Office, Nov. 8, 1917, PA Bonn, Gesandtschaft Stockholm 212. Riezler to Foreign Office, Nov. 9, 1917, PA Bonn, Europa gen. nr. 1, vol. 28. *Diaries,* Jan. 14, 1918, pp. 89, 455.

[39] Telegrams Riezler to Foreign Office, Nov. 25, 28, 1917, and letter Riezler to Bergen, Nov. 28, 1917, PA Bonn, Gesandtschaft Stockholm, Bolschewiki und Reichstagsmehrheit 1917, vol. 272, 10. Riezler, *Diaries,* Jan. 14, 1918, p. 454, and doc. 4. Zeman, *Germany and the Revolution,* docs. 89, 90, 99. Text of the "Peace Resolution of the German Reichstag," in Dollinger, *Der Erste Weltkrieg,* 3, p. 42. ˙

[40] After it was certain that the kind of separate peace with Russia which Riezler wanted could no longer be endangered by a socialist conference, Riezler advised the German government for tactical reasons not to reject publicly a socialist conference thereby burdening itself with the odium of having vetoed such a conference. PA Bonn, Gesandtschaft Stockholm, Sozialisten-Konferenz 1918, 212, vol. 16. Zeman, *Germany and the Revolution,* doc. 102. Scheidemann, *Memoiren,* pp. 126-27. Riezler, *Diaries,* Jan. 14, 1918, pp. 454-55.

[41] Riezler to Foreign Office, Jan. 3, 1918, PA Bonn, Gesandtschaft Stockholm, Sozialisten-Konferenz 1918, 212, vol. 16. Riezler to Nadolny, Dec. 3, 1917, PA Bonn, Russland 63, nr. 1, vol. 6. See Riezler's description of Bolshevik leaders in *Diaries,* doc. 3. See also *Diaries,* docs. 7, 8, and Jan. 14, 1918, p. 455. Zeman, *Germany and the Revolution,* docs. 81, 100, 103, 105-06. *Von Brest-Litovsk zur Deutschen November-Revolution. Aus den Tagebüchern, Briefen und Aufzeichnungen von Alfons Paquet, Wilhelm Groener und Albert Hopman März bis November 1918,* ed. by Winfried Baumgart, Deutsche Geschichtsquellen des 19. und 20. Jahrhunderts (Göttingen: Vandenhoeck & Ruprecht, 1971), p. 20. This book will hereafter be referred to as Paquet, *Tagebücher.* Paquet was a reporter for the *Frankfurter Zeitung* and later became press attaché under Riezler for the German legation in Moscow. Scheidemann, *Memoiren eines Sozialdemokraten,* pp. 127, 133.

[42] Fischer, *Lenin,* p. 159. Ritter, *Staatskunst,* 4, p. 109. For a short review of the literature on the Brest-Litovsk negotiations, see Konrad H. Jarausch, "Cooperation or Intervention?: Kurt Riezler and the Failure of German Ostpolitik, 1918," *Slavic Review,* 31 (June 1972). The chief works to see are Ritter, *Staatskunst,* 4; Fischer, *Griff nach der Weltmacht;* Winfried Baumgart, *Deutsche Ostpolitik 1918: Von Brest-*

Litovsk, bis zum Ende des Ersten Weltkrieges (Vienna: R. Oldenbourg Verlag, 1966); John W. Wheeler-Bennet, *Brest-Litovsk, The Forgotten Peach March 1918* (London: Macmillan, 1956). Werner Hahlweg, *Der Friede von Brest-Litovsk* (Düsseldorf: Droste Verlag, 1971). Oleh S. Fedyshyn mistakenly asserts that Riezler was in Brest-Litovsk on Jan. 4, 1918. See *Germany's Drive to the East and the Ukranian Revolution, 1917-1918* (New Brunswick, N.J.: Rutgers University Press, 1971), p. 65.

[43] Fischer, *Lenin*, p. 171.

[44] Fischer, *Griff nach der Weltmacht*, pp. 632-33. Ritter, *Staatskunst*, 4, pp. 93, 316-31. By January 1918, Russia had already suffered many secessions which the Bolsheviks were powerless to hinder. Fischer, *Lenin*, pp. 249-51. Stalin's proposal in G. Decker, *Die Selbstbestimmungsrecht der Nationen*, Anhang, and in Bruno Gebhardt, gen. ed., *Handbuch der Deutschen Geschichte*, Bd. 4: *Die Zeit der Weltkriege*, by Karl Dietrich Erdmann, 4 vols. (Stuttgart: Union Verlag, 1959), p. 67.

[45] Riezler, *Diaries*, Jan. 29, 1918, p. 457, and docs. 9, 11, 13. Ludendorff, *Ludendorff's Own Story*, pp. 167-75, in Fischer, *Lenin*, p. 175. Richard von Kühlmann, *Erinnerungen* (Heidelberg: Verlag Lambert Schneider, 1948), pp. 524-25.

[46] Social Revolutionaries and Marxist Social-Democracy were the two main streams of Russian socialism. The Social Revolutionaries (SRs) believed in a Russian national form of socialism rooted in the institution of communal property and direct democracy as was practiced in the Russian peasant community *(mir)*. There were many shades of dissent, and in 1917 the so-called Left SRs broke away from the main party. Marxist Social-Democracy split in 1903 into Mensheviks, who denounced conspiratorial and seditious methods of political warfare, and Bolsheviks, headed by Lenin. See the glossary of Russian institutions, parties, and movements in George Katkov, *Russia 1917. The February Revolution* (Oxford: Alden Press, 1967), pp. 465-70. Louis Fischer, *Lenin*, pp. 191-95. Fritz Fischer, *Griff nach der Weltmacht*, pp. 629-30. Trotsky, *Oktober Revolution*, pp. 37, 72-73. Riezler, *Diaries*, doc. 12.

[47] Riezler, *Diaries*, Jan. 14, 29, 1918, pp. 455-57.

[48] *Ibid.*, doc. 12. See also Jan. 24, 29, 1918, p. 456, and docs. 10, 11.

[49] Riezler, *Diaries*, Jan. 24, 1918, p. 456.

[50] Fischer, *Lenin*, pp. 195-202. Fischer, *Griff nach der Weltmacht*, pp. 632-44. Though he later denounced it, Riezler clearly favored a separate treaty with the Ukrainian puppet government at this time. See *Diaries*, doc. 13.

[51] Riezler, *Diaries*, docs. 13, 14.

[52] Fischer, *Lenin*, pp. 207-10. Possony, *Lenin*, p. 273.

[53] Erdmann, *Zeit der Weltkriege*, p. 67. Fischer, *Griff nach der Weltmacht*, p. 671. Wolfgang Steglich, *Die Friedenspolitik der Mittelmächte 1917/1918* (Wiesbaden: Franz Steiner Verlag, 1964), pp. 406-12. Scheidemann, *Zusammenbruch*, p. 153, and *Memoiren*, p. 158.

[54] Riezler, *Diaries*, doc. 14.

[55] Baumgart, *Deutsche Ostpolitik*, pp. 208-33. Riezler, *Diaries*, Apr. 24, 1918, p. 462. This aspect of Riezler's political career has been treated by Konrad H. Jarausch in "Cooperation or Intervention?"

[56] Riezler, *Diaries*, Apr. 24 and Sept. 12, 1918, pp. 462, 472. See Mirbach's first report from Moscow, Zeman, *Germany and the Revolution*, doc. 120. In a letter written to the Foreign Office May 14, 1918, Riezler stated that the mission's political aim was "to keep the Entente in check." He closed with the plea that "you please not leave us in the lurch and not let us perish in the desert." NA Washington microfilm, PA Deutschland, N. 135, nr. 4.

[57] Riezler, *Diaries*, Apr. 24 and Sept. 12, 1918, pp. 462, 472. Zeman, *Germany and the Revolution*, doc. 120.

[58] Riezler, *Diaries*, Sept. 12, 1918, pp. 474-75. The conflict between the Supreme Military Command and Foreign Office is the chief subject of Baumgart, *Deutsche Ostpolitik*.

[59] On May 11 Riezler complained of the "completely illegal" military advance in southern Russia, which might be "economically necessary" but which "pulls the rug out from under us, terrifies and greatly weakens the Bolsheviks, and gives the Entente and other socialist parties the opportunity for a great action." Riezler was referring to German military advances into the areas of Kharkov, Don, and Crimea which were not halted until May 22. *Diaries*, Apr. 24, May 11, 1918, pp. 463-64 and doc. 14. For Mirbach's reports and protests of these advances, see PA Bonn, Russland 61, vols. 151-52. Baumgart, *Deutsche Ostpolitik*, pp. 372-74. Zeman, *Germany and the Revolution*, doc. 122.

[60] Copy of letter Riezler to Frau Riezler, written May 1918, and located in Nachlass Haussmann, Büschel 54. See also Zeman, *Germany and the Revolution*, doc. 124.

[61] Zeman, *Germany and the Revolution*, docs. 123-24, 127-28. PA Bonn, Russland 61, vols. 153-54. Fischer, *Lenin*, pp. 222, 227-28.

[62] Riezler, *Diaries*, doc. 15. Zeman, *Germany and the Revolution*, doc. 132. Fischer, *Lenin*, pp. 266, 287.

⁶³ Riezler, *Diaries,* June 8, 1918, pp. 465-66. Zeman, *Germany and the Revolution,* doc. 134.

⁶⁴ Riezler, *Diaries,* doc. 16. Zeman, *Germany and the Revolution,* doc. 136. Fritz Klein, *Die Diplomatischen Beziehungen Deutschlands zur Sowjetunion 1917-1932* (Berlin: Rütten & Loening, 1953), p. 44. Kühlmann to Lersner, July 3, 1918, PA Bonn, Deutschland 131, vol. 42. Kühlmann did increase the funds for Riezler to use in counterrevolutionary activities. Baumgart, *Deutsche Ostpolitik,* pp. 80-85. See the anonymous article, "Für eine deutsch-russische Verständigung," in the *Frankfurter Zeitung und Handelsblatt,* June 26, 1918, p. 1, reporting great potential "for a lasting understanding with Russia" as soon as the Bolsheviks lose the reins of power. The "eminent expert of the contemporary situation" was Riezler.

⁶⁵ Riezler, *Diaries,* Aug. 28, 1918, p. 467. Fischer, *Lenin,* p. 242. Riezler disappeared before the most threatening speeches were given. Paquet, *Tagebücher,* pp. 52, 54. George F. Kennan, *Soviet-American Relations, 1917-1920: The Decision to Intervene,* 2 vols. (Princeton: Princeton University Press, 1958), 2, pp. 433-44.

⁶⁶ CHEKA was the abbreviation for All-Russian Extraordinary Commission for the Struggle against Counterrevolution, created in December 1917 by the Bolsheviks. The identification documents were stamped by Dzerzhinski's assistant, a Left SR. Both assassins were high CHEKA officials. Fischer, *Lenin,* p. 232. Karl von Bothmer, *Mit Graf Mirbach in Moskau* (Tübingen: Osianderische Buchhandlung, 1922), pp. 71-79, especially diagram on p. 77. In a letter to Haussmann written July 14, 1918, Riezler's wife reported that the assassins fired four times at Riezler: "It is an absolute wonder that nothing happened to him." Nachlass Haussmann, Büschel 54. Details of assassination from Riezler's verbal report of incident, *Diaries,* doc. 18. See also doc. 17, Aug. 28, 1918, p. 468. Jarausch, "Cooperation or Intervention," pp. 386-90. John G. Williamson, *Karl Helfferich 1874-1924: Economist, Financier, Politician* (Princeton: Princeton University Press, 1971), p. 174. Paquet, *Tagebücher,* p. 56. Gustav Hilger, *Wir und der Kriml, Deutsch-sowjetische Beziehungen 1919-1941. Erinnerungen eines Deutschen Diplomaten* (Frankfurt am Main: Alfred Metzner Verlag, 1955), pp. 11-19. See PA Bonn, Gr. H.Q., Russland 31 k., and Deutschland 131, Beziehungen zu Russland, vol. 42.

⁶⁷ Fischer, *Lenin,* pp. 232, 242-43. Baumgart, *Deutsche Ostpolitik,* pp. 224-33, 228-30. Klein, *Die Diplomatischen Beziehungen,* pp. 46-47. Kennan, *Soviet-American Relations,* p. 434. Paquet, *Tagebücher,* pp. 62-63. Alfons Paquet, *Im kommunistischen Russland, Briefe aus Moskau* (Jena: Eugen Diederichs, 1919), pp. 22-32. Refer to PA Bonn, Deutschland 131, vols. 42-44, Russland 61, vol. 158, Gr. H.Q., Russland 31k. Possony pointed to the "highly irregular and hence suspect" nature

of the entire Mirbach murder. It could have been a provocation by the Bolsheviks, who suspected an impending change in German policy and therefore ordered increased intelligence coverage of the German legation. The responsibility for this coverage was assigned to none other than Blyumkin, a member of the CHEKA and one of the assassins. Blyumkin managed to escape and was not found again until 1919. He was not arrested, and in 1921 was readmitted to the Communist Party and to the CHEKA. He became a special assistant to Trotsky in the Commissariat of War. Possony argued that the plot might have been directed by Lenin. Possony, *Lenin*, pp. 282-85. See also Jarausch, "Cooperation or Intervention?" pp. 387-90, for possible motives.

[68] Paquet, *Tagebücher*, pp. 87, 67, 84.

[69] Bothmer, *Mit Graf Mirbach*, p. 21.

[70] Riezler, *Diaries*, doc. 19. Zeman, *Germany and the Revolution*, docs. 129, 131, 133, 135. Supervision of espionage operations was one of Riezler's chief duties. On May 11, 1918, he noted in his diary "great activity involving agents with connections to the women of the very women-hungry Bolsheviks . . . briberies etc.," p. 463. PA Bonn, Deutschland 131, vol. 45. Paquet, *Tagebücher*, pp. 17, 67, 70.

[71] Riezler, *Diaries*, doc. 21. Fischer, *Lenin*, pp. 288-91. Baumgart, *Deutsche Ostpolitik*, pp. 52-60, 230-33. See Edwin P. Hoyt, *The Army Without a Country* (New York: Macmillan, 1967). After the assassination, Riezler requested either withdrawal of the mission from Moscow or the dispatching of one battalion of German troops to protect the mission. A reading of the documents leaves no doubt that Riezler wanted this battalion for use in the expected putsch against the Bolsheviks. The Bolsheviks saw this and understandably refused. PA Bonn, Gr. H.Q., Russland 31k and Deutschland 131, vols. 42-44.

[72] Riezler, *Diaries*, doc. 28. See also docs. 22-23, 25-26.

[73] Riezler, *Diaries*, docs. 29-31. PA Bonn, Deutschland 131, vol. 42. Baumgart, *Deutsche Ostpolitik*, pp. 249-50.

[74] Riezler, *Diaries*, Aug. 28, Sept. 12, 1918, pp. 469-71, and doc. 24. Baumgart, *Deutsche Ostpolitik*, pp. 225-26. Horst Günther Linke, *Deutsch-sowjetische Beziehungen bis Rapallo* (Cologne: Verlag Wissenschaft und Politik, 1970), p. 14. Paquet, *Tagebücher*, pp. 67, 84. Generalfeldmarschall an den Herrn Reichskanzler, July 13, 1918, in PA Bonn, Gr. H.Q., Russland 31k.

[75] Paquet, *Im kommunistischen Russland*, p. 57. Karl Helfferich, *Der Weltkrieg, Vom Eingreifen Amerikas bis zum Zusammenbruch*, 3 vols. (Berlin: Ullstein & Co., 1919), 3, p. 461.

[76] Riezler, *Diaries,* Sept. 12, 1918, p. 471. Williamson, *Karl Helfferich,* p. 274.

[77] Fischer, *Lenin,* pp. 268-69. Helfferich, *Der Weltkrieg,* 3, pp. 466-67. Helfferich to Foreign Office, Aug. 2, 1918. PA Bonn, Deutschland 131, Beziehungen zu Russland, vol. 44a.

[78] Riezler, *Diaries,* Sept. 12, 1918, p. 471. See also Sept. 27, 1915, p. 301. Foreign Office to Riezler, July 10, 1918, and Hintze to Helfferich, Aug. 4, 1918, in PA Bonn, Deutschland 131, vols. 42, 45. Also Helfferich, *Der Weltkrieg,* 3, pp. 480-81.

[79] Riezler, *Diaries,* Sept. 12, 1918, p. 471. Bothmer, *Mit Graf Mirbach,* p. 92. Baumgart, *Deutsche Ostpolitik,* p. 246. Karl Graf von Hertling, *Ein Jahr in der Reichskanzlei, Erinnerungen an die Kanzlerschaft meines Vaters* (Freiburg: Herdersche Verlagshandlung, 1919), p. 148.

[80] Riezler, *Diaries,* Sept. 12, 1918, pp. 471-72. Paquet, *Tagebücher,* pp. 100, 104. Also PA Bonn, Gr. H.Q., Russland 31k and Deutschland 131, vols. 44a, 45.

[81] Riezler, *Diaries,* Sept. 12, 1918, p. 472. See also doc. 13.

[82] *Ibid.,* pp. 473-74.

[83] *Ibid.,* p. 475.

[84] Hintze to Helfferich, Aug. 2, 1918, PA Bonn, Deutschland 131, vol. 44a. Jarausch wrote: "Though more realistic and restrained than the Supreme Command, the Foreign Office still played the dangerous game of establishing indirect German hegemony and did not struggle for an international order, acceptable to all, based on equality and noninterference. A disciple of sophisticated *Machtpolitik,* Riezler was chastened by the failure of Bethmann Hollweg's *Mitteleuropa,* and saw the latter course as the one in Germany's best interest." "Cooperation or Intervention?" pp. 396-97. Possony, *Lenin,* p. 294.

[85] Baumgart, *Deutsche Ostpolitik,* pp. 237-38.

[86] Ludendorff, *Ludendorff's Own Story,* in Fischer, *Lenin,* p. 303. The Rapallo Treaty between the Soviet Union and Germany was signed in April 1922. Mann, *Deutsche Geschichte,* p. 680. See also Riezler, "Rapallo and die russischen Länder," *Die Deutsche Nation,* 4 (May 1922).

CHAPTER SIX

[1] Riezler, *Diaries*, Sept. 13, 1918, p. 475.

[2] *Ibid.*, Sept. 30, 1918, pp. 478-79.

[3] *Ibid.*, Sept. 24, 30, 1918, pp. 477-78. Haussmann, *Schlaglichter*, p. 143.

[4] Riezler, *Diaries*, Oct. 2, 5, 13, 15, 19, 1918, pp. 480-85.

[5] F. A. Krummacher and Albert Wucher, *Die Weimarer Republik: Ihre Geschichte in Texten, Bildern und Dokumenten* (Munich: Verlag Kurt Desch GmbH, 1965), pp. 40, 42. Haussmann, *Schlaglichter*, pp. 244, 261.

[6] Riezler, *Diaries*, Oct. 1, 2, 5, 13, 1918, pp. 479-83.

[7] *Ibid.*, Oct. 22, 1918, p. 486.

[8] *Ibid.*, Oct. 15, 19, 22, Nov. 5, 1918, pp. 483-86. It was an unfortunate legacy for the Weimar Republic that constitutional change and democracy appeared as a demand of the victorious powers and not as the will of the majority of Germans.

[9] Riezler, *Diaries*, Oct. 13, 15, 19, 22, Nov. 5, 1918, pp. 482-86. Haussmann, *Schlaglichter*, pp. 143, 244. See Klaus Schwabe, *Deutsche Revolution und Wilson-Frieden: Die amerikanische und deutsche Friedenstrategie zwischen Ideologie und Machtpolitik 1918/19* (Düsseldorf: Droste Verlag, 1971), pp. 88-226.

[10] Riezler, *Diaries*, p. 119, and Oct. 1, 13, 1918, pp. 480, 482. Haussmann, *Schlaglichter*, p. 244.

[11] Riezler, *Diaries*, Nov. 5, 1918, pp. 486-87. Krummacher, *Weimarer Republik*, p. 45.

[12] Otto Friedrich, *Before the Deluge: A Portrait of Berlin in the 1920's* (New York: Harper and Row, 1972), p. 24.

[13] Ringer, *German Mandarins*, pp. 192-93, 202-03, 207-09, 252. Stern, *Failure of Illiberalism*, p. 23.

[14] Riezler, *Diaries*, Nov. 5, 1918, pp. 486-87.

[15] Friedrich, *Deluge*, p. 28. For a well-edited introduction to some of the different views taken by historians toward the German Revolution, see Richard N. Hunt, ed., *The Creation of the Weimar Republic: Still-*

born Democracy? Problems in European Civilization (Lexington: Heath, 1969). For a treatment of the councils, see Eberhard Kolb, *Die Arbeiterräte in der deutschen Innenpolitik 1918-1919* (Düsseldorf: Droste Verlag, 1962). Craig, *The Politics of the Prussian Army*, p. 343.

[16] Kessler, *Tagebücher*, pp. 83-84.

[17] *Ibid.*, p. 165.

[18] Allan Mitchell, *Revolution in Bavaria 1918-1919: The Eisner Regime and the Soviet Republic* (Princeton: Princeton University Press, 1965), pp. 272-74. Krummacher, *Weimarer Republik*, pp. 70-71. Wolfgang Benz, *Süddeutschland in der Weimarer Republik: Ein Beitrag zur deutschen Innenpolitik 1918-1923* (Berlin: Duncker und Humblot, 1970), p. 326. Karl-Ludwig Ay, *Appelle einer Revolution* (Munich: Süddeutscher Verlag, 1968).

[19] Mitchell, *Revolution in Bavaria*, pp. 280-82, 285-88.

[20] Kessler, *Tagebücher*, p. 170. Gajus [Kurt Riezler], "Bayerns Schande und Ende," *Die Deutsche Nation* (April 1919), 5-6.

[21] Zech and Riezler in Munich to Foreign Office (AA), March 9, 1919, in NA Washington microfilm, PA Bayern 50, Bd. 17-18, Roll 73. For the role of councils in revolutions, see Mark N. Hagopian, *The Phenomenon of Revolution* (New York: Dodd, Mead, 1974), p. 66.

[22] Zech and Riezler to AA, Mar. 9, 1919, in NA Washington microfilm, PA Bayern 50, Bd. 17-18, Roll 73. AA to Wedel, Mar. 12, 1919, in NA Washington microfilm, PA Bayern 50, Bd. 17-18, Roll 74. Kessler, *Tagebücher*, pp. 169-70. The "Riezler Plan" is described in Zech to AA, Mar. 9, 1919, in NA Washington microfilm, AA Weimar, V-10 to V-13, Bd. 1. T120, Roll A3.

[23] Mitchell, *Revolution in Bavaria*, pp. 298-99, 301.

[24] *Ibid.*, pp. 302-05, 310.

[25] *Ibid.*, pp. 309-10. Kessler reported that Riezler firmly believed on April 1, 1919, that a wave of revolution was coming westward, via Prague. Kessler, *Tagebücher*, p. 167.

[26] Mitchell, *Revolution in Bavaria*, p. 314.

[27] *Ibid.*, p. 315. Jordan to AA, Apr. 12, 1919, in NA Washington microfilm, AA Weimar, V-10 to V-13, Bd. 1. T120, Roll A3. Jordan was the Legation Secretary in Bamberg.

²⁸ Mitchell, *Revolution in Bavaria*, pp. 317-18.

²⁹ *Ibid.*, pp. 207-08, 313, 318-19.

³⁰ Riezler to AA, Apr. 12, 1919, in NA Washington microfilm, AA Weimar, V-10 to V-13, Bd. 1, T120, Roll A3. Also AA Memorandum, Apr. 19, 1919, in NA Washington microfilm, PA Bayern 50, Bd. 17-18, Roll 74. This memorandum records Riezler's report from a relative in Munich that the leaders of the "Munich Spartacists" were Russian and that 500-800 hostages had been taken.

³¹ Possony, *Lenin*, pp. 295-96, 303-04. See Walter Laqueur, *Deutschland und Russland* (Berlin: Propyläen Verlag, 1965), p. 22, and Radek, *In den Reihen*. For Moscow's role in the events in Munich, see Helmut Neubauer, *München und Moskau 1918/1919: Zur Geschichte der Rätebewegung in Bayern* (Munich: Isar Verlag, 1958). For Riezler's critique of Bolshevism, see Ruedorffer, *Drei Krisen*, pp. 47, 50, and "Political Decisions," 22.

³² Riezler to AA, Apr. 8, 1919, in NA Washington microfilm, PA Bayern 50, Bd. 17-18, Roll 73. Riezler to AA, Apr. 15, 1919, in NA Washington, microfilm, PA Bayern 50, Bd. 17-18, Roll 74. Mitchell, *Revolution in Bavaria*, p. 323.

³³ Riezler to AA, Apr. 13, 1919, NA Washington microfilm, PA Bayern 50, Bd. 17-18, Roll 74. Mitchell, *Revolution in Bavaria*, p. 324.

³⁴ Riezler to AA, Apr. 13, 1919, in NA Washington microfilm, PA Bayern 50, Bd. 17-18, Roll 74. Hans Beyer, *Von der Novemberrevolution zur Räterepublik in München* (Berlin: Rütten & Loening, 1957), p. 101.

³⁵ NA Washington microfilm: AA Memorandum, Apr. 12, 1919, in PA Bayern 50, Bd. 17-18, Roll 74; Riezler to AA, Apr. 13, 1919, in PA Bayern 50, Bd. 17-18, Roll 74; AA Memorandum, Apr. 14, 1919, in PA Bayern, Bd. 17-18, Roll 74; Riezler to AA, Apr. 25, 1919, in PA Bayern 50, Bd. 17-18, Roll 74; Riezler to AA, Apr. 28, 1919, in PA Bayern 50, Bd. 17-18, Roll 74; Riezler to AA, Apr. 12, 1919, in AA Weimar, V-10 to V-13, Bd. 1, T120, Roll A3. Mitchell, *Revolution in Bavaria*, pp. 295-98, 315-16, 321-22.

³⁶ Mitchell, *Revolution in Bavaria*, pp. 326-27. NA Washington microfilm, PA Bayern 50, Bd. 17-18, Roll 74.

³⁷ Hans Beyer, *München 1919: Der Kampf der Roten Armee in Bayern 1919* (Berlin: Verlag des Ministeriums für Nationale Verteidigung, 1956), p. 52. Mitchell, *Revolution in Bavaria*, p. 329. Neubauer, *München und Moskau*, p. 92.

[38] Beyer, *München 1919,* pp. 40-50, and Beyer, *Von der November-revolution,* p. 117. All but one (Eugen Leviné) of the Bavarian Soviet leaders were given sentences ranging from two years in prison to death. Leviné was convicted of treason and executed on June 5, 1919.

[39] Riezler to AA, May 6, 1919, in NA Washington microfilm, PA Bayern 50, Bd. 17-18, Roll 74. Mitchell, *Revolution in Bavaria,* pp. 330-31.

[40] Scheidemann's reaction to the murder of Rosa Luxemburg and Karl Liebknecht: "I sincerely regret the death of both, and indeed for good reasons. Day after day they called the *Volk* to arms and demanded the violent overthrow of the government. They have now become victims of their own bloody terror tactic." Scheidemann, *Der Zusammenbruch,* p. 238.

CHAPTER SEVEN

[1] Ruedorffer, *Drei Krisen,* p. 3.

[2] *Ibid.,* pp. 15, 20. Ruedorffer, "Vernunft oder Untergang," *Die Deutsche Nation* (May 1920), 321.

[3] Ruedorffer, *Drei Krisen,* p. 21. Benz, *Süddeutschland,* pp. 154-55. Riezler never changed his view of the Versailles Treaty. See Riezler's comment on Hans Speier's article, "The Future of German Nationalism," both published in *Social Research,* 14 (1947), 446.

[4] Ruedorffer, *Drei Krisen,* p. 22. For Riezler's views on Austria, see Riezler, "Deutschland und der Anschluss Österreichs," *Der Deutsche Volkswirt* (July 29, 1927), 1379-80.

[5] *Ibid.,* pp. 23-25. Riezler, "Gefahren und Hoffnungen. Europa zur Jahreswende," *Der Deutsche Volkswirt* (January 6, 1928), 419-21. See also Riezler, "Frankreichs Absichten," *Die Deutsche Nation* (July 1923), 498-501.

[6] Riezler, "Gefahren und Hoffnungen," p. 421.

[7] Riezler's letter of resignation to Foreign Minister Hermann Müller, June 23, 1919, in *Diaries,* pp. 737-38.

[8] *Die Deutsche Nation* was directed toward assembling "all those persons who unconditionally serve the new state." In addition to foreign policy objectives, the journal set out to dispose of the "obsolete class struggle" and to seek the collaboration of all classes to establish a socially just republic on a democratic foundation. Among those on the editorial staff were Bernhard W. von Bülow, later state secretary in the Foreign Office; historian Walter Goetz; Conrad Haussmann; Count Harry Kessler; and the subsequent mayor of Hamburg, Carl Petersen. See Nachlass Haussmann, Büschel 116. See also Riezler, *Diaries,* pp. 130-31.

[9] Ruedorffer, *Drei Krisen,* pp. 58, 61, 63, 65.

[10] *Ibid.,* p. 71. Ruedorffer, "Vernunft oder Untergang." On May 19, 1917, Riezler had pessimistically speculated about what Europeans might learn from the war: "Humanity will learn as much as nothing from all this misery; it will only wake up with a more confused head." *Diaries,* p. 435.

[11] Ruedorffer, *Drei Krisen,* pp. 8, 12, 13, 72.

[12] *Ibid.,* p. 72. For his later views on ideologies, see Riezler, "The Philosopher of History and the Modern Statesman," *Social Research,* 13 (September 1946), 370-72.

[13] Riezler, "Die Agonie des deutschen Parlamentarismus," *Die Deutsche Nation,* 4 (December 1922), 990. Ruedorffer, *Drei Krisen,* p. 60. The "stab in the back" legend received unwitting support from Friedrich Ebert, who greeted German troops returning to Berlin from the front as troops "undefeated on the battlefield." Krummacher, *Die Weimarer Republik,* p. 57.

[14] Riezler, "Gefahren und Hoffnungen," 421.

[15] Ruedorffer, *Drie Krisen,* p. 41. Gajus [Riezler], "Die Deutsche Nation," *Die Deutsche Nation* (January 1919), 10. Kessler, *Tagebücher,* p. 167.

[16] Ruedorffer, *Drei Krisen,* pp. 27, 37.

[17] Susanne Miller, Heinrich Potthoff, *Die Regierung der Volksbeauftragten 1918/19,* 2 vols. (Düsseldorf: Droste Verlag, 1969), 1, pp. 17, 251. Gajus, "Die Deutsche Nation," 12. Heuss, "A Word," 2.

[18] Riezler, *Diaries,* May 13, 1917, Apr. 15, 1918, Oct. 15, 1918, Nov. 5, 1918, pp. 434, 461, 483, 486.

[19] Kurt Riezler, "Die Schuld der Oberschicht," *Die Deutsche Nation* (August 1922), 623.

²⁰ Ruedorffer, *Drei Krisen,* p. 21. The German word *Land* will continue to be translated as "state." This is not to be confused with Riezler's "crisis of the state" which refers to the question of national organization.

²¹ Gajus [Riezler], "Zur deutschen Frage," *Die Deutsche Nation* (February 1922), 10-15. Benz, *Süddeutschland,* pp. 84-85, 108-09, 326, 329. Riezler so opposed the direction the negotiations were taking that he asked to be relieved of his role as the Foreign Office representative in the drafting of the constitution. See letter Riezler to Foreign Office, Feb. 6, 1919, in NA Washington microfilm, AA Weimar, I, Verfassung des Deutschen Reiches, T120, Roll 2411.

²² Riezler, *Diaries,* Mar. 22, 1916, Feb. 17, 1915, Jan. 18, 1916, pp. 343, 248, 325.

²³ Ruedorffer, *Drei Krisen,* pp. 31-32, 42. Also Ruedorffer, "Vernunft oder Untergang." Much later he pointed again to these dangers in "Political Decisions," p. 36.

²⁴ Ruedorffer, *Drei Krisen,* p. 44. By 1932, thirty-eight parties were represented in the Reichstag.

²⁵ Kurt Riezler, "Das Schicksal der sozialistischen Wirtschaftspolitik in Russland und Deutschland," *Die Deutsche Nation,* 326. Gajus [Riezler], "Zur Zeitgeschichte. Kabinettsbildungen," *Die Deutsche Nation* (March 1919), 1-2. Gajus [Riezler], "Ein Versuch," *Die Deutsche Nation* (April 1919), 11-12. Kurt Riezler, "Die Geldsackrepublik," *Die Deutsche Nation* (October 1922), 809. For Riezler's ideas in 1924 on how to weaken the German states, see Eberhard Pikart, "Ein Brief Kurt Riezlers an den Hamburger Bürgermeister Petersen vom 1. Februar 1924," in *Vierteljahrshefte für Zeitgeschichte,* 2 Heft (April 1967), p. 216.

²⁶ Gajus, "Ein Versuch," p. 11. See also Riezler, "Political Decisions," 51. Kessler, *Tagebücher,* p. 348.

²⁷ Kurt Riezler, "Hindenburgs Wahl," *Die Deutsche Nation* (May 1925). Haussmann, *Schlaglichter,* p. 129.

²⁸ In an unsigned article which appeared under the title "Deutsche Nation" in *Die Deutsche Nation* (1921), Riezler's phrase coined in the early days of August 1914 was distorted to describe postwar Germany: "Ich sehe keine Deutschen mehr, ich sehe nur Parteien." (I no longer see any Germans; I see only parties.) See Pikart, "Ein Brief Kurt Riezlers," p. 213. One reason why parties often did not compromise with each other is that Article 48 of the Constitution made it possible for parliamentary parties to avoid the responsibility for achieving compromise over important matters. When no compromise was possible or desired, the president of the Republic could decree a solution.

[29] Letter Riezler to Haussmann, Aug. 8, 1919, in Nachlass Haussmann, Büschel 116. Riezler, *Diaries,* Mar. 4, 1915, p. 254. Riezler, "Political Decisions," 33, 36. Riezler blamed the elites in Germany for the failure of the Weimar Republic. He told Staudinger that Hitler had come to power, "because the elite had failed." Interview with author, April 1975. See also Riezler, "Die Schuld der Oberschicht," *Die Deutsche Nation* (August 1922).

[30] Felix Hirsch, "Ein deutscher Lincoln oder der Stalin der SPD?" *Die Zeit,* March 7, 1975, p. 9. Pikart, "Ein Brief Kurt Riezlers," 215. The National Assembly elected Ebert by an overwhelming majority.

[31] Arnold Brecht, *Aus Nächster Nähe,* pp. 325-26.

[32] *Ibid.,* p. 326. Kessler, *Tagebücher,* p. 165. Heuss described Kessler as "full of ideas, but . . . somewhat vague in concrete evaluations." Heuss, *Erinnerungen,* p. 300.

[33] Erwin Redslob, *Von Weimar nach Europa, Erlebtes und Durchdachtes* (Berlin: Haude & Spendersche Verlagsbuchhandlung, 1972), pp. 166-67. Information concerning Riezler's and Ebert's differences from author's interview with Arnold Brecht in New York, April 1975.

[34] Mommsen in "Kurt Riezler," 209, and Kornhass in "Zwischen Kulturkritik und Machtverherrlichung," p. 105, mistakenly classified Riezler's political conception as close to the ideas of the "conservative revolution."

[35] Ruedorffer, "Vernunft oder Untergang," p. 322.

[36] In 1953 Riezler spoke of German impatience: "Germans are convinced by their own painful history as a nation that they always 'miss the bus.' It was so in the past, it is so now, and will be so in the future. They believe it their destiny to be too late. Hence a certain impatience and restiveness have characterized their political activities. This conviction was the source of their most conspicuous errors. Actually, by quietly waiting, they could have gotten what they could reasonably hope for. Such a belief, as a national way of thinking, is a powerful reality, guiding not only the opinions of the people but the actions of the rulers." See "Political Decisions," 30. Of course, impatience is not a typically German failing. It took the French decades to settle down to the Third Republic after the fall of Napoleon III, and many European democracies failed to survive the decade following the end of the First World War.

[37] Pikart, "Ein Brief Kurt Riezlers," 215-18.

[38] Riezler to AA, June 17, 1919, in NA Washington microfilm, PA Bayern 50, Bd. 17-18, Roll 74.

[39] Riezler, "Die Schuld der Oberschicht," 618.

[40] *Ibid.*, p. 617. On p. 25 of "Political Decisions," Riezler described how German disunity prepared the way for Hitler's rise.

[41] Riezler, "Die Schuld der Oberschicht," 619-23. Riezler wrote to Haussmann on December 19, 1921, that he would continue his attack against Ludendorff. Nachlass Haussmann, Büschel 116. Indeed, he devoted at least three articles to this attack: "Ludendorff und Bethmann," December 1921; "Noch einmal: Die Wahrheit und der General," January 1922; "Die Schuld der Oberschicht," August 1922. Ludendorff's books to which Riezler was referring were: *Meine Kriegserinnerungen 1914-1918* (Berlin: Ernst Siegfried Mittler und Sohn, 1919), and *Kriegführung und Politik* (Berlin: Verlag von E. S. Mittler & Sohn, 1922). Karl May was a popular German author of stories about the American West.

[42] Riezler, "Die Schuld der Oberschicht," 625, 627.

[43] Stern, *Cultural Despair,* p. xvi. Because this attack on many fronts was directed against modernity, Stern called it a "conservative revolution."

[44] Author's interviews with Brecht, Staudinger, and Lowe in New York, April 1975. See also Friedrich, *After the Deluge,* pp. 69, 71. Although the *Reichswehr* refused to oppose the putschists, it must be remembered that the Kapp Putsch failed chiefly because the German army and civil service refused to support the putschists. Meissner to Ebert, Apr. 1, 1920; on Kapp events from March 13, 1920: Regierungsrat Dr. Doehle to Ebert, Mar. 16, 1920; and Riezler to Ebert, Mar. 18, 1920. All three documents in ZStA Potsdam, Büro des Reichspräsidenten, 1, nr. 218.

[45] Johannes Erger, *Der Kapp-Lüttwitz Putsch, Ein Beitrag zur deutschen Innenpolitik 1919-20* (Düsseldorf: Droste Verlag, 1967), pp. 255-56. Riezler, *Diaries,* pp. 128-29, and "Die Schuld der Oberschicht," 621. There were Spartacist uprisings in various German cities after the Kapp Putsch in Berlin. The most threatening were in the Ruhr area, where *Freikorps* units containing Kapp putschists were actually deployed against the rebels. See Robert G. L. Waite, *Vanguard of Nazism: The Free Corps Movement in Postwar Germany 1918-1923* (New York: Norton, 1969), pp. 171-72, and J. H. Morgan, *Assize of Arms* (New York: Oxford University Press, 1946), p. 93. ZStA Potsdam, Reichskanzlei, nr. 1493, Kabinettsprotokolle, April 1, 1920. Erwin Könnemann, Hans-Joachim Krusch, *Aktionseinheit contra Kapp-Putsch* (Berlin: Dietz Verlag, 1972), pp. 451-52.

[46] Riezler to Ebert, Mar. 18, 1920, in ZStA Potsdam, Büro des Reichspräsidenten, 1, nr. 218.

[47] Riezler, "Die Schuld der Oberschicht," 620-21. Krummacher, *Die Weimarer Republik,* p. 134.

[48] Kurt Riezler, "The Psychology of the Modern Revolution," *Social Research,* 10 (1943), 320, 335, and "Political Decisions," 18, 23. Riezler was extremely critical of Chancellor Brüning, who understood nothing of Keynesian economics and who sought to balance the government's budget, instead of incurring spending deficits to increase employment and to stimulate the economy. This policy merely drove millions of desperate Germans into the arms of extremist parties. Author's interview with Hans Staudinger, New York, April 1975.

[49] Riezler described one kind of good outcast—"The voluntary and cheerful outcast who refuses to conform but bears no grudge. He is the salt and pepper of any society, and its most important member, though he does not regard himself as a member. He is the spur of a horse that likes to fall asleep." Clearly, Riezler considered himself just such an outcast. "Psychology of Modern Revolution," 324-25. Riezler, "Political Decisions," 23.

[50] Riezler, "Psychology of Modern Revolution," 325, 328-31. Henry A. Turner, Jr., "Big Business and the Rise of Hitler," in Turner, ed., *Nazism and the Third Reich* (New York: Quadrangle Books, 1972). Stern, *Cultural Despair,* p. 290. For Nazi elimination of the popular movement, see Karl Dietrich Bracher, "Gleichschaltung of the Universities," in *The German Dilemma: The Throes of Political Emancipation* (London: Weidenfeld and Nicolson, 1974), pp. 86-103. See David Schoenbaum, *Hitler's Social Revolution: Class and Status in Nazi Germany* (Garden City: Doubleday, 1966).

[51] Riezler, "Die Schuld der Oberschicht," 618.

[52] Toni Stolper, *Ein Leben in Brennpunkten unserer Zeit, Wien, Berlin, New York: Gustav Stolper 1888-1947* (Tübingen: Rainer Wunderlich Verlag, Hermann Leins, 1960), pp. 204, 419. Riezler, *Diaries,* p. 132. Heuss, "A Word," 2, and *Erinnerungen,* p. 377. Kessler, *Tagebücher,* p. 169.

[53] Riezler's job was not only to mediate between the faculty, which was autonomous in academic affairs, and the university administration, but also between the university and the Frankfurt and Prussian administrations. Paul Kluke, *Die Stiftungsuniversität Frankfurt am Main 1914-1932* (Frankfurt am M.: Im Verlag von Waldemar Kramer, 1972), pp. 471, 474. Heuss, "A Word," 2. Adolf Lowe, who was brought to the University of Frankfurt by Riezler, explained that the office of *Kurator* is not to be confused with the American office of president of a university. "It was a bureaucratic institution. The holder of the post was appointed jointly by the Prussian Ministry of Culture and the Mayor of the city and was not responsible to the faculty." Letter Lowe to author, Apr. 3, 1976.

⁵⁴ Author's interview with Adolf Lowe in New York, April 1975. Also, Kluke, *Frankfurt,* pp. 492, 494-95.

⁵⁵ Riezler, *Diaries,* pp. 142-43. Kluke, *Frankfurt,* p. 476.

⁵⁶ Author's interview with Adolf Lowe in New York, April 1975. After Riezler had been dismissed from his post by the National Socialists due to alleged "national unreliability," Riezler wrote, in order to receive his pension, that as *Kurator* he had tried to attract Heidegger and Carl Schmitt to Frankfurt. Letter from Riezler to Walter Platzhoff, Dec. 3, 1933, in Riezler, *Diaries,* p. 144. Lowe knew nothing about a Heidegger appointment, but he indicated that although Riezler respected Schmitt's brilliance, Riezler "rejected Schmitt because of his declared sympathy with the Nazis." Of course, there would have been nothing wrong with recruiting Heidegger and Schmitt in the 1920s. As late as 1932, the latter was appointed to a chair at the University of Cologne by Mayor Konrad Adenauer and Dean Hans Kelsen, a Jew. According to Hans Speier, Riezler also recommended Herbert Marcuse to Horkheimer. Letter Speier to author, Sept. 23, 1975. See also Martin Jay, *The Dialectical Imagination: A History of the Frankfurt School and the Institute of Social Research, 1923-1950* (Boston: Little, Brown, 1973), pp. 24, 28. Among those in Riezler's circle were Walter F. Otto, Kurt Burchard, F. Drevemann, K. Rheindorf, Karl Reinhardt, Ernst Kantorowicz, Max Wertheimer, Max Horkheimer, Fritz Pollock, Theodor Adorno, and Leo Löwenthal. Kluke reports that for some of the members of this circle, "following the master, the feeling of an arrogant superiority over the unprivileged was very natural." Kluke, *Frankfurt,* pp. 477-78.

⁵⁷ Riezler, *Diaries,* p. 144. The entire *Institut für Sozialforschung* sought refuge in the United States during the war and then returned to Germany again after Hitler's defeat. Erich Hula recalled tense relations between the *Institut,* which was composed largely of Marxists, and the New School for Social Research. Author's interview with Hula in New York, April 1976. See also Jay, *Dialectical Imagination.*

⁵⁸ Karl Reinhardt, *Die Krise des Helden, Beiträge zur Literatur und Zeitgeschichte* (Munich: Deutscher Taschenbuch Verlag, GmbH, 1962), p. 160. Also, author's interview with Lowe.

⁵⁹ Draft letter written by Riezler for Reinhardt, quoted in Riezler, *Diaries,* p. 149. See Reinhardt, *Die Krise des Helden,* pp. 160-63, for the aftermath of Riezler's dismissal. Between 1933-34, an estimated 1,684 scholars, including 1,145 university professors were dismissed. The percentages of university dismissals were: Berlin and Frankfurt am Main, over 32%; Heidelberg, 24%; Breslau, 22%; Göttingen, Freiburg, Hamburg, Cologne, 18-19%. The size of the student body fell by about one-half. Karl Dietrich Bracher, *The German Dictatorship* (New York: Praeger, 1970), p. 267. Ringer, *German Mandarins,* pp. 436-48.

· ⁶⁰ Stern, *Cultural Despair,* p. xi.

CHAPTER EIGHT

[1] After Hitler's rise to power, Riezler sent the bulk of the paintings to a showing of impressionists in Holland with a secret understanding as to ultimate property rights. Letter Toni Stolper to author, May 9, 1976.

[2] Walter Schmitthenner, Hans Buchheim, ed., *Der deutsche Widerstand gegen Hitler* (Cologne and Berlin: Verlag Kiepenheuer & Wietsch, 1966), pp. 45-58. Gerhard Ritter, *The German Resistance: Carl Goerdeler's Struggle against Tyranny* (New York: Praeger, 1958), pp. 226-27. Information concerning Riezler's generalization about Americans from author's interview with Adolf Lowe, April 1975.

[3] Harold C. Deutsch, *The Conspiracy Against Hitler in the Twilight War* (Minneapolis: University of Minnesota Press, 1968), pp. 6, 16-25. Joachim von Ribbentrop was Hitler's foreign minister.

[4] Carl Goerdeler was Lord Mayor of Leipzig; he was executed on February 2, 1945, by the Nazis for his role in the resistance. For Trott, see his biography by Christopher Sykes, *Tormented Loyalty: The Story of a German Patriot who Defied Hitler* (New York: Harper & Row, 1969), pp. 290-91, 296. Ritter, *German Resistance,* pp. 156-67, 193, 227, 263-69, 286-87. Gottfried R. Treviranus, *Für Deutschland im Exil* (Düsseldorf: Econ Verlag, 1973), pp. 152-54. At the New School for Social Research, Simons was the dean of the School of Politics from 1943-50 and president from 1950-60.

[5] Deutsch, *Conspiracy Against Hitler,* pp. 152-53. Sykes, *Tormented Loyalty,* p. 298. Riezler's daughter, Mrs. Marie White, described her father as a man "against Hitler, but for Germany." Interview with author, April 1975.

[6] Deutsch, *Conspiracy Against Hitler,* pp. 151-52. Sykes, *Tormented Loyalty,* pp. 301-02. Treviranus, *Für Deutschland,* p. 153

[7] Suspicion that Trott was an agent of Hitler was certainly not dispelled by the president's wife, Eleanor Roosevelt, who invited Trott to a tea in the White House. Mrs. Roosevelt loudly announced to her guests, who were mostly unknown to Trott: "Why now this is Mr. von Trott who is going to tell us all about Mr. Hitler." Sykes, *Tormented Loyalty,* pp. 302-05, 307. Deutsch, *Conspiracy Against Hitler,* p. 152. Treviranus, *Für Deutschland,* p. 153.

[8] Lecture published in *Social Research,* September 1946. Quotation on p. 368. According to one of Riezler's closest American students, Richard Kennington, Riezler did not discuss politics with young Americans because they had no concept of the political setting in which he had acted. Interview with author, February 1976.

⁹ Riezler, "Modern Statesman," 368.

¹⁰ *Ibid.*, 369-71. Drawing from his own experience, he wrote in 1953 that "no man who ever acted in history ever believed in a completely determined order of events—he knows that man's knowledge is limited—and to him things are what they are to man." "Political Decisions," 4. See also p. 53.

¹¹ Riezler, "Modern Statesman," 372-73.

¹² *Ibid.*, 374-77. For his final treatment of the context within which the statesman must operate, see "Political Decisions," 1-8. He wrote that "political action of each and every acting ruler, be it an individual or a collectivity, occurs in a human context, which ties together the necessary, the possible, and the desirable; man cannot help looking at each one of these three under the aspect of the two others." "Man in political action is man in his totality." Pp. 2-3.

¹³ Riezler, "Political Decisions," 4, 53. Riezler, "Modern Statesman," 375, 379-80.

¹⁴ Both Hans Speier, "Future of German Nationalism," and Kurt Riezler, "Comment," were published in *Social Research,* 14 (1947). See pp. 446-54.

¹⁵ Walter Riezler's remark in Riezler, *Diaries,* p. 12.

¹⁶ The "University in Exile" was renamed the Graduate Faculty of Political and Social Science in 1934. Exiled French scholars established the École Libre des Hautes Études in 1941. Although this institution was modeled on the Graduate Faculty and cooperated with the latter faculty, it remained officially independent.

¹⁷ Strauss, "Kurt Riezler," pp. 234-35.

¹⁸ Author's interview with Kennington, February 1976.

¹⁹ Letter Riezler to Heuss, Aug. 21, year unknown, in Riezler, *Diaries,* p. 156.

²⁰ Letter Riezler to Heuss, Mar. 10, year unknown, in Riezler, *Diaries,* p. 155. Letter Hans Speier to author, Sept. 23, 1975. Letter Riezler to Karl Reinhardt, Feb. 2, 1939, and letter Riezler to Heuss, Mar. 10, year unknown, both in Riezler, *Diaries,* p. 155. Speier wrote in a letter to Riezler from Washington, D.C., on Feb. 3, 1944: "I think it admirable that you are able to concentrate on anything non-political."

²¹ Kurt Riezler, *Physics and Reality: Lectures of Aristotle on Modern Physics at an International Congress of Scientists. 679 Olymp.*

Cambridge 1940 (New Haven: Yale University Press, 1940). Kurt Riezler, "Die Krise des physikalischen Weltbegriffs," *Deutsche Vierteljahrsschriften für Literatur, Wissenschaft und Geistesgeschichte,* 6 (1928), 23-24. Strauss, "Kurt Riezler," pp. 241-45. Kurt Riezler, *Man Mutable and Immutable, The Fundamental Structure of Social Life* (Chicago: Regnery, 1950), p. vii. In this book Riezler dealt with man, who is a social animal, and his environment. See especially pp. 3-8, 73-93.

[22] Riezler, *Physics and Reality,* p. 5. Strauss, "Kurt Riezler," pp. 245-48, 253. Kurt Riezler, *Parmenides.* Werner Marx related that Riezler had known Heidegger earlier, but that they had had a falling out which, Marx recalled, had not been due exclusively to Heidegger's political activity. In any case, Marx remembered that Riezler was always irritated whenever Marx brought up the subject of Heidegger.

[23] Letter Riezler to Hans Speier, Feb. 29, 1952.

[24] Riezler, "Political Decisions," 41, 48-50.

[25] *Ibid.,* 41-42. Riezler had traveled to Shanghai in 1914 over the Trans-Siberian Railway and returned by ship through the Suez Canal.

[26] Riezler, "Political Decisions," 21-22, 46-47, 51-53.

[27] *Ibid.,* 52-53. Riezler, "What is Public Opinion?" *Social Research,* 11 (1944).

[28] Author's interview with Werner Marx, June 1974. Letter Kurt Riezler to Karl Reinhardt, Dec. 26, 1953, in *Diaries,* p. 159.

[29] Heuss, "A Word," 2. The quotation in Italian means: "Of tomorrow nothing is certain."

Bibliography

Bethmann Hollweg, Theobald von. *Betrachtungen zum Weltkriege.* 2 vols. Berlin: Verlag von Reimar Hobbing, 1919 & 1921.

Craig, Gordon A. Review of *Kurt Riezler, Tagebücher, Aufsätze, Dokumente.* Ed. by Karl Dietrich Erdmann. *American Historical Review* 78 (October 1973).

Erdmann, Karl Dietrich. "Begehrtes Tagebuch." *Die Zeit* (January 12, 1968).

_____, ed. *Kurt Riezler, Tagebücher, Aufsätze, Dokumente.* Deutsche Geschichtsquellen des 19. und 20. Jahrhunderts, Band 48. Göttingen: Vandenhoeck & Ruprecht, 1972.

Fischer, Fritz. *Griff nach der Weltmacht: Die Kriegszielpolitik des kaiserlichen Deutschland 1914-1918.* 4th ed. Düsseldorf: Droste Verlag, 1971.

_____. *Krieg der Illusionen: Die deutsche Politik von 1911 bis 1914.* Düsseldorf: Droste Verlag, 1969.

Geiss, Imanuel. *Julikrise und Kriegsausbruch 1914.* 2 vols. Hannover: Verlag für Literatur und Zeitgeschehen GmbH, 1963-64.

_____. "Kurt Riezler Tagebücher." Review of *Kurt Riezler, Tagebücher, Aufsätze, Dokumente. Jahrbuch Institut Deutsche Geschichte* 2 (1973).

_____. "Kurt Riezler und der erste Weltkrieg." *Deutschland in der Weltpolitik des 19. und 20. Jahrhunderts.* Ed. by Imanuel Geiss and B. J. Wendt. Düsseldorf: Bertelsmann Universitätsverlag, 1973.

_____. "Weltherrschaft durch Hegemonie: Die deutsche Politik im I. Weltkrieg nach den Riezler-Tagebüchern." *Parlament* 22 (1972).

Hahlweg, Werner, ed. *Lenins Rückkehr nach Russland 1917: Die Deutschen Akten.* Leiden: E. J. Brill, 1957.

Haussmann, Conrad. *Schlaglichter, Reichstagsbriefe und Aufzeichnungen.* Frankfurt am Main: Frankfurter Societäts-Druckerei, GmbH, 1924.

Herzfeld, Hans. Review of *Kurt Riezler, Tagebücher, Aufsätze, Dokumente. Historische Zeitschrift* 217 (1973).

Heuss, Theodor. "A Word in Memory of Kurt Riezler." *Social Research* 23 (1956).

Hillgruber, Andreas. "Riezlers Theorie des kalkulierten Risikos und Bethmann Hollwegs politische Konzeption in der Julikrise 1914." *Historische Zeitschrift* 202 (1966).

Jarausch, Konrad H. "Cooperation or Intervention?: Kurt Riezler and the Failure of German Ostpolitik, 1918." *Slavic Review* 31 (June 1972).

_____. *The Enigmatic Chancellor: Bethmann Hollweg and the Hubris of Imperial Germany.* New Haven: Yale University Press, 1973.

_____. "Die Alldeutschen und die Regierung Bethmann Hollweg. Eine Denkschrift Kurt Riezlers vom Herbst 1916." *Vierteljahrshefte für Zeitgeschichte* 4 (October 1973).

Klein, Fritz. "Bemerkungen zum Riezler Tagebuch," Review of *Kurt Riezler, Tagebücher, Aufsätze, Dokumente. Zeitschrift für Geschichtswissenschaft* 21 (1973).

Kornhass, Eike-Wolfgang. "Zwischen Kulturkritik und Machtverherrlichung: Kurt Riezler." In Vondung, Klaus. *Das wilhelmische Bildungsbürgertum: Zur Sozialgeschichte seiner Ideen.* Göttingen: Vandenhoeck & Ruprecht, 1976.

Mommsen, Wolfgang J. "Kurt Riezler, ein Intellektueller im Dienste Wilhelminischer Machtpolitik." *Geschichte in Wissenschaft und Unterricht* (April 1974).

Moses, John A. "Karl Dietrich Erdmann, the Riezler Diary and the Fischer Controversy." *Journal of European Studies* 3 (1973).

Pikart, Eberhard. "Ein Brief Kurt Riezlers an den Hamburger Bürgermeister Petersen vom 1. Februar 1924." *Vierteljahrshefte für Zeitgeschichte* 2 (April 1967).

Riezler, Kurt. *Über Finanzen und Monopole im alten Griechenland: Zur Theorie und Geschichte der antiken Stadtwirtschaft.* Berlin: Puttkammer & Mühlbrecht, 1907.

———. *Die Erforderlichkeit des Unmöglichen: Prolegomena zu einer Theorie der Politik und zu anderen Theorien.* Munich: Müller Verlag, 1913.

———. *Gestalt und Gesetz: Entwurf einer Metaphysik der Freiheit.* Munich: Musarion-Verlag, 1924.

———. *Über Gebundenheit und Freiheit des gegenwärtigen Zeitalters.* Bonn: F. Cohen, 1929.

———. *Parmenides.* Quellen der Philosophie 12. 2d ed. Frankfurt am Main: Vittorio Klostermann, 1970. This book was first published in 1934.

———. *Traktat vom Schönen: Zur Ontologie der Kunst.* Frankfurt am Main: Vittorio Klostermann, 1935.

———. *Physics and Reality: Lectures of Aristotle on Modern Physics at an International Congress of Scientists. 679 Olymp. Cambridge 1940.* New Haven: Yale University Press, 1940.

———. *Man: Mutable and Immutable, The Fundamental Structure of Social Life.* Chicago: Regnery, 1950.

———. "Political Decisions in Modern Society." *Ethics* 44 (January 1954). Delivered as public lectures under the Charles R. Walgreen Foundation for the Study of American Institutions. University of Chicago, February, 1953.

Ruedorffer, J. J. [Kurt Riezler]. *Grundzüge der Weltpolitik in der Gegenwart.* Stuttgart: Deutsche Verlags-Anstalt, 1914.

———. *Die drei Krisen: Eine Untersuchung über den gegenwärtigen politischen Weltzustand.* Stuttgart: Deutsche Verlags-Anstalt, 1920.

Ritter, Gerhard. *Staatskunst und Kriegshandwerk: Das Problem des "Militarismus" in Deutschland.* Vols. 2-4. Munich: Verlag R. Oldenbourg, 1964-68.

Strauss, Leo. "Kurt Riezler." In *What is Political Philosophy.* Glencoe, Ill.: Free Press, 1959.

Thompson, Wayne C. Review of *Kurt Riezler Tagebücher, Aufsätze, Dokumente. American Political Science Review* 67 (December 1973).

———. "The September Program: Reflections on the Evidence." *Central European History* 11 (December 1978).

———. "Inner Reform and National Power: Kurt Riezler's Domestic Policy Proposals 1914-1917." *German Studies Review* 2 (May 1979).

———. "Chinese and Japanese Nationalism in the Age of Imperialism: The

Views of Kurt Riezler." *Asian Studies—Occasional Papers of the Virginia Consortium for Asian Studies* 1 (Spring 1979).

———. "France: A Land of Frightened Pensioners? A View from across the Rhine." *Contemporary French Civilization* 4 (Fall 1979).

———. "Voyage on Uncharted Seas: Kurt Riezler and German Policy toward Russia, 1914-1918." *East European Quarterly* 14 (June 1980).

Zeman, Z. A. B., ed. *Germany and the Revolution in Russia 1915-1918: Documents from the Archives of the German Foreign Ministry.* London: Oxford University Press, 1958.